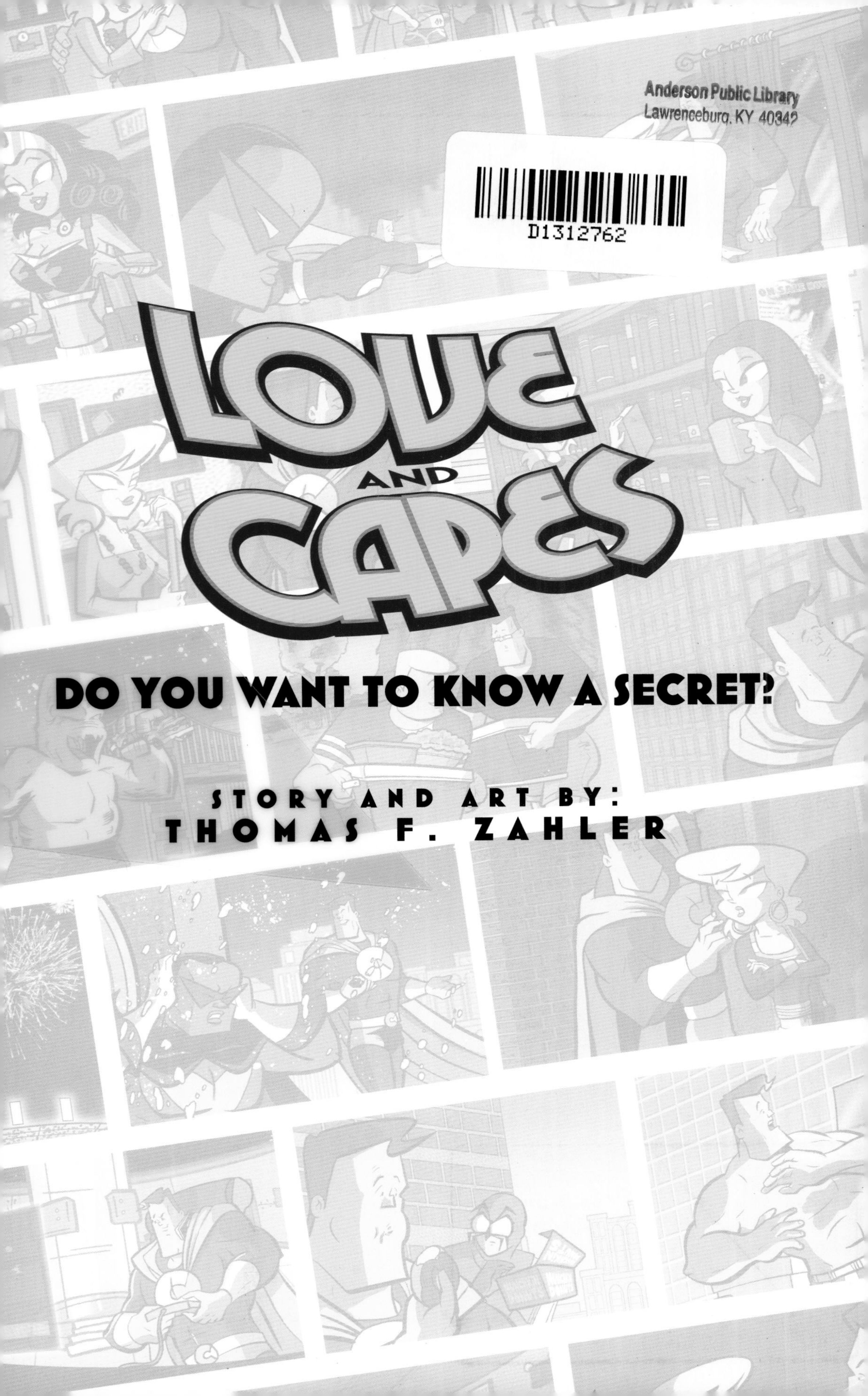

LOVE AND CAPES

DO YOU WANT TO KNOW A SECRET?

STORY AND ART BY:
THOMAS F. ZAHLER

INTRODUCTION

Thom Zahler infuriates me.

Really, it's all I can do to contain myself when I see his smiling, cheerful mug across the convention floor. And that happens a lot. Generally, the way it plays out is that he comes up to me to say something catty and snide like, "Good to see you again, Mr. Waid!" or "Again, I cannot tell you what an inspiration you've been to me, Mr. Waid!" or "It's really an honor to be in your presence, can I get you something to drink, Mr. Waid?" I respond by donning my Porcelain Mask of Feigned Enthusiasm and glad-hand him. Then, after the show has closed for the night, in some alleyway behind the convention center, far away from the hounding fans and their YouTube-linked cameraphones, I gut a homeless guy with his own broken bottle.

But enough about me.

Zahler's real crime was that he fooled me. He really did. The first time he handed me a copy of **_"Love and Capes,"_** I patted him consdescendingly on his flaxen-haired head, swore to him that **of course I would read it and get back to him,** and, naturally, had every intention of simply leaving it with the hotel maid in lieu of a tip. That was my plan. Instead, it accidentally fell into my carry-on bag and, starved for entertainment, I read it on the bumpy flight back home from PetalumaCon.

And it was GREAT.

No, honestly, it was great. And each ensuing issue just got better and more engaging. I really liked Mark and Abby and, by the end of that first issue, I was deeply invested in their romance and eager to see what complications would ensue. Zahler's a skilled author who writes about people first and capes second, and his insights into what makes a relationship work are genuine. *"Love and Capes"* is written with heart, it's whip-smart, and most importantly, Zahler and his artistic talents never once let you relax complacently into believing it's all about the jokes--not when Thom throws a curveball of heartbreak at you totally out of the blue, just like real heartbreak works.

Zahler has taken a simple idea--the tumultuous romance between a super-hero and an ordinary gal--and writes it probably better than anyone else in comics could. He certainly writes it better than I could. Better than I ever could.

Thom Zahler infuriates me.

MARK WAID, writer of KINGDOM COME, THE FLASH, JLA and SUPERMAN, is careful never to leave fingerprints and is not wanted for any known felonies. Currently, he serves as Editor-In-Chief of Boom! Studios in Los Angeles and remembers wistfully the days when people used to describe him as "flaxen-haired."

DEDICATED TO MY FAMILY

FROM ALL OF YOU I DRAW
MY HUMOR, MY STRENGTH, MY LOVE, AND MY SKILLS

YOU'RE LIKE MY "SHAZAM," BUT WITHOUT THE COOL ACRONYM.

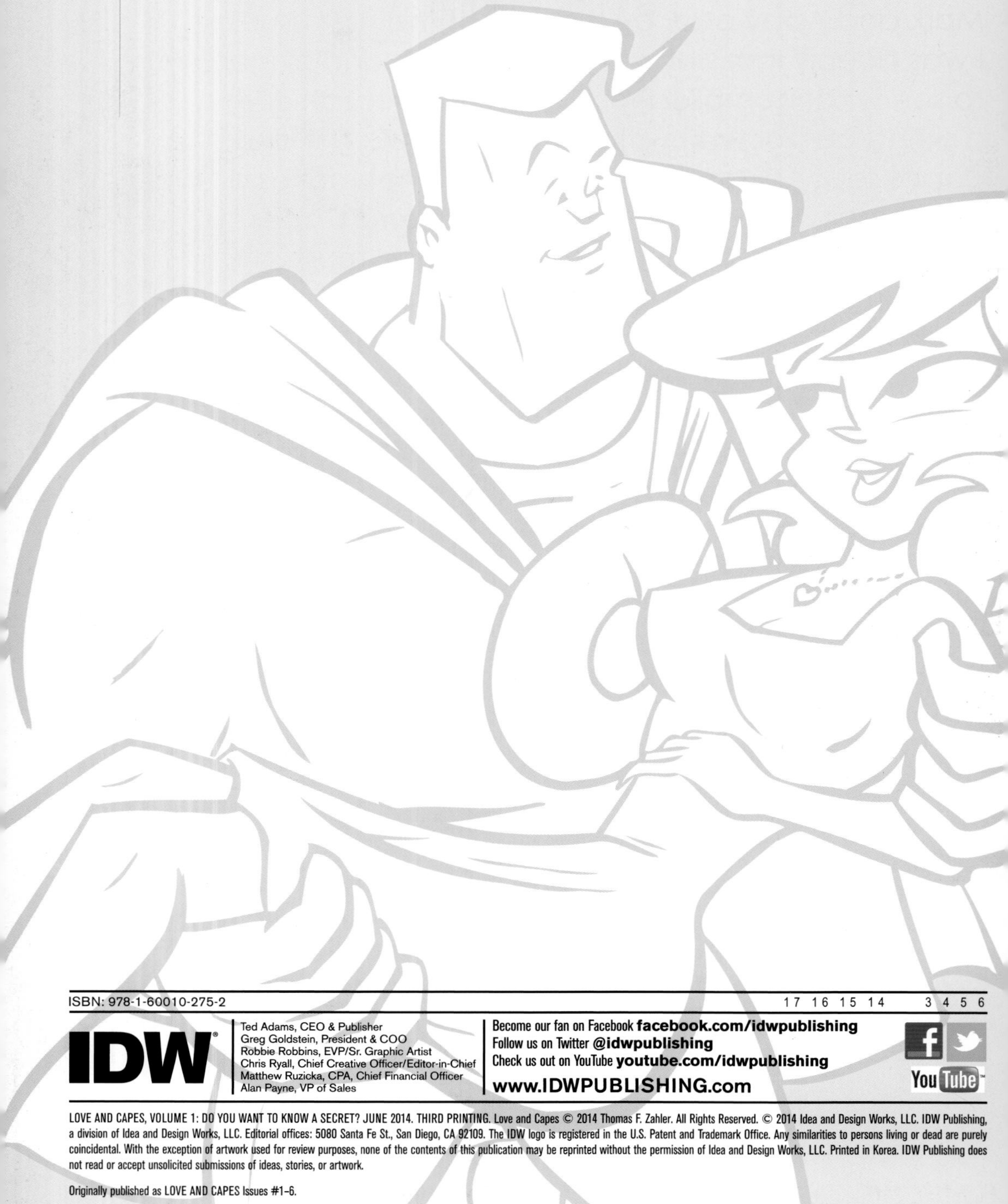

ISBN: 978-1-60010-275-2

17 16 15 14 3 4 5 6

IDW

Ted Adams, CEO & Publisher
Greg Goldstein, President & COO
Robbie Robbins, EVP/Sr. Graphic Artist
Chris Ryall, Chief Creative Officer/Editor-in-Chief
Matthew Ruzicka, CPA, Chief Financial Officer
Alan Payne, VP of Sales

Become our fan on Facebook **facebook.com/idwpublishing**
Follow us on Twitter **@idwpublishing**
Check us out on YouTube **youtube.com/idwpublishing**
www.IDWPUBLISHING.com

Originally published as LOVE AND CAPES Issues #1–6.

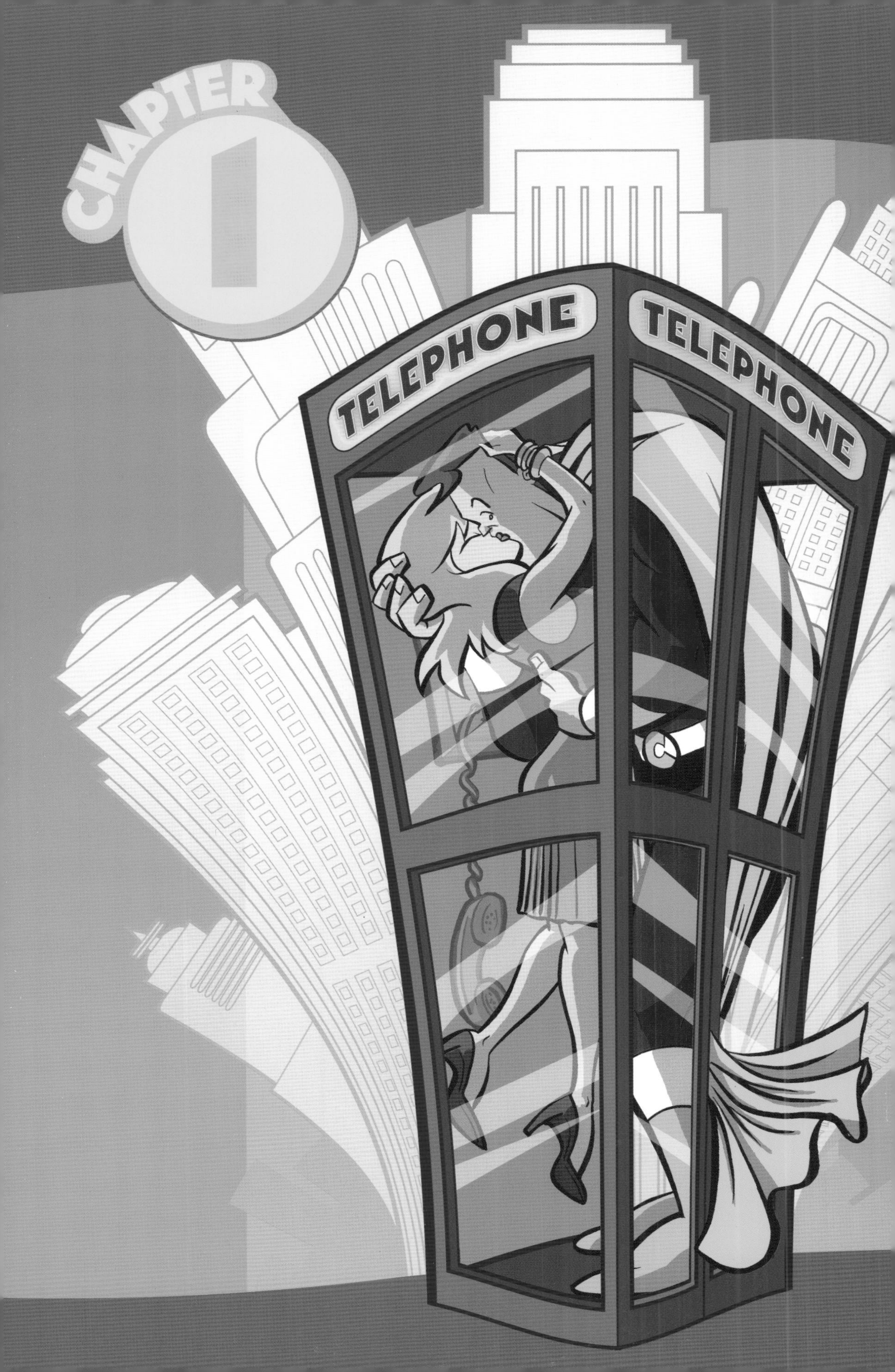
CHAPTER 1
TELEPHONE
TELEPHONE
TELEPHONE

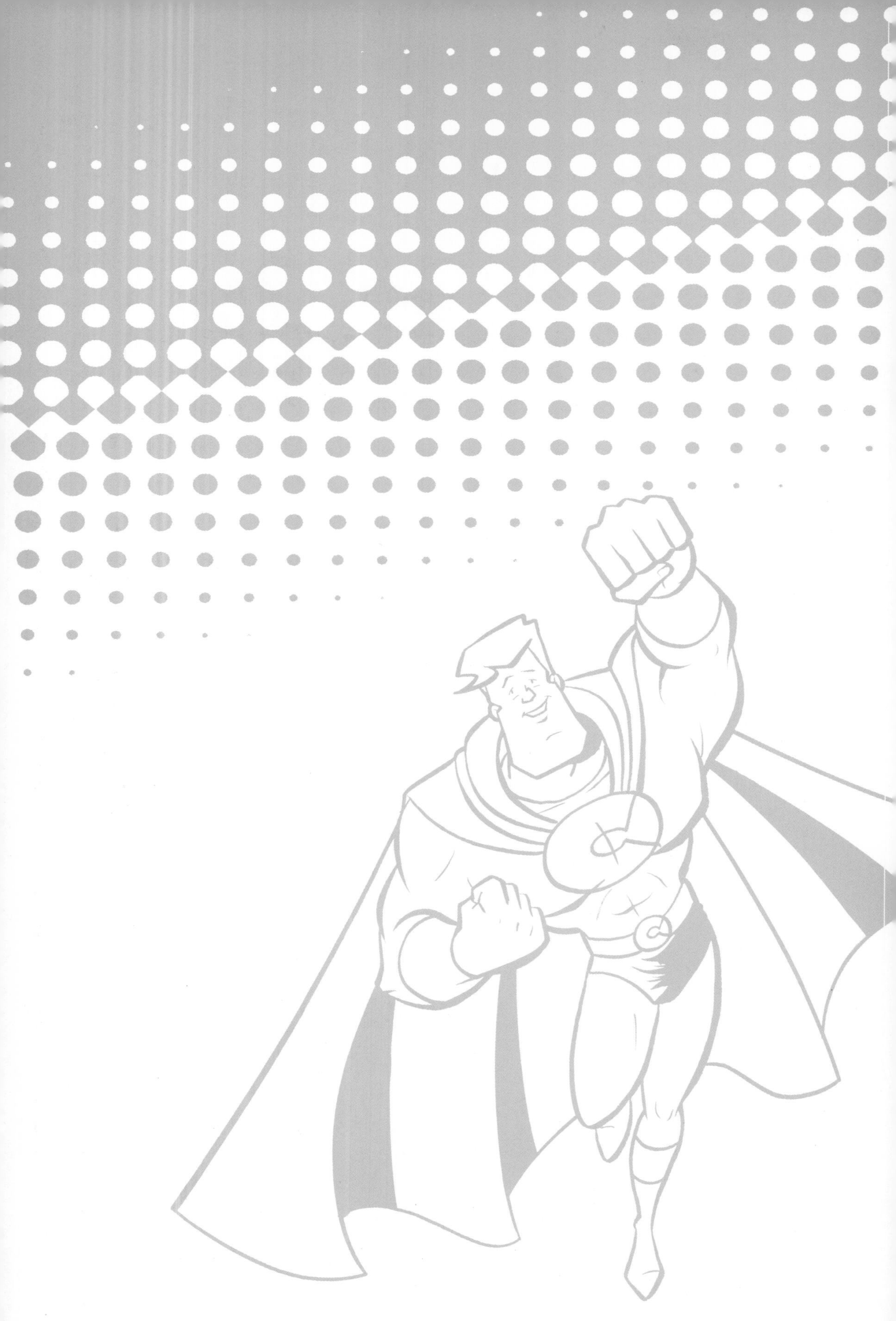

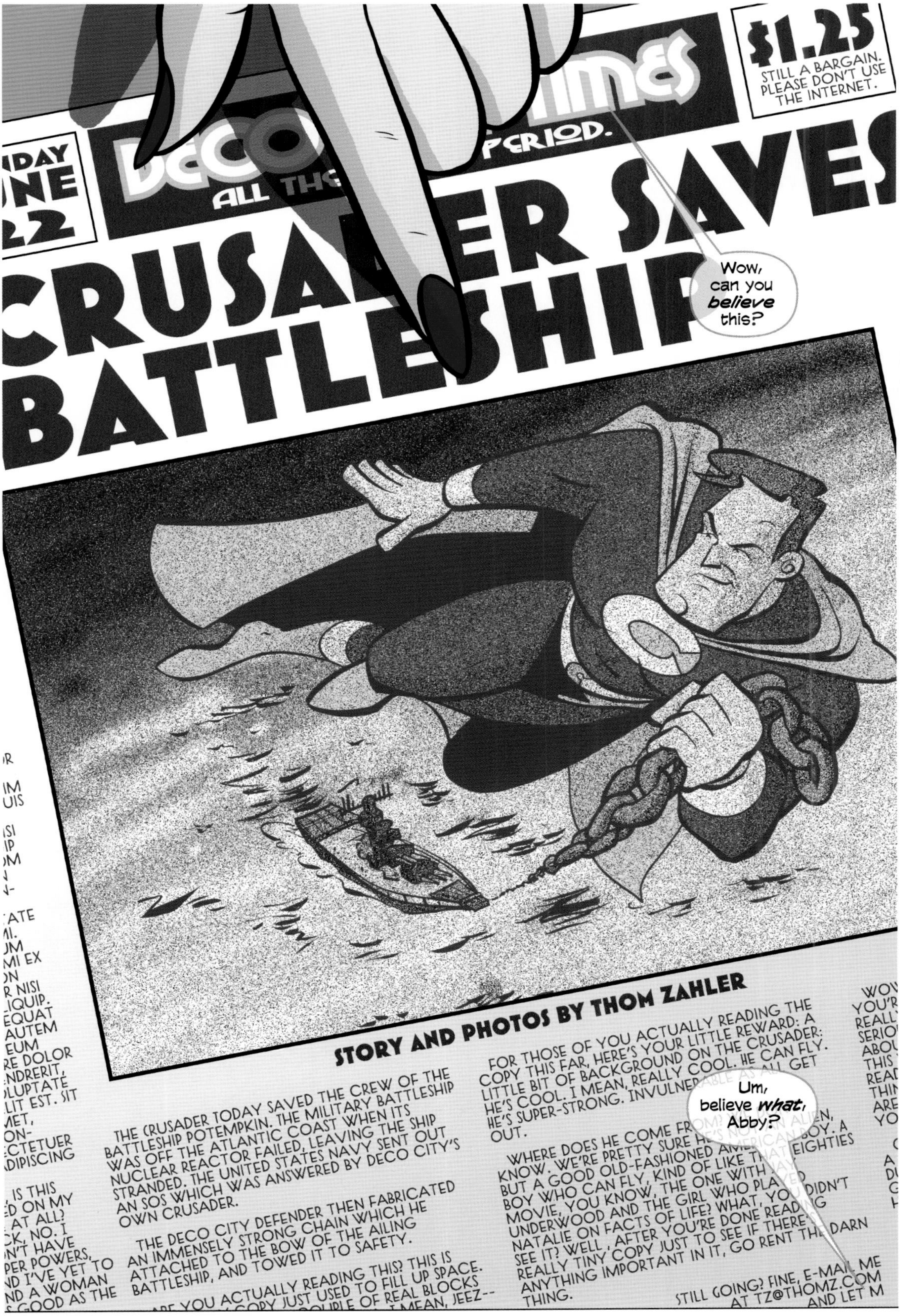
$1.25
STILL A BARGAIN. PLEASE DON'T USE THE INTERNET.
PERIOD.
CRUSADER SAVES BATTLESHIP
Wow, can you *believe* this?
STORY AND PHOTOS BY THOM ZAHLER
THE CRUSADER TODAY SAVED THE CREW OF THE BATTLESHIP POTEMPKIN. THE MILITARY BATTLESHIP WAS OFF THE ATLANTIC COAST WHEN ITS NUCLEAR REACTOR FAILED, LEAVING THE SHIP STRANDED. THE UNITED STATES NAVY SENT OUT AN SOS WHICH WAS ANSWERED BY DECO CITY'S OWN CRUSADER.
THE DECO CITY DEFENDER THEN FABRICATED AN IMMENSELY STRONG CHAIN WHICH HE ATTACHED TO THE BOW OF THE AILING BATTLESHIP, AND TOWED IT TO SAFETY.
FOR THOSE OF YOU ACTUALLY READING THE COPY THIS FAR, HERE'S YOUR LITTLE REWARD: A LITTLE BIT OF BACKGROUND ON THE CRUSADER: HE'S COOL. I MEAN, REALLY COOL. HE CAN FLY. HE'S SUPER-STRONG.
Um, believe ***what***, Abby?
STILL GOING? FINE, E-MAIL ME AT TZ@THOMZ.COM

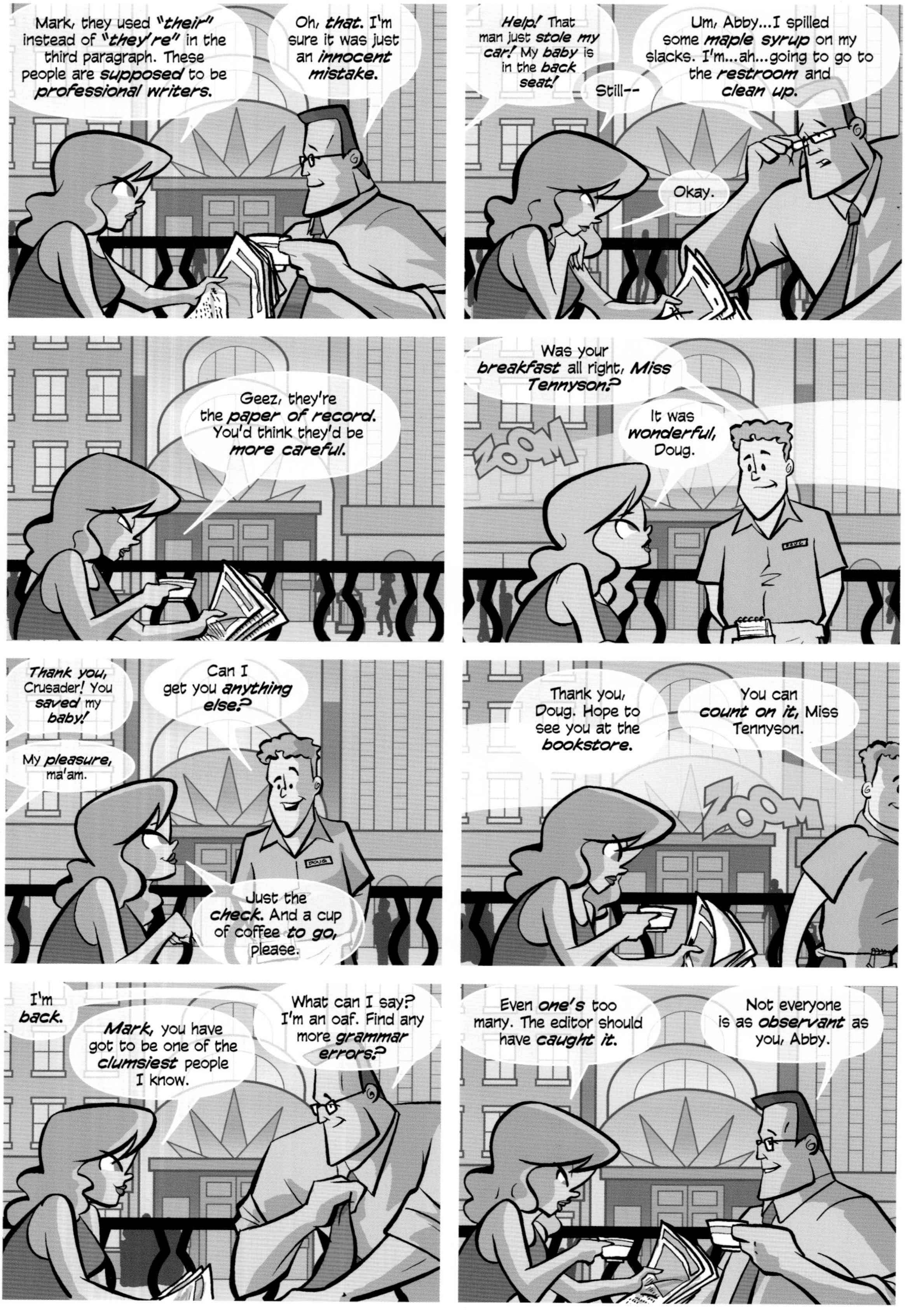
Mark, they used "their" instead of "they're" in the third paragraph. These people are supposed to be professional writers.
Oh, that. I'm sure it was just an innocent mistake.
Help! That man just stole my car! My baby is in the back seat!
Still--
Um, Abby...I spilled some maple syrup on my slacks. I'm...ah...going to go to the restroom and clean up.
Okay.
Geez, they're the paper of record. You'd think they'd be more careful.
Was your breakfast all right, Miss Tennyson?
ZOOM
It was wonderful, Doug.
Thank you, Crusader! You saved my baby!
Can I get you anything else?
My pleasure, ma'am.
Just the check. And a cup of coffee to go, please.
Thank you, Doug. Hope to see you at the bookstore.
You can count on it, Miss Tennyson.
ZOOM
I'm back.
Mark, you have got to be one of the clumsiest people I know.
What can I say? I'm an oaf. Find any more grammar errors?
Even one's too many. The editor should have caught it.
Not everyone is as observant as you, Abby.

LATER--

Thanks for meeting me for *breakfast*, Mark.

I *love* starting the day with *you*.

I've got a meeting with a *client* that's going to *run late* but would you like to meet for some late coffee?

I'm at the *bookstore* until ten tonight. Give me a call *after* that.

Count on it.

See you *tonight*.

Whoa. He is still a *super* kisser.

And he *said* "I *love you*"...even if those words were *separated* by "starting the day with."

Hey, *Charlotte*, it's *Abby.* I'm running a little late.

Yes, I was with *Mark.*

Sheesh. Why are you *so hard* on him? He's *great*...so *down to earth.*

MEANWHILE IN CHRONOPOLIS--

So you're going to *tell* her...?

Absolutely, Paul. I've never felt *so sure* about *anything*.

Sure, telling someone you *love* them leaves you *vulnerable*... and that's not exactly a feeling *I'm* used to, but--

I *meant* tell her your *secret identity.*

I *have* to, don't you thi--

It's the *Danger Alarm!*

Beep! Beep! Beep!

ALA
ANK A
2144 MONR
ROBBERY IN

Let's get *into* character.

I should *never* have gotten you the *"Pulp Fiction"* DVD for your *birthday.*

9

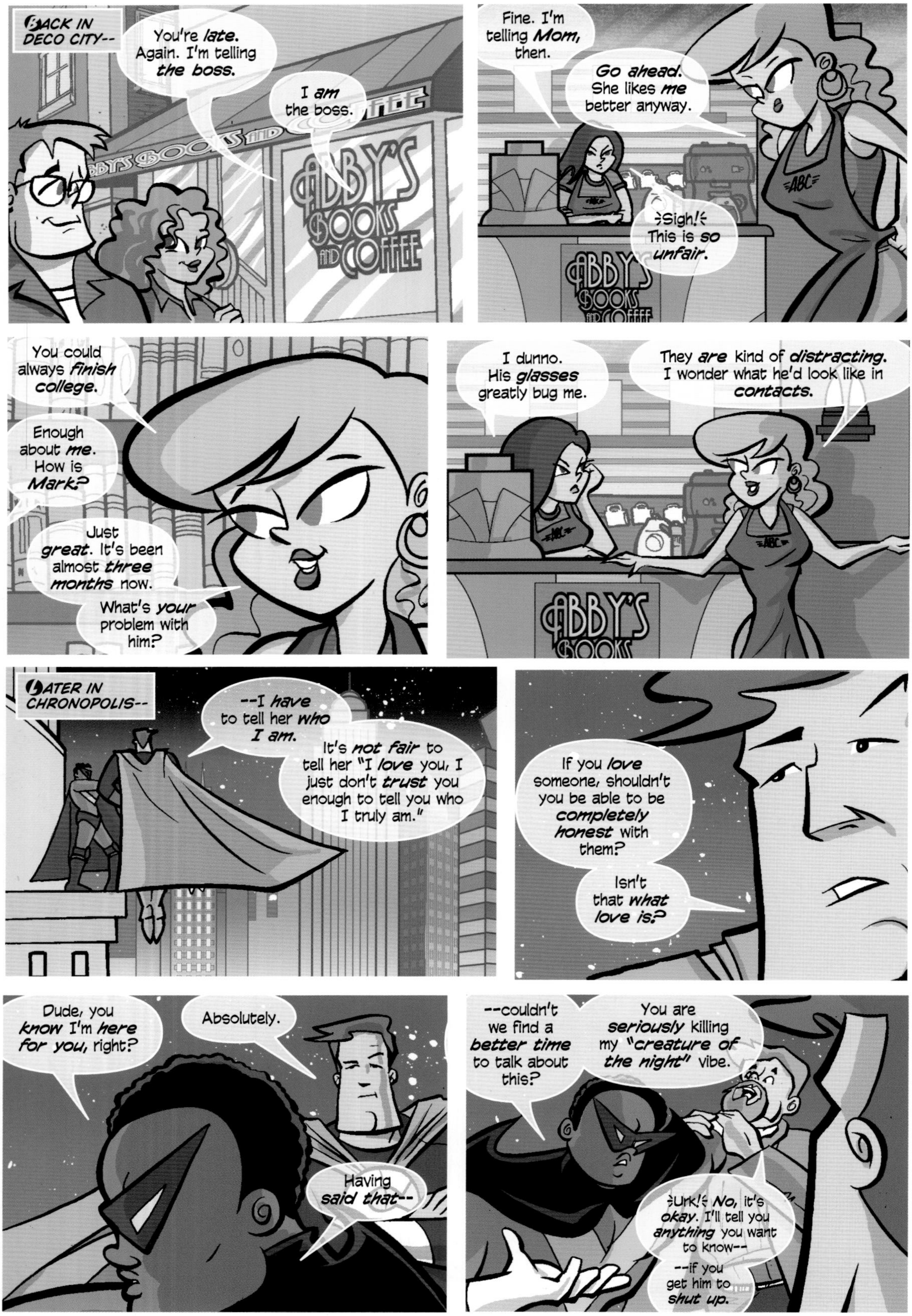
BACK IN DECO CITY--
You're late. Again. I'm telling the boss.
I am the boss.
ABBY'S BOOKS AND COFFEE
Fine. I'm telling Mom, then.
Go ahead. She likes me better anyway.
Sigh! This is so unfair.
You could always finish college.
Enough about me. How is Mark?
Just great. It's been almost three months now.
What's your problem with him?
I dunno. His glasses greatly bug me.
They are kind of distracting. I wonder what he'd look like in contacts.
ABBY'S BOOKS
LATER IN CHRONOPOLIS--
--I have to tell her who I am.
It's not fair to tell her "I love you, I just don't trust you enough to tell you who I truly am."
If you love someone, shouldn't you be able to be completely honest with them?
Isn't that what love is?
Dude, you know I'm here for you, right?
Absolutely.
Having said that--
--couldn't we find a better time to talk about this?
You are seriously killing my "creature of the night" vibe.
Urk! No, it's okay. I'll tell you anything you want to know--
--if you get him to shut up.

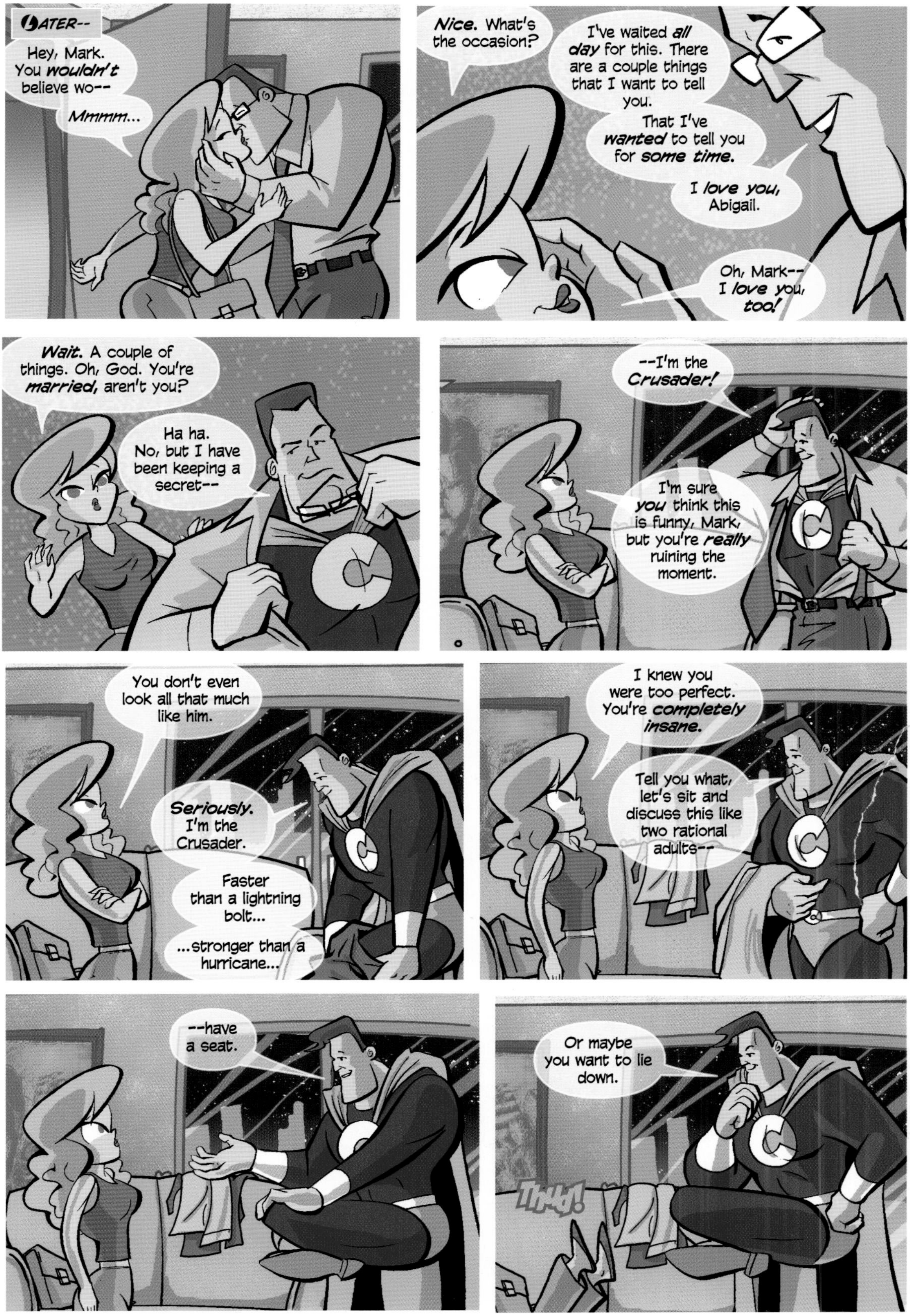
LATER--
Hey, Mark. You wouldn't believe wo--
Mmmm...
Nice. What's the occasion?
I've waited all day for this. There are a couple things that I want to tell you.
That I've wanted to tell you for some time.
I love you, Abigail.
Oh, Mark-- I love you, too!
Wait. A couple of things. Oh, God. You're married, aren't you?
Ha ha. No, but I have been keeping a secret--
--I'm the Crusader!
I'm sure you think this is funny, Mark, but you're really ruining the moment.
You don't even look all that much like him.
Seriously. I'm the Crusader.
Faster than a lightning bolt...
...stronger than a hurricane...
I knew you were too perfect. You're completely insane.
Tell you what, let's sit and discuss this like two rational adults--
--have a seat.
Or maybe you want to lie down.
THUD!

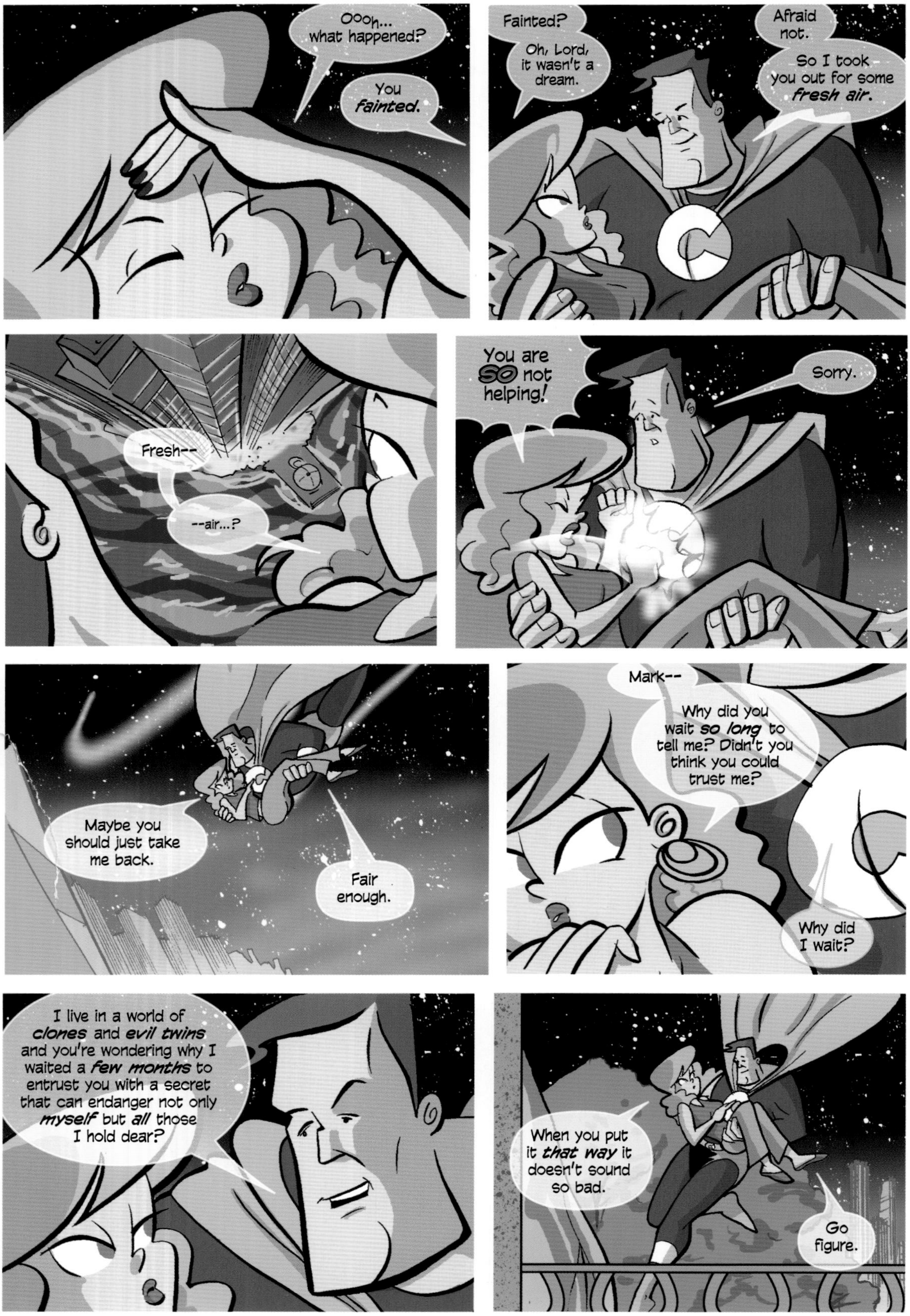
Oooh... what happened?
You *fainted.*
Fainted?
Oh, Lord, it wasn't a dream.
Afraid not.
So I took you out for some *fresh air.*
Fresh--
--air...?
You are *SO* not helping!
Sorry.
Maybe you should just take me back.
Fair enough.
Mark--
Why did you wait *so long* to tell me? Didn't you think you could trust me?
Why did I wait?
I live in a world of *clones* and *evil twins* and you're wondering why I waited a *few months* to entrust you with a secret that can endanger not only *myself* but *all* those I hold dear?
When you put it *that way* it doesn't sound so bad.
Go figure.

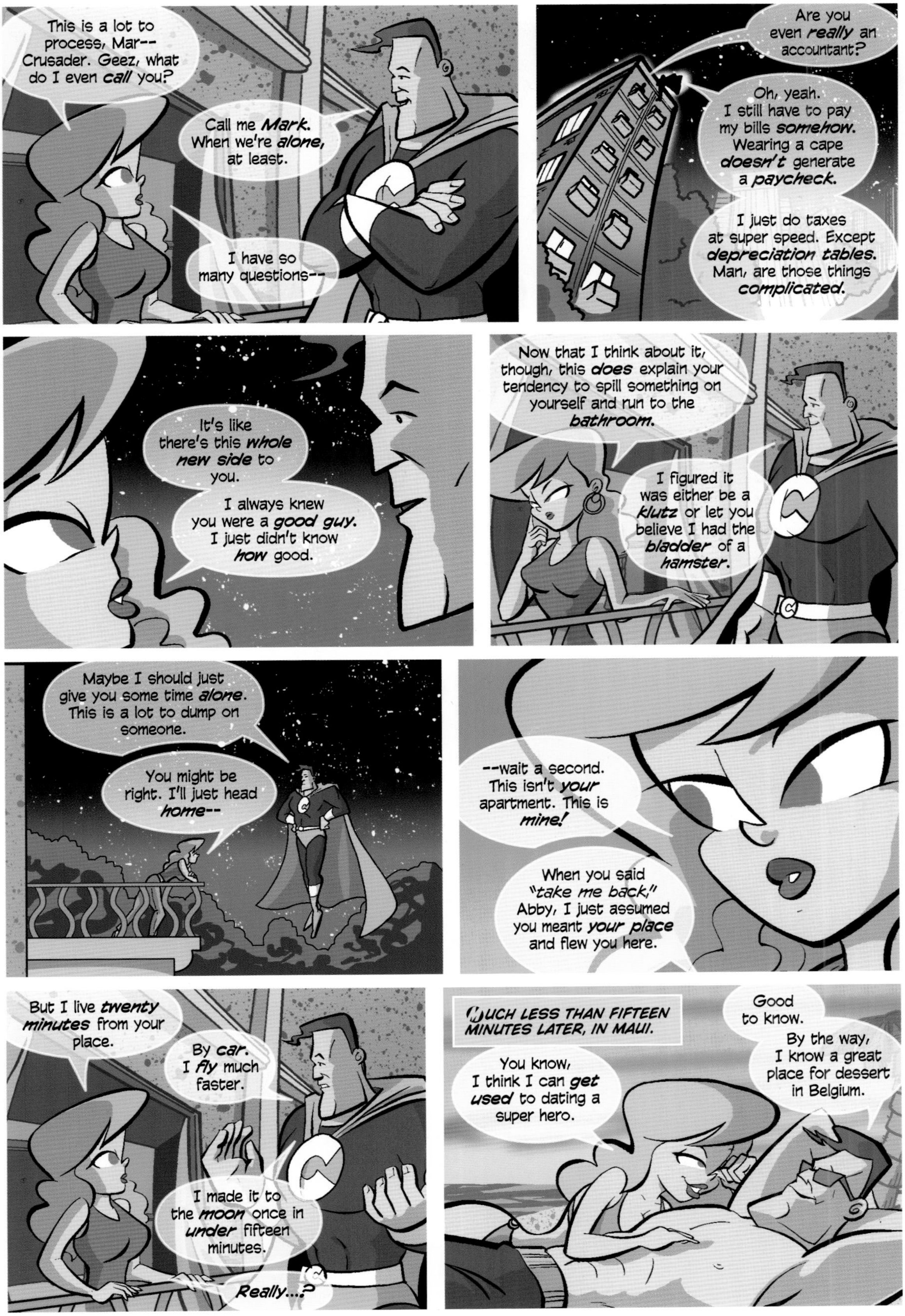
This is a lot to process, Mar-- Crusader. Geez, what do I even *call* you?
Call me *Mark*. When we're *alone*, at least.
I have so many questions--
Are you even *really* an accountant?
Oh, yeah. I still have to pay my bills *somehow*. Wearing a cape *doesn't* generate a *paycheck*.
I just do taxes at super speed. Except *depreciation tables*. Man, are those things *complicated*.
It's like there's this *whole new side* to you.
I always knew you were a *good guy*. I just didn't know *how* good.
Now that I think about it, though, this *does* explain your tendency to spill something on yourself and run to the *bathroom*.
I figured it was either be a *klutz* or let you believe I had the *bladder* of a *hamster*.
Maybe I should just give you some time *alone*. This is a lot to dump on someone.
You might be right. I'll just head *home*--
--wait a second. This isn't *your* apartment. This is *mine!*
When you said *"take me back,"* Abby, I just assumed you meant *your place* and flew you here.
But I live *twenty minutes* from your place.
By *car*. I *fly* much faster.
I made it to the *moon* once in *under* fifteen minutes.
Really...?
MUCH LESS THAN FIFTEEN MINUTES LATER, IN MAUI.
You know, I think I can *get used* to dating a super hero.
Good to know.
By the way, I know a great place for dessert in Belgium.

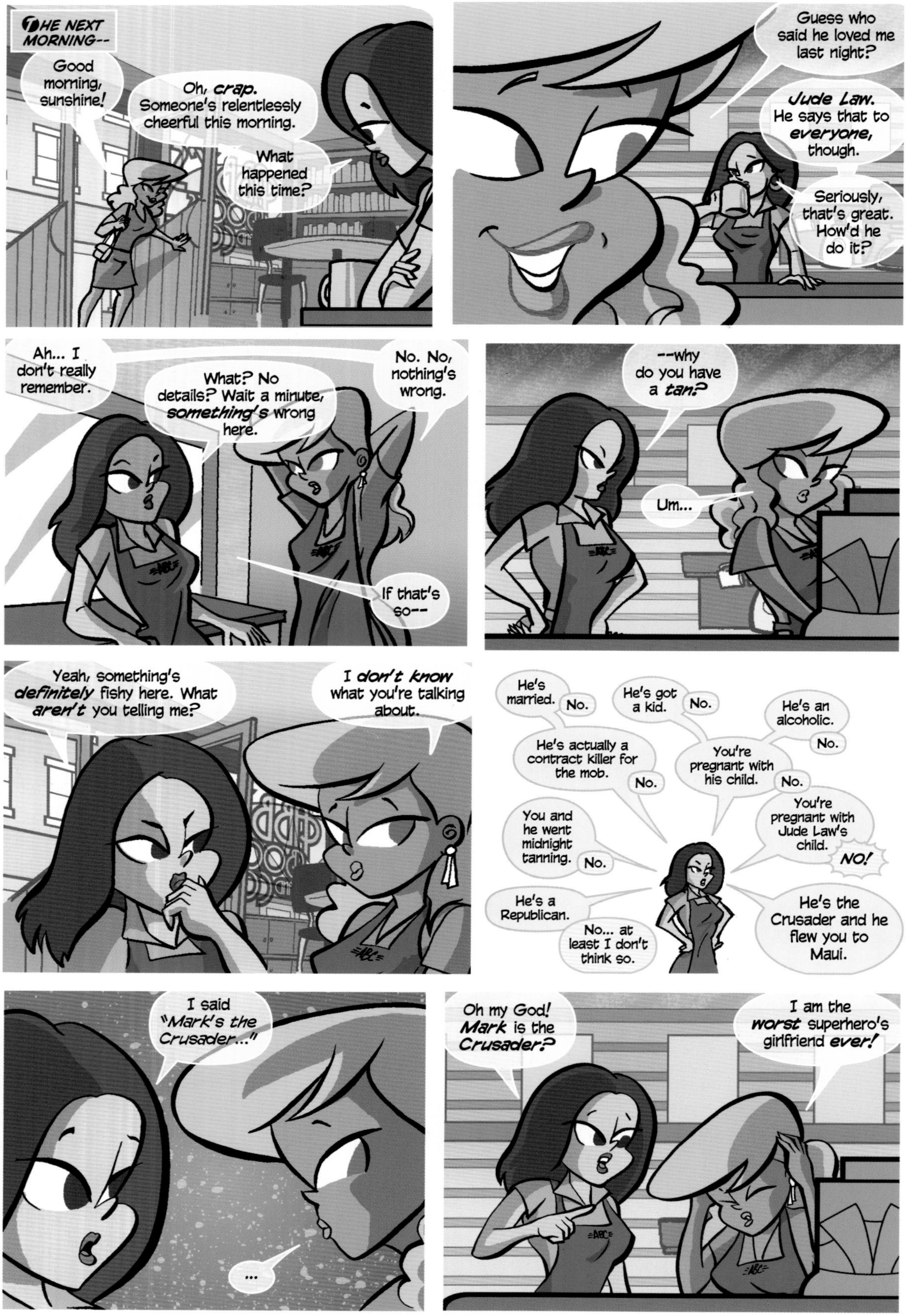
THE NEXT MORNING--
Good morning, sunshine!
Oh, crap. Someone's relentlessly cheerful this morning.
What happened this time?
Guess who said he loved me last night?
Jude Law. He says that to everyone, though.
Seriously, that's great. How'd he do it?
Ah... I don't really remember.
What? No details? Wait a minute, something's wrong here.
No. No, nothing's wrong.
If that's so--
--why do you have a tan?
Um...
Yeah, something's definitely fishy here. What aren't you telling me?
I don't know what you're talking about.
He's married.
No.
He's got a kid.
No.
He's an alcoholic.
No.
He's actually a contract killer for the mob.
No.
You're pregnant with his child.
No.
You and he went midnight tanning.
No.
You're pregnant with Jude Law's child.
NO!
He's a Republican.
No... at least I don't think so.
He's the Crusader and he flew you to Maui.
I said "Mark's the Crusader..."
...
Oh my God! Mark is the Crusader?
I am the worst superhero's girlfriend ever!

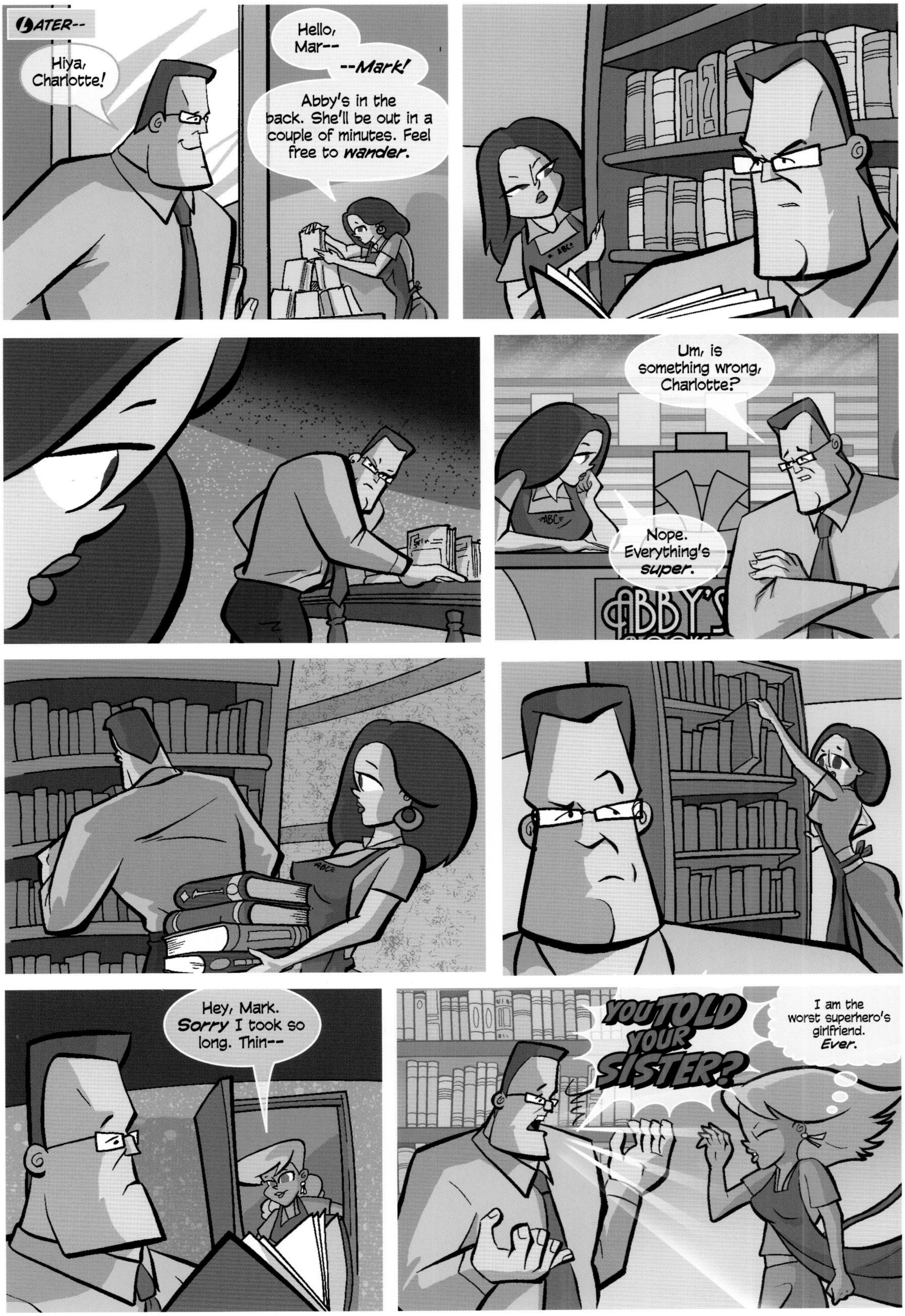
LATER--
Hiya, Charlotte!
Hello, Mar--
--Mark!
Abby's in the back. She'll be out in a couple of minutes. Feel free to *wander*.
Um, is something wrong, Charlotte?
Nope. Everything's *super*.
ABBY'S
Hey, Mark. *Sorry* I took so long. Thin--
YOU TOLD YOUR SISTER?
I am the worst superhero's girlfriend. *Ever*.

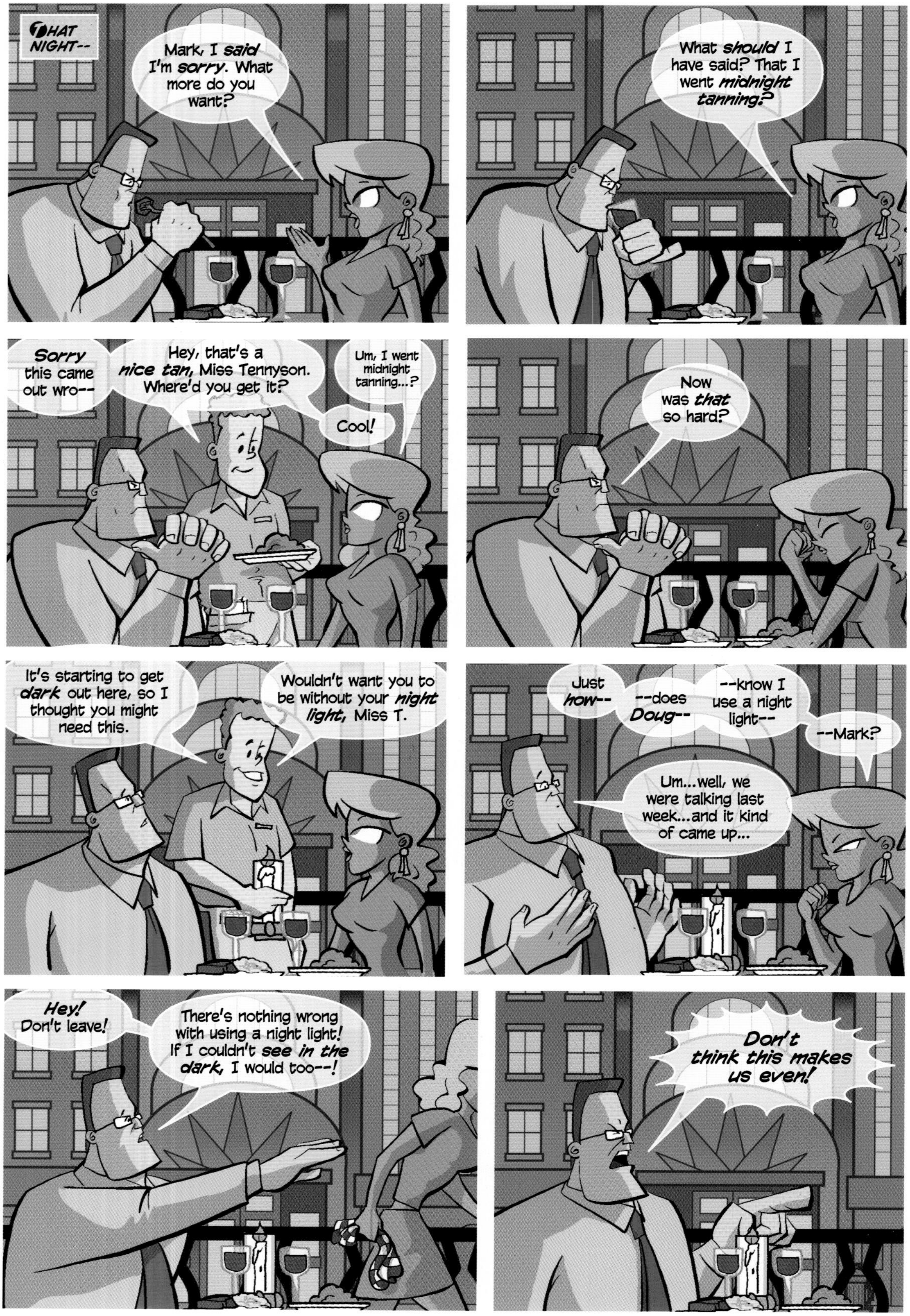
THAT NIGHT--
Mark, I said I'm sorry. What more do you want?
What should I have said? That I went midnight tanning?
Sorry this came out wro--
Hey, that's a nice tan, Miss Tennyson. Where'd you get it?
Um, I went midnight tanning...?
Cool!
Now was that so hard?
It's starting to get dark out here, so I thought you might need this.
Wouldn't want you to be without your night light, Miss T.
Just how--
--does Doug--
--know I use a night light--
--Mark?
Um...well, we were talking last week...and it kind of came up...
Hey! Don't leave!
There's nothing wrong with using a night light! If I couldn't see in the dark, I would too--!
Don't think this makes us even!

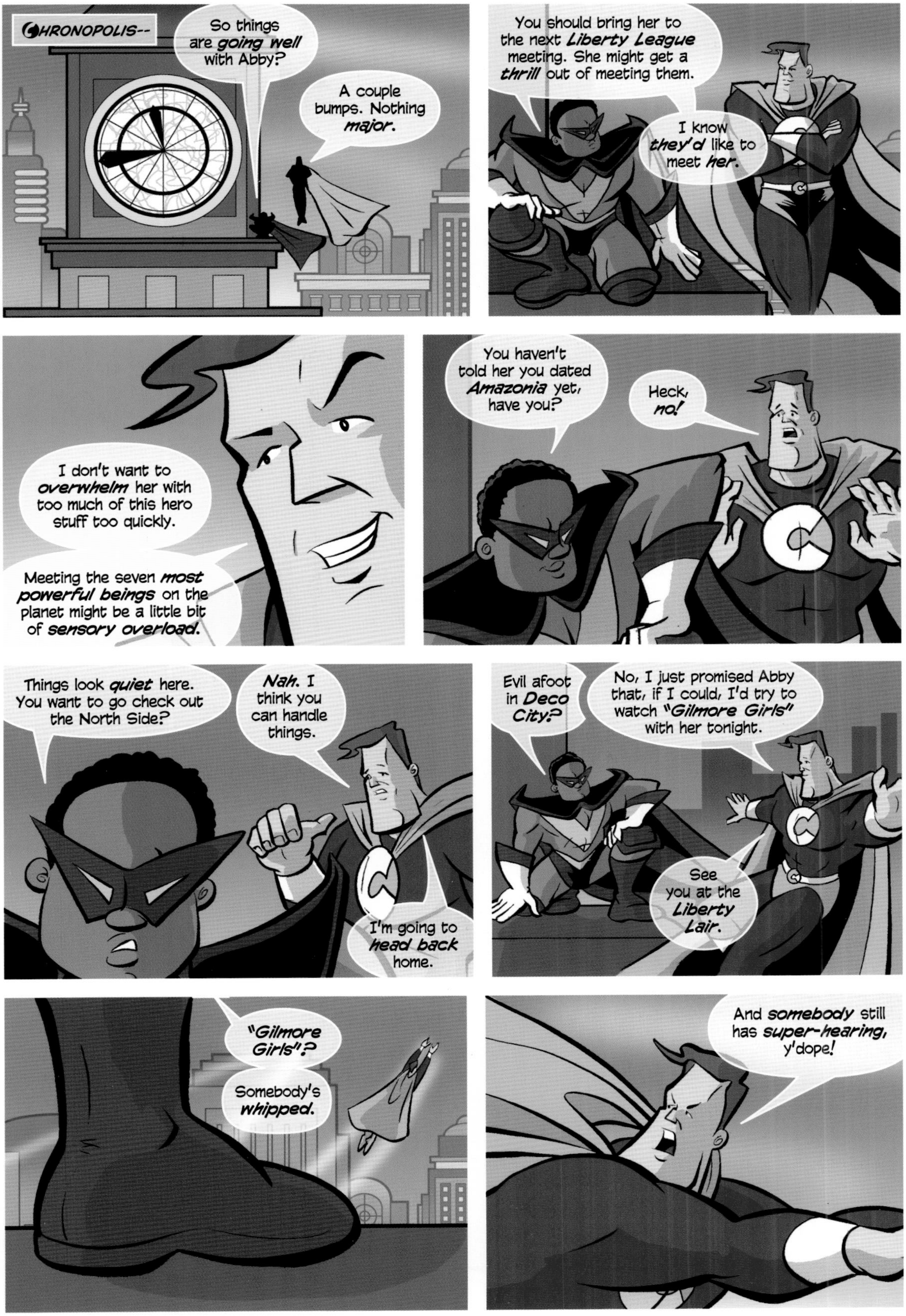
CHRONOPOLIS--
So things are going well with Abby?
A couple bumps. Nothing major.
You should bring her to the next Liberty League meeting. She might get a thrill out of meeting them.
I know they'd like to meet her.
I don't want to overwhelm her with too much of this hero stuff too quickly.
Meeting the seven most powerful beings on the planet might be a little bit of sensory overload.
You haven't told her you dated Amazonia yet, have you?
Heck, no!
Things look quiet here. You want to go check out the North Side?
Nah. I think you can handle things.
I'm going to head back home.
Evil afoot in Deco City?
No, I just promised Abby that, if I could, I'd try to watch "Gilmore Girls" with her tonight.
See you at the Liberty Lair.
"Gilmore Girls"?
Somebody's whipped.
And somebody still has super-hearing, y'dope!

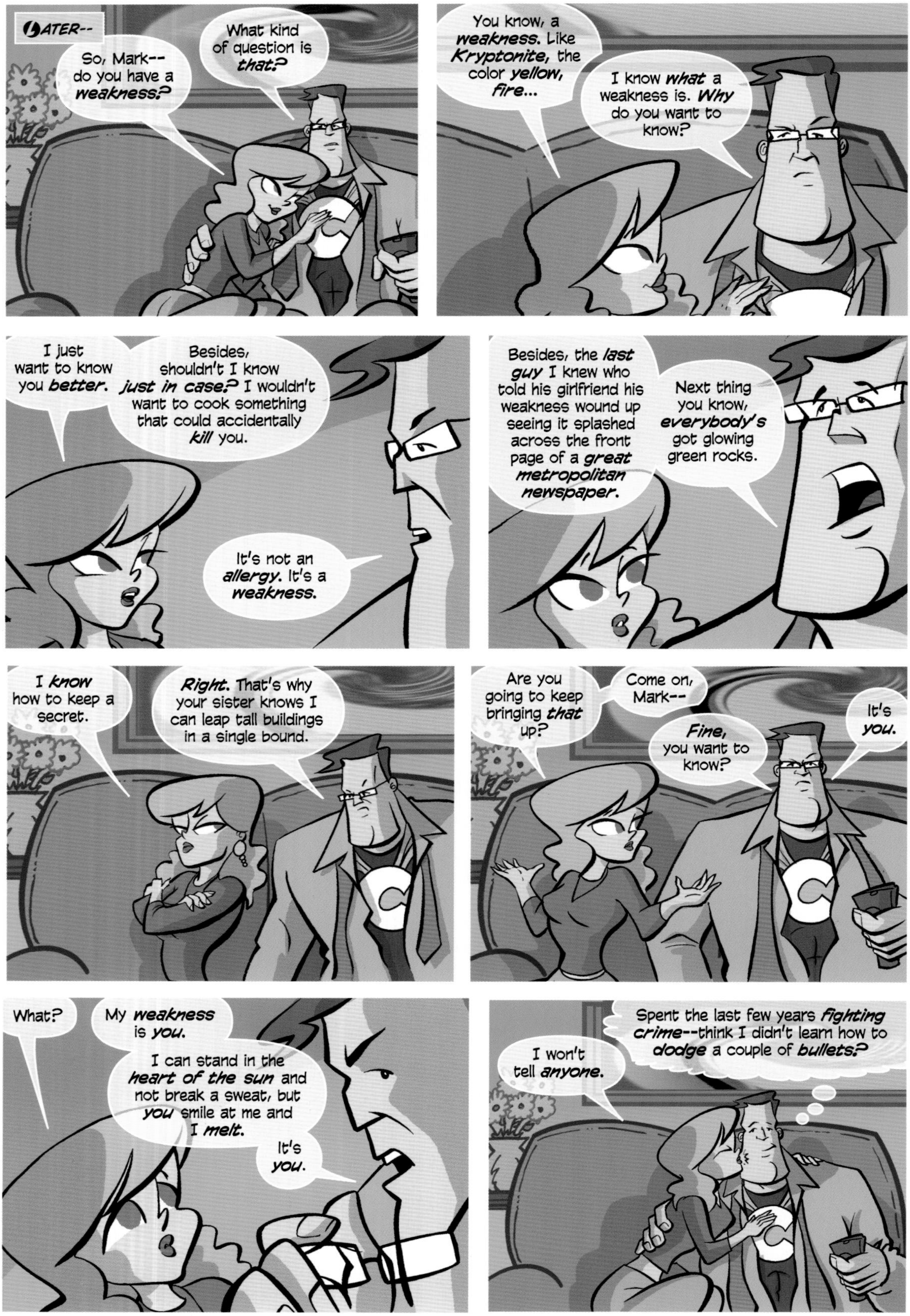
LATER--
So, Mark-- do you have a weakness?
What kind of question is that?
You know, a weakness. Like Kryptonite, the color yellow, fire...
I know what a weakness is. Why do you want to know?
I just want to know you better.
Besides, shouldn't I know just in case? I wouldn't want to cook something that could accidentally kill you.
It's not an allergy. It's a weakness.
Besides, the last guy I knew who told his girlfriend his weakness wound up seeing it splashed across the front page of a great metropolitan newspaper.
Next thing you know, everybody's got glowing green rocks.
I know how to keep a secret.
Right. That's why your sister knows I can leap tall buildings in a single bound.
Are you going to keep bringing that up?
Come on, Mark--
Fine, you want to know?
It's you.
What?
My weakness is you.
I can stand in the heart of the sun and not break a sweat, but you smile at me and I melt.
It's you.
I won't tell anyone.
Spent the last few years fighting crime--think I didn't learn how to dodge a couple of bullets?

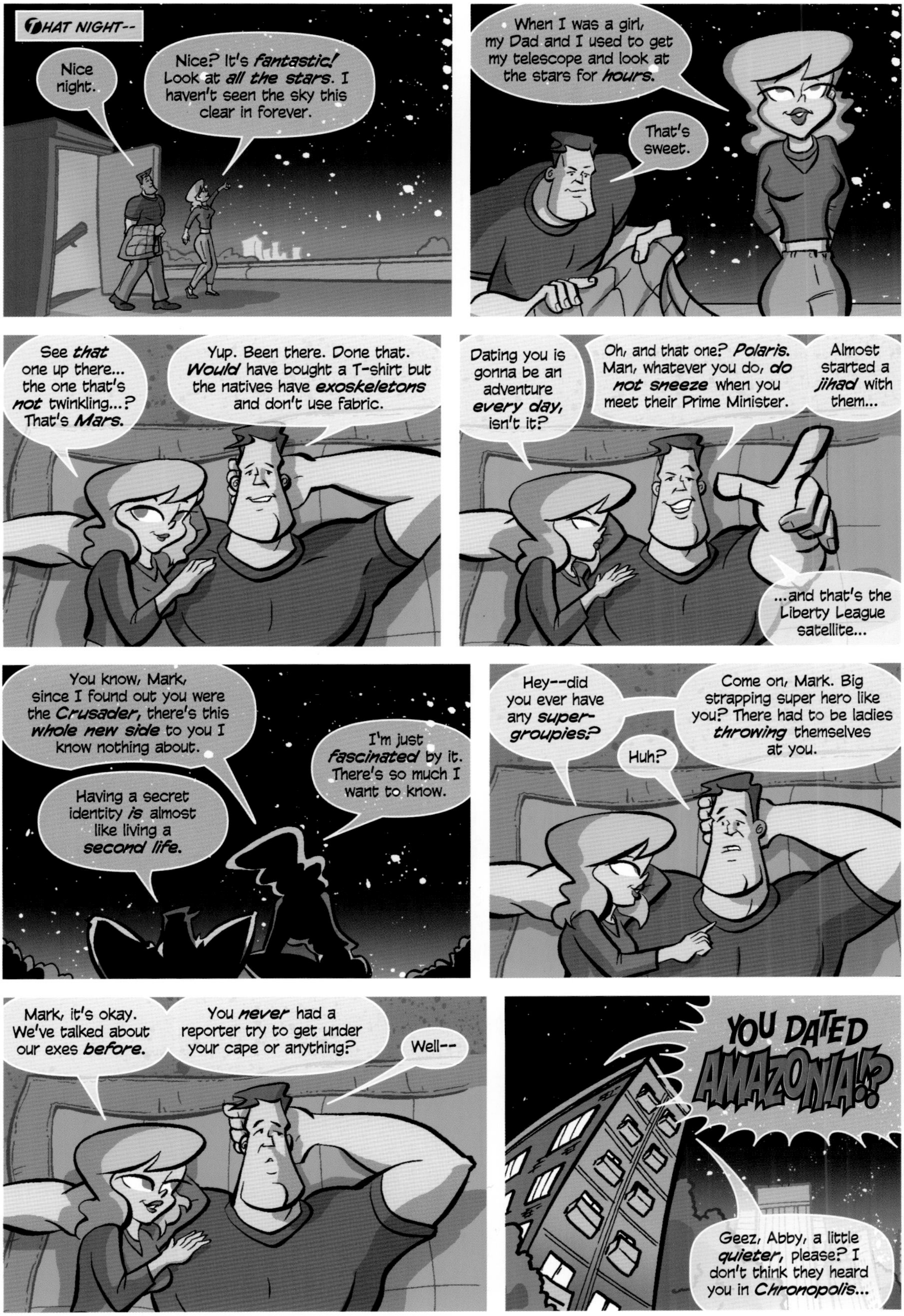
THAT NIGHT--
Nice night.
Nice? It's fantastic! Look at all the stars. I haven't seen the sky this clear in forever.
When I was a girl, my Dad and I used to get my telescope and look at the stars for hours.
That's sweet.
See that one up there... the one that's not twinkling...? That's Mars.
Yup. Been there. Done that. Would have bought a T-shirt but the natives have exoskeletons and don't use fabric.
Dating you is gonna be an adventure every day, isn't it?
Oh, and that one? Polaris. Man, whatever you do, do not sneeze when you meet their Prime Minister.
Almost started a jihad with them...
...and that's the Liberty League satellite...
You know, Mark, since I found out you were the Crusader, there's this whole new side to you I know nothing about.
Having a secret identity is almost like living a second life.
I'm just fascinated by it. There's so much I want to know.
Hey--did you ever have any super-groupies?
Huh?
Come on, Mark. Big strapping super hero like you? There had to be ladies throwing themselves at you.
Mark, it's okay. We've talked about our exes before.
You never had a reporter try to get under your cape or anything?
Well--
YOU DATED AMAZONIA!?
Geez, Abby, a little quieter, please? I don't think they heard you in Chronopolis...

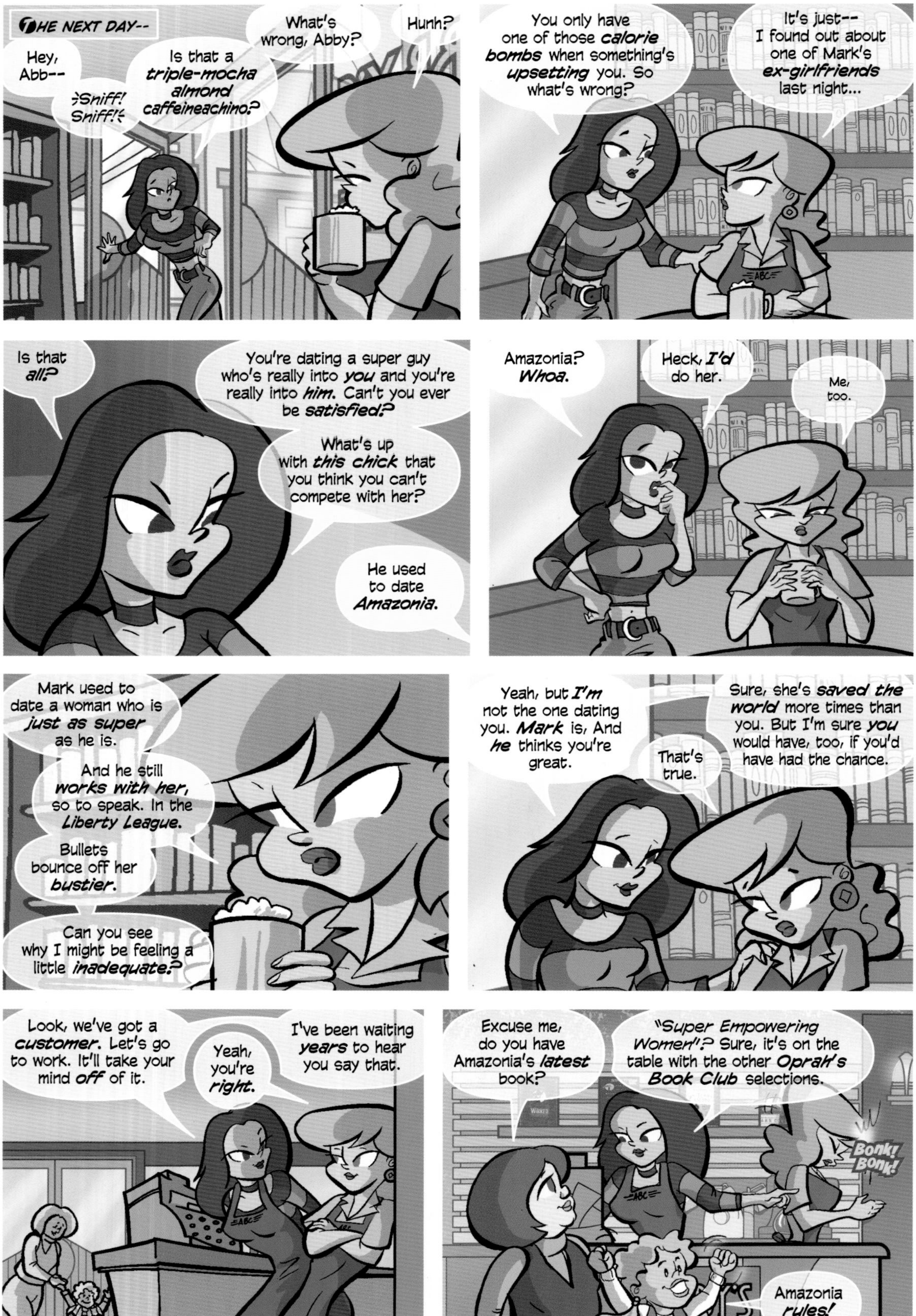
THE NEXT DAY--
Hey, Abb--
Sniff! Sniff!
Is that a triple-mocha almond caffeineachino?
What's wrong, Abby?
Hunh?
You only have one of those calorie bombs when something's upsetting you. So what's wrong?
It's just-- I found out about one of Mark's ex-girlfriends last night...
Is that all?
You're dating a super guy who's really into you and you're really into him. Can't you ever be satisfied?
What's up with this chick that you think you can't compete with her?
He used to date Amazonia.
Amazonia? Whoa.
Heck, I'd do her.
Me, too.
Mark used to date a woman who is just as super as he is.
And he still works with her, so to speak. In the Liberty League.
Bullets bounce off her bustier.
Can you see why I might be feeling a little inadequate?
Yeah, but I'm not the one dating you. Mark is, And he thinks you're great.
That's true.
Sure, she's saved the world more times than you. But I'm sure you would have, too, if you'd have had the chance.
Look, we've got a customer. Let's go to work. It'll take your mind off of it.
Yeah, you're right.
I've been waiting years to hear you say that.
Excuse me, do you have Amazonia's latest book?
"Super Empowering Women"? Sure, it's on the table with the other Oprah's Book Club selections.
BONK! BONK!
Amazonia rules!

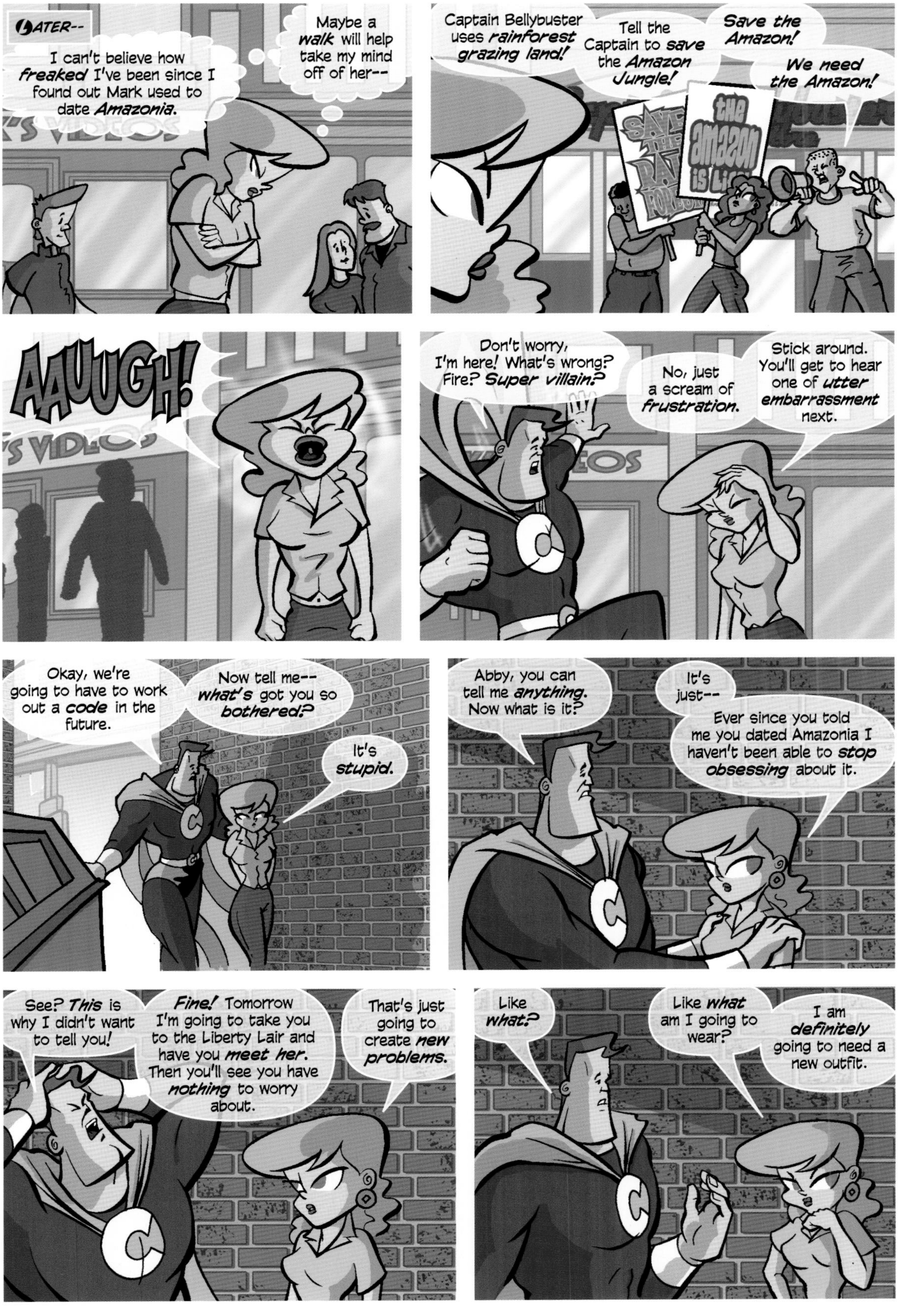
LATER--
I can't believe how freaked I've been since I found out Mark used to date Amazonia.
Maybe a walk will help take my mind off of her--
Captain Bellybuster uses rainforest grazing land!
Tell the Captain to save the Amazon Jungle!
Save the Amazon!
We need the Amazon!
SAVE THE RAIN FOREST
the amazon is Li
AAUUGH!
Don't worry, I'm here! What's wrong? Fire? Super villain?
No, just a scream of frustration.
Stick around. You'll get to hear one of utter embarrassment next.
Okay, we're going to have to work out a code in the future.
Now tell me-- what's got you so bothered?
It's stupid.
Abby, you can tell me anything. Now what is it?
It's just--
Ever since you told me you dated Amazonia I haven't been able to stop obsessing about it.
See? This is why I didn't want to tell you!
Fine! Tomorrow I'm going to take you to the Liberty Lair and have you meet her. Then you'll see you have nothing to worry about.
That's just going to create new problems.
Like what?
Like what am I going to wear?
I am definitely going to need a new outfit.

THE NEXT NIGHT, ABOARD THE LIBERTY LAIR--

Don't worry, Abby, almost everybody *throws up* their first time on the teleporter.

You could have *warned* me.

Then you wouldn't have come.

Abby, this is my friend *Darkblade.* He protects Chronopolis.

I didn't know *you'd* be here tonight.

Hello, Crusader.

I had to finally meet *legendary Abby.*

Mark talks about you *all the time.*

I wish I could *say the same.* Mark *hasn't* mentioned you at all.

That's as it *should* be, for *I* am a *creature of the night,* living in the shadows--

Mostly it's "*for you are a dork.*"

LATER--

--and this is *Amazonia,* Abby.

Abby owns a bookstore in Deco City.

Nice to meet you, Abby. Hey, that's a *great* outfit.

Thanks. That's, um, a nice *tiara.*

That's wonderful!

Mark, she's *adorable!*

Chirp!

Crusader! We have a problem!

Adora--?

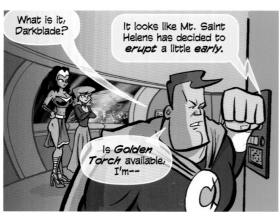

What is it, Darkblade?

It looks like Mt. Saint Helens has decided to *erupt* a little *early.*

Is *Golden Torch* available, I'm--

Mark, go *save Seattle.* Abby and I can hang out here. We'll have some *girl talk.*

Sure. Shoes... guys...

...um, *arch enemies?*

Be back in a *few minutes!*

22

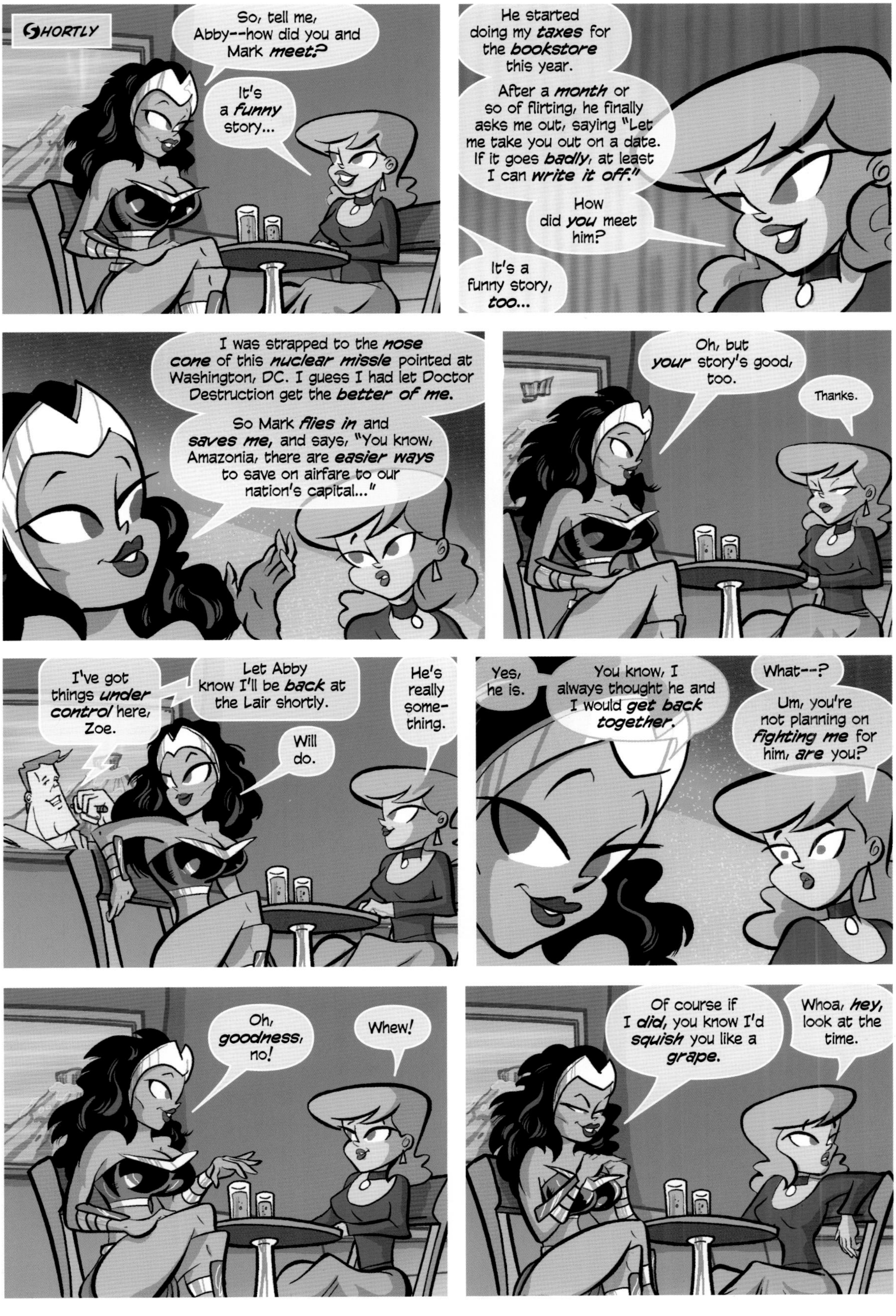
SHORTLY
So, tell me, Abby--how did you and Mark meet?
It's a funny story...
He started doing my taxes for the bookstore this year.
After a month or so of flirting, he finally asks me out, saying "Let me take you out on a date. If it goes badly, at least I can write it off."
How did you meet him?
It's a funny story, too...
I was strapped to the nose cone of this nuclear missle pointed at Washington, DC. I guess I had let Doctor Destruction get the better of me.
So Mark flies in and saves me, and says, "You know, Amazonia, there are easier ways to save on airfare to our nation's capital..."
Oh, but your story's good, too.
Thanks.
I've got things under control here, Zoe.
Let Abby know I'll be back at the Lair shortly.
Will do.
He's really some-thing.
Yes, he is.
You know, I always thought he and I would get back together.
What--?
Um, you're not planning on fighting me for him, are you?
Oh, goodness, no!
Whew!
Of course if I did, you know I'd squish you like a grape.
Whoa, hey, look at the time.

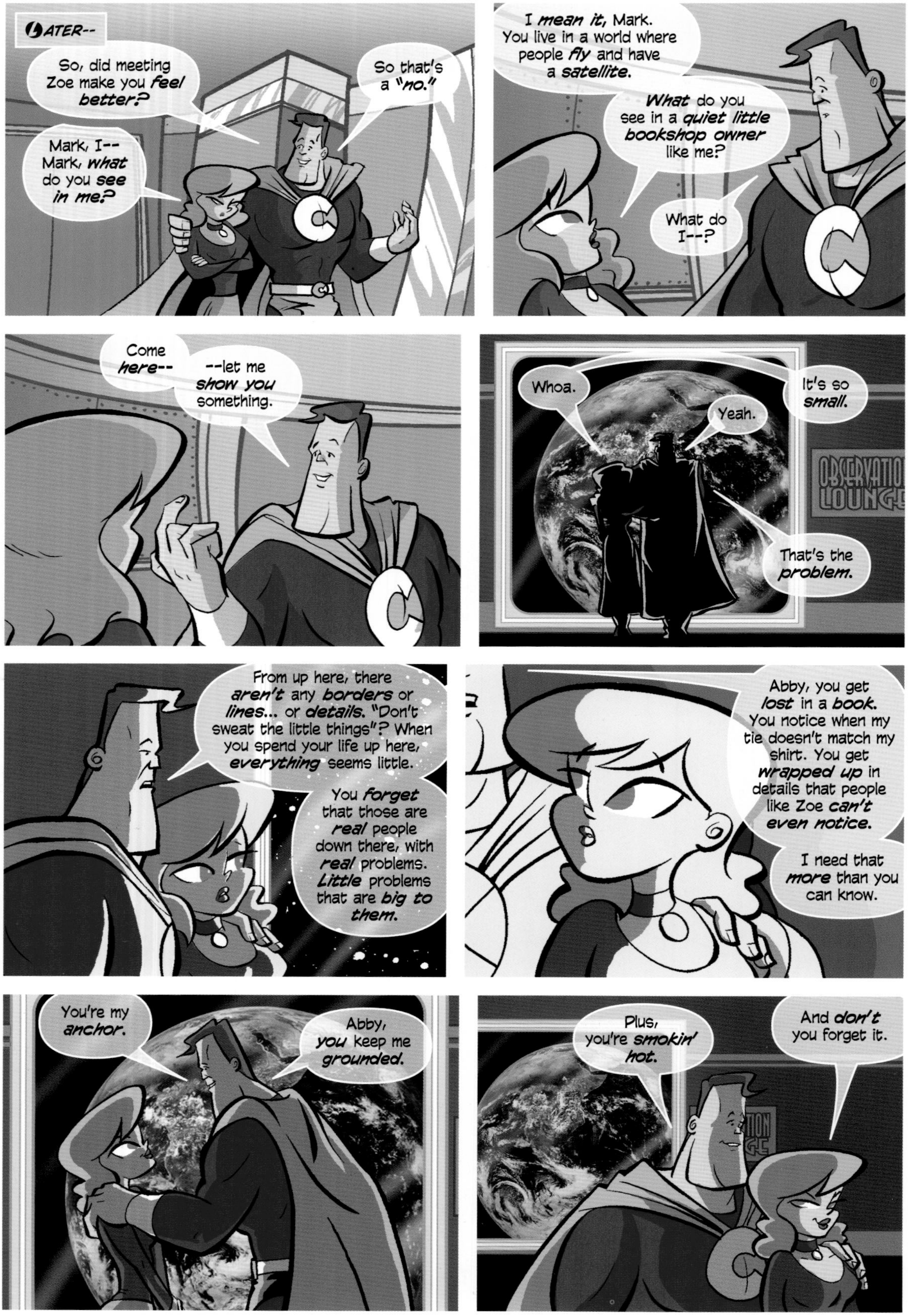
LATER--
So, did meeting Zoe make you feel better?
Mark, I-- Mark, what do you see in me?
So that's a "no."
I mean it, Mark. You live in a world where people fly and have a satellite.
What do you see in a quiet little bookshop owner like me?
What do I--?
Come here--
--let me show you something.
Whoa.
It's so small.
Yeah.
That's the problem.
From up here, there aren't any borders or lines... or details. "Don't sweat the little things"? When you spend your life up here, everything seems little.
You forget that those are real people down there, with real problems. Little problems that are big to them.
Abby, you get lost in a book. You notice when my tie doesn't match my shirt. You get wrapped up in details that people like Zoe can't even notice.
I need that more than you can know.
You're my anchor.
Abby, you keep me grounded.
Plus, you're smokin' hot.
And don't you forget it.

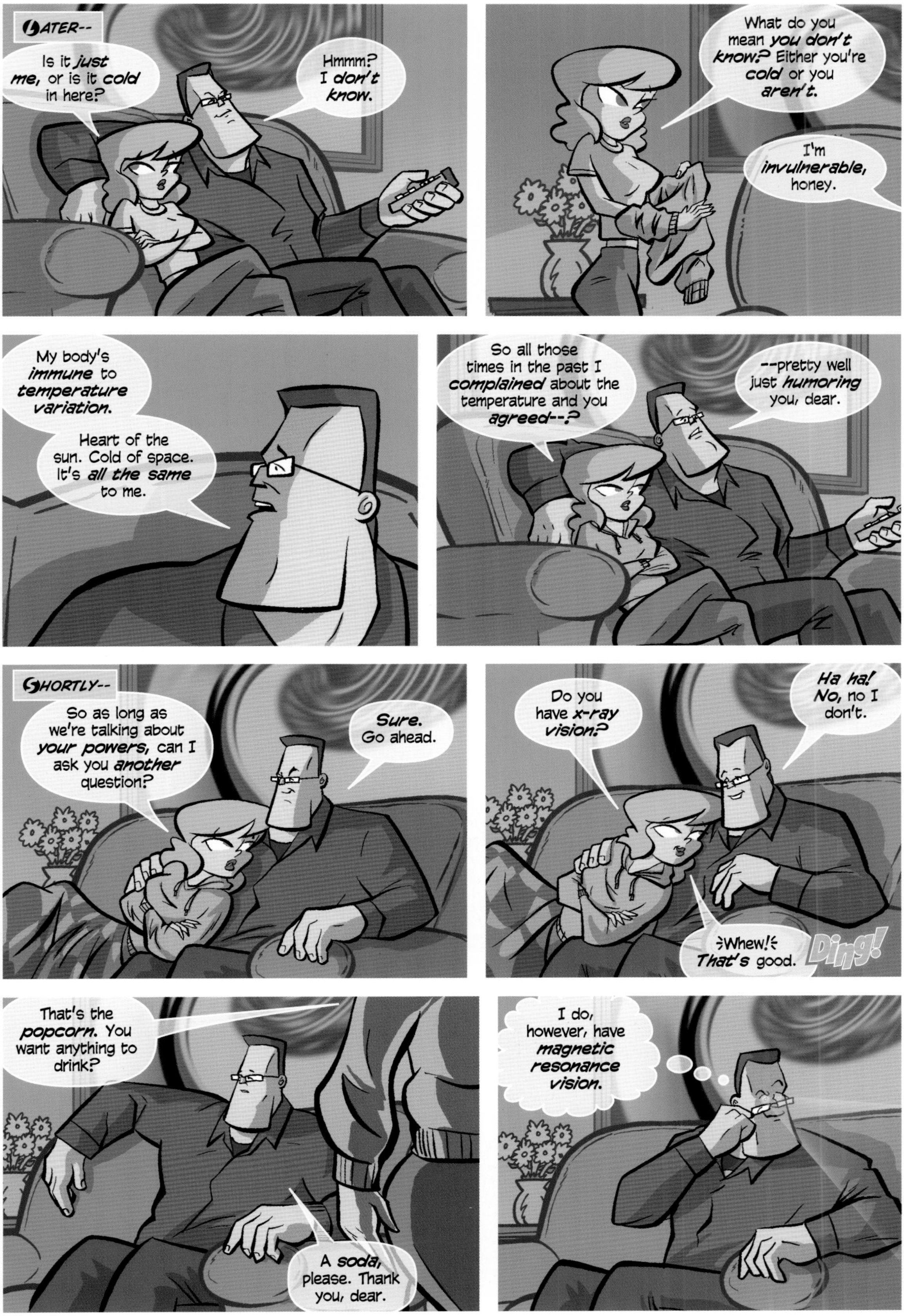
LATER--
Is it just me, or is it cold in here?
Hmmm? I don't know.
What do you mean you don't know? Either you're cold or you aren't.
I'm invulnerable, honey.
My body's immune to temperature variation.
Heart of the sun. Cold of space. It's all the same to me.
So all those times in the past I complained about the temperature and you agreed--?
--pretty well just humoring you, dear.
SHORTLY--
So as long as we're talking about your powers, can I ask you another question?
Sure. Go ahead.
Do you have x-ray vision?
Ha ha! No, no I don't.
Whew! That's good.
Ding!
That's the popcorn. You want anything to drink?
A soda, please. Thank you, dear.
I do, however, have magnetic resonance vision.

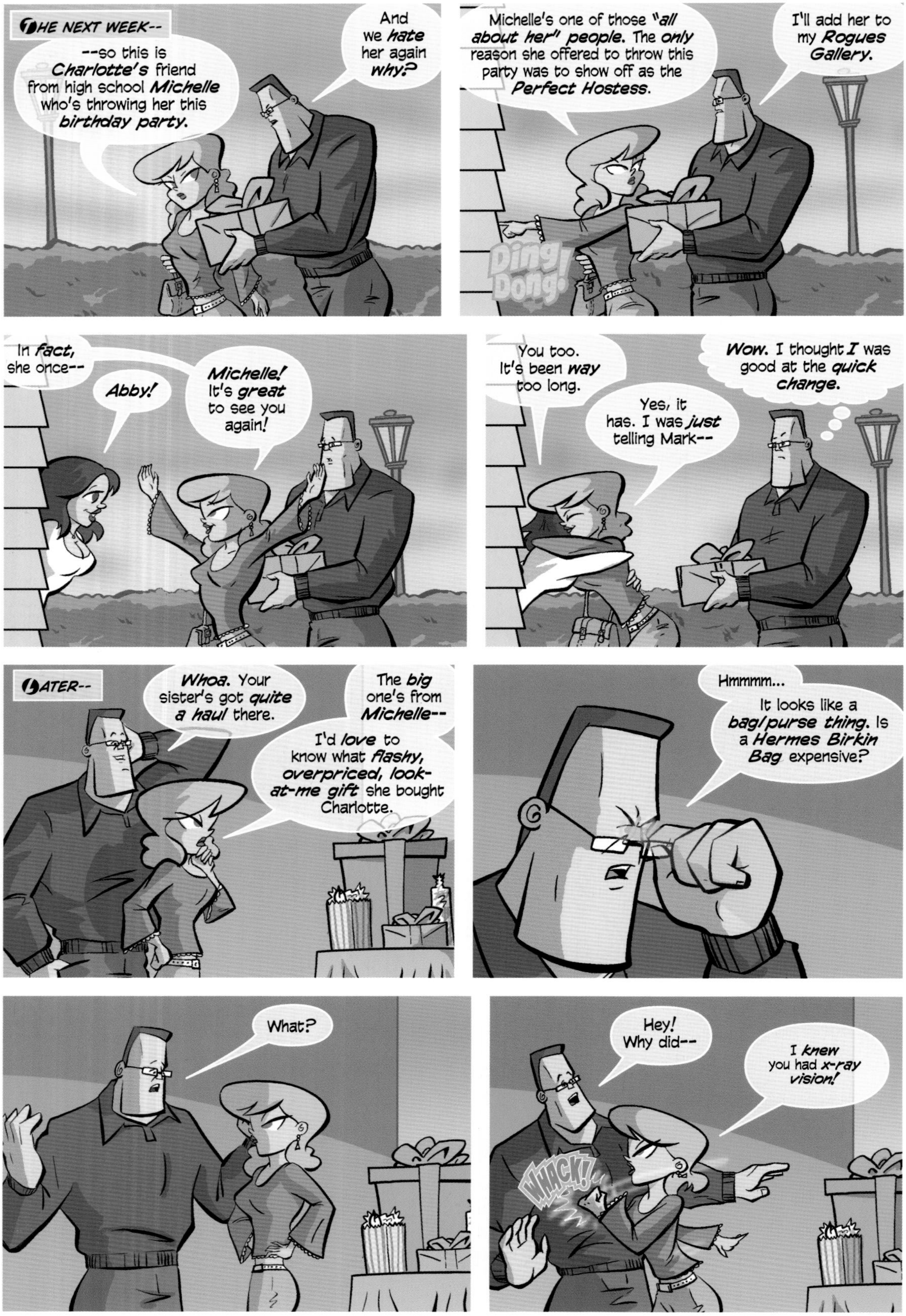
THE NEXT WEEK--
--so this is Charlotte's friend from high school Michelle who's throwing her this birthday party.
And we hate her again why?
Michelle's one of those "all about her" people. The only reason she offered to throw this party was to show off as the Perfect Hostess.
I'll add her to my Rogues Gallery.
Ding Dong!
In fact, she once--
Abby!
Michelle! It's great to see you again!
You too. It's been way too long.
Yes, it has. I was just telling Mark--
Wow. I thought I was good at the quick change.
LATER--
Whoa. Your sister's got quite a haul there.
The big one's from Michelle--
I'd love to know what flashy, overpriced, look-at-me gift she bought Charlotte.
Hmmmm...
It looks like a bag/purse thing. Is a Hermes Birkin Bag expensive?
What?
Hey! Why did--
WHACK!
I knew you had x-ray vision!

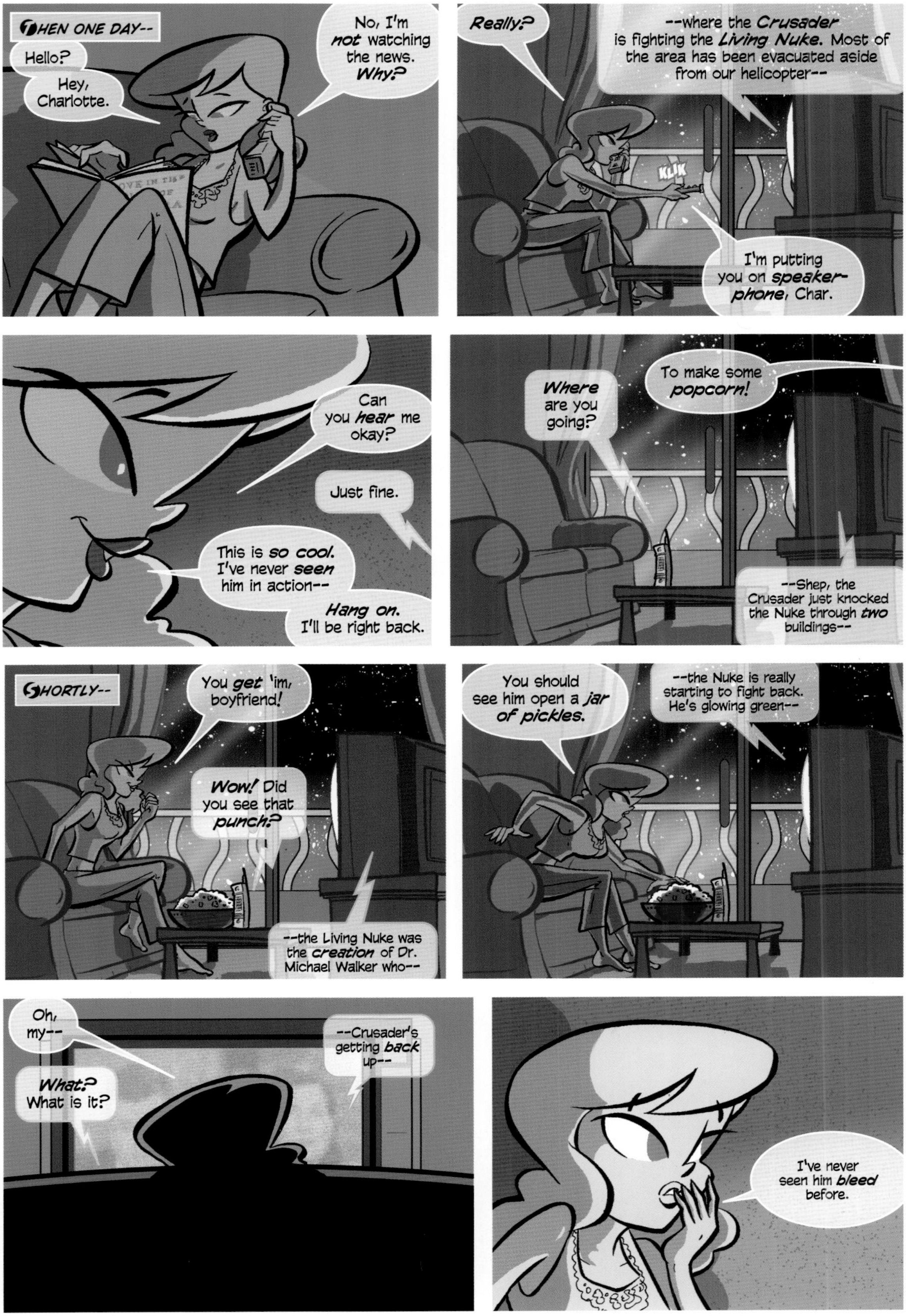
THEN ONE DAY--
Hello?
Hey, Charlotte.
No, I'm *not* watching the news. *Why?*
Really?
--where the *Crusader* is fighting the *Living Nuke.* Most of the area has been evacuated aside from our helicopter--
KLIK
I'm putting you on *speaker-phone,* Char.
Can you *hear* me okay?
Just fine.
This is *so cool.* I've never *seen* him in action--
Hang on. I'll be right back.
Where are you going?
To make some *popcorn!*
--Shep, the Crusader just knocked the Nuke through *two* buildings--
SHORTLY--
You *get* 'im, boyfriend!
Wow! Did you see that *punch?*
--the Living Nuke was the *creation* of Dr. Michael Walker who--
You should see him open a *jar of pickles.*
--the Nuke is really starting to fight back. He's glowing green--
Oh, my--
What? What is it?
--Crusader's getting *back* up--
I've never seen him *bleed* before.

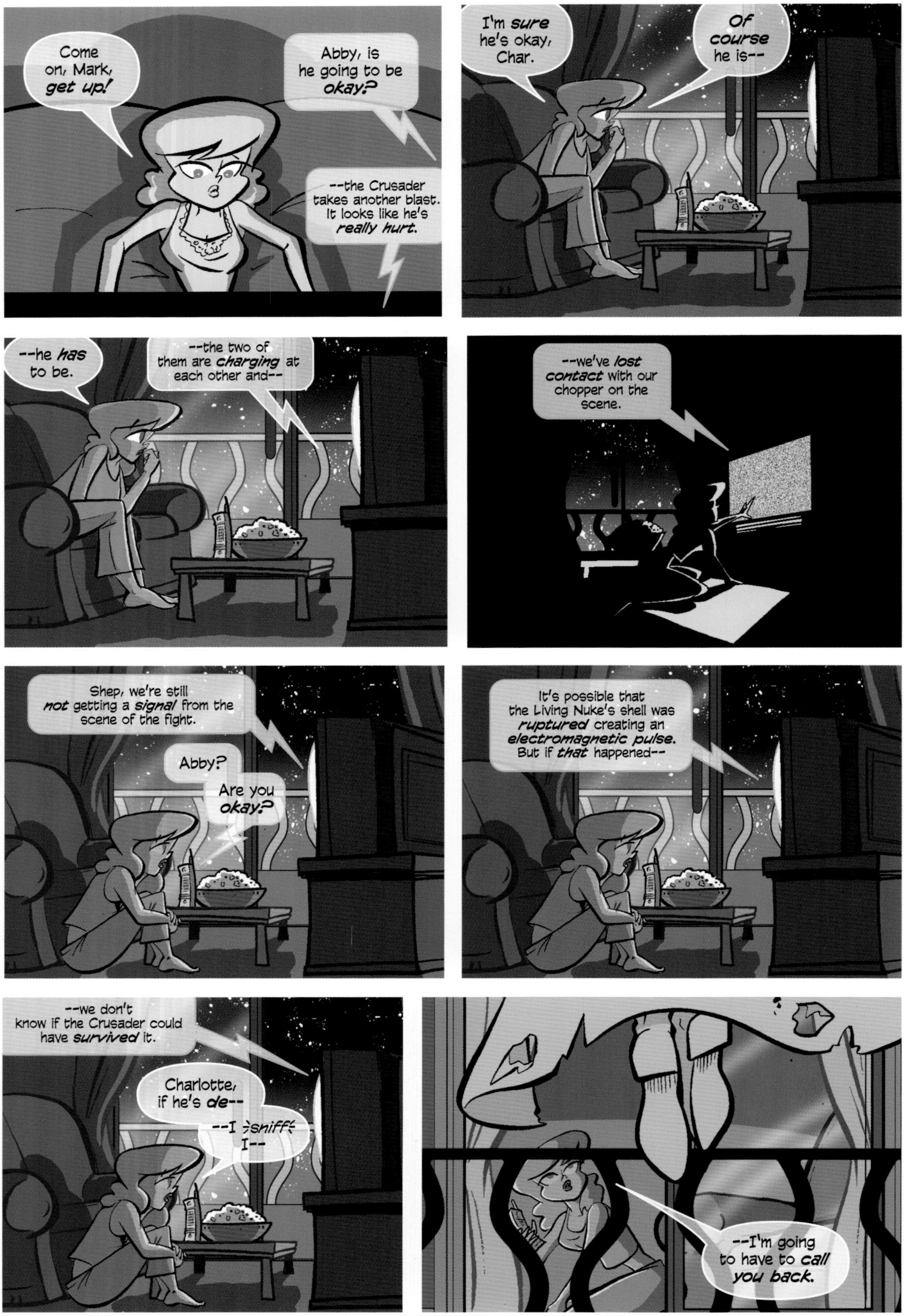
Come on, Mark, get up!
Abby, is he going to be okay?
--the Crusader takes another blast. It looks like he's really hurt.
I'm sure he's okay, Char.
Of course he is--
--he has to be.
--the two of them are charging at each other and--
--we've lost contact with our chopper on the scene.
Shep, we're still not getting a signal from the scene of the fight.
Abby?
Are you okay?
It's possible that the Living Nuke's shell was ruptured creating an electromagnetic pulse. But if that happened--
--we don't know if the Crusader could have survived it.
Charlotte, if he's de--
--I ⫘sniff⫘ I--
--I'm going to have to call you back.

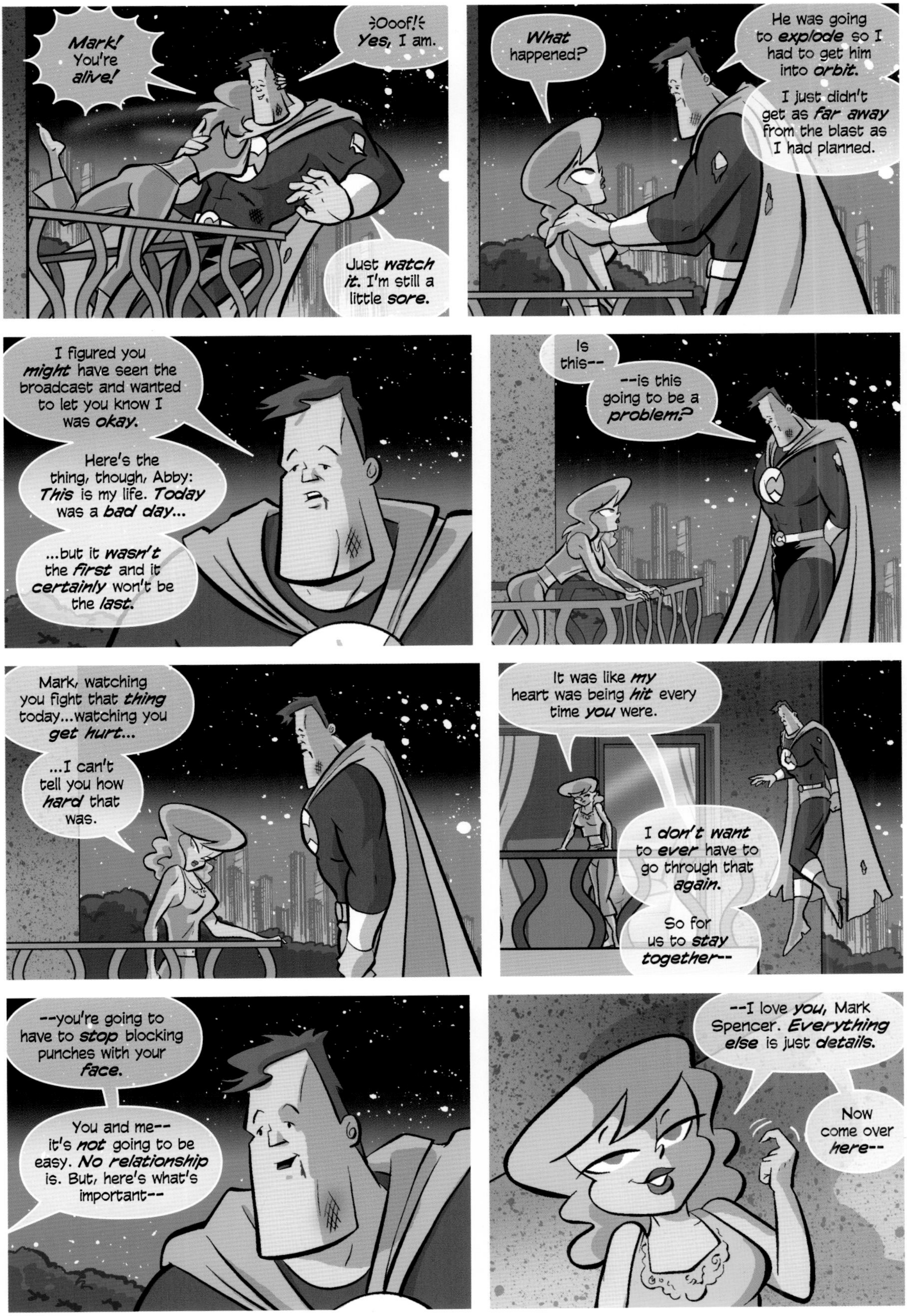
Mark! You're alive!
Ooof! Yes, I am.
Just watch it. I'm still a little sore.
What happened?
He was going to explode so I had to get him into orbit.
I just didn't get as far away from the blast as I had planned.
I figured you might have seen the broadcast and wanted to let you know I was okay.
Here's the thing, though, Abby: This is my life. Today was a bad day...
...but it wasn't the first and it certainly won't be the last.
Is this--
--is this going to be a problem?
Mark, watching you fight that thing today...watching you get hurt...
...I can't tell you how hard that was.
It was like my heart was being hit every time you were.
I don't want to ever have to go through that again.
So for us to stay together--
--you're going to have to stop blocking punches with your face.
You and me--it's not going to be easy. No relationship is. But, here's what's important--
--I love you, Mark Spencer. Everything else is just details.
Now come over here--

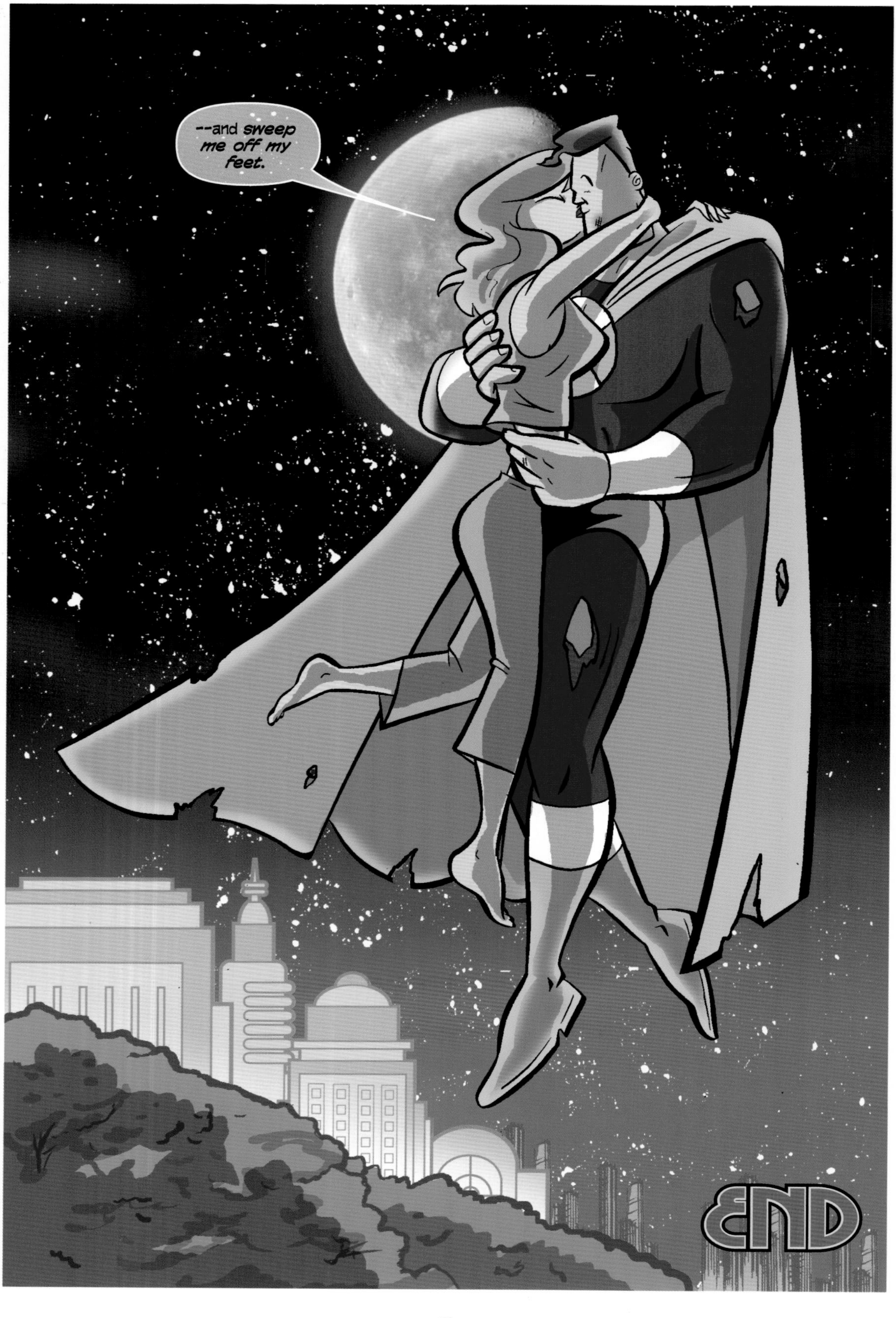
--and sweep me off my feet.
END

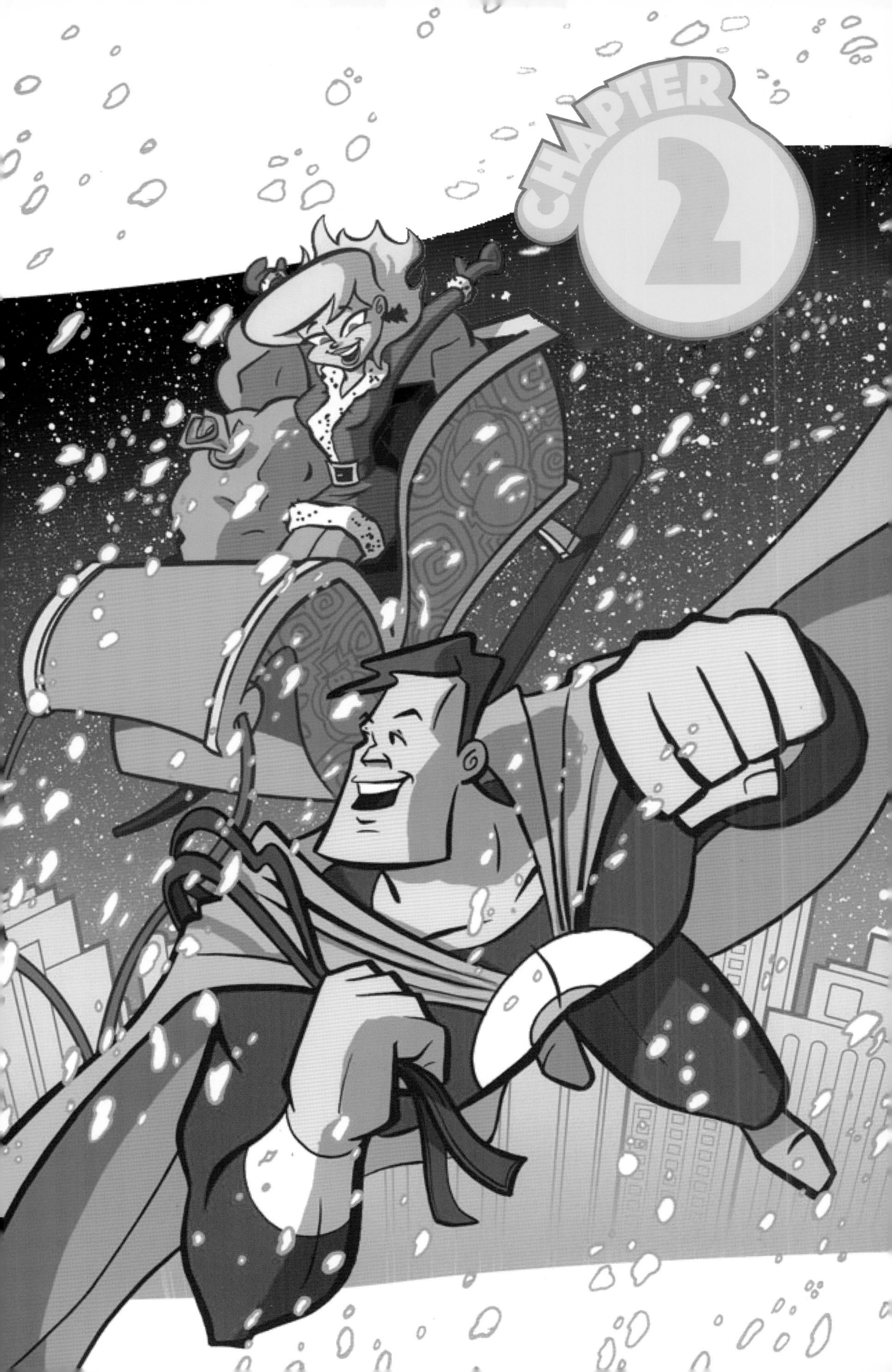
CHAPTER
2

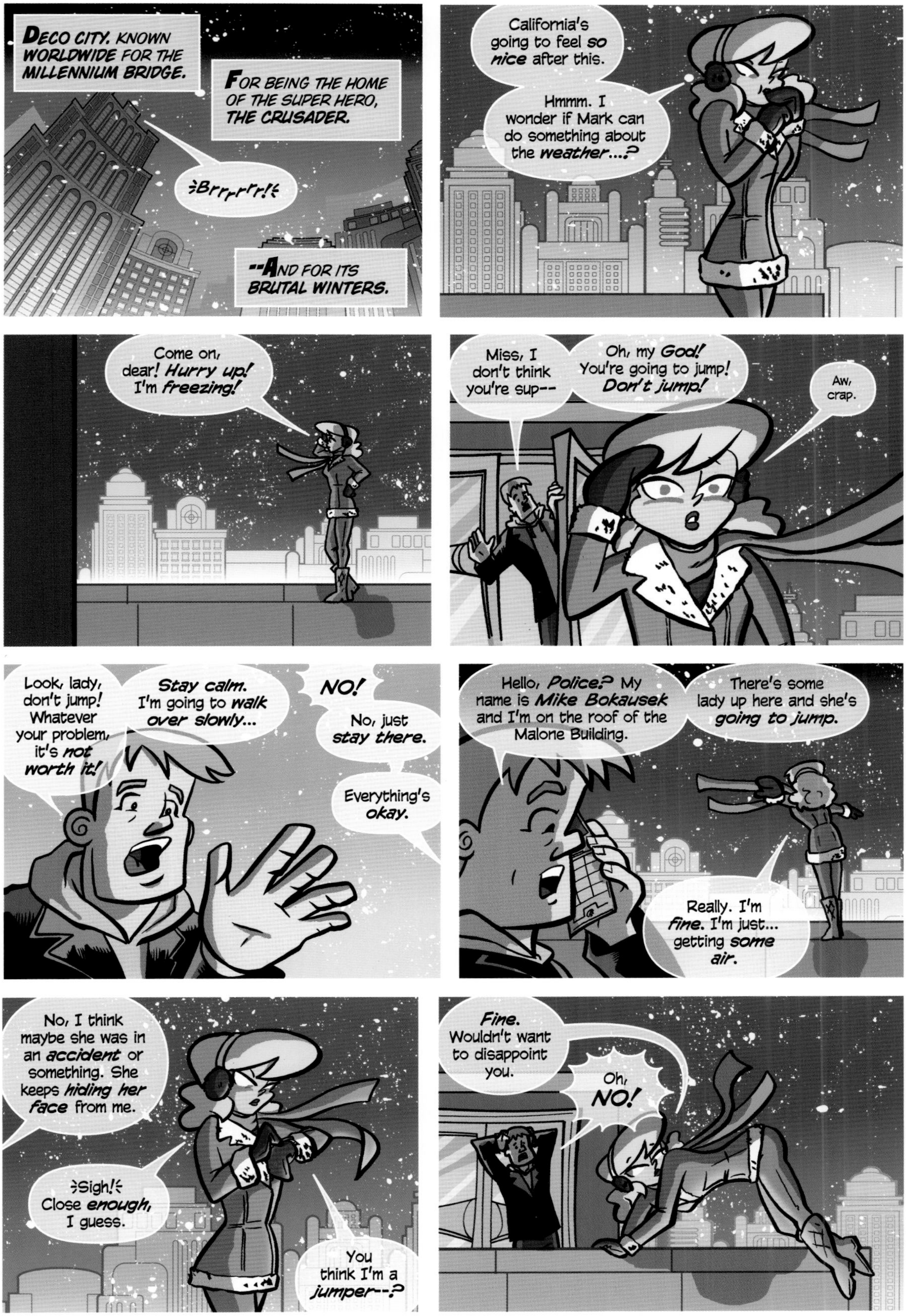
DECO CITY. KNOWN WORLDWIDE FOR THE MILLENNIUM BRIDGE.
FOR BEING THE HOME OF THE SUPER HERO, THE CRUSADER.
Brrrrrr!
--AND FOR ITS BRUTAL WINTERS.
California's going to feel so nice after this.
Hmmm. I wonder if Mark can do something about the weather...?
Come on, dear! Hurry up! I'm freezing!
Miss, I don't think you're sup--
Oh, my God! You're going to jump! Don't jump!
Aw, crap.
Look, lady, don't jump! Whatever your problem, it's not worth it!
Stay calm. I'm going to walk over slowly...
NO!
No, just stay there.
Everything's okay.
Hello, Police? My name is Mike Bokausek and I'm on the roof of the Malone Building.
There's some lady up here and she's going to jump.
Really. I'm fine. I'm just... getting some air.
No, I think maybe she was in an accident or something. She keeps hiding her face from me.
Sigh! Close enough, I guess.
You think I'm a jumper--?
Fine. Wouldn't want to disappoint you.
Oh, NO!

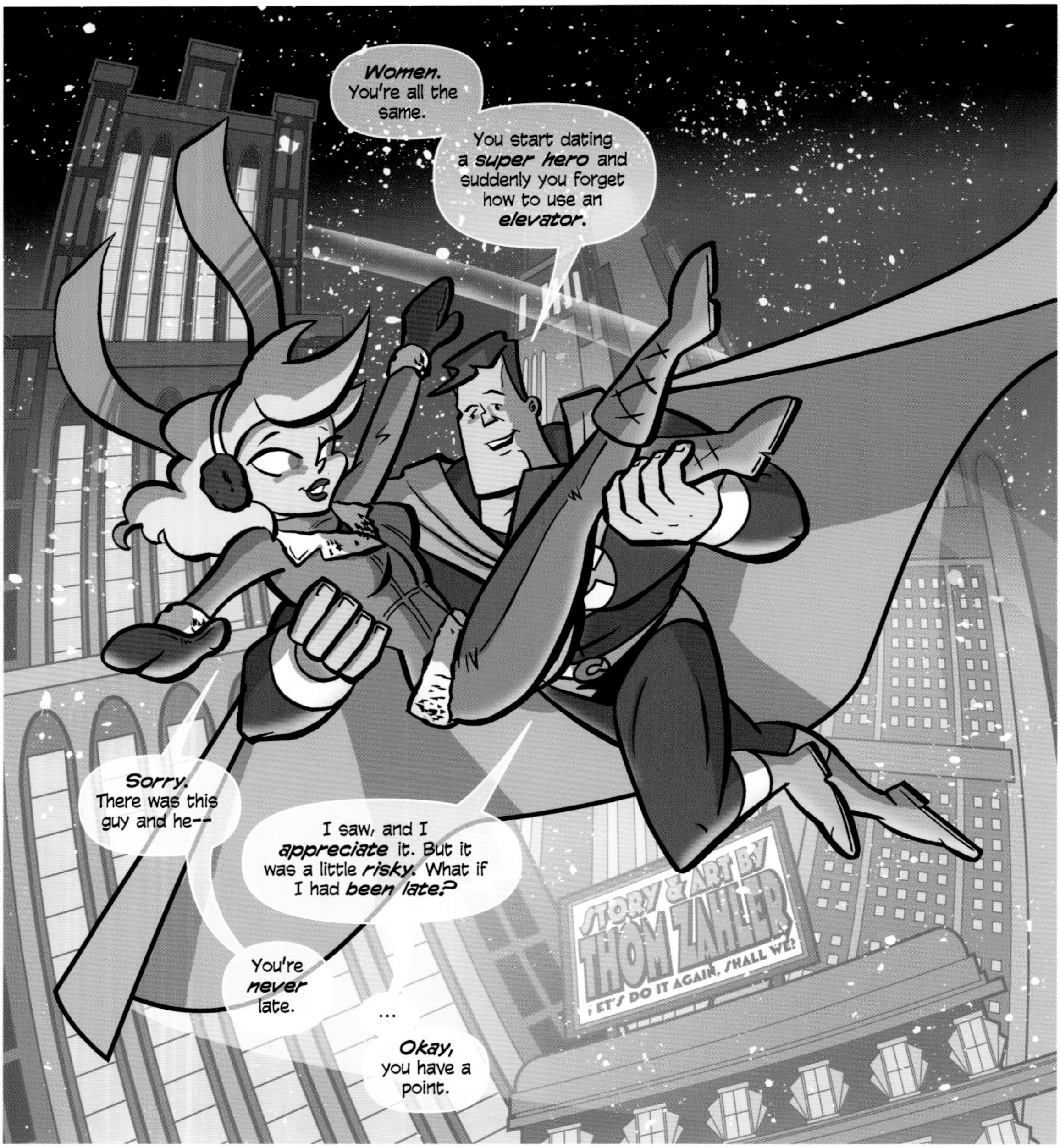
Women. You're all the same.
You start dating a super hero and suddenly you forget how to use an elevator.
Sorry. There was this guy and he--
I saw, and I appreciate it. But it was a little risky. What if I had been late?
You're never late.
...
Okay, you have a point.
STORY & ART BY THOM ZAHLER
ET'S DO IT AGAIN, SHALL WE?

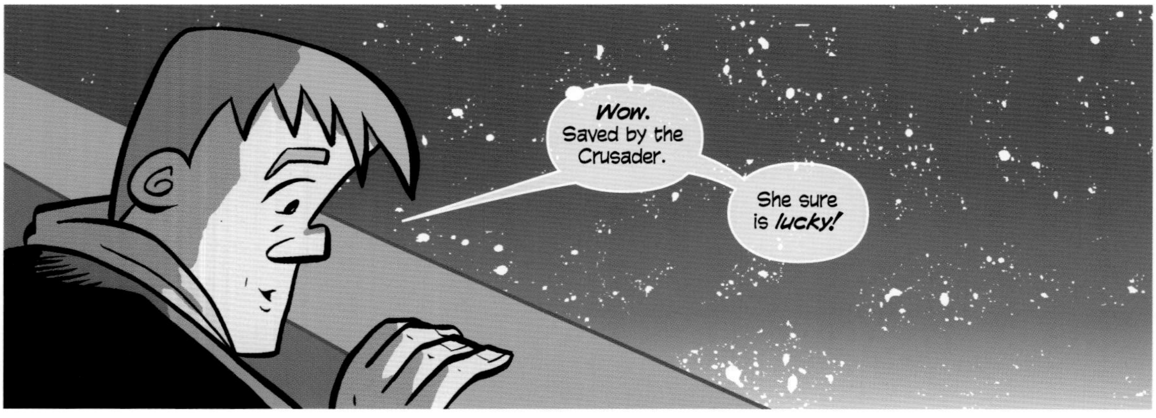
Wow. Saved by the Crusader.
She sure is lucky!

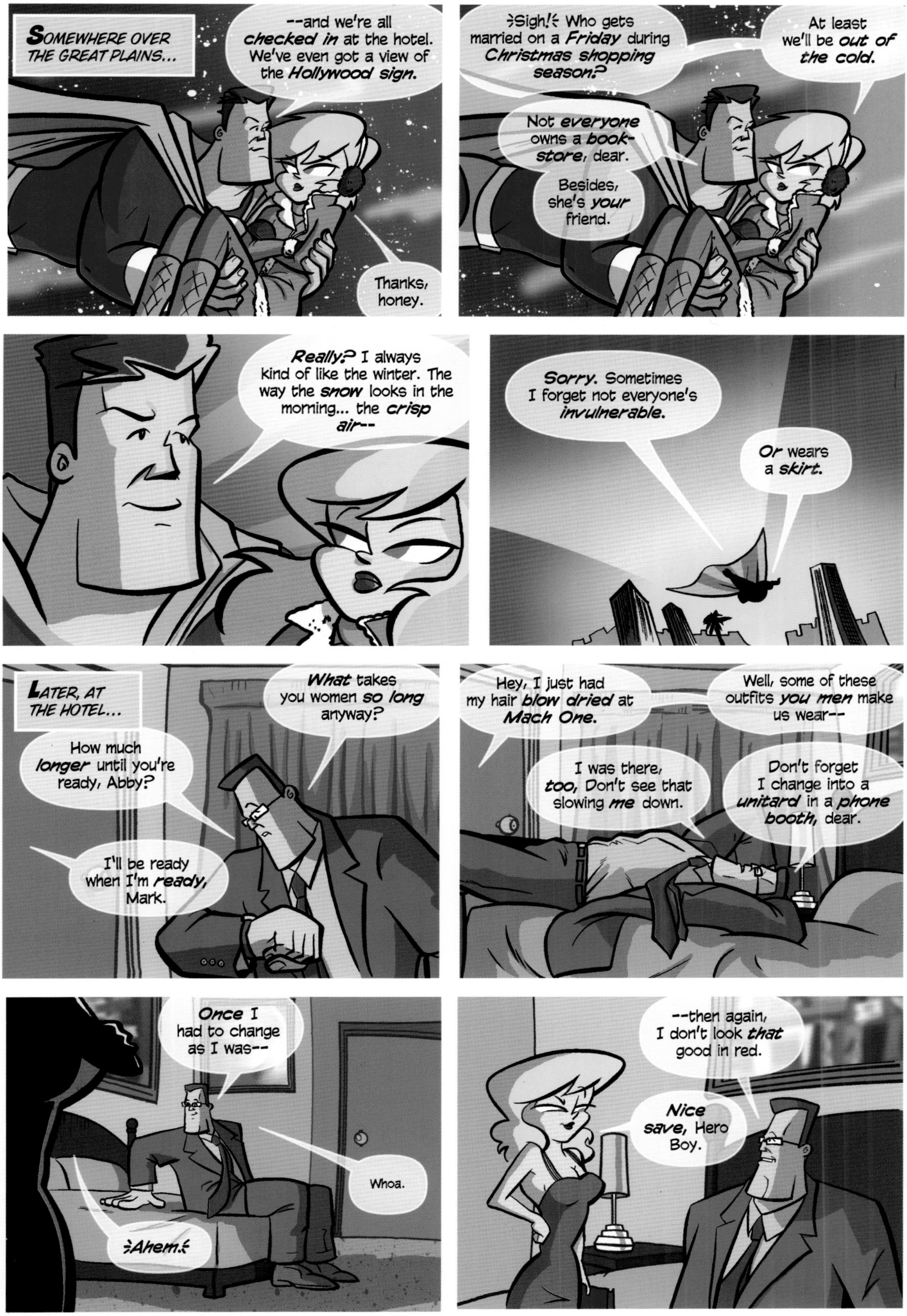

SOMEWHERE OVER THE GREAT PLAINS...
--and we're all checked in at the hotel. We've even got a view of the Hollywood sign.
Thanks, honey.
Sigh! Who gets married on a Friday during Christmas shopping season?
At least we'll be out of the cold.
Not everyone owns a book-store, dear.
Besides, she's your friend.
Really? I always kind of like the winter. The way the snow looks in the morning... the crisp air--
Sorry. Sometimes I forget not everyone's invulnerable.
Or wears a skirt.
LATER, AT THE HOTEL...
What takes you women so long anyway?
How much longer until you're ready, Abby?
I'll be ready when I'm ready, Mark.
Hey, I just had my hair blow dried at Mach One.
Well, some of these outfits you men make us wear--
I was there, too, Don't see that slowing me down.
Don't forget I change into a unitard in a phone booth, dear.
Once I had to change as I was--
Whoa.
Ahem.
--then again, I don't look that good in red.
Nice save, Hero Boy.

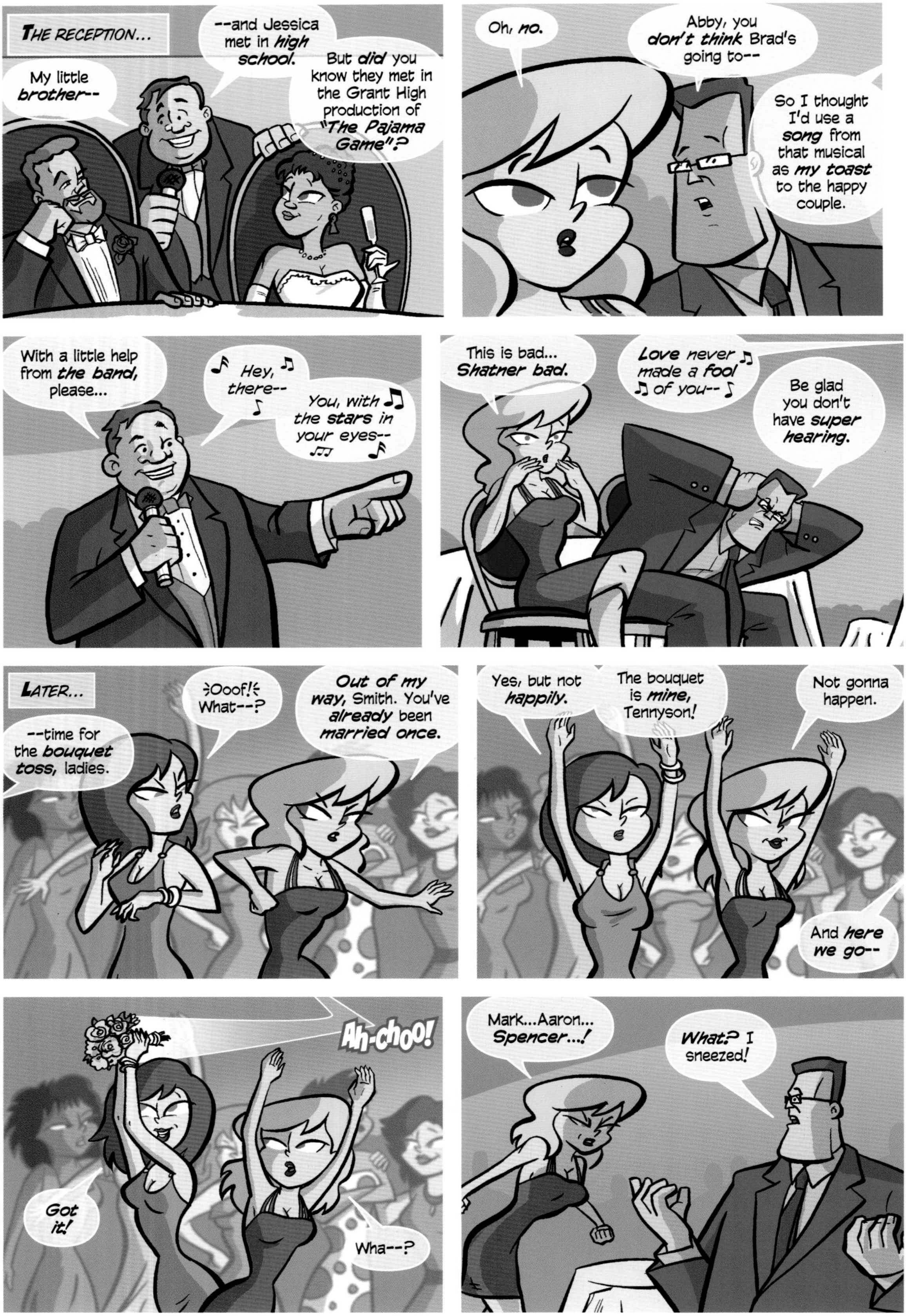
THE RECEPTION...
My little brother--
--and Jessica met in high school.
But did you know they met in the Grant High production of "The Pajama Game"?
Oh, no.
Abby, you don't think Brad's going to--
So I thought I'd use a song from that musical as my toast to the happy couple.
With a little help from the band, please...
Hey, there--
You, with the stars in your eyes--
This is bad... Shatner bad.
Love never made a fool of you--
Be glad you don't have super hearing.
LATER...
--time for the bouquet toss, ladies.
Ooof! What--?
Out of my way, Smith. You've already been married once.
Yes, but not happily.
The bouquet is mine, Tennyson!
Not gonna happen.
And here we go--
Ah-choo!
Got it!
Wha--?
Mark...Aaron... Spencer...!
What? I sneezed!

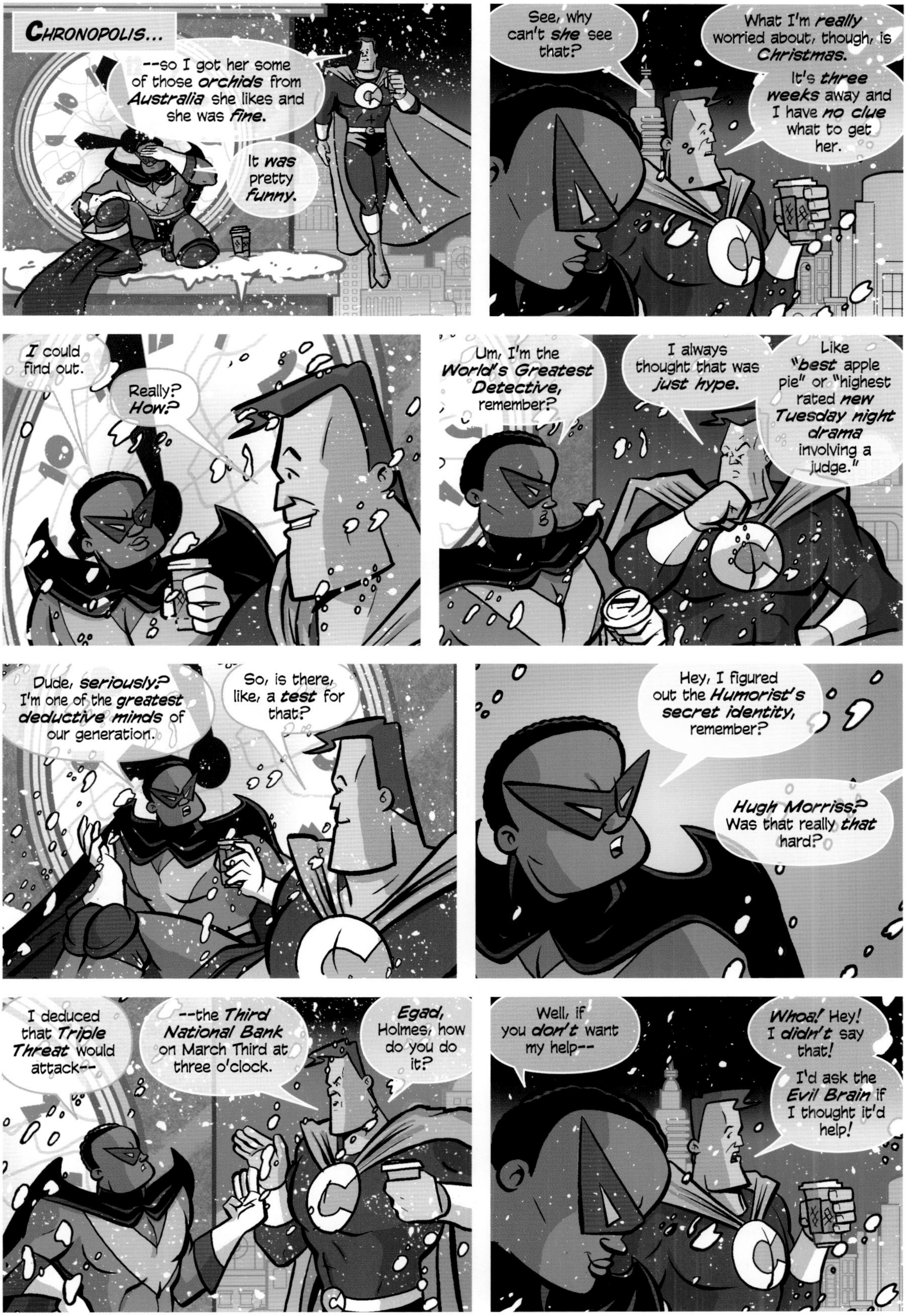

CHRONOPOLIS...
--so I got her some of those orchids from Australia she likes and she was fine.
It was pretty funny.
See, why can't she see that?
What I'm really worried about, though, is Christmas.
It's three weeks away and I have no clue what to get her.
I could find out.
Really? How?
Um, I'm the World's Greatest Detective, remember?
I always thought that was just hype.
Like "best apple pie" or "highest rated new Tuesday night drama involving a judge."
Dude, seriously? I'm one of the greatest deductive minds of our generation.
So, is there, like, a test for that?
Hey, I figured out the Humorist's secret identity, remember?
Hugh Morriss? Was that really that hard?
I deduced that Triple Threat would attack--
--the Third National Bank on March Third at three o'clock.
Egad, Holmes, how do you do it?
Well, if you don't want my help--
Whoa! Hey! I didn't say that!
I'd ask the Evil Brain if I thought it'd help!

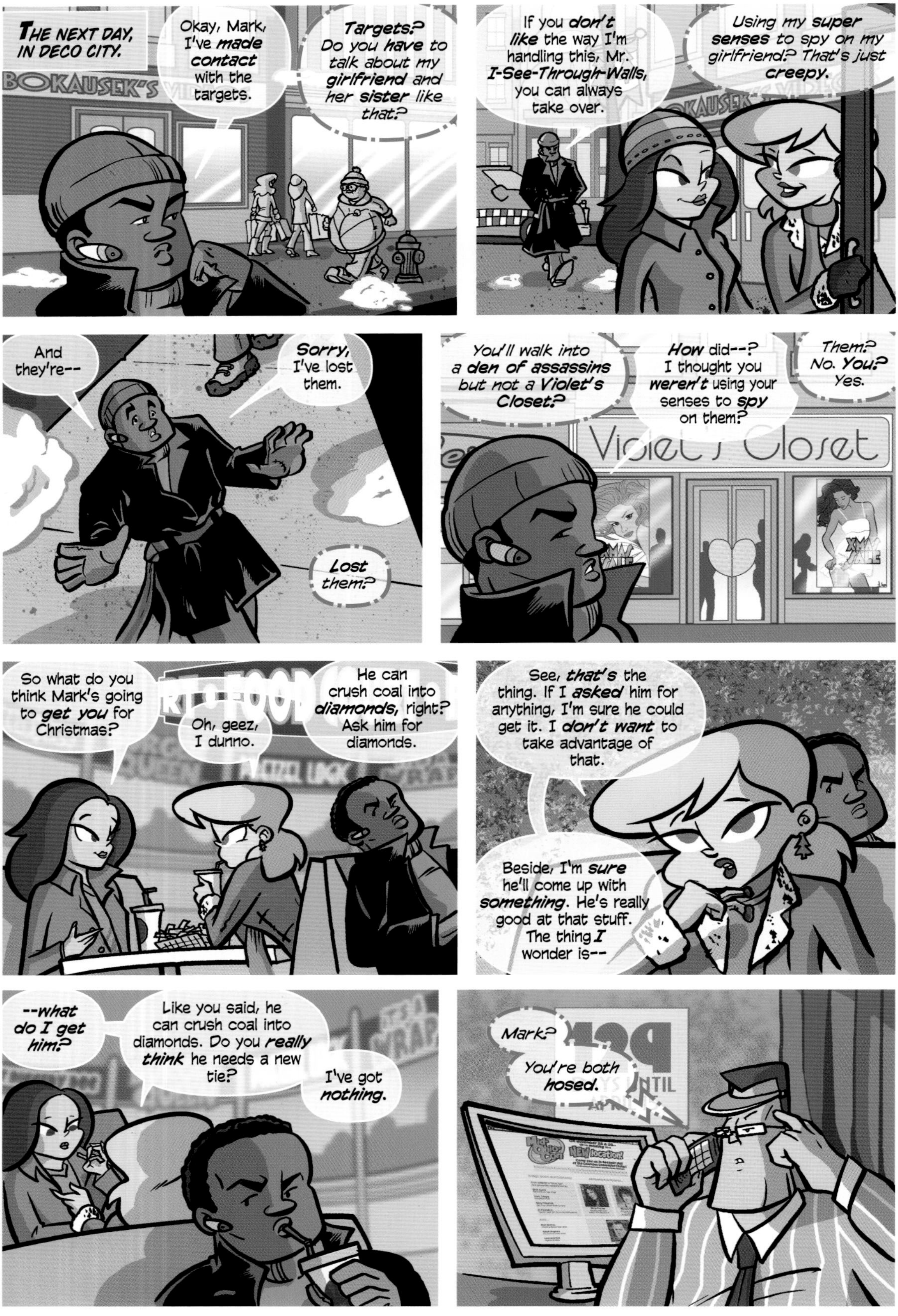
THE NEXT DAY, IN DECO CITY.
BOKAUSEK'S
Okay, Mark, I've made contact with the targets.
Targets? Do you have to talk about my girlfriend and her sister like that?
If you don't like the way I'm handling this, Mr. I-See-Through-Walls, you can always take over.
Using my super senses to spy on my girlfriend? That's just creepy.
And they're--
Sorry, I've lost them.
Lost them?
You'll walk into a den of assassins but not a Violet's Closet?
How did--? I thought you weren't using your senses to spy on them?
Them? No. You? Yes.
Violet's Closet
So what do you think Mark's going to get you for Christmas?
Oh, geez, I dunno.
He can crush coal into diamonds, right? Ask him for diamonds.
See, that's the thing. If I asked him for anything, I'm sure he could get it. I don't want to take advantage of that.
Beside, I'm sure he'll come up with something. He's really good at that stuff. The thing I wonder is--
--what do I get him?
Like you said, he can crush coal into diamonds. Do you really think he needs a new tie?
I've got nothing.
Mark?
You're both hosed.

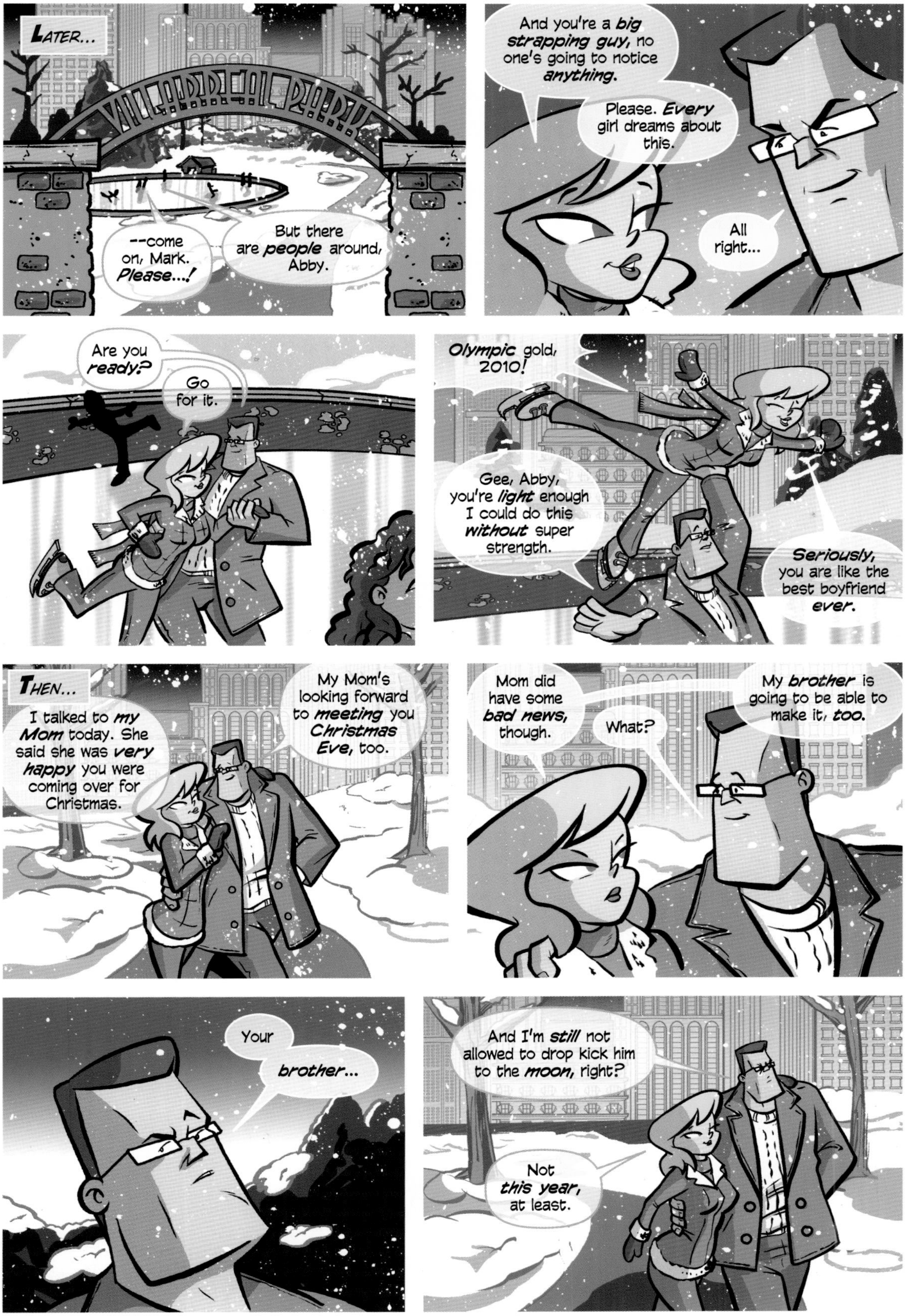
LATER...
--come on, Mark. *Please...!*
But there are *people* around, Abby.
And you're a *big strapping guy,* no one's going to notice *anything.*
Please. *Every* girl dreams about this.
All right...
Are you *ready?*
Go for it.
Olympic gold, 2010!
Gee, Abby, you're *light* enough I could do this *without* super strength.
Seriously, you are like the best boyfriend *ever.*
THEN...
I talked to *my Mom* today. She said she was *very happy* you were coming over for Christmas.
My Mom's looking forward to *meeting* you *Christmas Eve,* too.
Mom did have some *bad news,* though.
What?
My *brother* is going to be able to make it, *too.*
Your *brother...*
And I'm *still* not allowed to drop kick him to the *moon,* right?
Not *this year,* at least.

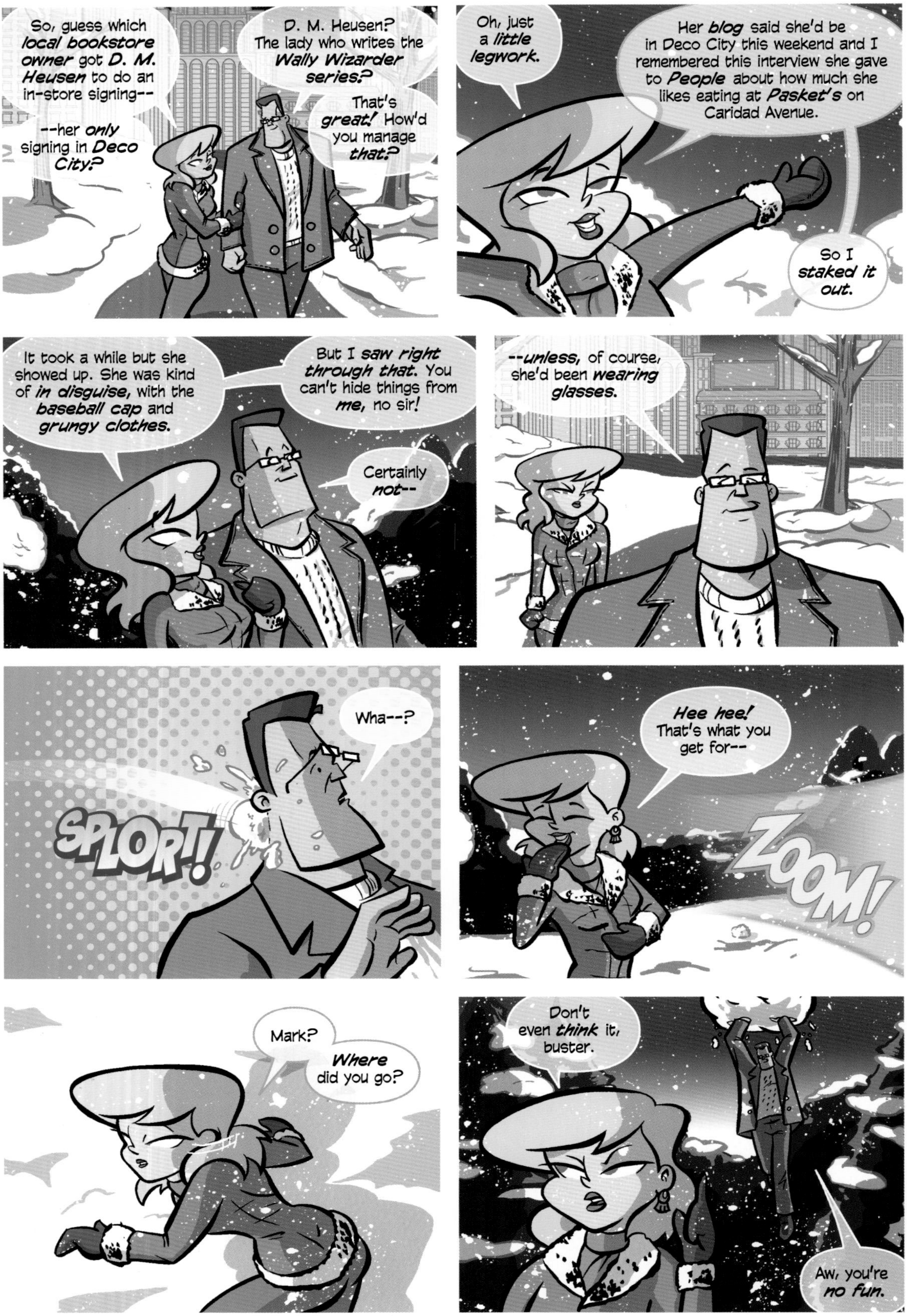
So, guess which local bookstore owner got D. M. Heusen to do an in-store signing--
--her only signing in Deco City?
D. M. Heusen? The lady who writes the Wally Wizarder series?
That's great! How'd you manage that?
Oh, just a little legwork.
Her blog said she'd be in Deco City this weekend and I remembered this interview she gave to People about how much she likes eating at Pasket's on Caridad Avenue.
So I staked it out.
It took a while but she showed up. She was kind of in disguise, with the baseball cap and grungy clothes.
But I saw right through that. You can't hide things from me, no sir!
Certainly not--
--unless, of course, she'd been wearing glasses.
Wha--?
SPLORT!
Hee hee! That's what you get for--
ZOOM!
Mark? Where did you go?
Don't even think it, buster.
Aw, you're no fun.

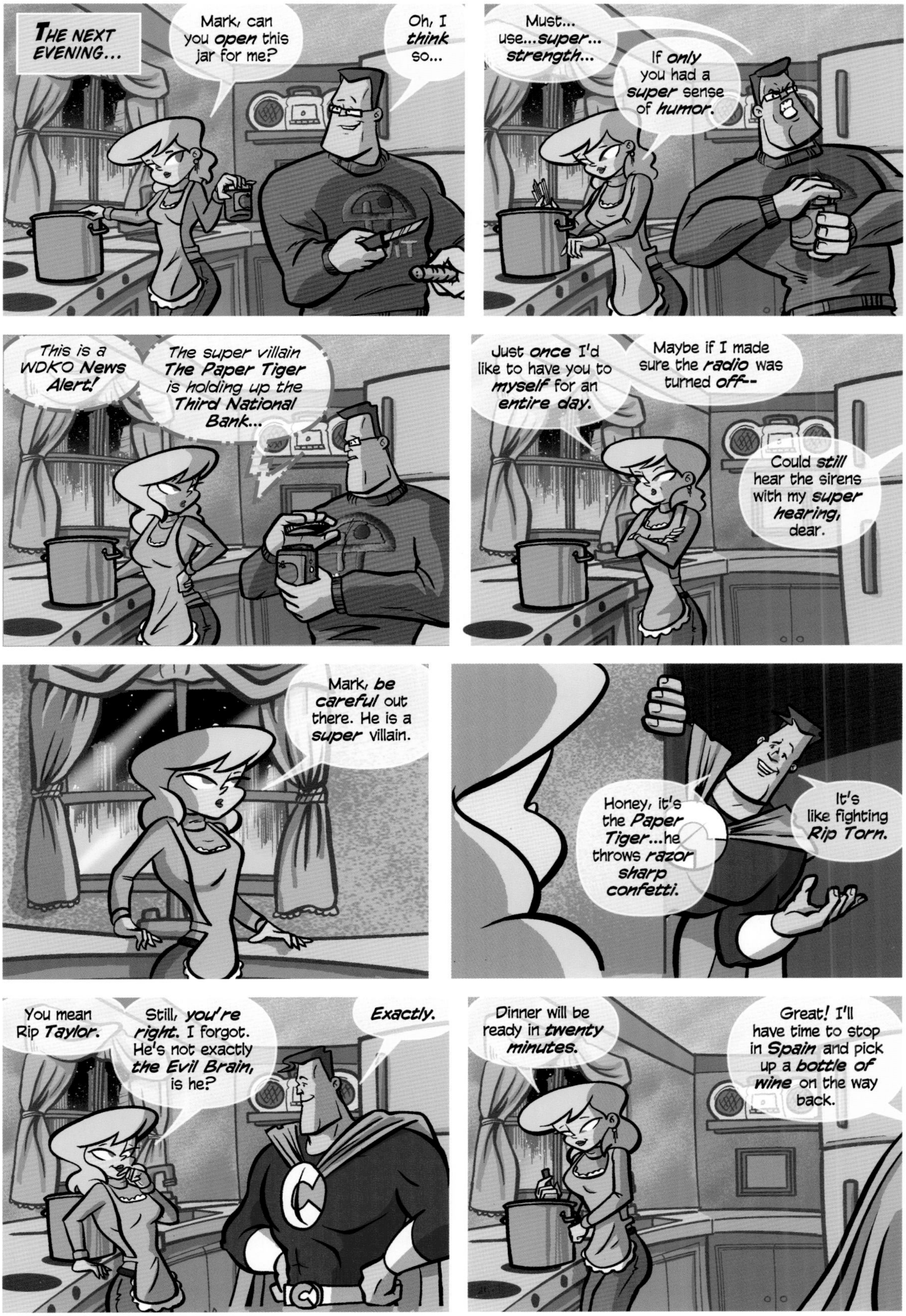
THE NEXT EVENING...
Mark, can you open this jar for me?
Oh, I think so...
Must... use...super... strength...
If only you had a super sense of humor.
This is a WDKO News Alert!
The super villain The Paper Tiger is holding up the Third National Bank...
Just once I'd like to have you to myself for an entire day.
Maybe if I made sure the radio was turned off--
Could still hear the sirens with my super hearing, dear.
Mark, be careful out there. He is a super villain.
Honey, it's the Paper Tiger...he throws razor sharp confetti.
It's like fighting Rip Torn.
You mean Rip Taylor.
Still, you're right. I forgot. He's not exactly the Evil Brain, is he?
Exactly.
Dinner will be ready in twenty minutes.
Great! I'll have time to stop in Spain and pick up a bottle of wine on the way back.

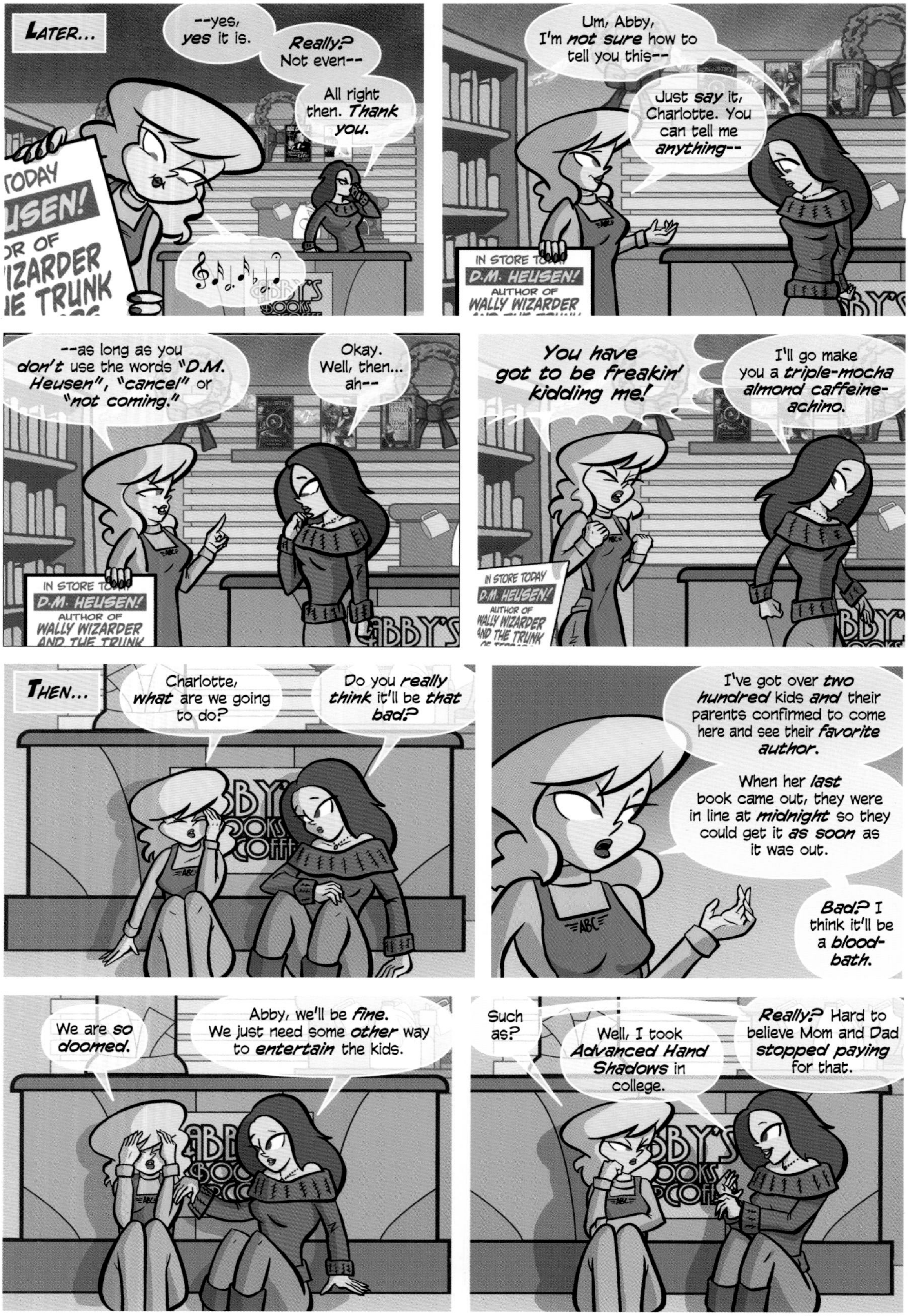
LATER...
--yes, yes it is.
Really? Not even--
All right then. Thank you.
Um, Abby, I'm not sure how to tell you this--
Just say it, Charlotte. You can tell me anything--
D.M. HEUSEN!
AUTHOR OF
WALLY WIZARDER
--as long as you don't use the words "D.M. Heusen", "cancel" or "not coming."
Okay. Well, then... ah--
You have got to be freakin' kidding me!
I'll go make you a triple-mocha almond caffeine-achino.
THEN...
Charlotte, what are we going to do?
Do you really think it'll be that bad?
I've got over two hundred kids and their parents confirmed to come here and see their favorite author.
When her last book came out, they were in line at midnight so they could get it as soon as it was out.
Bad? I think it'll be a blood-bath.
We are so doomed.
Abby, we'll be fine. We just need some other way to entertain the kids.
Such as?
Well, I took Advanced Hand Shadows in college.
Really? Hard to believe Mom and Dad stopped paying for that.

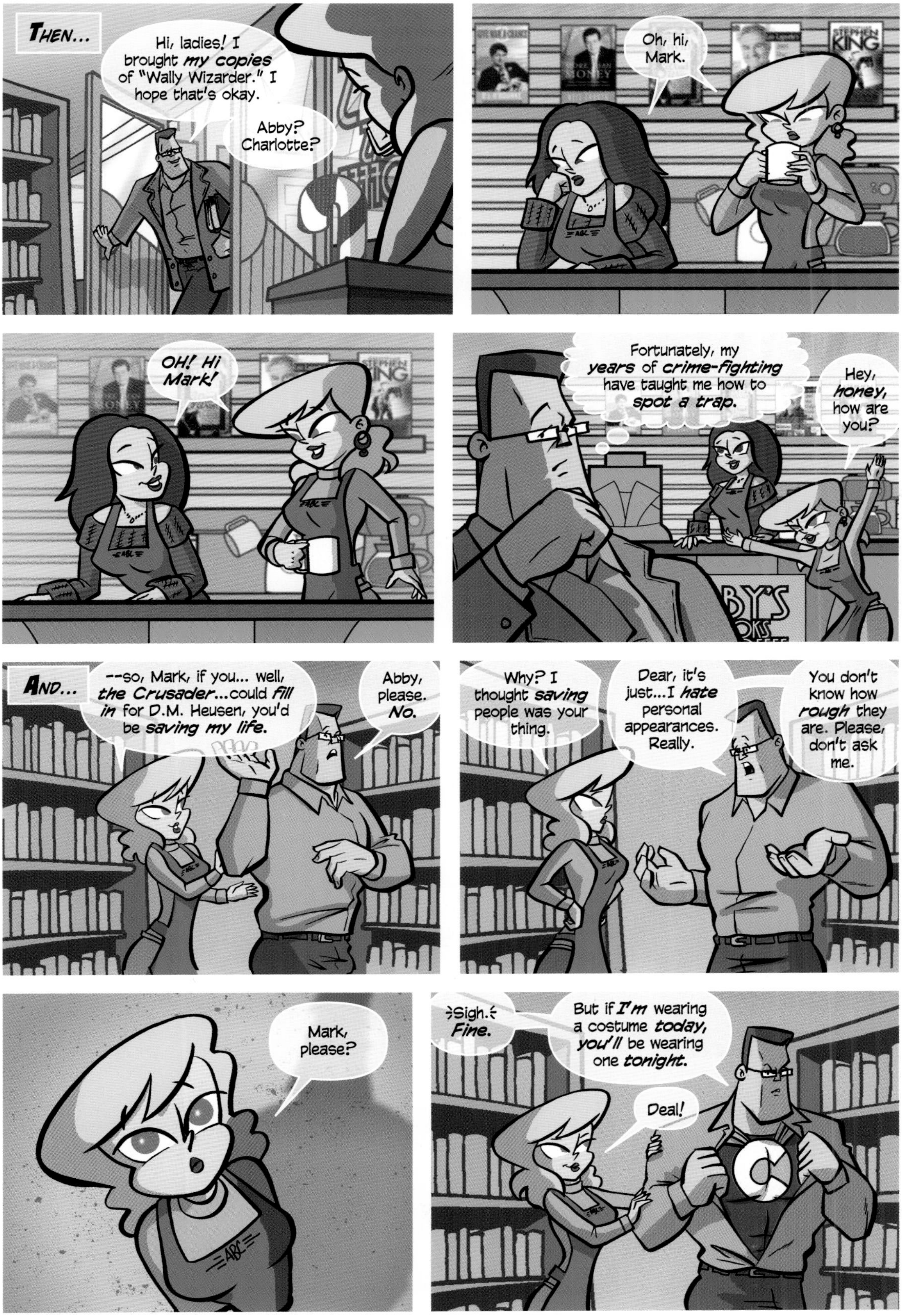
THEN...
Hi, ladies! I brought my copies of "Wally Wizarder." I hope that's okay.
Abby? Charlotte?
STEPHEN KING
Oh, hi, Mark.
OH! Hi Mark!
Fortunately, my years of crime-fighting have taught me how to spot a trap.
Hey, honey, how are you?
AND...
--so, Mark, if you... well, the Crusader...could fill in for D.M. Heusen, you'd be saving my life.
Abby, please. No.
Why? I thought saving people was your thing.
Dear, it's just...I hate personal appearances. Really.
You don't know how rough they are. Please, don't ask me.
Mark, please?
Sigh. Fine.
But if I'm wearing a costume today, you'll be wearing one tonight.
Deal!

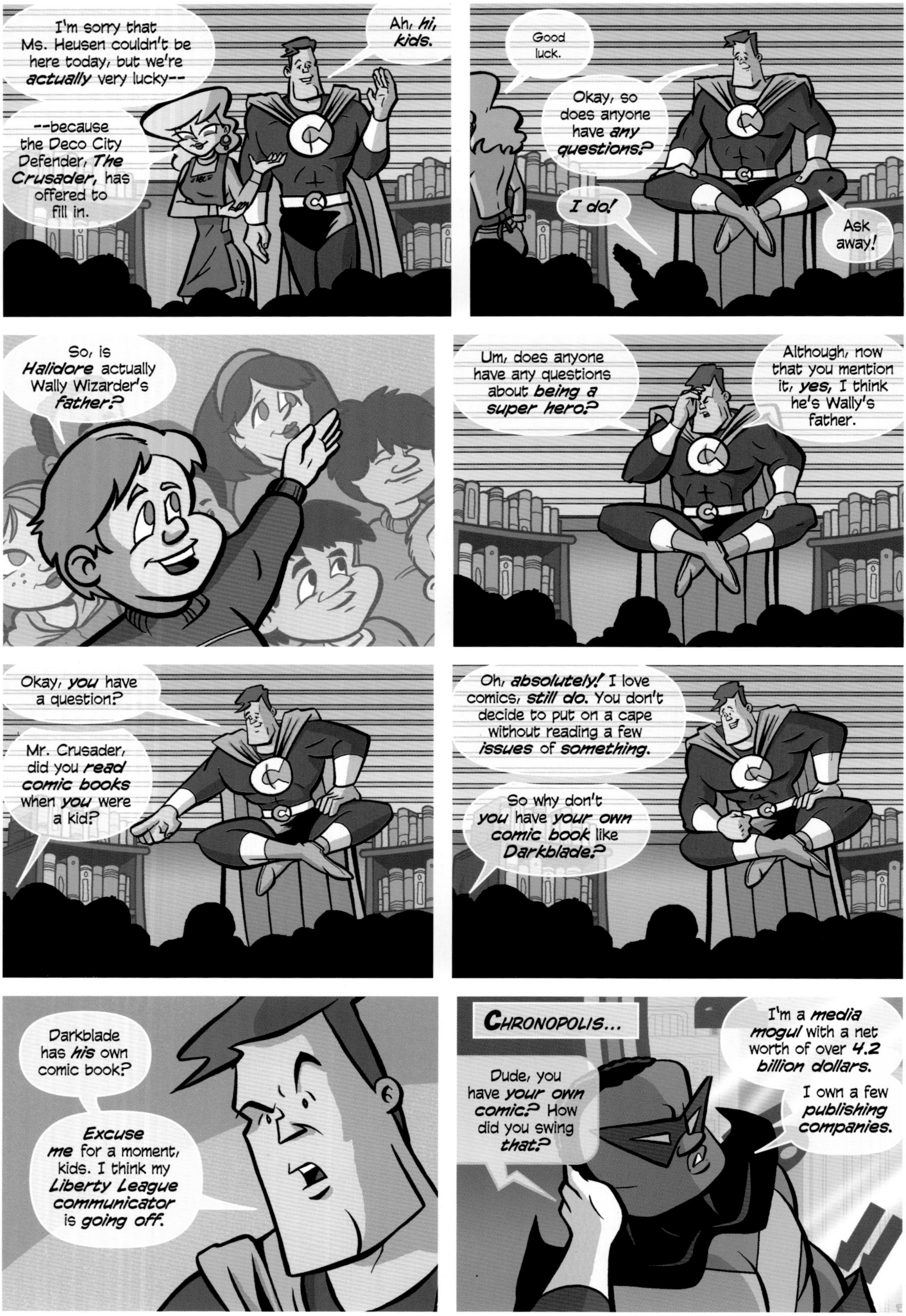
I'm sorry that Ms. Heusen couldn't be here today, but we're *actually* very lucky--
--because the Deco City Defender, *The Crusader*, has offered to fill in.
Ah, *hi, kids.*
Good luck.
Okay, so does anyone have *any questions?*
I do!
Ask away!
So, is *Halidore* actually Wally Wizarder's *father?*
Um, does anyone have any questions about *being a super hero?*
Although, now that you mention it, *yes,* I think he's Wally's father.
Okay, *you* have a question?
Mr. Crusader, did you *read comic books* when *you* were a kid?
Oh, *absolutely!* I love comics, *still do.* You don't decide to put on a cape without reading a few *issues* of *something*.
So why don't *you* have *your own comic book* like *Darkblade?*
Darkblade has *his* own comic book?
Excuse me for a moment, kids. I think my *Liberty League communicator* is *going off.*
CHRONOPOLIS...
Dude, you have *your own comic?* How did you swing *that?*
I'm a *media mogul* with a net worth of over *4.2 billion dollars.*
I own a few *publishing companies.*

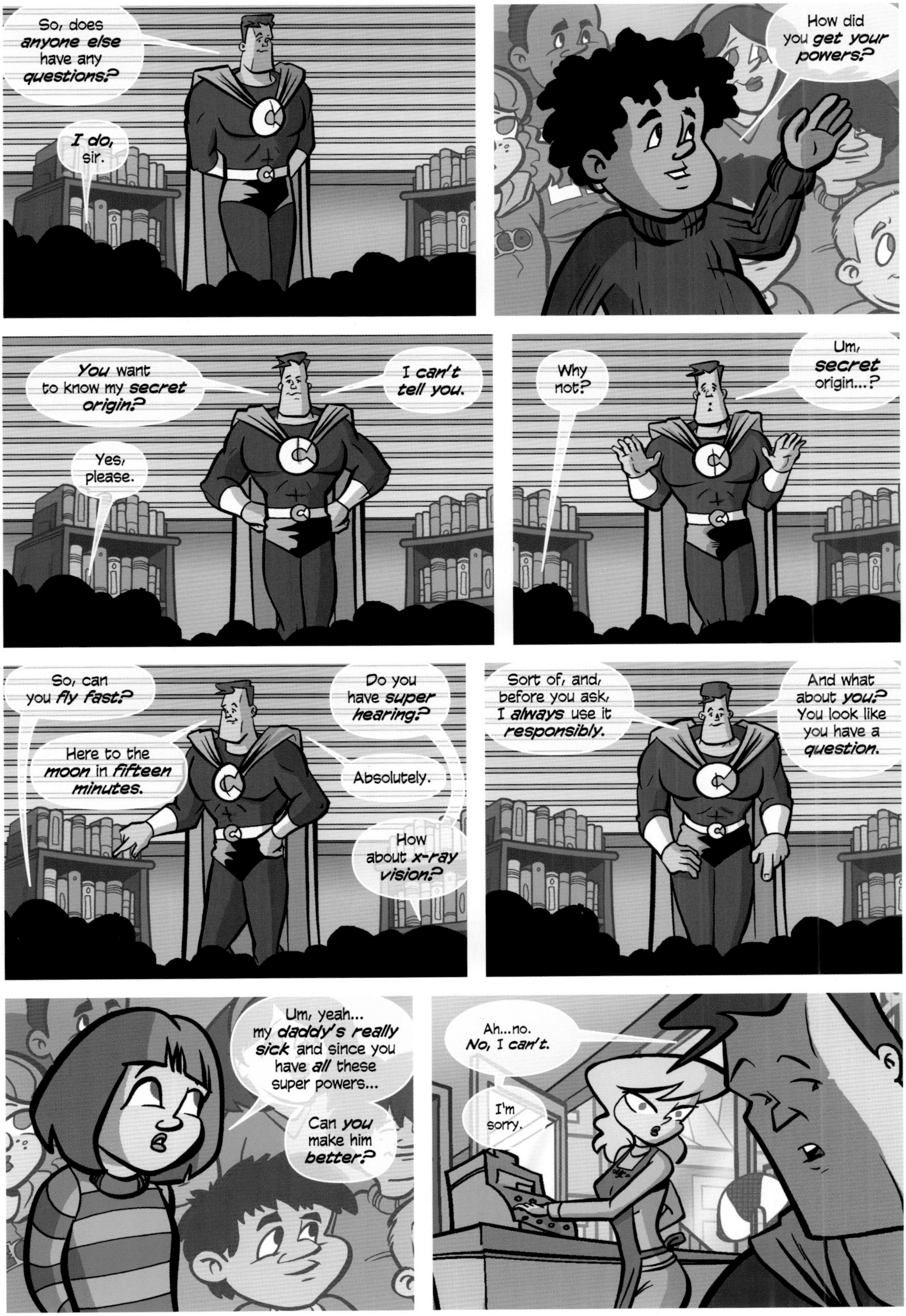
So, does anyone else have any questions?
I do, sir.
How did you get your powers?
You want to know my secret origin?
Yes, please.
I can't tell you.
Why not?
Um, secret origin...?
So, can you fly fast?
Here to the moon in fifteen minutes.
Do you have super hearing?
Absolutely.
How about x-ray vision?
Sort of, and, before you ask, I always use it responsibly.
And what about you? You look like you have a question.
Um, yeah... my daddy's really sick and since you have all these super powers...
Can you make him better?
Ah...no. No, I can't.
I'm sorry.

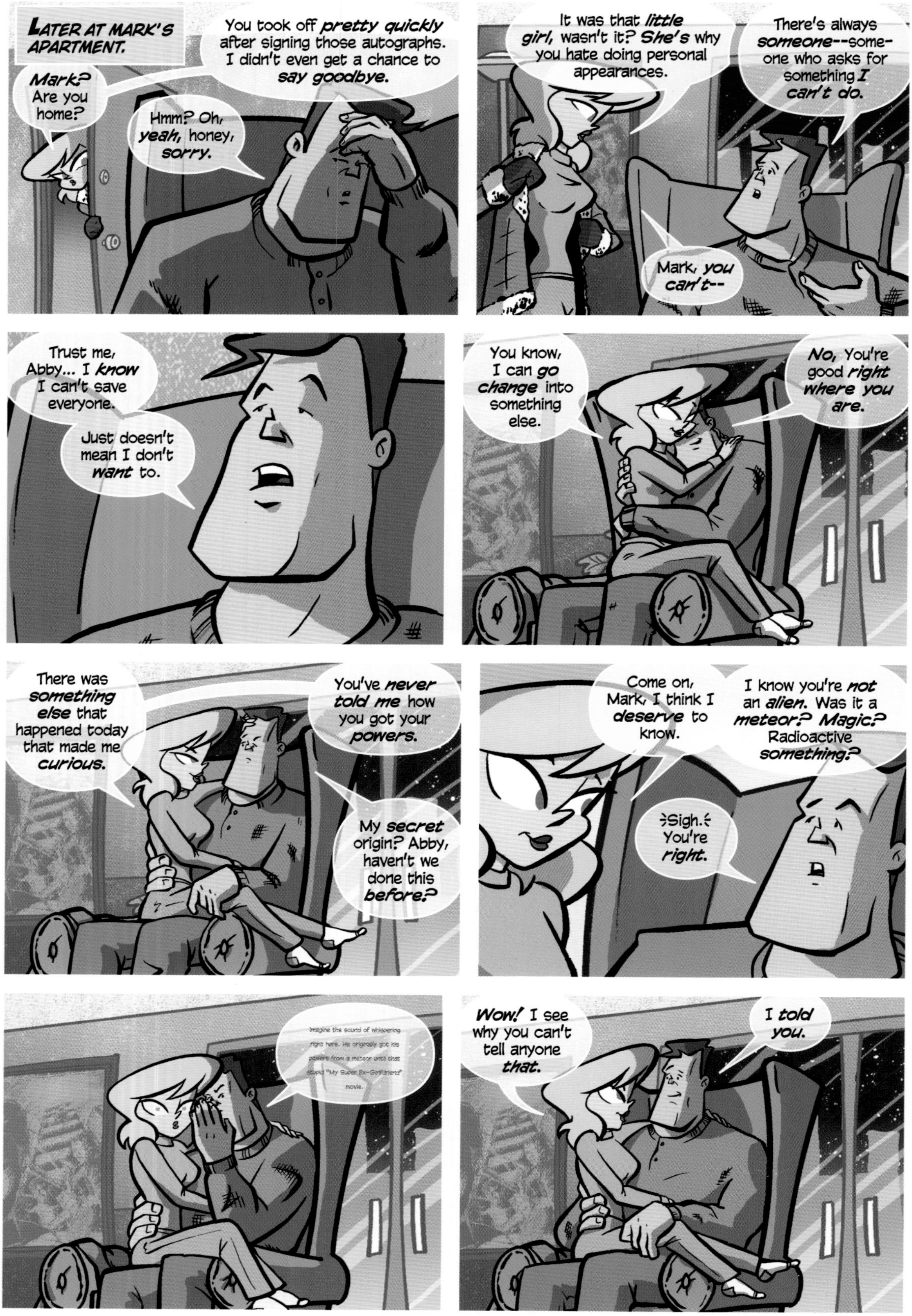
LATER AT MARK'S APARTMENT.
Mark? Are you home?
You took off pretty quickly after signing those autographs. I didn't even get a chance to say goodbye.
Hmm? Oh, yeah, honey, sorry.
It was that little girl, wasn't it? She's why you hate doing personal appearances.
There's always someone--someone who asks for something I can't do.
Mark, you can't--
Trust me, Abby... I know I can't save everyone.
Just doesn't mean I don't want to.
You know, I can go change into something else.
No, You're good right where you are.
There was something else that happened today that made me curious.
You've never told me how you got your powers.
My secret origin? Abby, haven't we done this before?
Come on, Mark, I think I deserve to know.
I know you're not an alien. Was it a meteor? Magic? Radioactive something?
Sigh. You're right.
Imagine the sound of whispering right here. He originally got his powers from a meteor until that stupid "My Super Ex-Girlfriend" movie.
Wow! I see why you can't tell anyone that.
I told you.

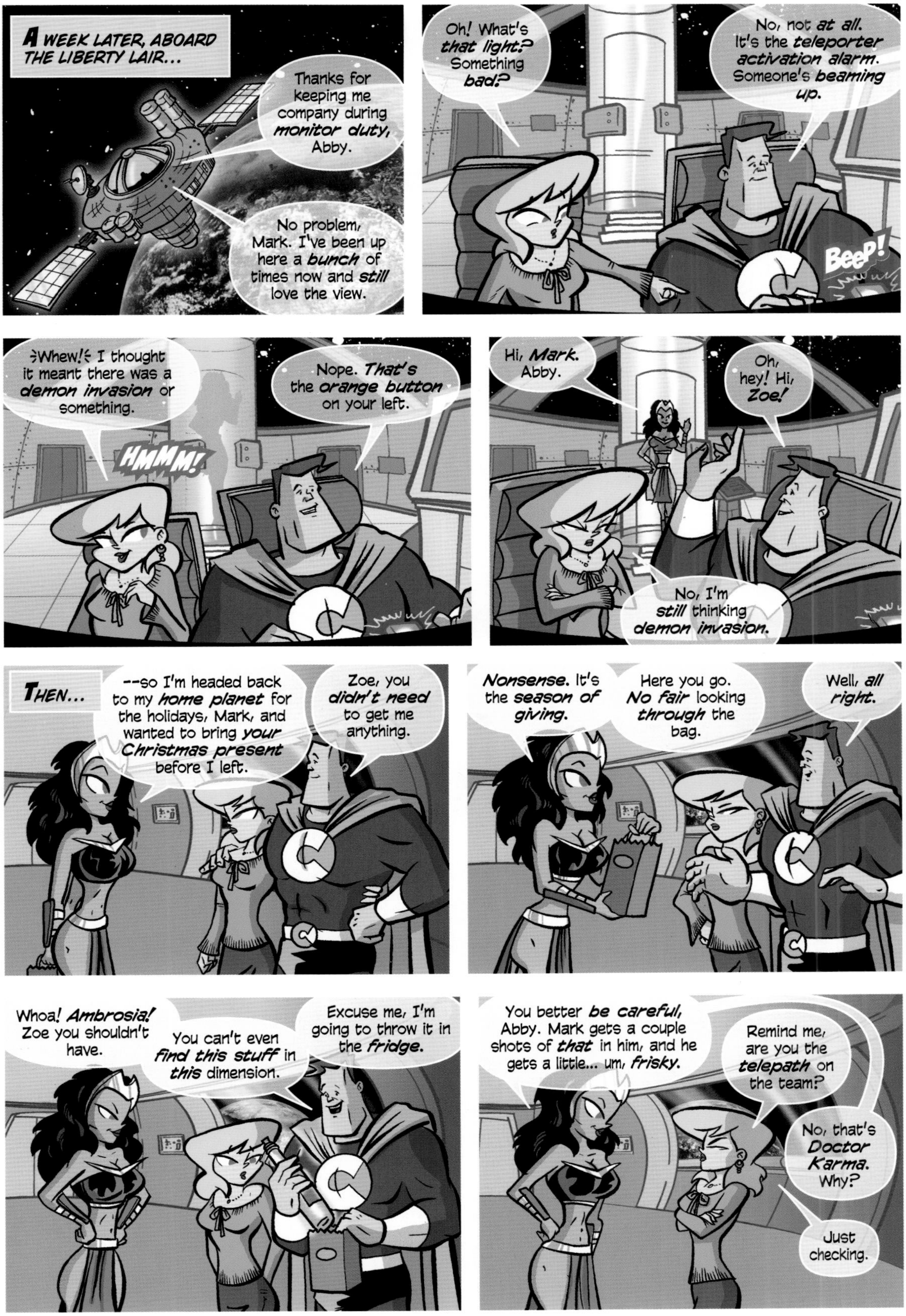
A WEEK LATER, ABOARD THE LIBERTY LAIR...
Thanks for keeping me company during monitor duty, Abby.
No problem, Mark. I've been up here a bunch of times now and still love the view.
Oh! What's that light? Something bad?
No, not at all. It's the teleporter activation alarm. Someone's beaming up.
BEEP!
Whew! I thought it meant there was a demon invasion or something.
HMMM!
Nope. That's the orange button on your left.
Hi, Mark. Abby.
Oh, hey! Hi, Zoe!
No, I'm still thinking demon invasion.
THEN...
--so I'm headed back to my home planet for the holidays, Mark, and wanted to bring your Christmas present before I left.
Zoe, you didn't need to get me anything.
Nonsense. It's the season of giving.
Here you go. No fair looking through the bag.
Well, all right.
Whoa! Ambrosia! Zoe you shouldn't have.
You can't even find this stuff in this dimension.
Excuse me, I'm going to throw it in the fridge.
You better be careful, Abby. Mark gets a couple shots of that in him, and he gets a little... um, frisky.
Remind me, are you the telepath on the team?
No, that's Doctor Karma. Why?
Just checking.

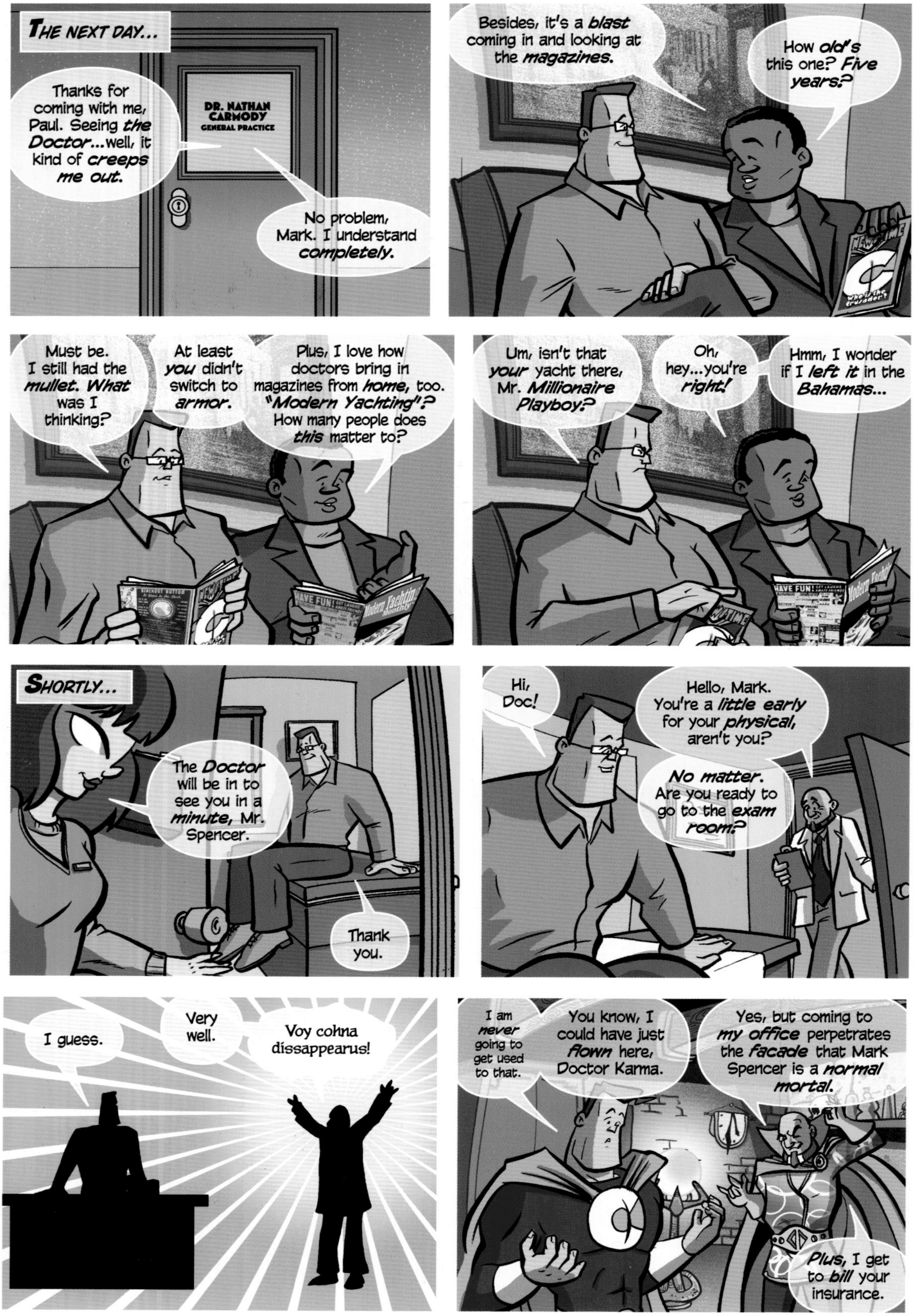
THE NEXT DAY...
Thanks for coming with me, Paul. Seeing the Doctor...well, it kind of creeps me out.
DR. NATHAN CARMODY
GENERAL PRACTICE
No problem, Mark. I understand completely.
Besides, it's a blast coming in and looking at the magazines.
How old's this one? Five years?
Must be. I still had the mullet. What was I thinking?
At least you didn't switch to armor.
Plus, I love how doctors bring in magazines from home, too. "Modern Yachting"? How many people does this matter to?
HAVE FUN!
Modern Yachting Monthly
Um, isn't that your yacht there, Mr. Millionaire Playboy?
Oh, hey...you're right!
Hmm, I wonder if I left it in the Bahamas...
SHORTLY...
The Doctor will be in to see you in a minute, Mr. Spencer.
Thank you.
Hi, Doc!
Hello, Mark. You're a little early for your physical, aren't you?
No matter. Are you ready to go to the exam room?
I guess.
Very well.
Voy cohna dissappearus!
I am never going to get used to that.
You know, I could have just flown here, Doctor Karma.
Yes, but coming to my office perpetrates the facade that Mark Spencer is a normal mortal.
Plus, I get to bill your insurance.

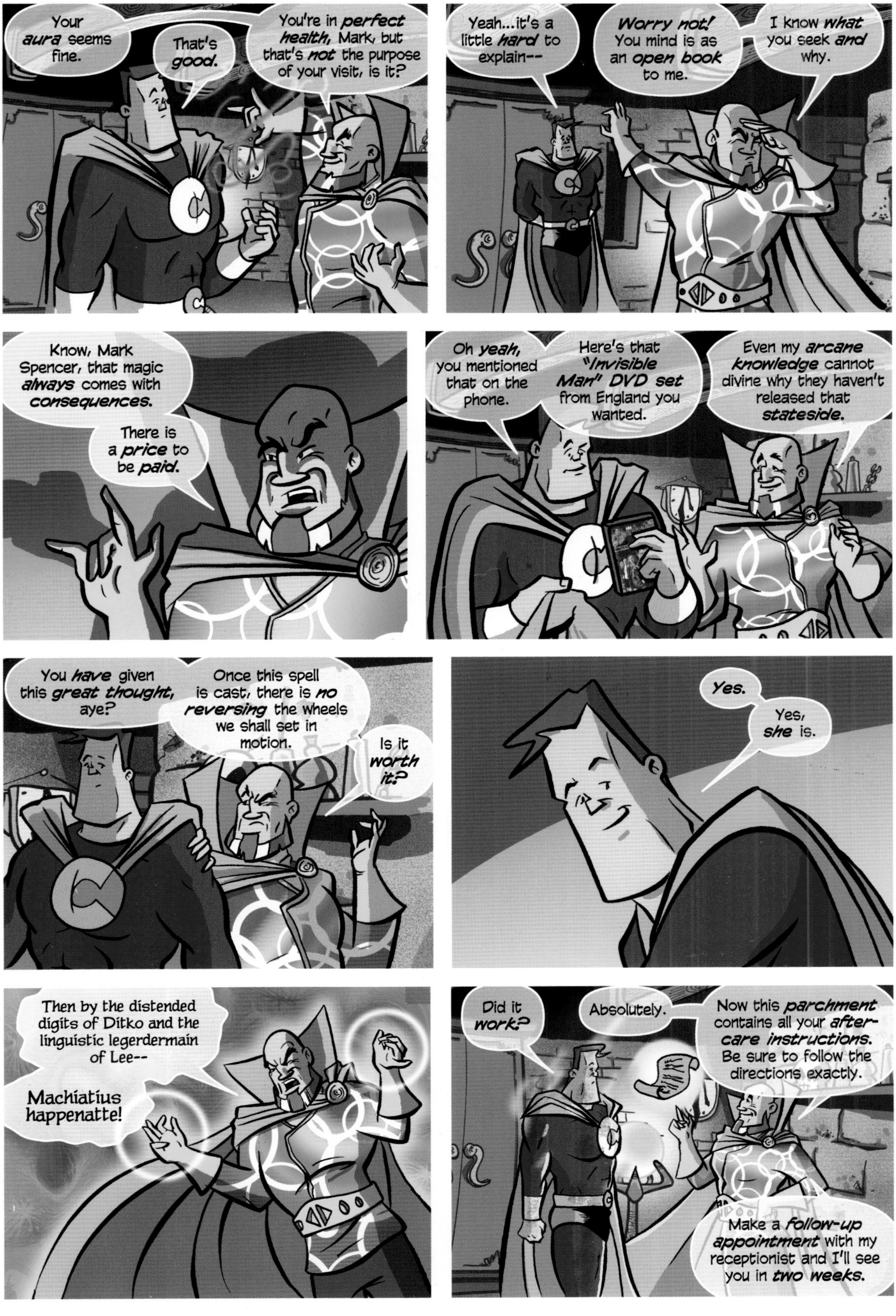
Your aura seems fine.
That's good.
You're in perfect health, Mark, but that's not the purpose of your visit, is it?
Yeah...it's a little hard to explain--
Worry not! You mind is as an open book to me.
I know what you seek and why.
Know, Mark Spencer, that magic always comes with consequences.
There is a price to be paid.
Oh yeah, you mentioned that on the phone.
Here's that "Invisible Man" DVD set from England you wanted.
Even my arcane knowledge cannot divine why they haven't released that stateside.
You have given this great thought, aye?
Once this spell is cast, there is no reversing the wheels we shall set in motion.
Is it worth it?
Yes.
Yes, she is.
Then by the distended digits of Ditko and the linguistic legerdermain of Lee--
Machiatius happenatte!
Did it work?
Absolutely.
Now this parchment contains all your after-care instructions. Be sure to follow the directions exactly.
Make a follow-up appointment with my receptionist and I'll see you in two weeks.

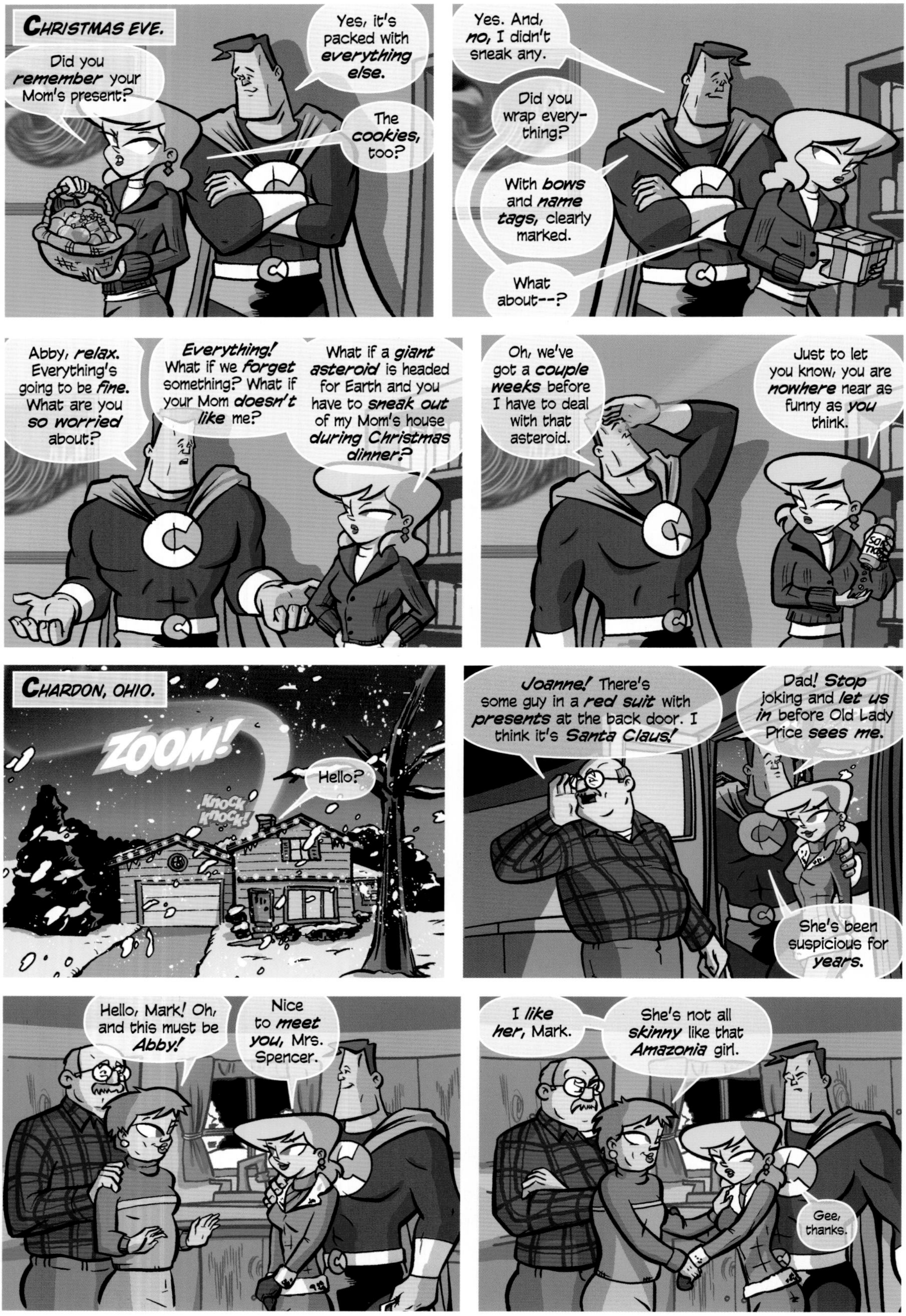
CHRISTMAS EVE.
Did you remember your Mom's present?
Yes, it's packed with everything else.
The cookies, too?
Yes. And, no, I didn't sneak any.
Did you wrap everything?
With bows and name tags, clearly marked.
What about--?
Abby, relax. Everything's going to be fine. What are you so worried about?
Everything! What if we forget something? What if your Mom doesn't like me?
What if a giant asteroid is headed for Earth and you have to sneak out of my Mom's house during Christmas dinner?
Oh, we've got a couple weeks before I have to deal with that asteroid.
Just to let you know, you are nowhere near as funny as you think.
CHARDON, OHIO.
ZOOM!
KNOCK KNOCK!
Hello?
Joanne! There's some guy in a red suit with presents at the back door. I think it's Santa Claus!
Dad! Stop joking and let us in before Old Lady Price sees me.
She's been suspicious for years.
Hello, Mark! Oh, and this must be Abby!
Nice to meet you, Mrs. Spencer.
I like her, Mark.
She's not all skinny like that Amazonia girl.
Gee, thanks.

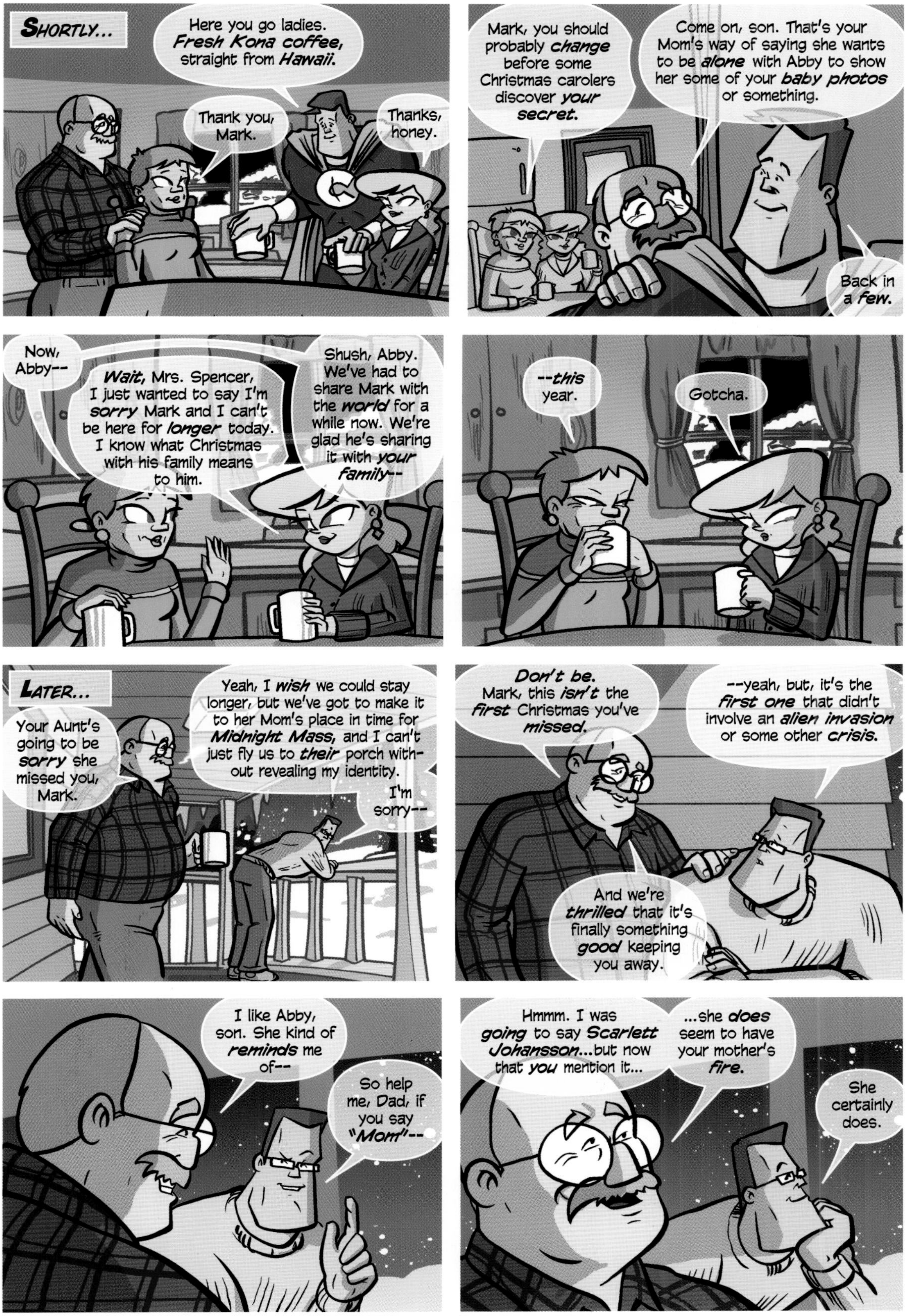
SHORTLY...
Here you go ladies. Fresh Kona coffee, straight from Hawaii.
Thank you, Mark.
Thanks, honey.
Mark, you should probably change before some Christmas carolers discover your secret.
Come on, son. That's your Mom's way of saying she wants to be alone with Abby to show her some of your baby photos or something.
Back in a few.
Now, Abby--
Wait, Mrs. Spencer, I just wanted to say I'm sorry Mark and I can't be here for longer today. I know what Christmas with his family means to him.
Shush, Abby. We've had to share Mark with the world for a while now. We're glad he's sharing it with your family--
--this year.
Gotcha.
LATER...
Your Aunt's going to be sorry she missed you, Mark.
Yeah, I wish we could stay longer, but we've got to make it to her Mom's place in time for Midnight Mass, and I can't just fly us to their porch without revealing my identity.
I'm sorry--
Don't be. Mark, this isn't the first Christmas you've missed.
--yeah, but, it's the first one that didn't involve an alien invasion or some other crisis.
And we're thrilled that it's finally something good keeping you away.
I like Abby, son. She kind of reminds me of--
So help me, Dad, if you say "Mom"--
Hmmm. I was going to say Scarlett Johansson...but now that you mention it...
...she does seem to have your mother's fire.
She certainly does.

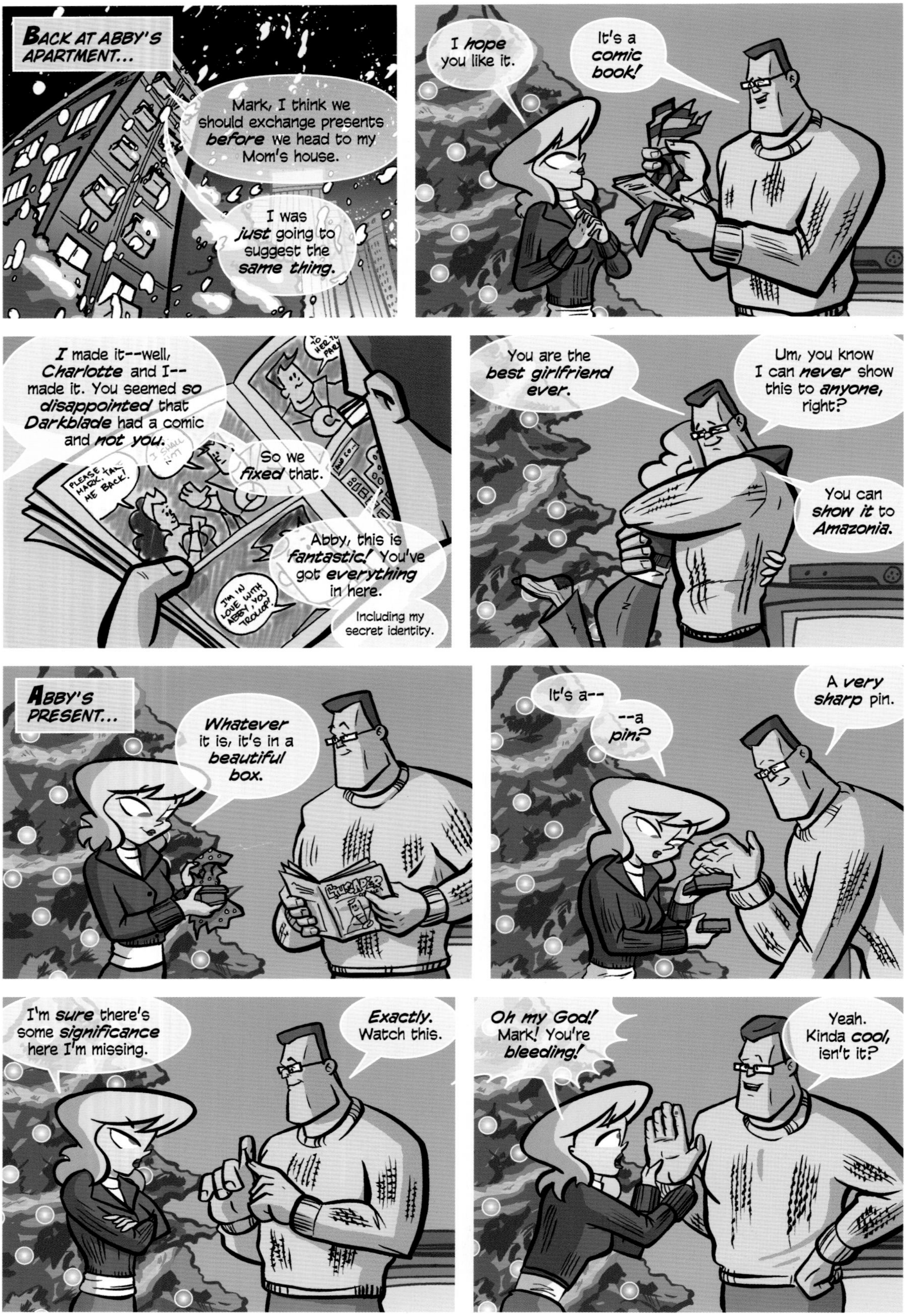
BACK AT ABBY'S APARTMENT...
Mark, I think we should exchange presents *before* we head to my Mom's house.
I was *just* going to suggest the *same thing.*
I *hope* you like it.
It's a *comic book!*
I made it--well, *Charlotte* and I--made it. You seemed *so disappointed* that *Darkblade* had a comic and *not you.*
PLEASE MARK, TAKE ME BACK!
I SHALL NOT!
So we *fixed* that.
Abby, this is *fantastic!* You've got *everything* in here.
I'M IN LOVE WITH ABBY, YOU TROLLOP!
Including my secret identity.
You are the *best girlfriend ever.*
Um, you know I can *never* show this to *anyone,* right?
You can *show it* to *Amazonia.*
ABBY'S PRESENT...
Whatever it is, it's in a *beautiful box.*
It's a--
--a *pin?*
A *very sharp* pin.
I'm *sure* there's some *significance* here I'm missing.
Exactly. Watch this.
Oh my God! Mark! You're *bleeding!*
Yeah. Kinda *cool,* isn't it?

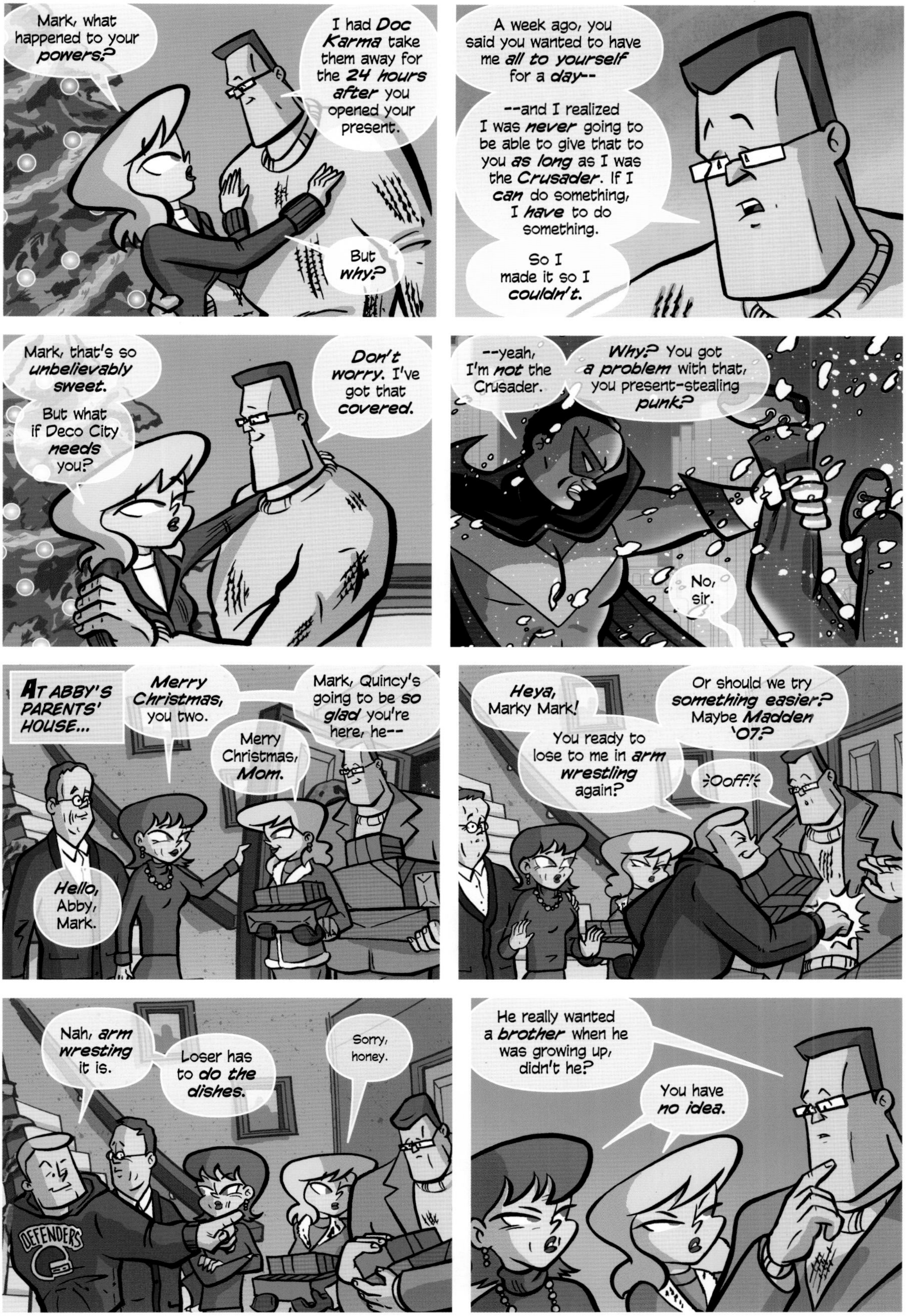
Mark, what happened to your powers?
I had Doc Karma take them away for the 24 hours after you opened your present.
But why?
A week ago, you said you wanted to have me all to yourself for a day--
--and I realized I was never going to be able to give that to you as long as I was the Crusader. If I can do something, I have to do something.
So I made it so I couldn't.
Mark, that's so unbelievably sweet.
But what if Deco City needs you?
Don't worry. I've got that covered.
--yeah, I'm not the Crusader.
Why? You got a problem with that, you present-stealing punk?
No, sir.
AT ABBY'S PARENTS' HOUSE...
Merry Christmas, you two.
Mark, Quincy's going to be so glad you're here, he--
Merry Christmas, Mom.
Hello, Abby, Mark.
Heya, Marky Mark!
You ready to lose to me in arm wrestling again?
Or should we try something easier? Maybe Madden '07?
Ooff!
Nah, arm wresting it is.
Loser has to do the dishes.
Sorry, honey.
DEFENDERS
He really wanted a brother when he was growing up, didn't he?
You have no idea.

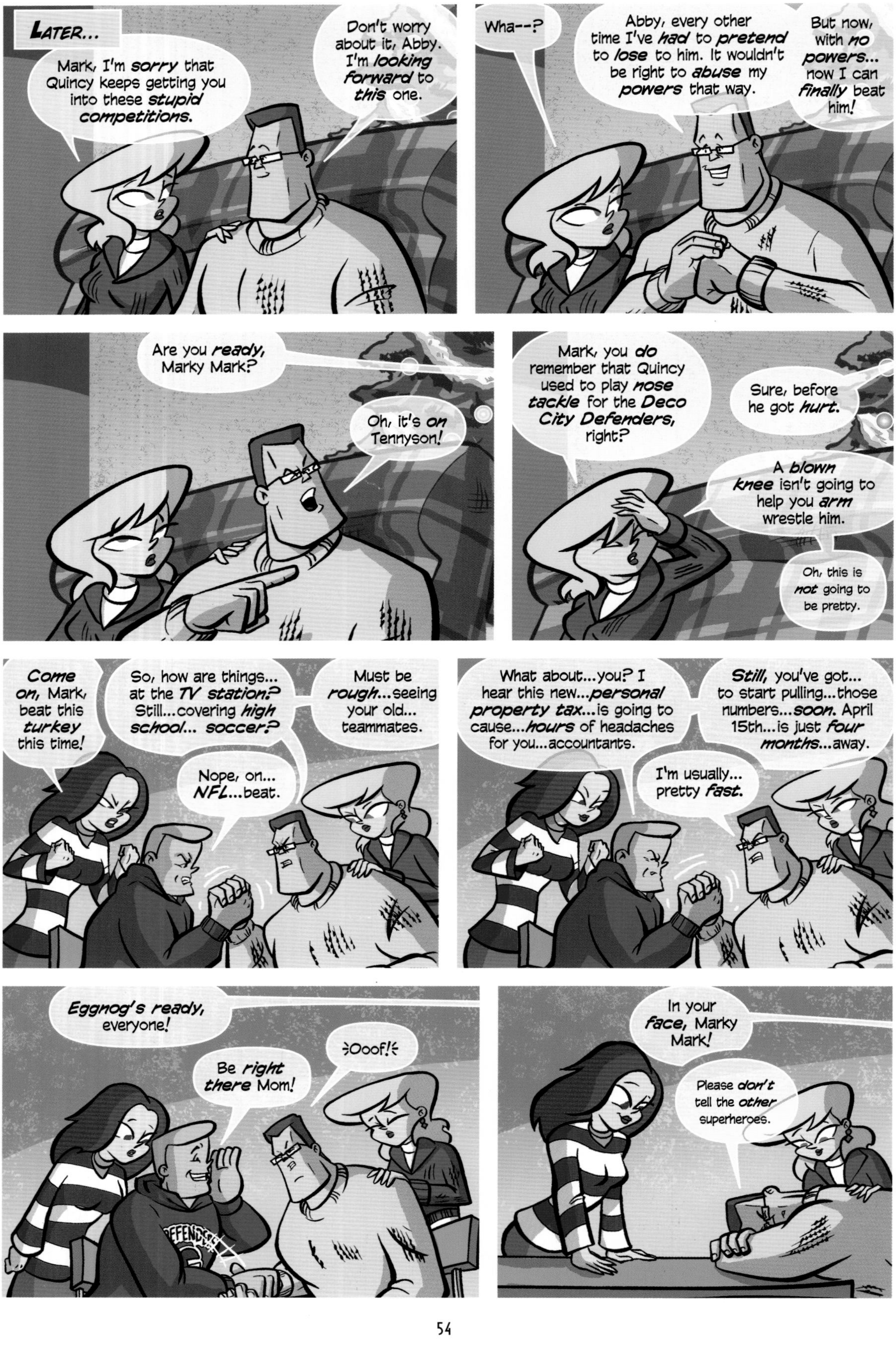
LATER...
Mark, I'm sorry that Quincy keeps getting you into these stupid competitions.
Don't worry about it, Abby. I'm looking forward to this one.
Wha--?
Abby, every other time I've had to pretend to lose to him. It wouldn't be right to abuse my powers that way.
But now, with no powers... now I can finally beat him!
Are you ready, Marky Mark?
Oh, it's on Tennyson!
Mark, you do remember that Quincy used to play nose tackle for the Deco City Defenders, right?
Sure, before he got hurt.
A blown knee isn't going to help you arm wrestle him.
Oh, this is not going to be pretty.
Come on, Mark, beat this turkey this time!
So, how are things... at the TV station? Still...covering high school... soccer?
Must be rough...seeing your old... teammates.
Nope, on... NFL...beat.
What about...you? I hear this new...personal property tax...is going to cause...hours of headaches for you...accountants.
Still, you've got... to start pulling...those numbers...soon. April 15th...is just four months...away.
I'm usually... pretty fast.
Eggnog's ready, everyone!
Be right there Mom!
Ooof!
DEFENDERS
In your face, Marky Mark!
Please don't tell the other superheroes.

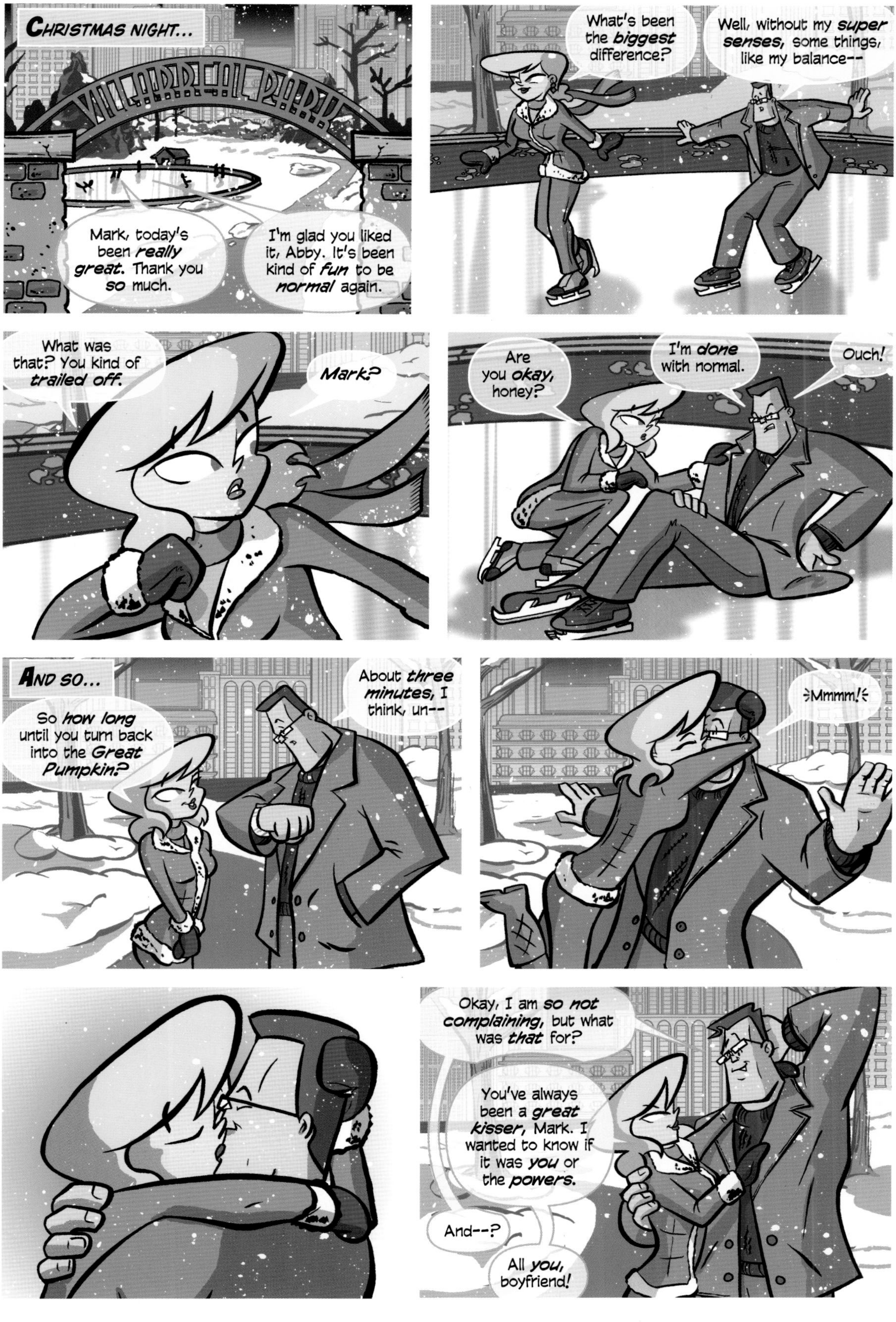
CHRISTMAS NIGHT...
Mark, today's been really great. Thank you so much.
I'm glad you liked it, Abby. It's been kind of fun to be normal again.
What's been the biggest difference?
Well, without my super senses, some things, like my balance--
What was that? You kind of trailed off.
Mark?
Are you okay, honey?
I'm done with normal.
Ouch!
AND SO...
So how long until you turn back into the Great Pumpkin?
About three minutes, I think, un--
Mmmm!
Okay, I am so not complaining, but what was that for?
You've always been a great kisser, Mark. I wanted to know if it was you or the powers.
And--?
All you, boyfriend!

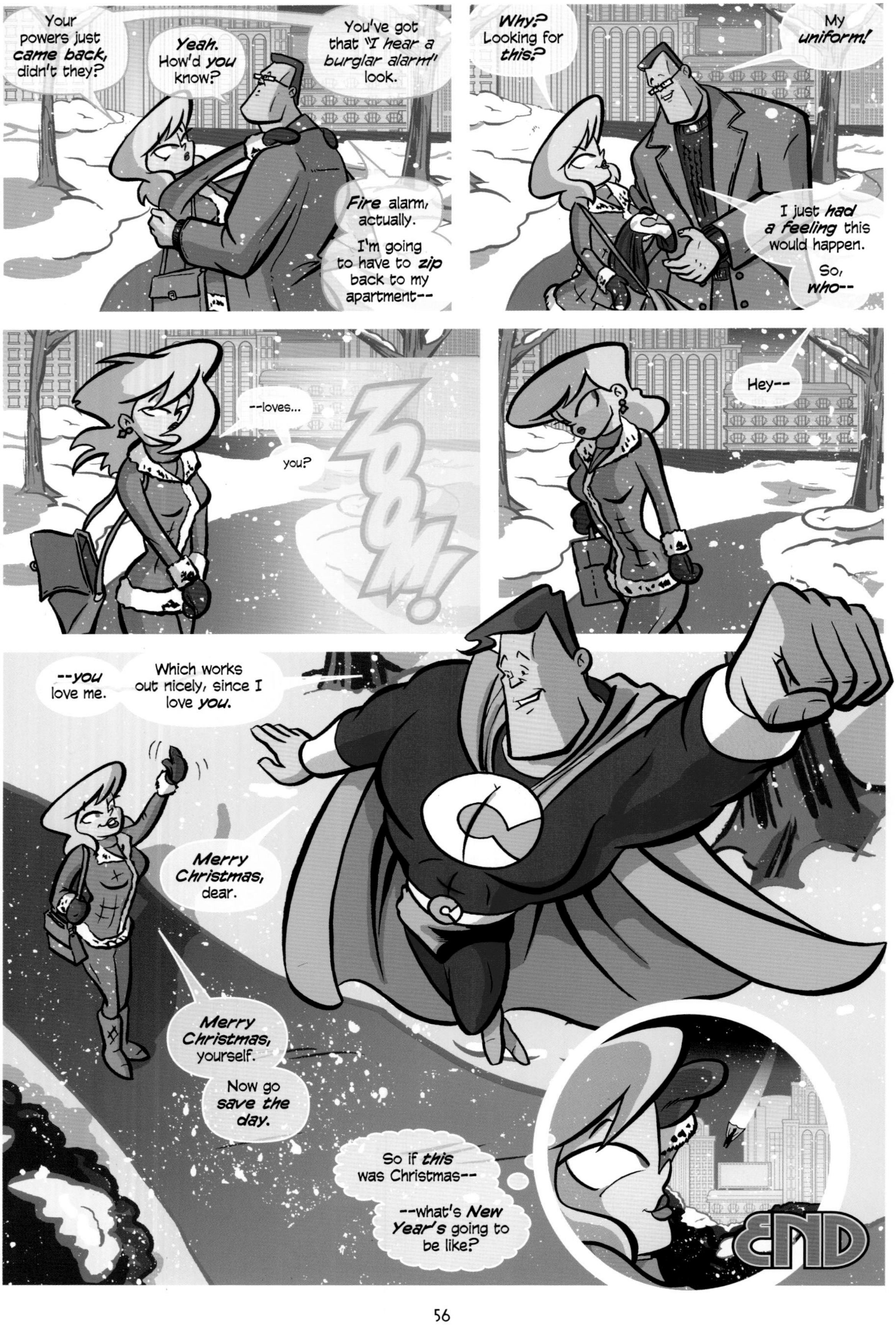
Your powers just came back, didn't they?
Yeah. How'd you know?
You've got that "I hear a burglar alarm" look.
Fire alarm, actually.
I'm going to have to zip back to my apartment--
Why? Looking for this?
My uniform!
I just had a feeling this would happen.
So, who--
--loves...
you?
ZOOM!
Hey--
--you love me.
Which works out nicely, since I love you.
Merry Christmas, dear.
Merry Christmas, yourself.
Now go save the day.
So if this was Christmas--
--what's New Year's going to be like?
END

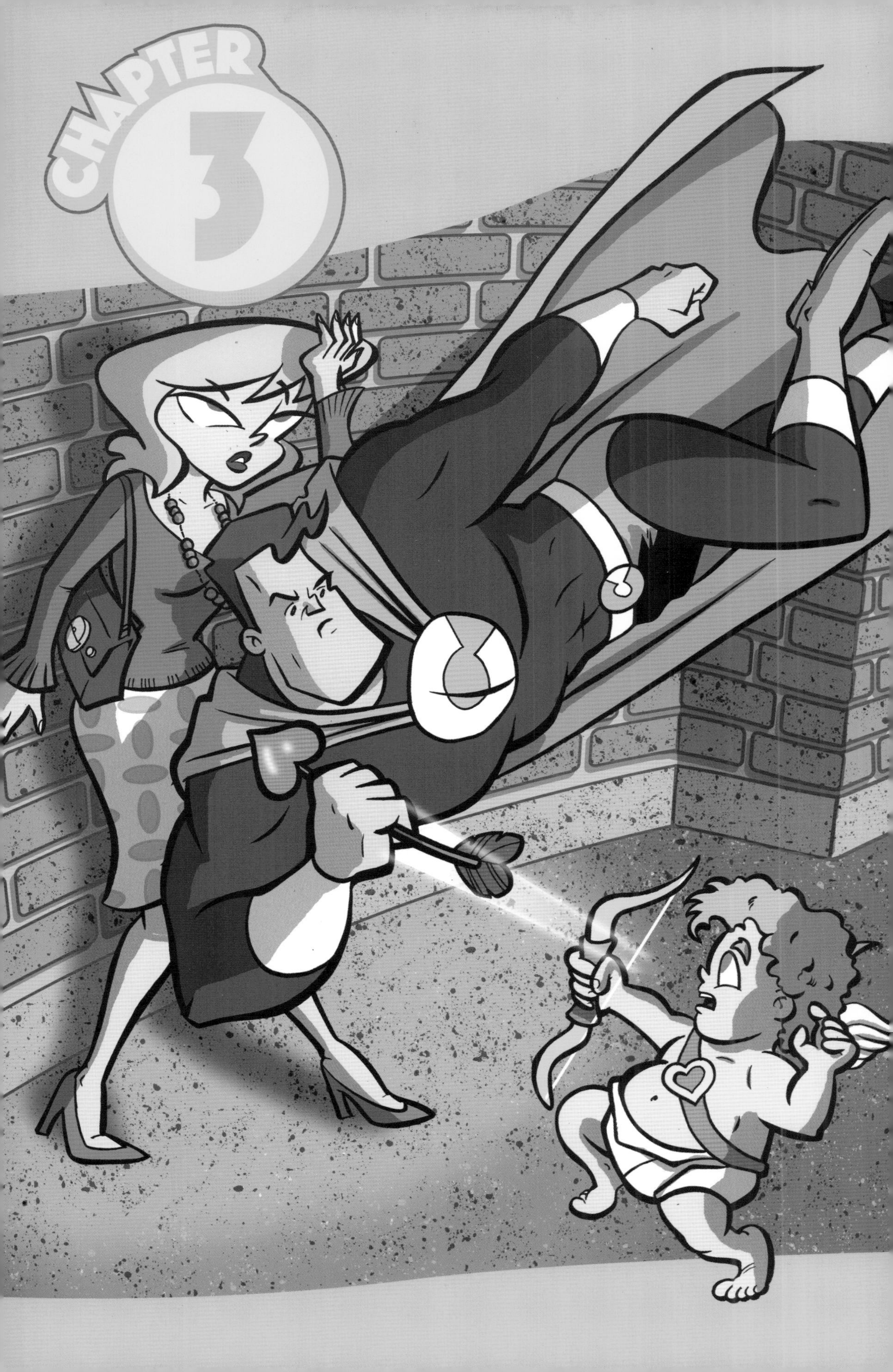
CHAPTER 3

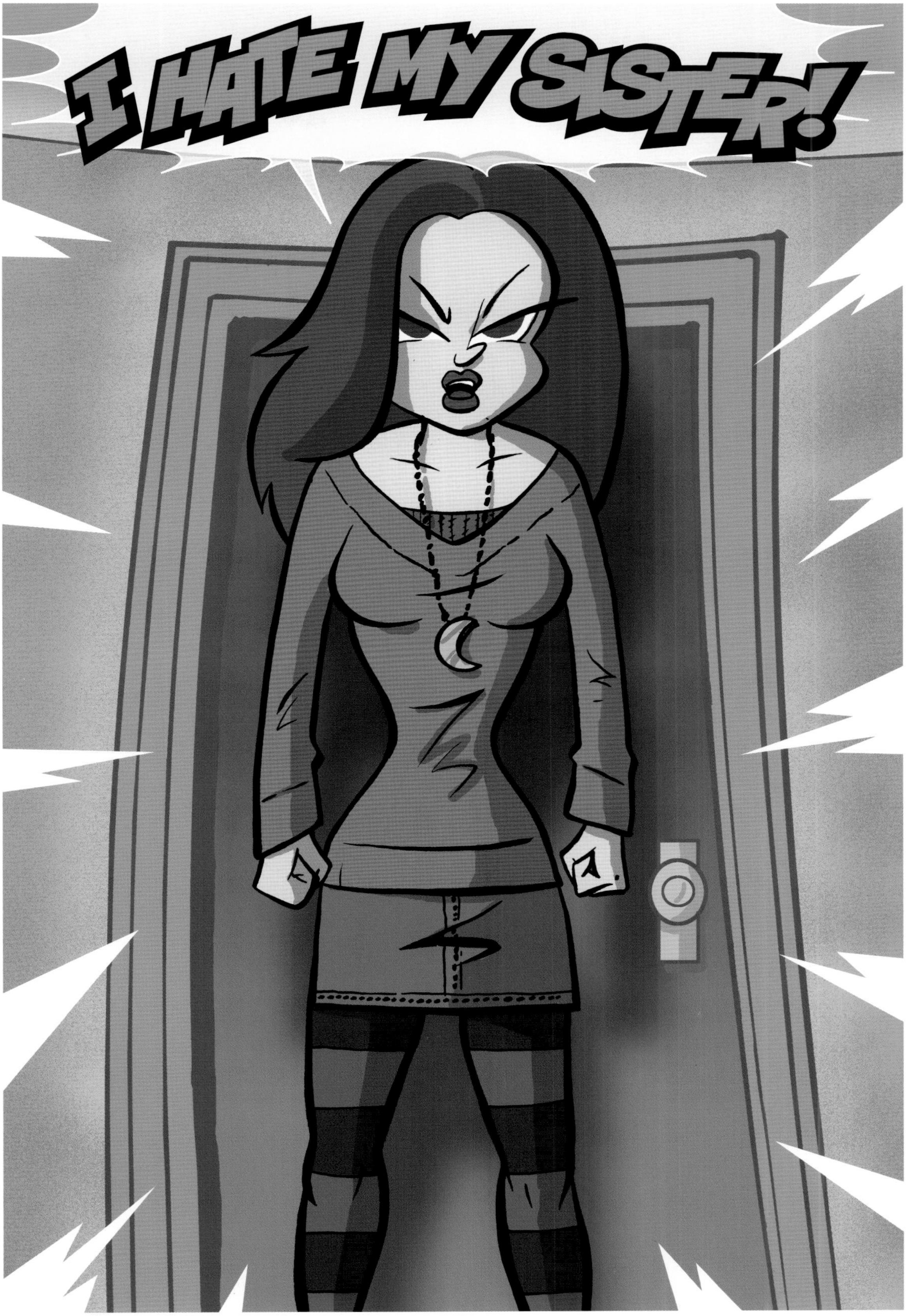
I HATE MY SISTER!

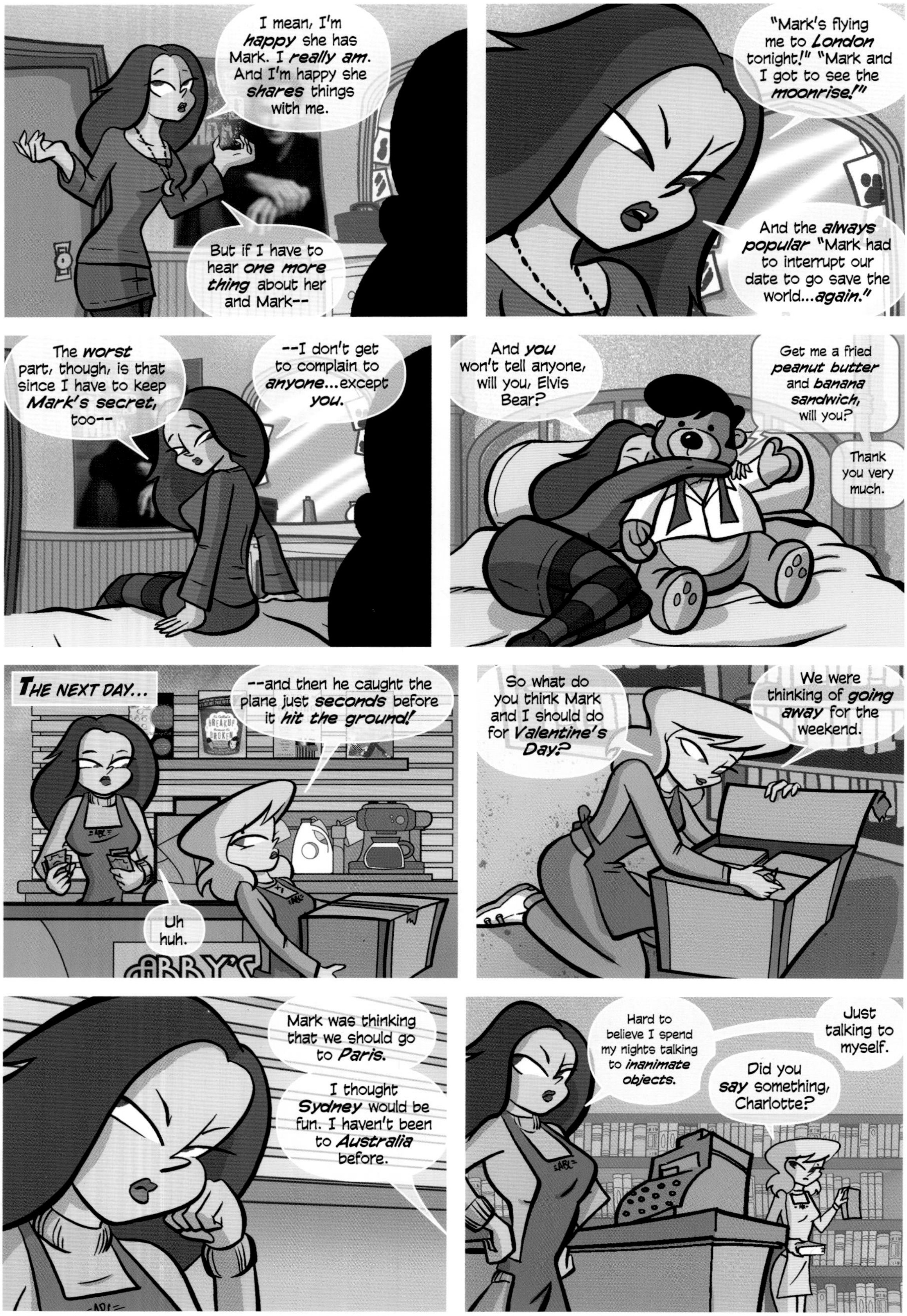

I mean, I'm happy she has Mark. I really am. And I'm happy she shares things with me.
But if I have to hear one more thing about her and Mark--
"Mark's flying me to London tonight!" "Mark and I got to see the moonrise!"
And the always popular "Mark had to interrupt our date to go save the world...again."
The worst part, though, is that since I have to keep Mark's secret, too--
--I don't get to complain to anyone...except you.
And you won't tell anyone, will you, Elvis Bear?
Get me a fried peanut butter and banana sandwich, will you?
Thank you very much.
THE NEXT DAY...
--and then he caught the plane just seconds before it hit the ground!
Uh huh.
So what do you think Mark and I should do for Valentine's Day?
We were thinking of going away for the weekend.
Mark was thinking that we should go to Paris.
I thought Sydney would be fun. I haven't been to Australia before.
Hard to believe I spend my nights talking to inanimate objects.
Did you say something, Charlotte?
Just talking to myself.

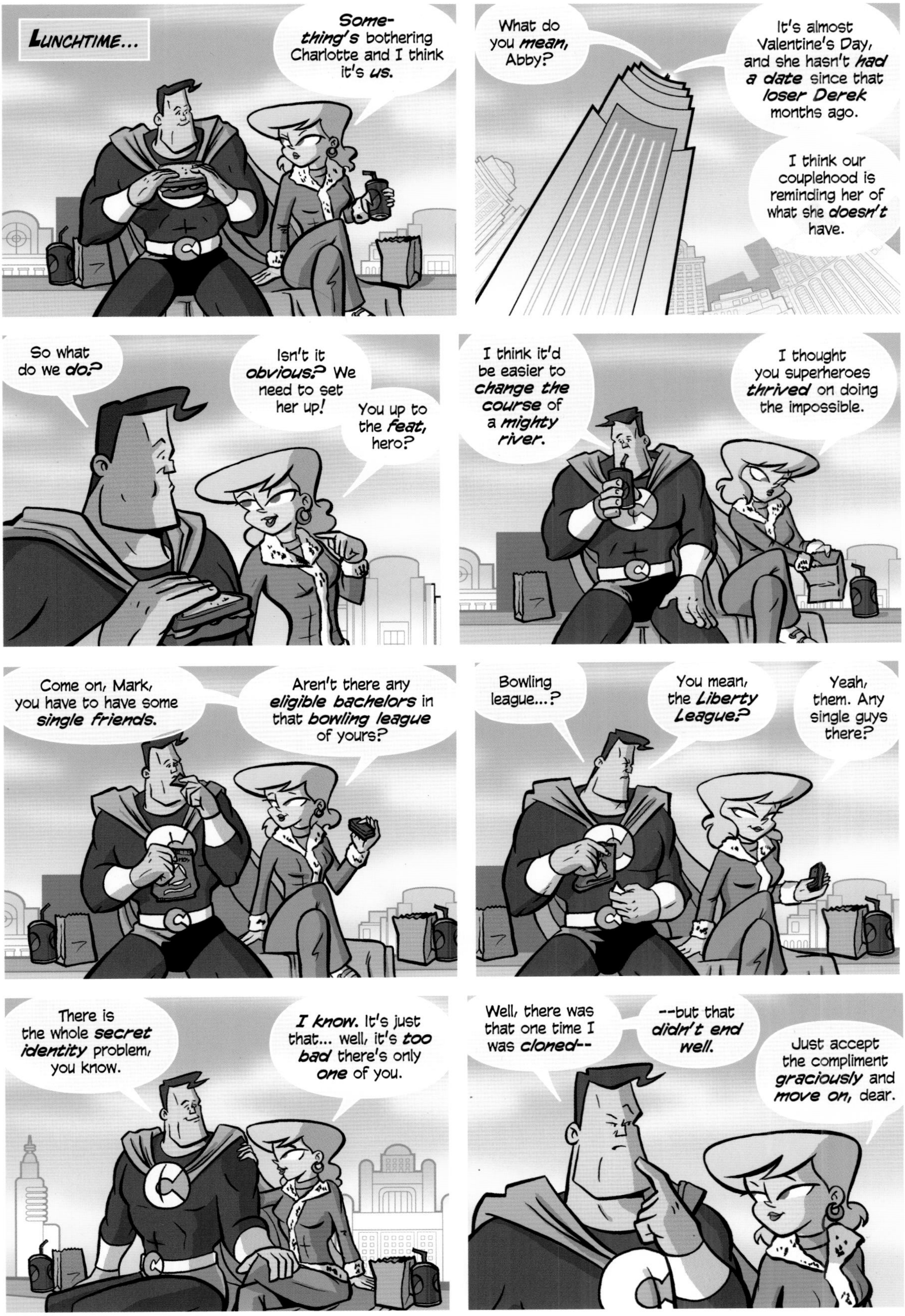
LUNCHTIME...
Something's bothering Charlotte and I think it's us.
What do you mean, Abby?
It's almost Valentine's Day, and she hasn't had a date since that loser Derek months ago.
I think our couplehood is reminding her of what she doesn't have.
So what do we do?
Isn't it obvious? We need to set her up!
You up to the feat, hero?
I think it'd be easier to change the course of a mighty river.
I thought you superheroes thrived on doing the impossible.
Come on, Mark, you have to have some single friends.
Aren't there any eligible bachelors in that bowling league of yours?
Bowling league...?
You mean, the Liberty League?
Yeah, them. Any single guys there?
There is the whole secret identity problem, you know.
I know. It's just that... well, it's too bad there's only one of you.
Well, there was that one time I was cloned--
--but that didn't end well.
Just accept the compliment graciously and move on, dear.

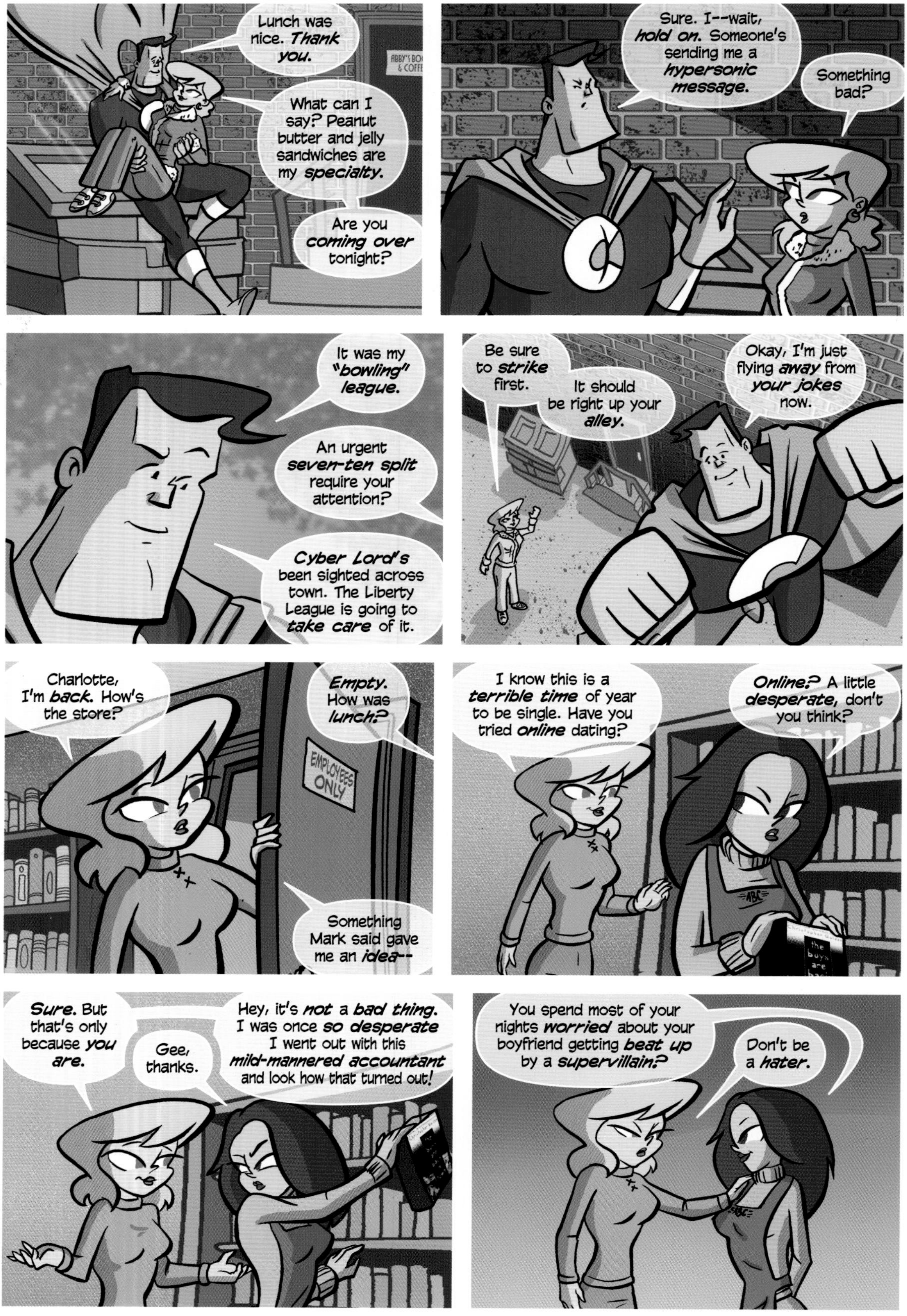
Lunch was nice. Thank you.
What can I say? Peanut butter and jelly sandwiches are my specialty.
Are you coming over tonight?
Sure. I--wait, hold on. Someone's sending me a hypersonic message.
Something bad?
It was my "bowling" league.
An urgent seven-ten split require your attention?
Cyber Lord's been sighted across town. The Liberty League is going to take care of it.
Be sure to strike first.
It should be right up your alley.
Okay, I'm just flying away from your jokes now.
Charlotte, I'm back. How's the store?
Empty. How was lunch?
EMPLOYEES ONLY
Something Mark said gave me an idea--
I know this is a terrible time of year to be single. Have you tried online dating?
Online? A little desperate, don't you think?
Sure. But that's only because you are.
Gee, thanks.
Hey, it's not a bad thing. I was once so desperate I went out with this mild-mannered accountant and look how that turned out!
You spend most of your nights worried about your boyfriend getting beat up by a supervillain?
Don't be a hater.

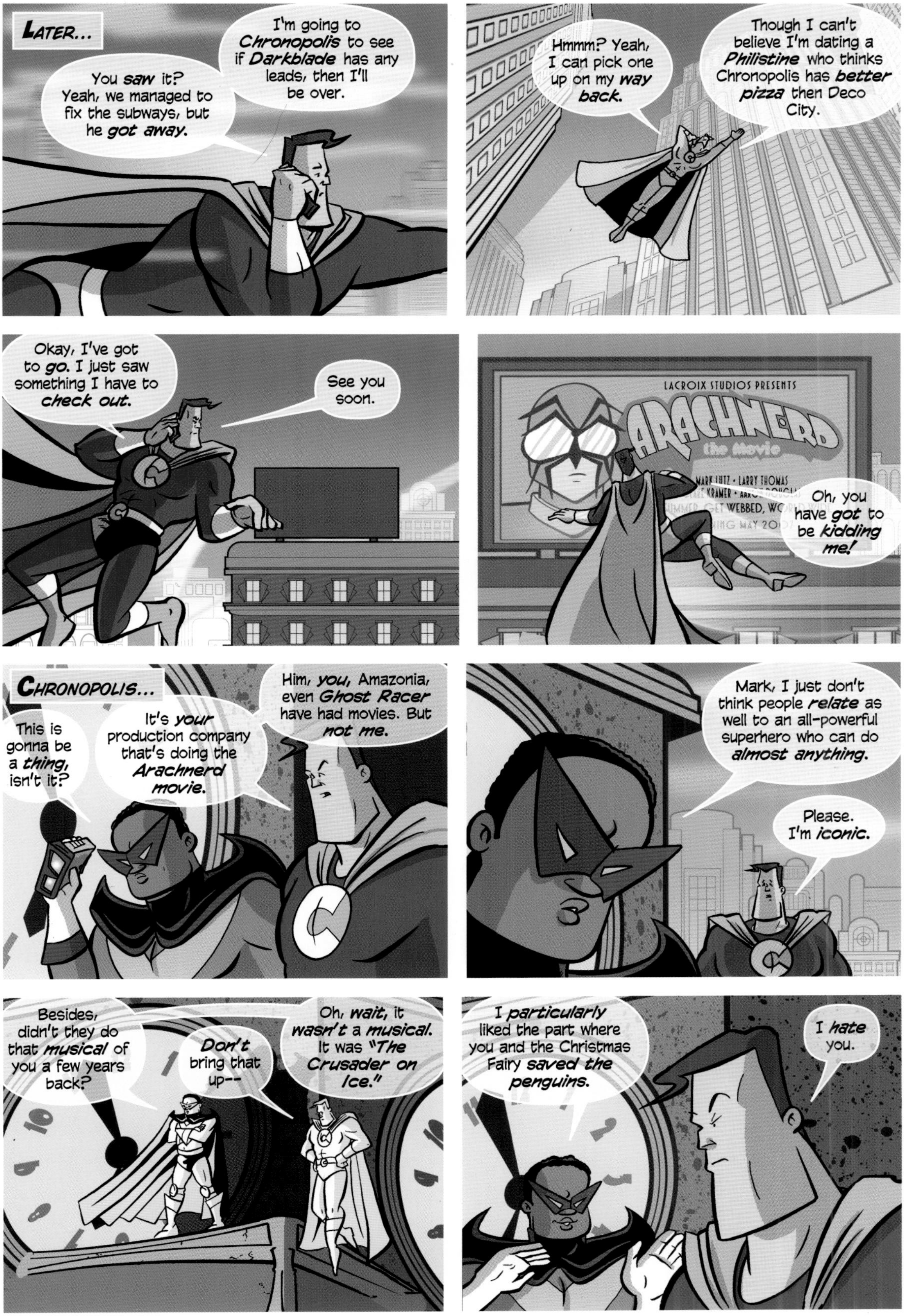

LATER...
You *saw* it? Yeah, we managed to fix the subways, but he *got away.*
I'm going to *Chronopolis* to see if *Darkblade* has any leads, then I'll be over.
Hmmm? Yeah, I can pick one up on my *way back.*
Though I can't believe I'm dating a *Philistine* who thinks Chronopolis has *better pizza* then Deco City.
Okay, I've got to *go.* I just saw something I have to *check out.*
See you soon.
LACROIX STUDIOS PRESENTS
ARACHNERD
the Movie
MARK LUTZ • LARRY THOMAS
Oh, you have *got* to be *kidding me!*
CHRONOPOLIS...
This is gonna be a *thing,* isn't it?
It's *your* production company that's doing the *Arachnerd movie.*
Him, *you,* Amazonia, even *Ghost Racer* have had movies. But *not me.*
Mark, I just don't think people *relate* as well to an all-powerful superhero who can do *almost anything.*
Please. I'm *iconic.*
Besides, didn't they do that *musical* of you a few years back?
Don't bring that up--
Oh, *wait,* it *wasn't* a *musical.* It was *"The Crusader on Ice."*
I *particularly* liked the part where you and the Christmas Fairy *saved the penguins.*
I *hate* you.

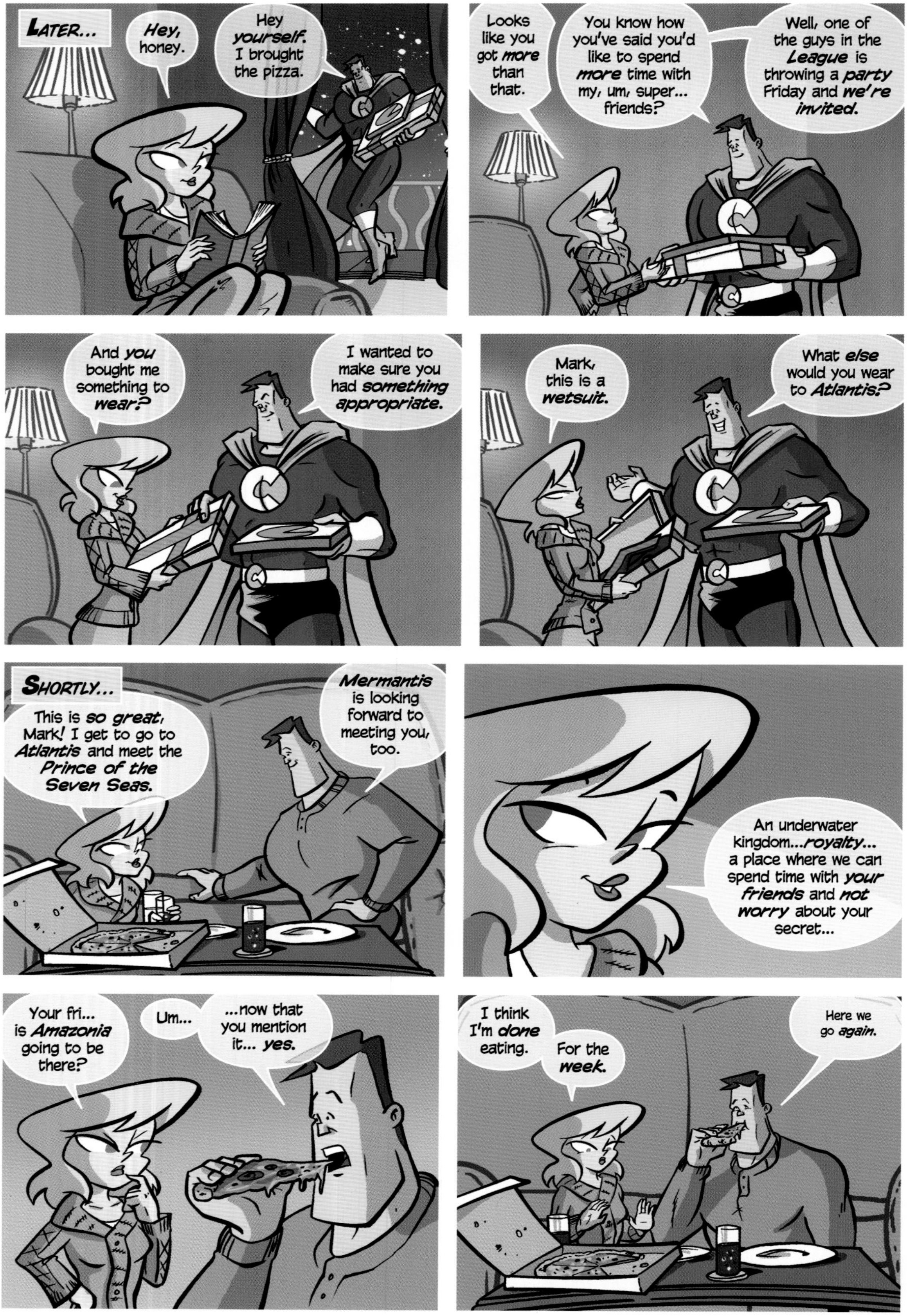
LATER...
Hey, honey.
Hey yourself. I brought the pizza.
Looks like you got more than that.
You know how you've said you'd like to spend more time with my, um, super... friends?
Well, one of the guys in the League is throwing a party Friday and we're invited.
And you bought me something to wear?
I wanted to make sure you had something appropriate.
Mark, this is a wetsuit.
What else would you wear to Atlantis?
SHORTLY...
This is so great, Mark! I get to go to Atlantis and meet the Prince of the Seven Seas.
Mermantis is looking forward to meeting you, too.
An underwater kingdom...royalty... a place where we can spend time with your friends and not worry about your secret...
Your fri... is Amazonia going to be there?
Um...
...now that you mention it... yes.
I think I'm done eating.
For the week.
Here we go again.

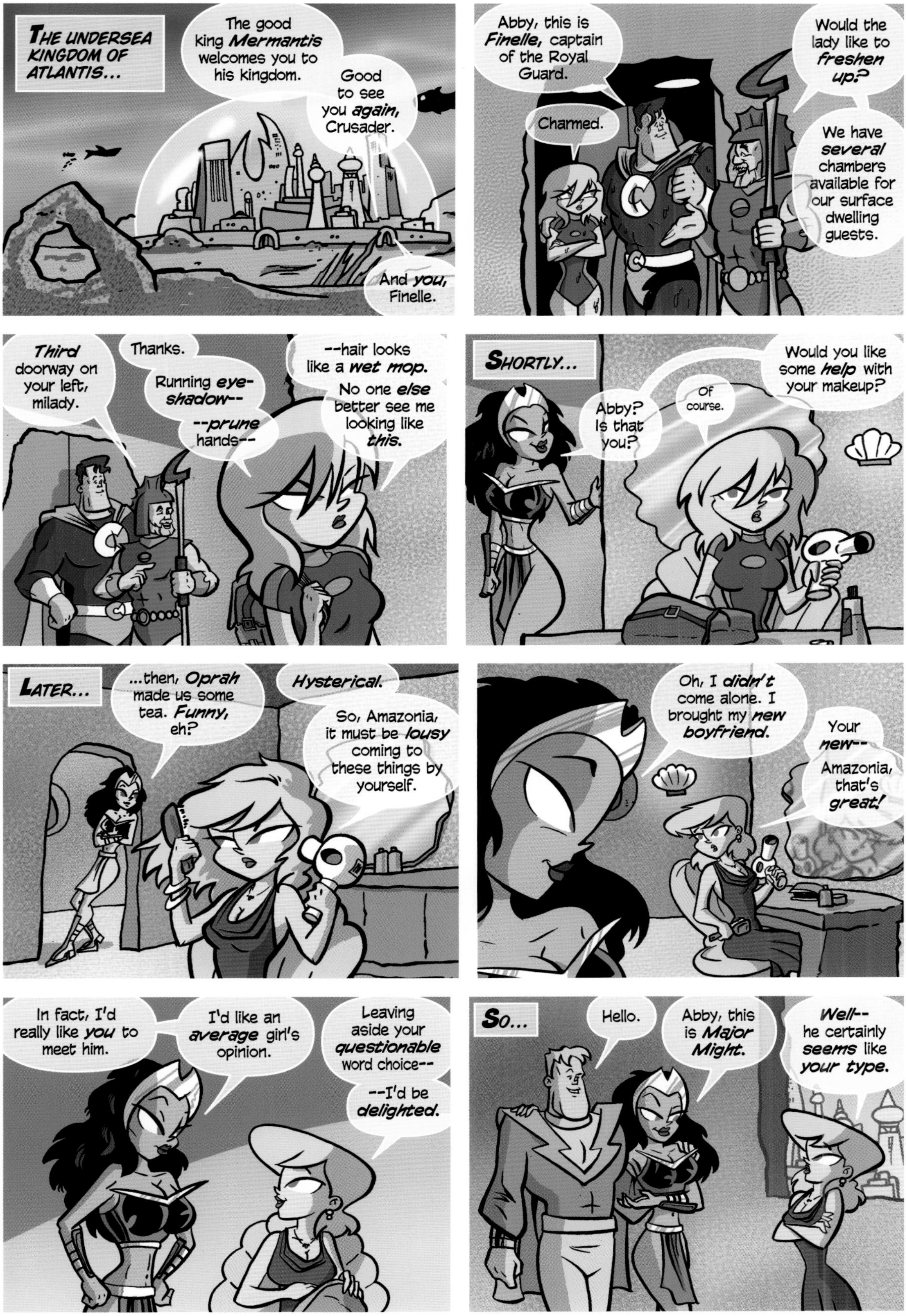

THE UNDERSEA KINGDOM OF ATLANTIS...
The good king Mermantis welcomes you to his kingdom.
Good to see you again, Crusader.
And you, Finelle.
Abby, this is Finelle, captain of the Royal Guard.
Charmed.
Would the lady like to freshen up?
We have several chambers available for our surface dwelling guests.
Third doorway on your left, milady.
Thanks.
Running eye-shadow--
--prune hands--
--hair looks like a wet mop.
No one else better see me looking like this.
SHORTLY...
Abby? Is that you?
Of course.
Would you like some help with your makeup?
LATER...
...then, Oprah made us some tea. Funny, eh?
Hysterical.
So, Amazonia, it must be lousy coming to these things by yourself.
Oh, I didn't come alone. I brought my new boyfriend.
Your new--
Amazonia, that's great!
In fact, I'd really like you to meet him.
I'd like an average girl's opinion.
Leaving aside your questionable word choice--
--I'd be delighted.
SO...
Hello.
Abby, this is Major Might.
Well-- he certainly seems like your type.

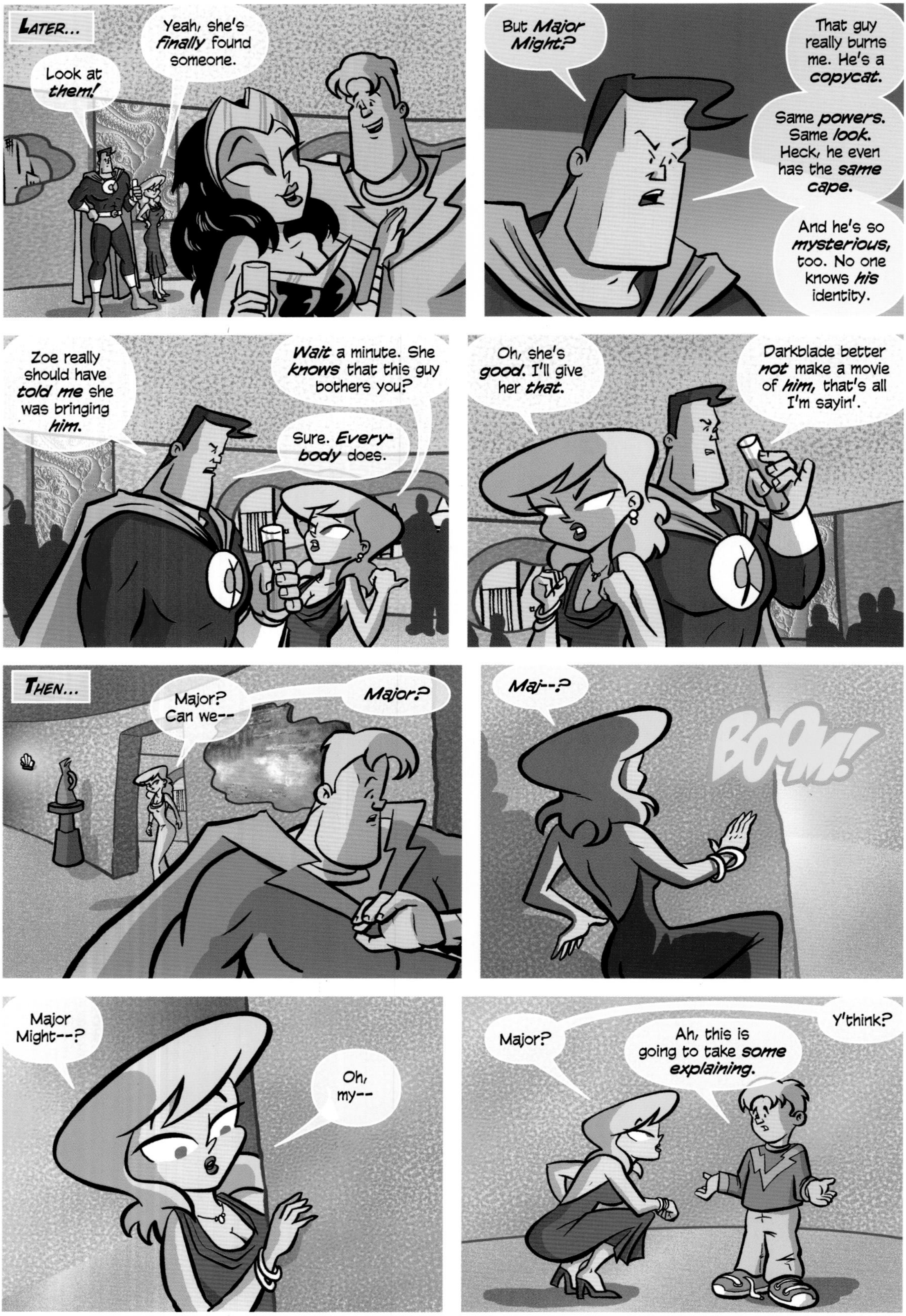
Later...
Look at them!
Yeah, she's finally found someone.
But Major Might?
That guy really burns me. He's a copycat.
Same powers. Same look. Heck, he even has the same cape.
And he's so mysterious, too. No one knows his identity.
Zoe really should have told me she was bringing him.
Wait a minute. She knows that this guy bothers you?
Sure. Everybody does.
Oh, she's good. I'll give her that.
Darkblade better not make a movie of him, that's all I'm sayin'.
Then...
Major? Can we--
Major?
Maj--?
BOOM!
Major Might--?
Oh, my--
Major?
Ah, this is going to take some explaining.
Y'think?

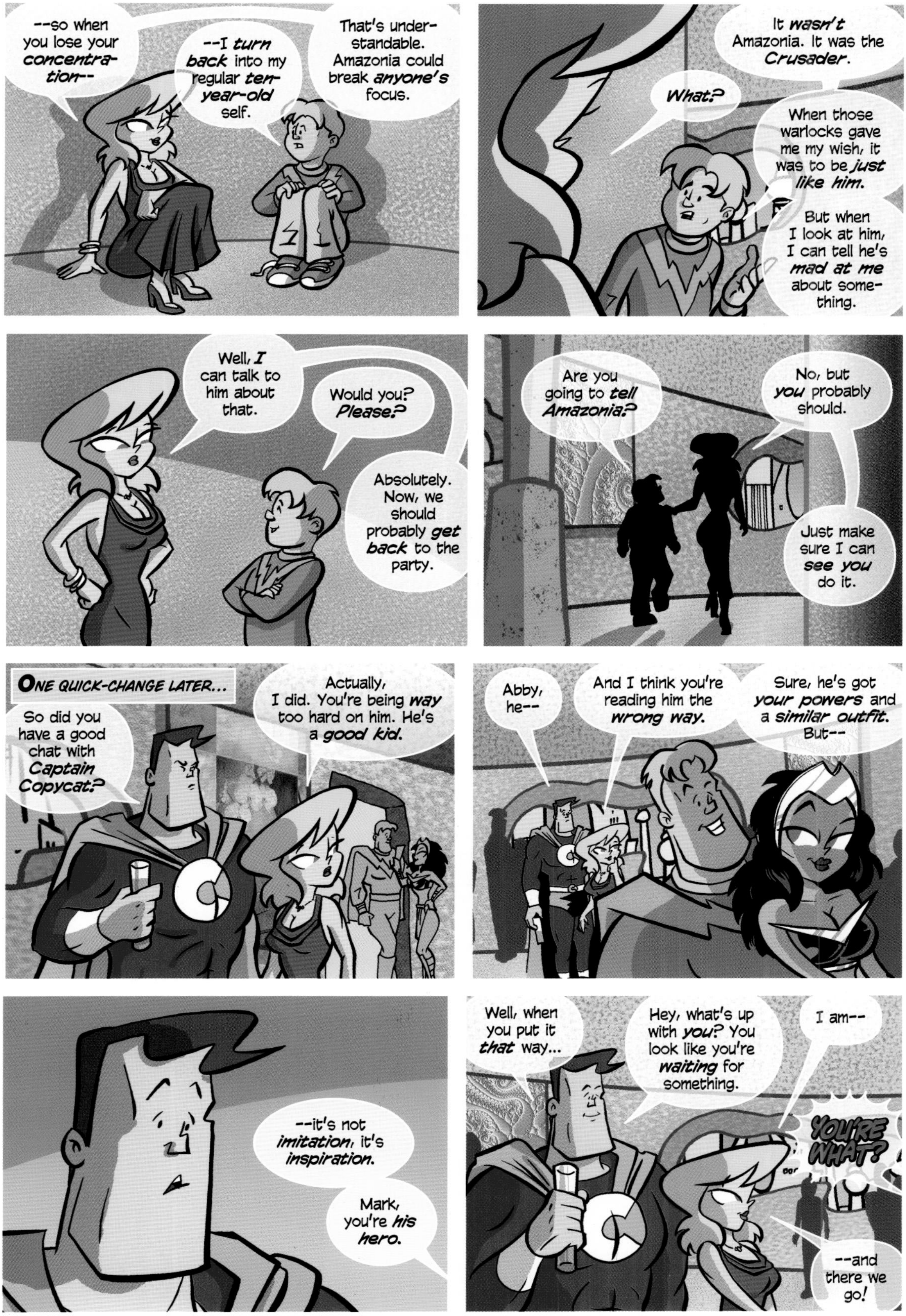
--so when you lose your concentration--
--I turn back into my regular ten-year-old self.
That's understandable. Amazonia could break anyone's focus.
It wasn't Amazonia. It was the Crusader.
What?
When those warlocks gave me my wish, it was to be just like him.
But when I look at him, I can tell he's mad at me about something.
Well, I can talk to him about that.
Would you? Please?
Absolutely. Now, we should probably get back to the party.
Are you going to tell Amazonia?
No, but you probably should.
Just make sure I can see you do it.
ONE QUICK-CHANGE LATER...
So did you have a good chat with Captain Copycat?
Actually, I did. You're being way too hard on him. He's a good kid.
Abby, he--
And I think you're reading him the wrong way.
Sure, he's got your powers and a similar outfit. But--
--it's not imitation, it's inspiration.
Mark, you're his hero.
Well, when you put it that way...
Hey, what's up with you? You look like you're waiting for something.
I am--
YOU'RE WHAT?
--and there we go!

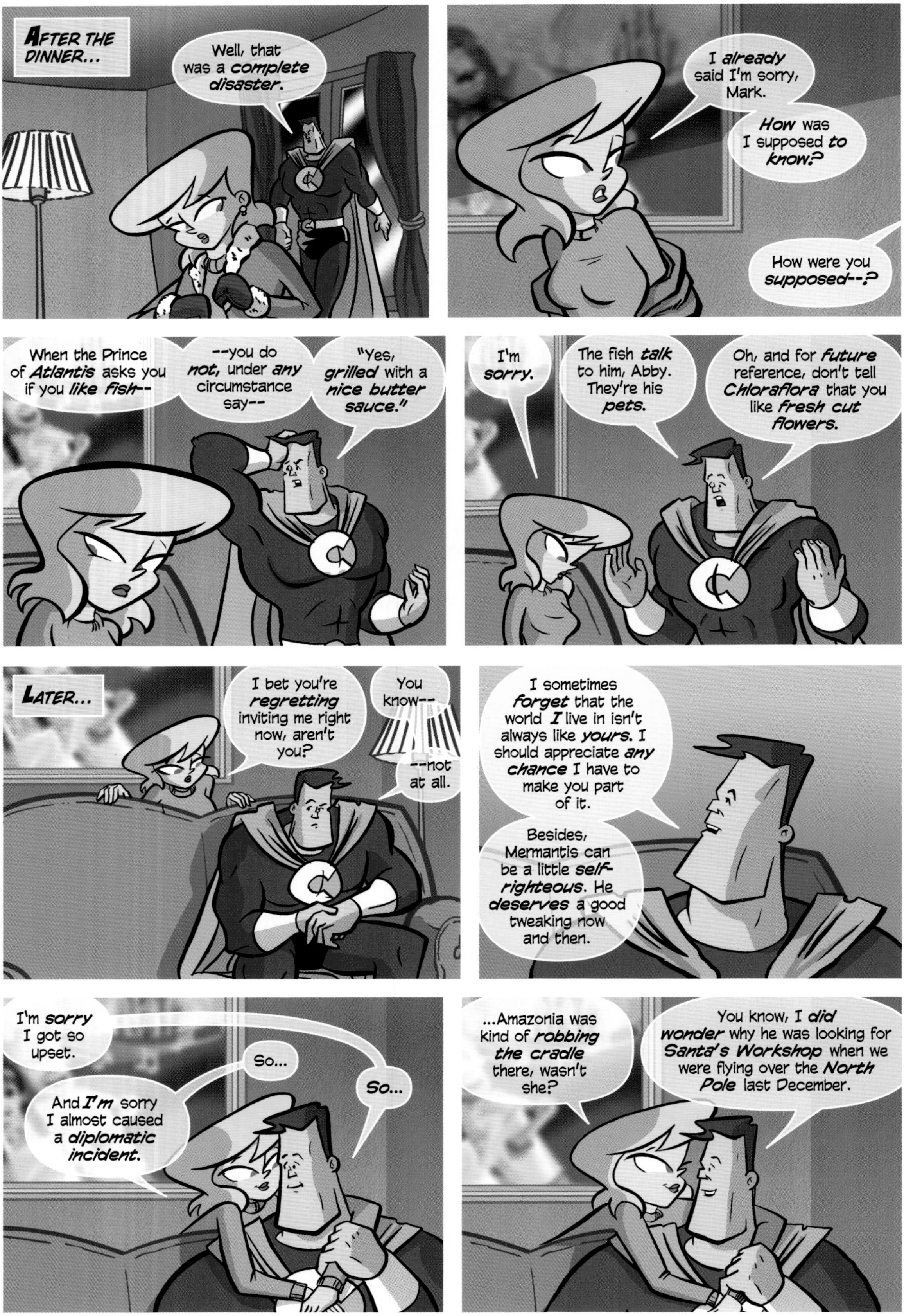
AFTER THE DINNER...
Well, that was a complete disaster.
I already said I'm sorry, Mark.
How was I supposed to know?
How were you supposed--?
When the Prince of Atlantis asks you if you like fish--
--you do not, under any circumstance say--
"Yes, grilled with a nice butter sauce."
I'm sorry.
The fish talk to him, Abby. They're his pets.
Oh, and for future reference, don't tell Chloraflora that you like fresh cut flowers.
LATER...
I bet you're regretting inviting me right now, aren't you?
You know--
--not at all.
I sometimes forget that the world I live in isn't always like yours. I should appreciate any chance I have to make you part of it.
Besides, Mermantis can be a little self-righteous. He deserves a good tweaking now and then.
I'm sorry I got so upset.
So...
And I'm sorry I almost caused a diplomatic incident.
So...
...Amazonia was kind of robbing the cradle there, wasn't she?
You know, I did wonder why he was looking for Santa's Workshop when we were flying over the North Pole last December.

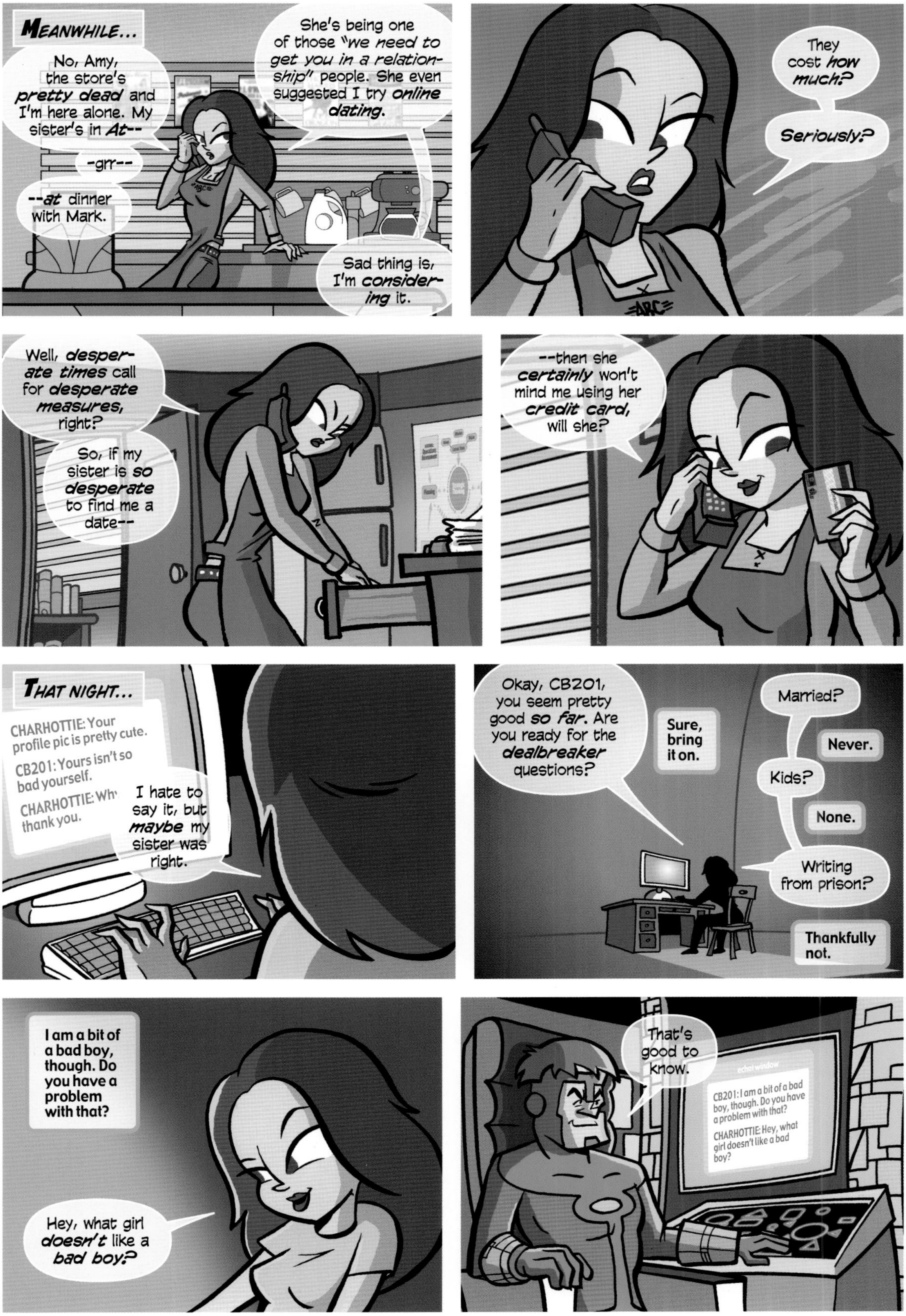
MEANWHILE...
No, Amy, the store's *pretty dead* and I'm here alone. My sister's in *At*--
-grr--
--*at* dinner with Mark.
She's being one of those *"we need to get you in a relationship"* people. She even suggested I try *online dating*.
Sad thing is, I'm *considering* it.
They cost *how much?*
Seriously?
Well, *desperate times* call for *desperate measures*, right?
So, if my sister is *so desperate* to find me a date--
--then she *certainly* won't mind me using her *credit card*, will she?
THAT NIGHT...
CHARHOTTIE: Your profile pic is pretty cute.
CB201: Yours isn't so bad yourself.
CHARHOTTIE: Wh
thank you.
I hate to say it, but *maybe* my sister was right.
Okay, CB201, you seem pretty good *so far*. Are you ready for the *dealbreaker* questions?
Sure, bring it on.
Married?
Never.
Kids?
None.
Writing from prison?
Thankfully not.
I am a bit of a bad boy, though. Do you have a problem with that?
Hey, what girl *doesn't* like a *bad boy?*
That's good to know.
CB201: I am a bit of a bad boy, though. Do you have a problem with that?
CHARHOTTIE: Hey, what girl doesn't like a bad boy?

A FEW DAYS LATER...

...and there I was, sopping wet.

OMG, I can't believe I just told you that story! I'm so embarrassed.

Don't be. It's endearing.

You know, I did pretty well on *Wall Street* today.

Want to go to dinner and *celebrate?* Say, *to-morrow?*

NASDAQ access granted!

AMEX access granted!

NYSE access granted!

FUNDS TRANSFER:
$1,000,0000 to account 17011864...
$3,000,0000 to account 17011864...
$2,000,0000 to account 17011864...
$9,000,000 to account 17011864...

Say, tomorrow
CHARHOTTIE: Y
mean finally m
person?

You mean finally meet in person?

Absolutely. How about *Chez Ferrer?*

You *sure* know how to *impress* someone. That's the *toughest ticket* in town.

Can you even score us *reservations?*

Chez Ferrer

USER: Ferrerboss
PASS: *******

FRIDAY RESERVATIONS
7:00 Haley Party (2)
7:30 Panosian Party (4)
8:00 DELETING...
8:30 Wray Party (1)

Oh, I don't see *that* as being a *problem.*

AT MARK'S APARTMENT...

Hello, Mark.

Hi, honey. How was work?

Not bad. Hey, I have a *favor* to ask.

Charlotte met a guy online. They're *going out* to dinner tomorrow night.

That's *good,* right?

I *think* so. But I'd like you to *check up* on the guy. Make sure he's *not trouble.*

Somebody's been watching *"Dateline"* again.

I'm *protective.* Sue me.

I think you mean *over*-protective.

You know I'm *not* a *detective,* right?

But, as I recall, your best friend *is.*

Oh, I see, you just want another *pizza* from *Chronopolis.*

That, and I like watching you *take your shirt off.*

70

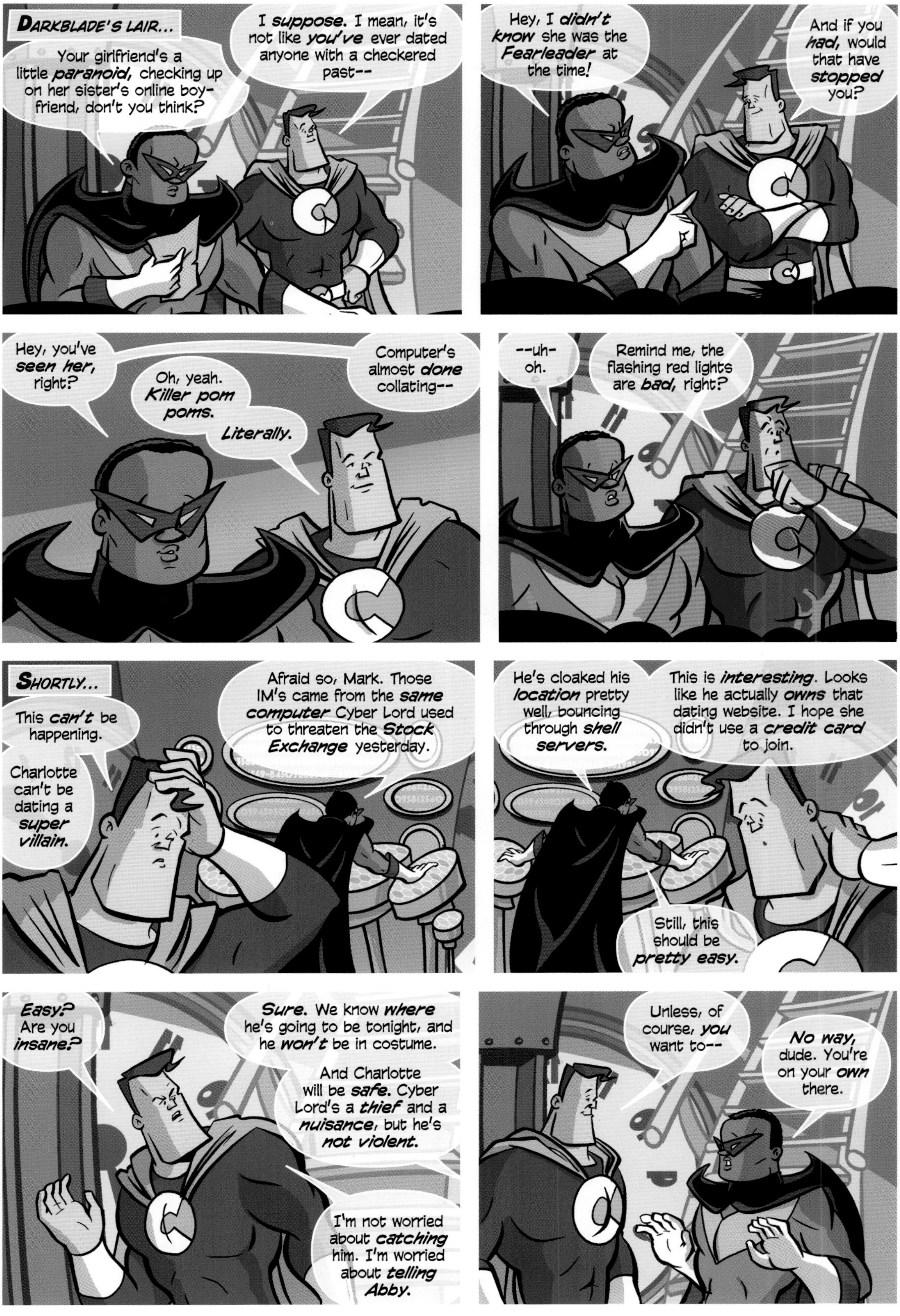
DARKBLADE'S LAIR...
Your girlfriend's a little *paranoid,* checking up on her sister's online boy-friend, don't you think?
I *suppose.* I mean, it's not like *you've* ever dated anyone with a checkered past--
Hey, I *didn't know* she was the *Fearleader* at the time!
And if you *had,* would that have *stopped* you?
Hey, you've *seen her,* right?
Oh, yeah. *Killer pom poms.*
Literally.
Computer's almost *done* collating--
--uh-oh.
Remind me, the flashing red lights are *bad,* right?
SHORTLY...
This *can't* be happening.
Charlotte can't be dating a *super villain.*
Afraid so, Mark. Those IM's came from the *same computer* Cyber Lord used to threaten the *Stock Exchange* yesterday.
He's cloaked his *location* pretty well, bouncing through *shell servers.*
This is *interesting.* Looks like he actually *owns* that dating website. I hope she didn't use a *credit card* to join.
Still, this should be *pretty easy.*
Easy? Are you *insane?*
Sure. We know *where* he's going to be tonight, and he *won't* be in costume.
And Charlotte will be *safe.* Cyber Lord's a *thief* and a *nuisance,* but he's *not violent.*
I'm not worried about *catching* him. I'm worried about *telling Abby.*
Unless, of course, *you* want to--
No way, dude. You're on your *own* there.

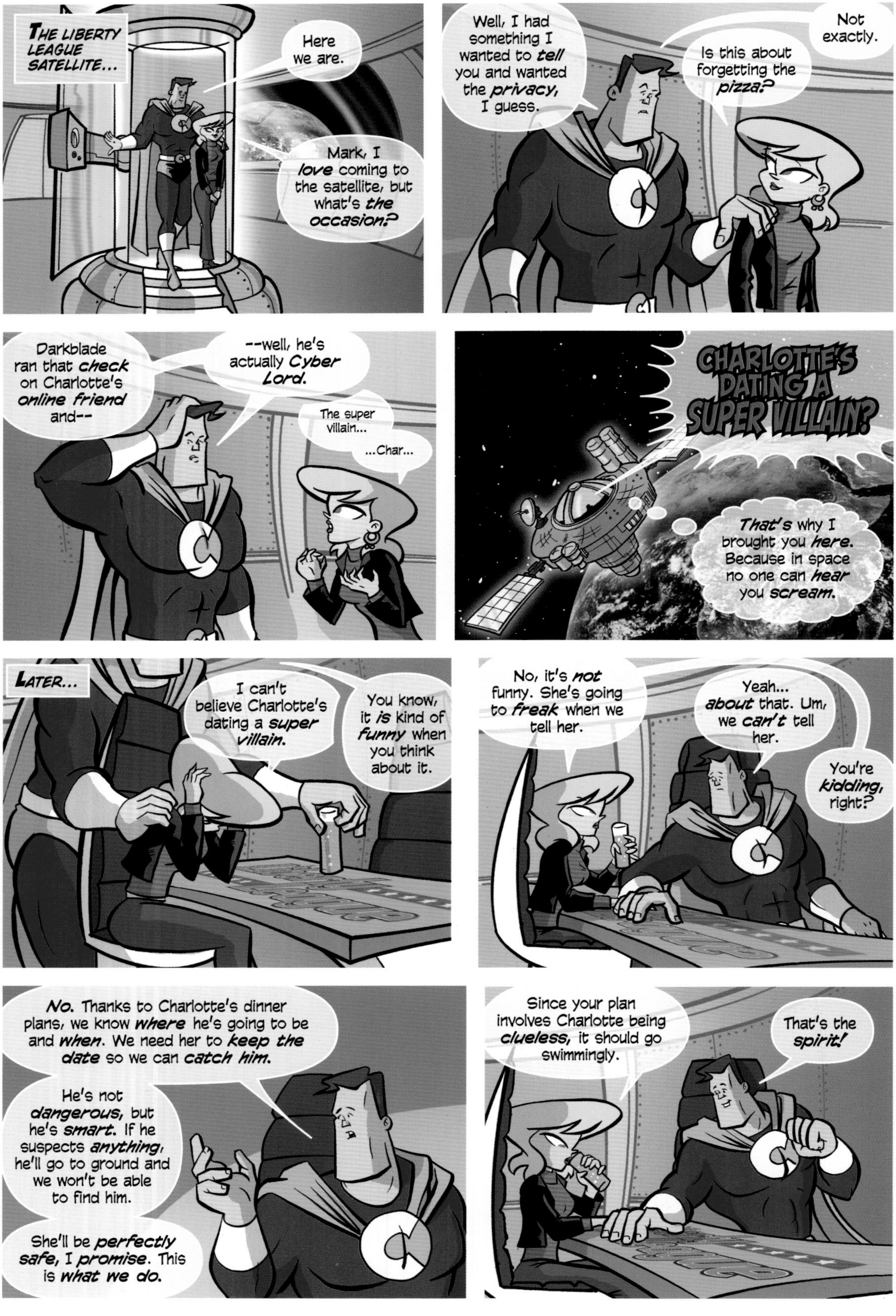
THE LIBERTY LEAGUE SATELLITE...
Here we are.
Mark, I love coming to the satellite, but what's the occasion?
Well, I had something I wanted to tell you and wanted the privacy, I guess.
Is this about forgetting the pizza?
Not exactly.
Darkblade ran that check on Charlotte's online friend and--
--well, he's actually Cyber Lord.
The super villain...
...Char...
CHARLOTTE'S DATING A SUPER VILLAIN?
That's why I brought you here. Because in space no one can hear you scream.
LATER...
I can't believe Charlotte's dating a super villain.
You know, it is kind of funny when you think about it.
No, it's not funny. She's going to freak when we tell her.
Yeah... about that. Um, we can't tell her.
You're kidding, right?
No. Thanks to Charlotte's dinner plans, we know where he's going to be and when. We need her to keep the date so we can catch him.
He's not dangerous, but he's smart. If he suspects anything, he'll go to ground and we won't be able to find him.
She'll be perfectly safe, I promise. This is what we do.
Since your plan involves Charlotte being clueless, it should go swimmingly.
That's the spirit!

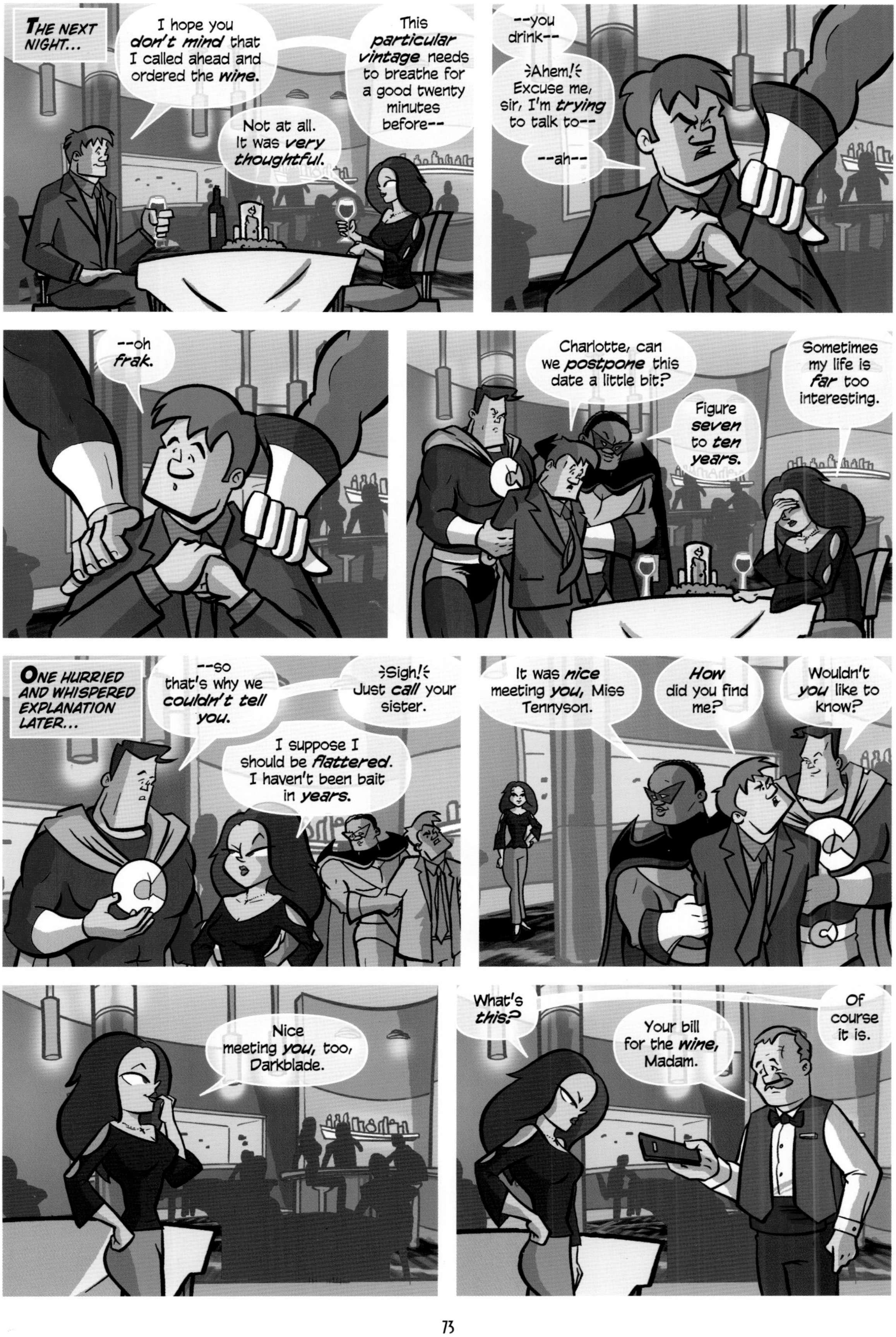

THE NEXT NIGHT...
I hope you don't mind that I called ahead and ordered the wine.
Not at all. It was very thoughtful.
This particular vintage needs to breathe for a good twenty minutes before--
--you drink--
Ahem! Excuse me, sir, I'm trying to talk to--
--ah--
--oh frak.
Charlotte, can we postpone this date a little bit?
Figure seven to ten years.
Sometimes my life is far too interesting.
ONE HURRIED AND WHISPERED EXPLANATION LATER...
--so that's why we couldn't tell you.
Sigh! Just call your sister.
I suppose I should be flattered. I haven't been bait in years.
It was nice meeting you, Miss Tennyson.
How did you find me?
Wouldn't you like to know?
Nice meeting you, too, Darkblade.
What's this?
Your bill for the wine, Madam.
Of course it is.

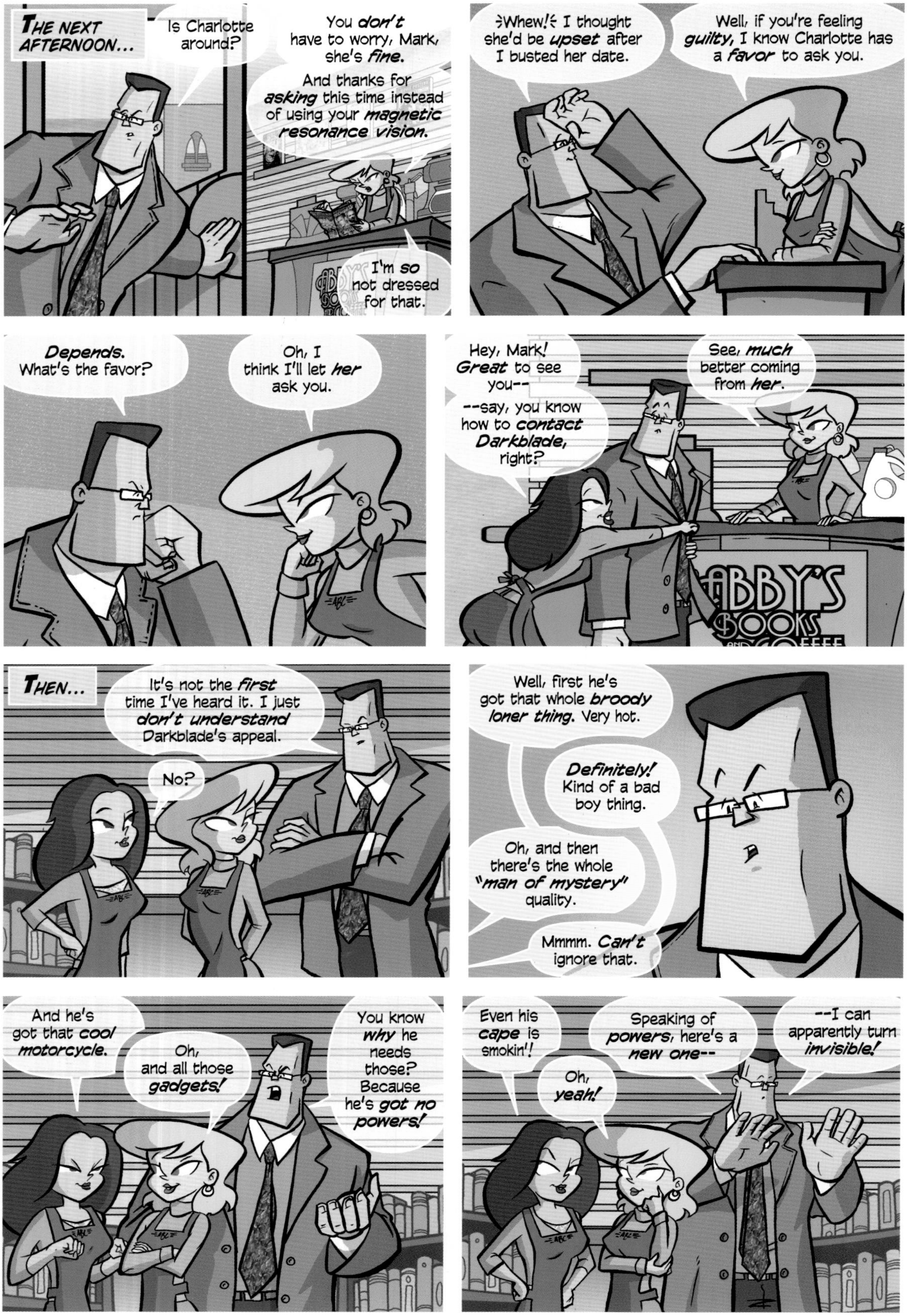
THE NEXT AFTERNOON...
Is Charlotte around?
You don't have to worry, Mark, she's fine.
And thanks for asking this time instead of using your magnetic resonance vision.
I'm so not dressed for that.
Whew! I thought she'd be upset after I busted her date.
Well, if you're feeling guilty, I know Charlotte has a favor to ask you.
Depends. What's the favor?
Oh, I think I'll let her ask you.
Hey, Mark! Great to see you--
--say, you know how to contact Darkblade, right?
See, much better coming from her.
ABBY'S BOOKS AND COFFEE
THEN...
It's not the first time I've heard it. I just don't understand Darkblade's appeal.
No?
Well, first he's got that whole broody loner thing. Very hot.
Definitely! Kind of a bad boy thing.
Oh, and then there's the whole "man of mystery" quality.
Mmmm. Can't ignore that.
And he's got that cool motorcycle.
Oh, and all those gadgets!
You know why he needs those? Because he's got no powers!
Even his cape is smokin'!
Oh, yeah!
Speaking of powers, here's a new one--
--I can apparently turn invisible!

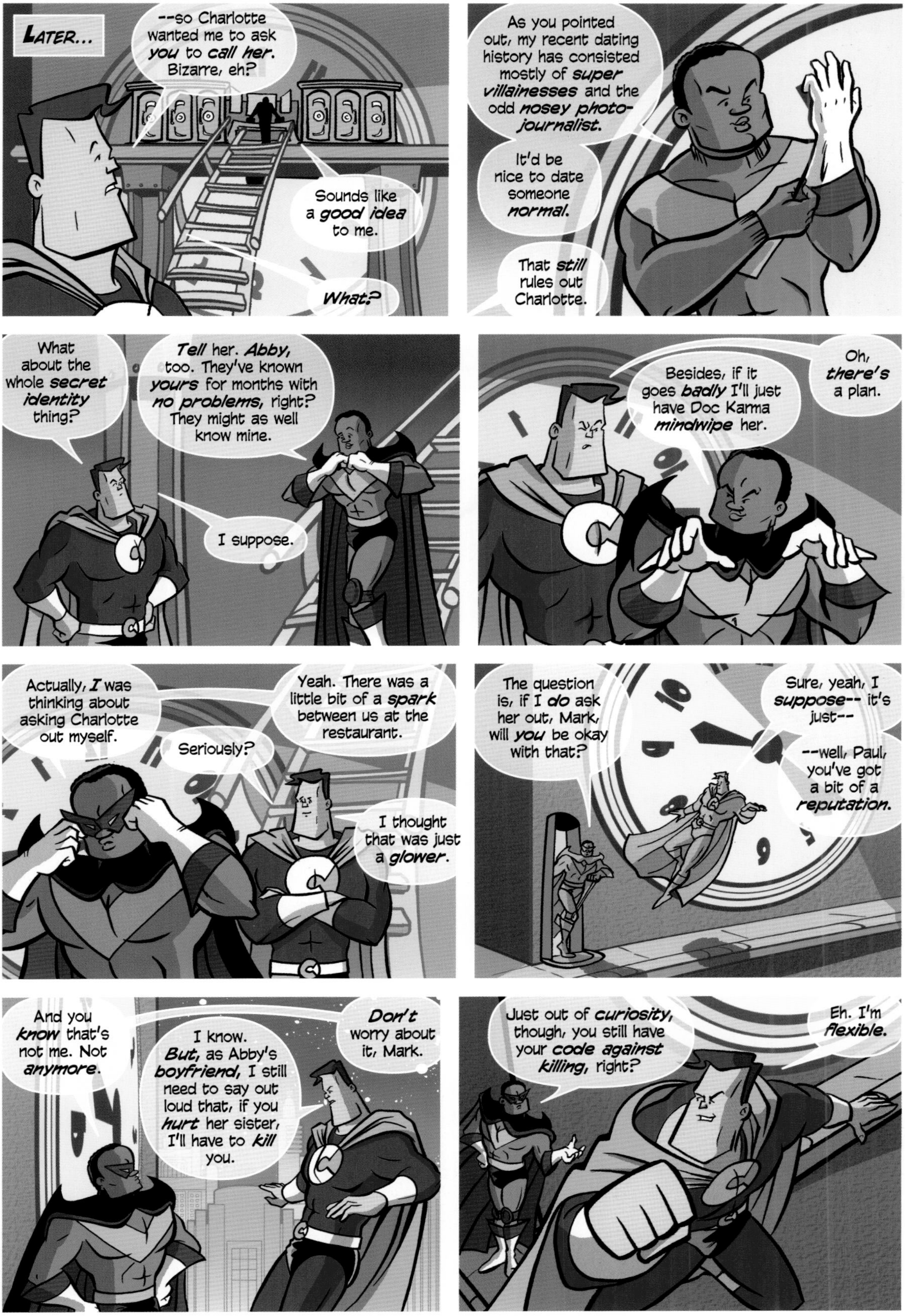
LATER...
--so Charlotte wanted me to ask you to call her. Bizarre, eh?
Sounds like a good idea to me.
What?
As you pointed out, my recent dating history has consisted mostly of super villainesses and the odd nosey photo-journalist.
It'd be nice to date someone normal.
That still rules out Charlotte.
What about the whole secret identity thing?
Tell her. Abby, too. They've known yours for months with no problems, right? They might as well know mine.
I suppose.
Besides, if it goes badly I'll just have Doc Karma mindwipe her.
Oh, there's a plan.
Actually, I was thinking about asking Charlotte out myself.
Seriously?
Yeah. There was a little bit of a spark between us at the restaurant.
I thought that was just a glower.
The question is, if I do ask her out, Mark, will you be okay with that?
Sure, yeah, I suppose-- it's just--
--well, Paul, you've got a bit of a reputation.
And you know that's not me. Not anymore.
I know. But, as Abby's boyfriend, I still need to say out loud that, if you hurt her sister, I'll have to kill you.
Don't worry about it, Mark.
Just out of curiosity, though, you still have your code against killing, right?
Eh. I'm flexible.

LATER...

--so I talked to Darkblade and he said he'd like to go out with *you*, too

He *even* said to go ahead and tell you his *secret identity*.

Now remember, Charlotte, this is a *big responsibility*. He's got *plenty* of enemies.

I've got it, Mark, now *spill!*

He's *Paul Lacroix* from Chronopolis.

Wait... *the* Paul Lacroix? The *Boy Mogul?*

One of *People's Fifty Most Attractive...*

And *rich*, too. Wow, you sure are *lucky!*

...um, of course not as lucky as *I* am, Sweetie.

Nice save, Bookstore Girl.

So, *what* are you going to *wear?*

Geez, I *don't know*, Abby. He hasn't even actually *called* yet.

Still--

Dear, *please.* "Studio 60" is on.

BREEP! BREEP!

--my *Liberty League* comlink!

Mark, is that--?

BREEP! BREEP!

I'd better grab that.

So, anything I *need* to *know* about dating a superhero?

First off, prepare to be interrupted. *A lot.*

Darkblade? What is it?

Charlotte?

Yes?

It's for *you.*

76

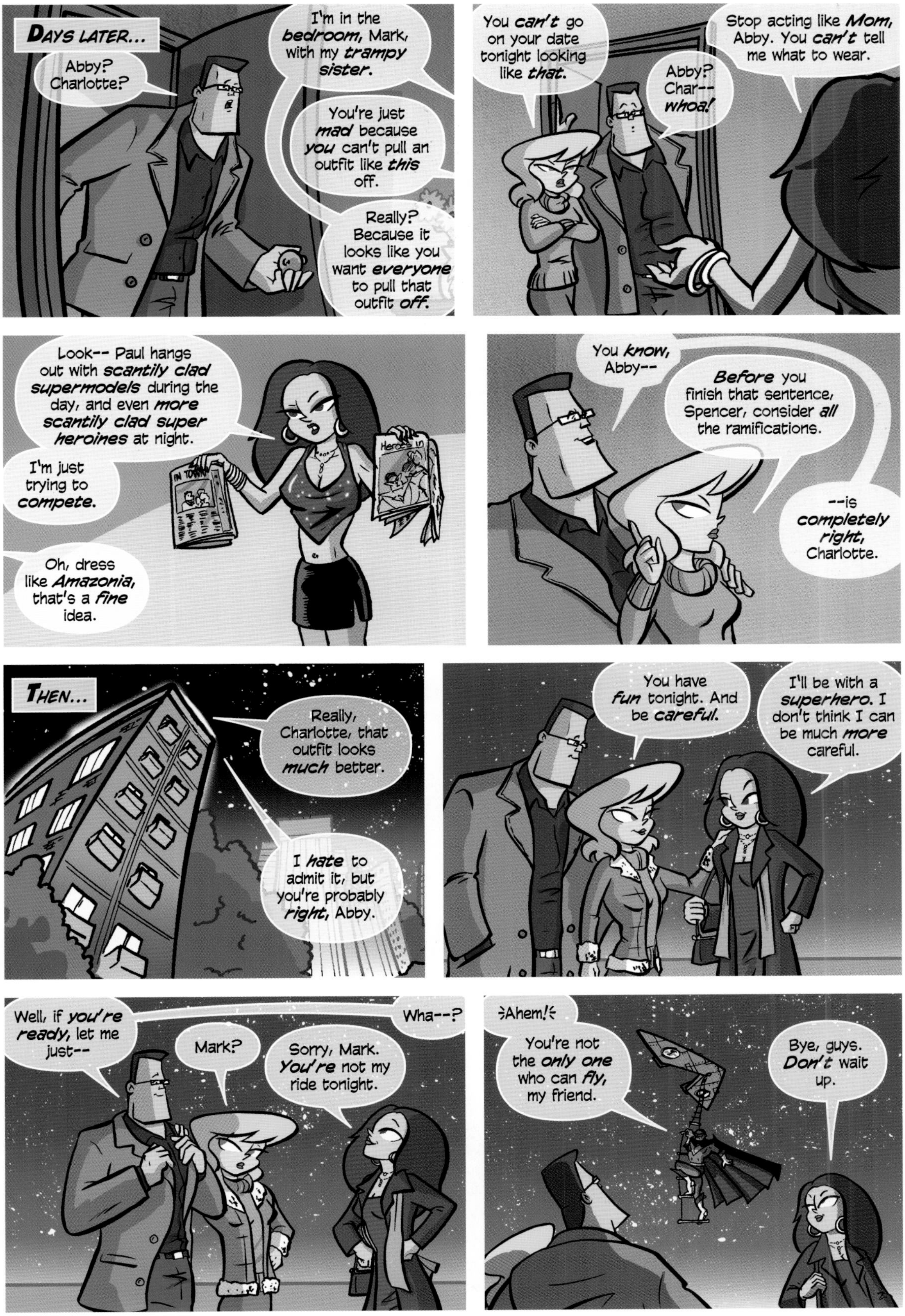
DAYS LATER...
Abby? Charlotte?
I'm in the *bedroom,* Mark, with my *trampy sister.*
You're just *mad* because *you* can't pull an outfit like *this* off.
Really? Because it looks like you want *everyone* to pull that outfit *off.*
You *can't* go on your date tonight looking like *that.*
Abby? Char-- *whoa!*
Stop acting like *Mom,* Abby. You *can't* tell me what to wear.
Look-- Paul hangs out with *scantily clad supermodels* during the day, and even *more scantily clad super heroines* at night.
I'm just trying to *compete.*
Oh, dress like *Amazonia,* that's a *fine* idea.
You *know,* Abby--
Before you finish that sentence, Spencer, consider *all* the ramifications.
--is *completely right,* Charlotte.
THEN...
Really, Charlotte, that outfit looks *much* better.
I *hate* to admit it, but you're probably *right,* Abby.
You have *fun* tonight. And be *careful.*
I'll be with a *superhero.* I don't think I can be much *more* careful.
Well, if *you're ready,* let me just--
Wha--?
Mark?
Sorry, Mark. *You're* not my ride tonight.
Ahem!
You're not the *only one* who can *fly,* my friend.
Bye, guys. *Don't* wait up.

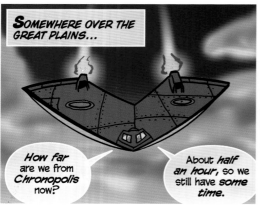

SOMEWHERE OVER THE GREAT PLAINS...

How far are we from Chronopolis now?

About half an hour, so we still have some time.

Is that enough time to tell me how you became Darkblade?

Sure. It's not something I normally get to tell my dates.

Back in the day, I was quite the wild child. Think Paris Hilton meets Jude Law. My father tried everything to get through to me, but nothing worked.

But my father is a man of means--

--so he contracted an order of warrior priests and hired them to kidnap me and teach me some humility and respect.

It actually took better than my father thought. The priests wound up training me to be the next champion in the order of the Lanna Na Hoíche or Darkblade.

Wow. Thanksgiving dinner with your folks must be weird.

You have no idea.

LATER...

So what do you have planned for our date, Paul?

Well--

I was thinking we could go to my mansion and I'll fix you dinner. Oddly, those priests were good chefs, too.

My first thought was to take you to The Top of the Town in downtown Chronopolis, but I'm famous even without the mask. I figured that wouldn't work--

--unless your idea of a good time is being surrounded by paparazzi and being stared at all night.

So...

How's the risotto?

Just perfect.

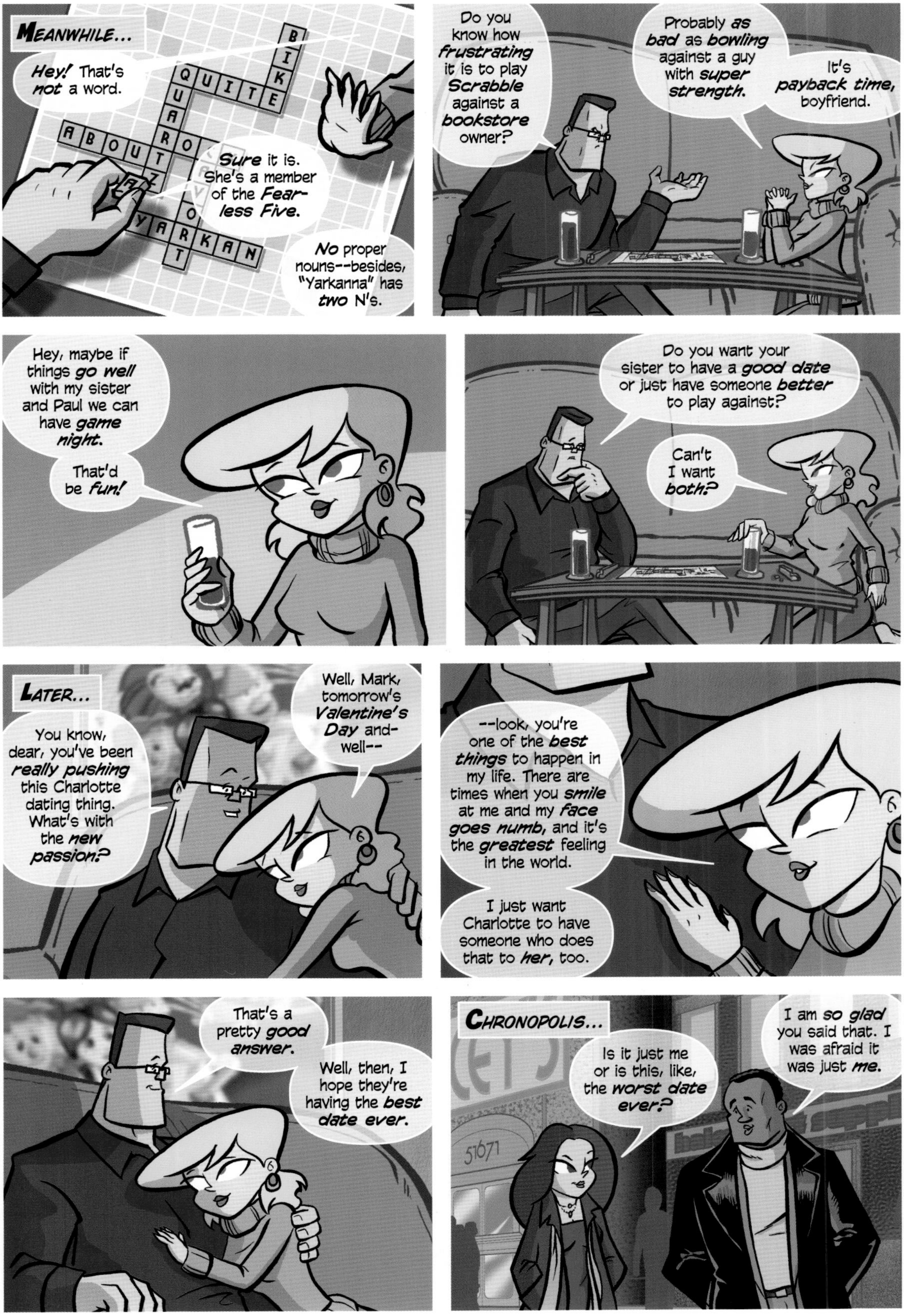
MEANWHILE...
Hey! That's not a word.
BIKE
QUITE
QUARTZ
ABOUT
YARKAN
Sure it is. She's a member of the Fear-less Five.
No proper nouns--besides, "Yarkanna" has two N's.
Do you know how frustrating it is to play Scrabble against a bookstore owner?
Probably as bad as bowling against a guy with super strength.
It's payback time, boyfriend.
Hey, maybe if things go well with my sister and Paul we can have game night.
That'd be fun!
Do you want your sister to have a good date or just have someone better to play against?
Can't I want both?
LATER...
You know, dear, you've been really pushing this Charlotte dating thing. What's with the new passion?
Well, Mark, tomorrow's Valentine's Day and-well--
--look, you're one of the best things to happen in my life. There are times when you smile at me and my face goes numb, and it's the greatest feeling in the world.
I just want Charlotte to have someone who does that to her, too.
That's a pretty good answer.
Well, then, I hope they're having the best date ever.
CHRONOPOLIS...
Is it just me or is this, like, the worst date ever?
I am so glad you said that. I was afraid it was just me.

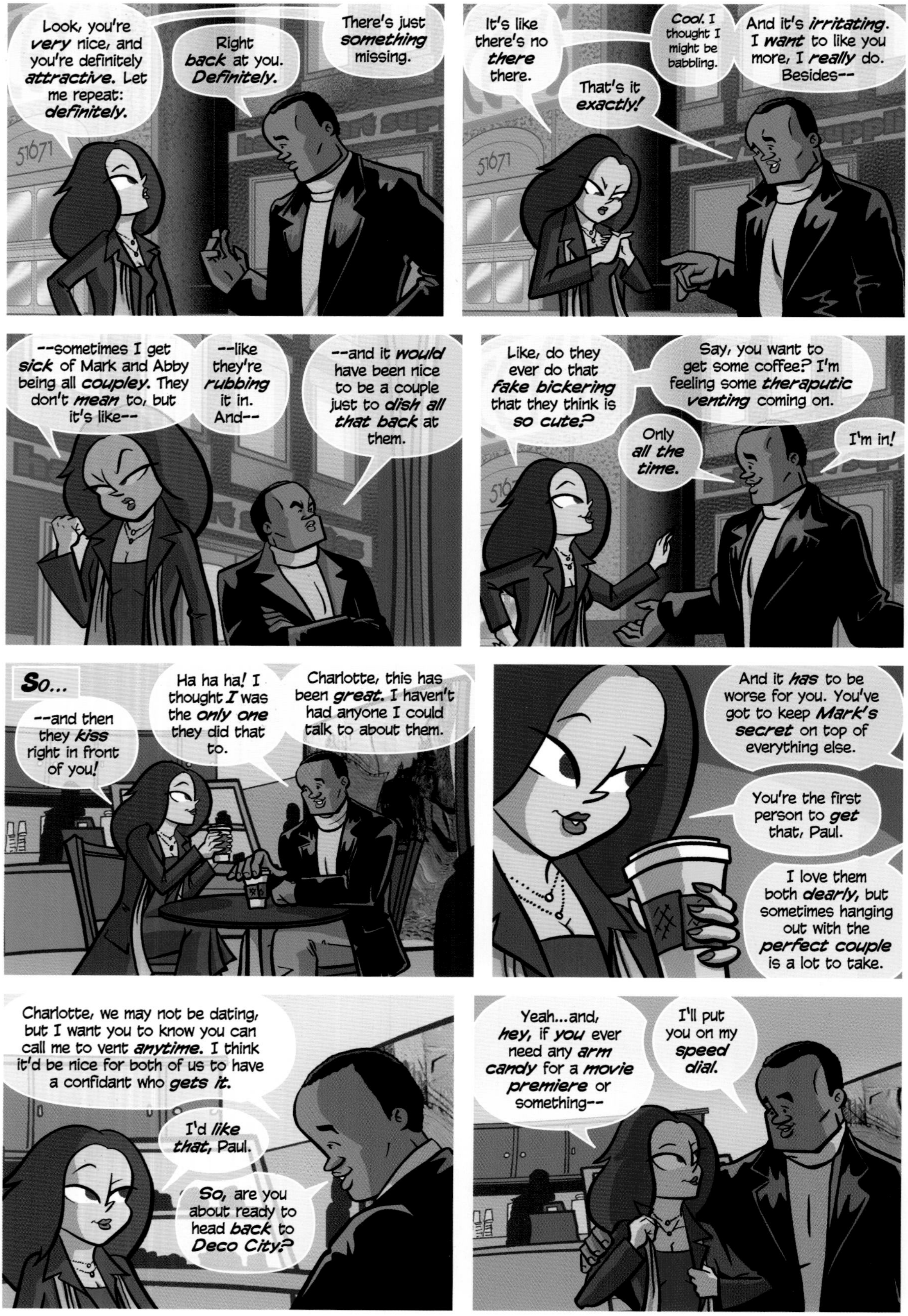

Look, you're very nice, and you're definitely attractive. Let me repeat: definitely.
Right back at you. Definitely.
There's just something missing.
51671
It's like there's no there there.
That's it exactly!
Cool. I thought I might be babbling.
And it's irritating. I want to like you more, I really do. Besides--
51671
--sometimes I get sick of Mark and Abby being all coupley. They don't mean to, but it's like--
--like they're rubbing it in. And--
--and it would have been nice to be a couple just to dish all that back at them.
Like, do they ever do that fake bickering that they think is so cute?
Say, you want to get some coffee? I'm feeling some theraputic venting coming on.
Only all the time.
I'm in!
So...
--and then they kiss right in front of you!
Ha ha ha! I thought I was the only one they did that to.
Charlotte, this has been great. I haven't had anyone I could talk to about them.
And it has to be worse for you. You've got to keep Mark's secret on top of everything else.
You're the first person to get that, Paul.
I love them both dearly, but sometimes hanging out with the perfect couple is a lot to take.
Charlotte, we may not be dating, but I want you to know you can call me to vent anytime. I think it'd be nice for both of us to have a confidant who gets it.
I'd like that, Paul.
So, are you about ready to head back to Deco City?
Yeah...and, hey, if you ever need any arm candy for a movie premiere or something--
I'll put you on my speed dial.

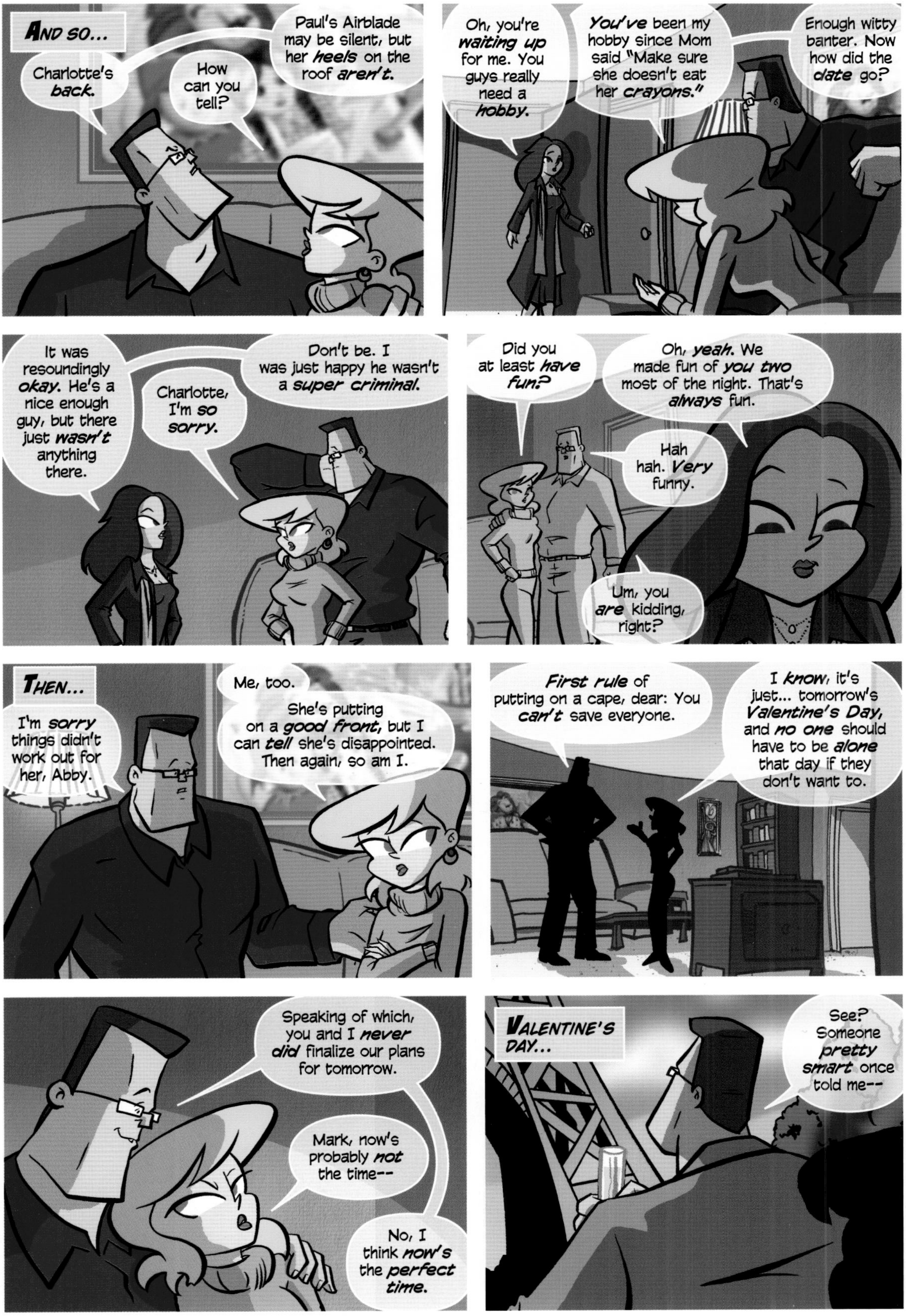
AND SO...
Charlotte's back.
How can you tell?
Paul's Airblade may be silent, but her heels on the roof aren't.
Oh, you're waiting up for me. You guys really need a hobby.
You've been my hobby since Mom said "Make sure she doesn't eat her crayons."
Enough witty banter. Now how did the date go?
It was resoundingly okay. He's a nice enough guy, but there just wasn't anything there.
Charlotte, I'm so sorry.
Don't be. I was just happy he wasn't a super criminal.
Did you at least have fun?
Oh, yeah. We made fun of you two most of the night. That's always fun.
Hah hah. Very funny.
Um, you are kidding, right?
THEN...
I'm sorry things didn't work out for her, Abby.
Me, too.
She's putting on a good front, but I can tell she's disappointed. Then again, so am I.
First rule of putting on a cape, dear: You can't save everyone.
I know, it's just... tomorrow's Valentine's Day, and no one should have to be alone that day if they don't want to.
Speaking of which, you and I never did finalize our plans for tomorrow.
Mark, now's probably not the time--
No, I think now's the perfect time.
VALENTINE'S DAY...
See? Someone pretty smart once told me--

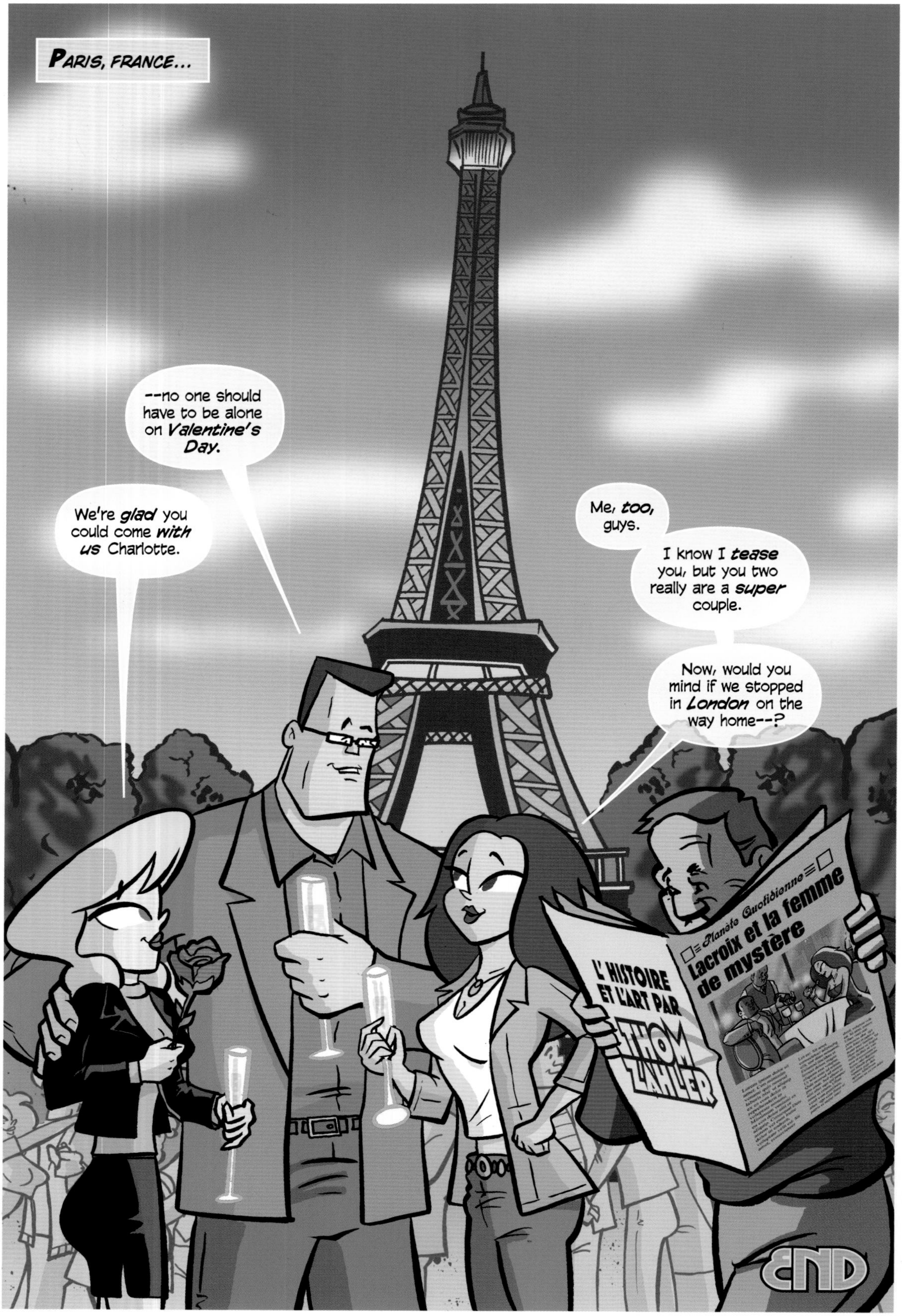
PARIS, FRANCE...
We're *glad* you could come *with us* Charlotte.
--no one should have to be alone on *Valentine's Day.*
Me, *too,* guys.
I know I *tease* you, but you two really are a *super* couple.
Now, would you mind if we stopped in *London* on the way home--?
Planète Quotidienne
Lacroix et la femme de mystère
L'HISTOIRE ET L'ART PAR THOM ZAHLER
END

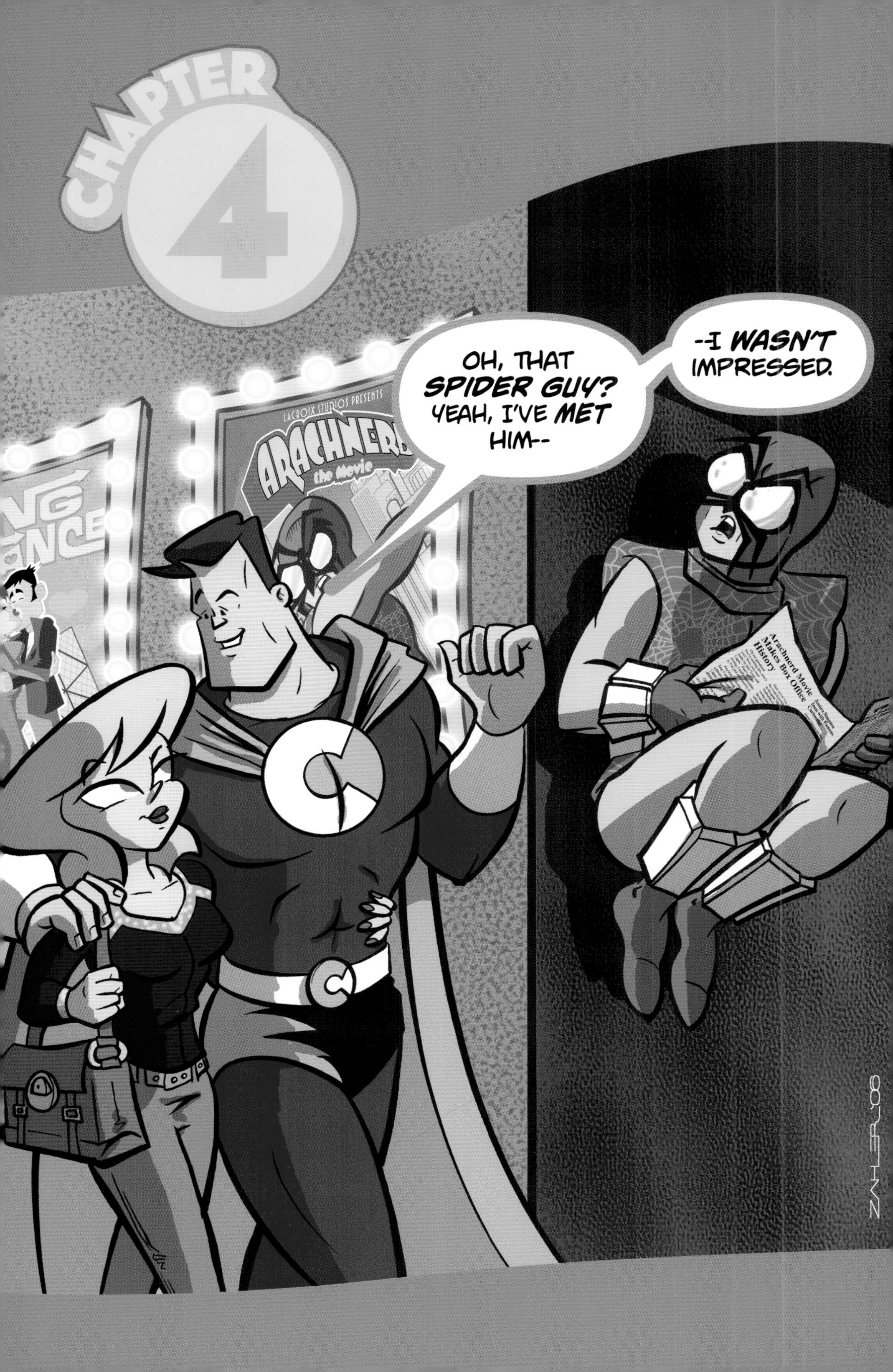
CHAPTER 4
LACROIX STUDIOS PRESENTS
ARACHNERD the Movie
OH, THAT SPIDER GUY? YEAH, I'VE MET HIM--
-I WASN'T IMPRESSED.
Arachnerd Movie Makes Box Office History
ZAHLER '06

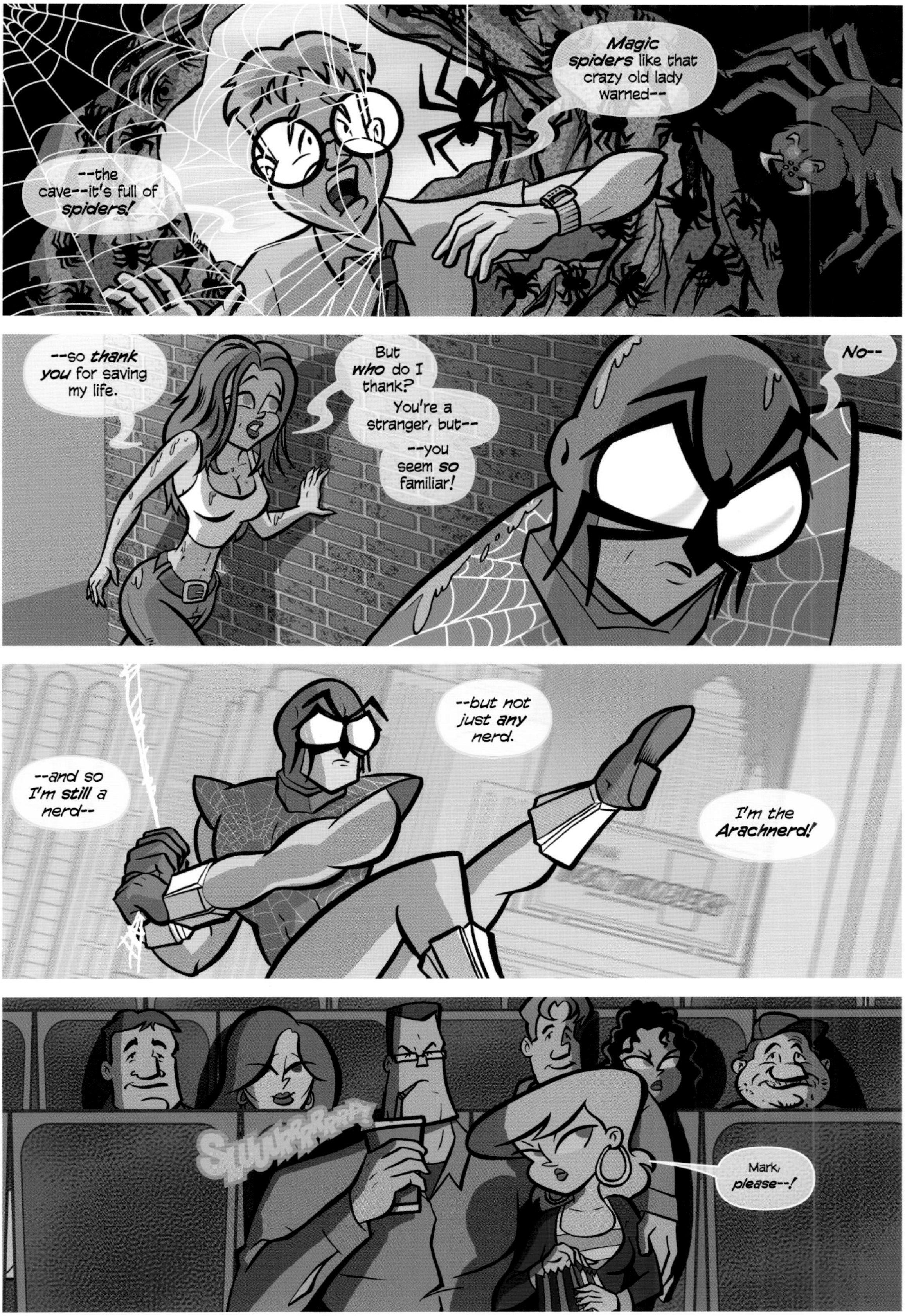

--the cave--it's full of *spiders!*
Magic spiders like that crazy old lady warned--
--so ***thank you*** for saving my life.
But ***who*** do I thank?
You're a stranger, but--
--you seem ***so*** familiar!
No--
*--and so I'm **still** a nerd--*
*--but not just **any** nerd.*
*I'm the **Arachnerd!***
SLUUURRRRRRP!
Mark, ***please--!***

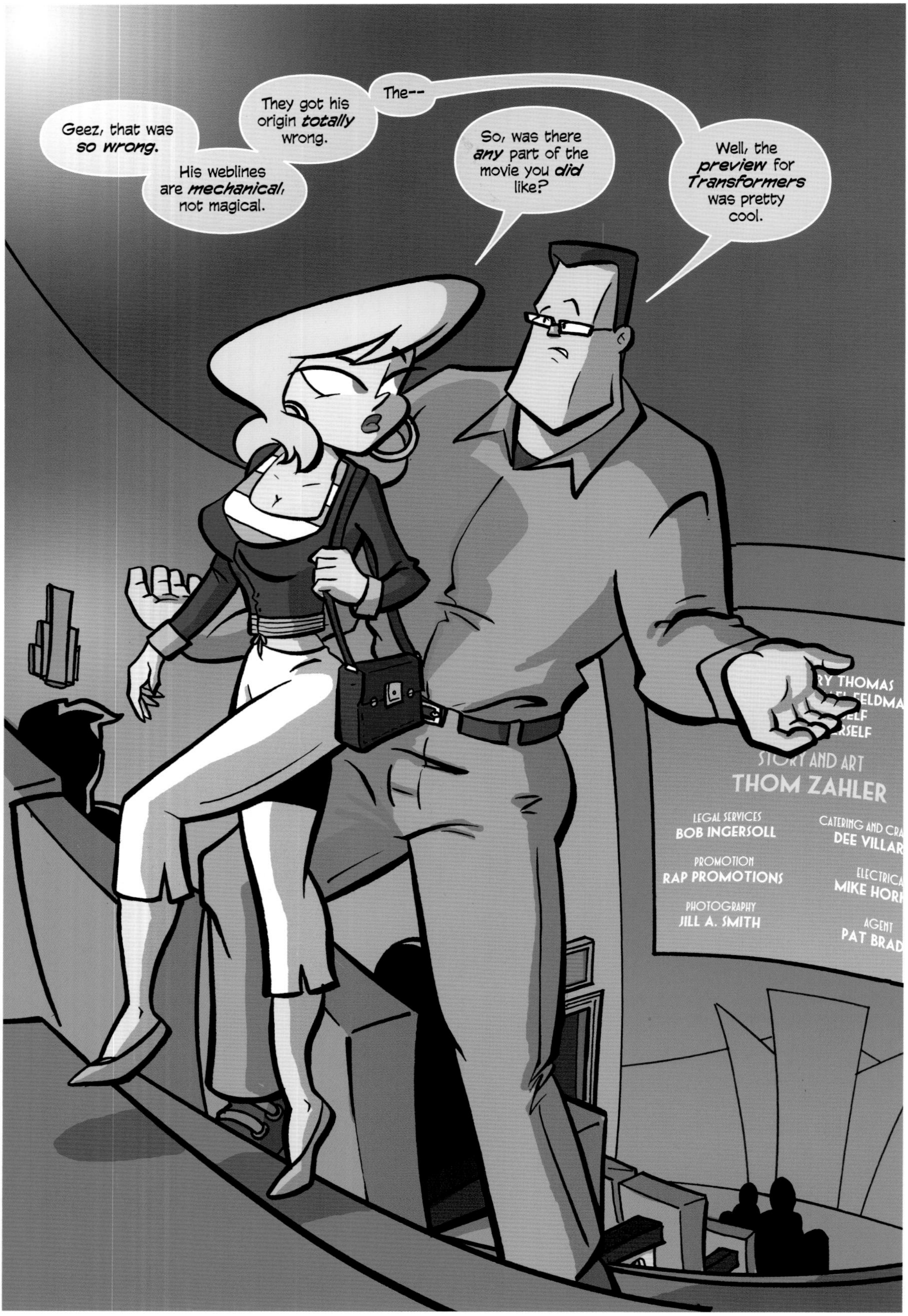
Geez, that was *so wrong.*
His weblines are *mechanical,* not magical.
They got his origin *totally* wrong.
The--
So, was there *any* part of the movie you *did* like?
Well, the *preview* for *Transformers* was pretty cool.
STORY AND ART
THOM ZAHLER
LEGAL SERVICES
BOB INGERSOLL
PROMOTION
RAP PROMOTIONS
PHOTOGRAPHY
JILL A. SMITH
AGENT

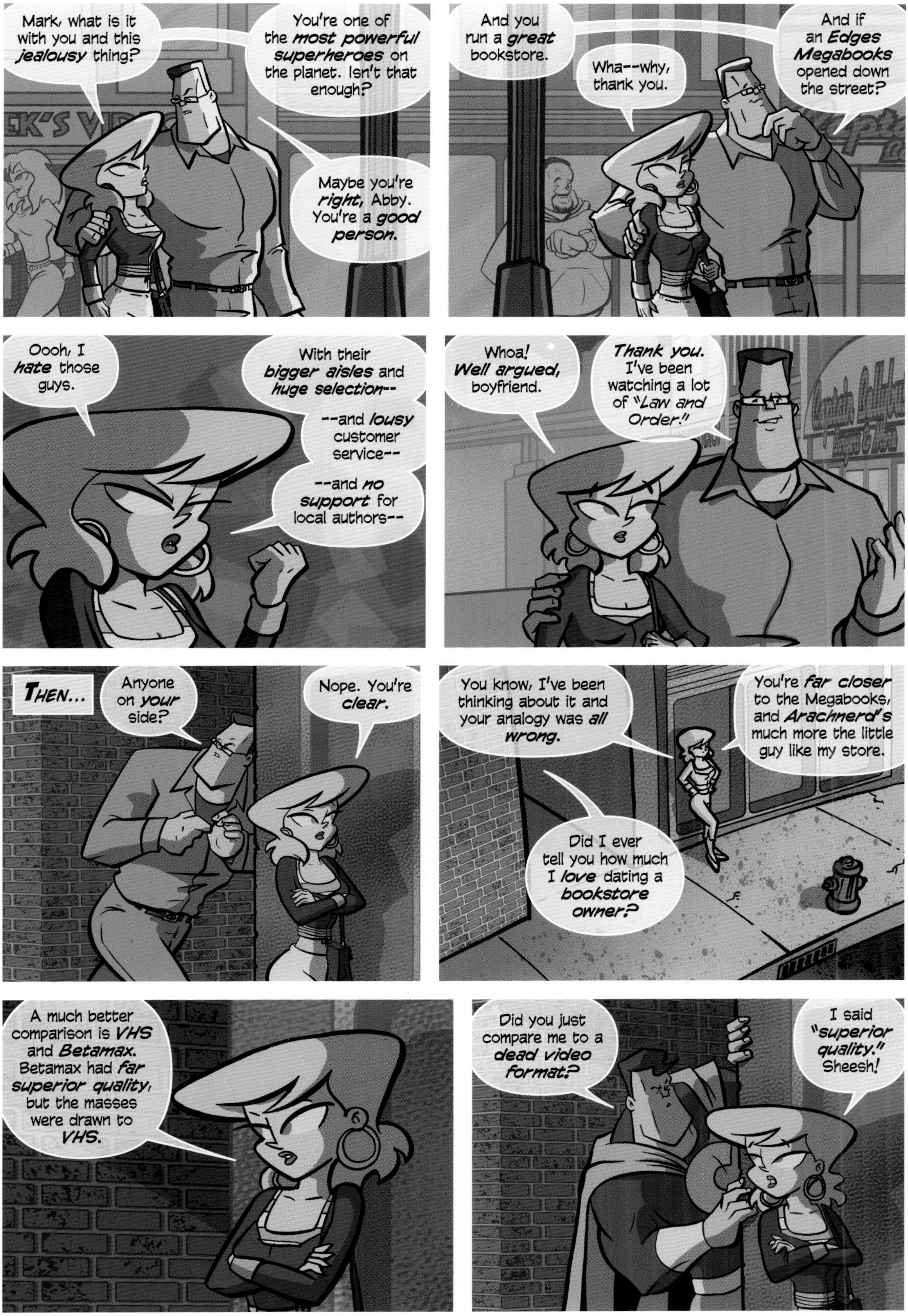
Mark, what is it with you and this *jealousy* thing?
You're one of the *most powerful superheroes* on the planet. Isn't that enough?
Maybe you're *right,* Abby. You're a *good person.*
And you run a *great* bookstore.
Wha--why, thank you.
And if an *Edges Megabooks* opened down the street?
Oooh, I *hate* those guys.
With their *bigger aisles* and *huge selection--*
--and *lousy* customer service--
--and *no support* for local authors--
Whoa! *Well argued,* boyfriend.
Thank you. I've been watching a lot of "*Law and Order.*"
THEN...
Anyone on *your* side?
Nope. You're *clear.*
You know, I've been thinking about it and your analogy was *all wrong.*
You're *far closer* to the Megabooks, and *Arachnerd's* much more the little guy like my store.
Did I ever tell you how much I *love* dating a *bookstore owner?*
A much better comparison is *VHS* and *Betamax.* Betamax had *far superior quality,* but the masses were drawn to *VHS.*
Did you just compare me to a *dead video format?*
I said "*superior quality.*" Sheesh!

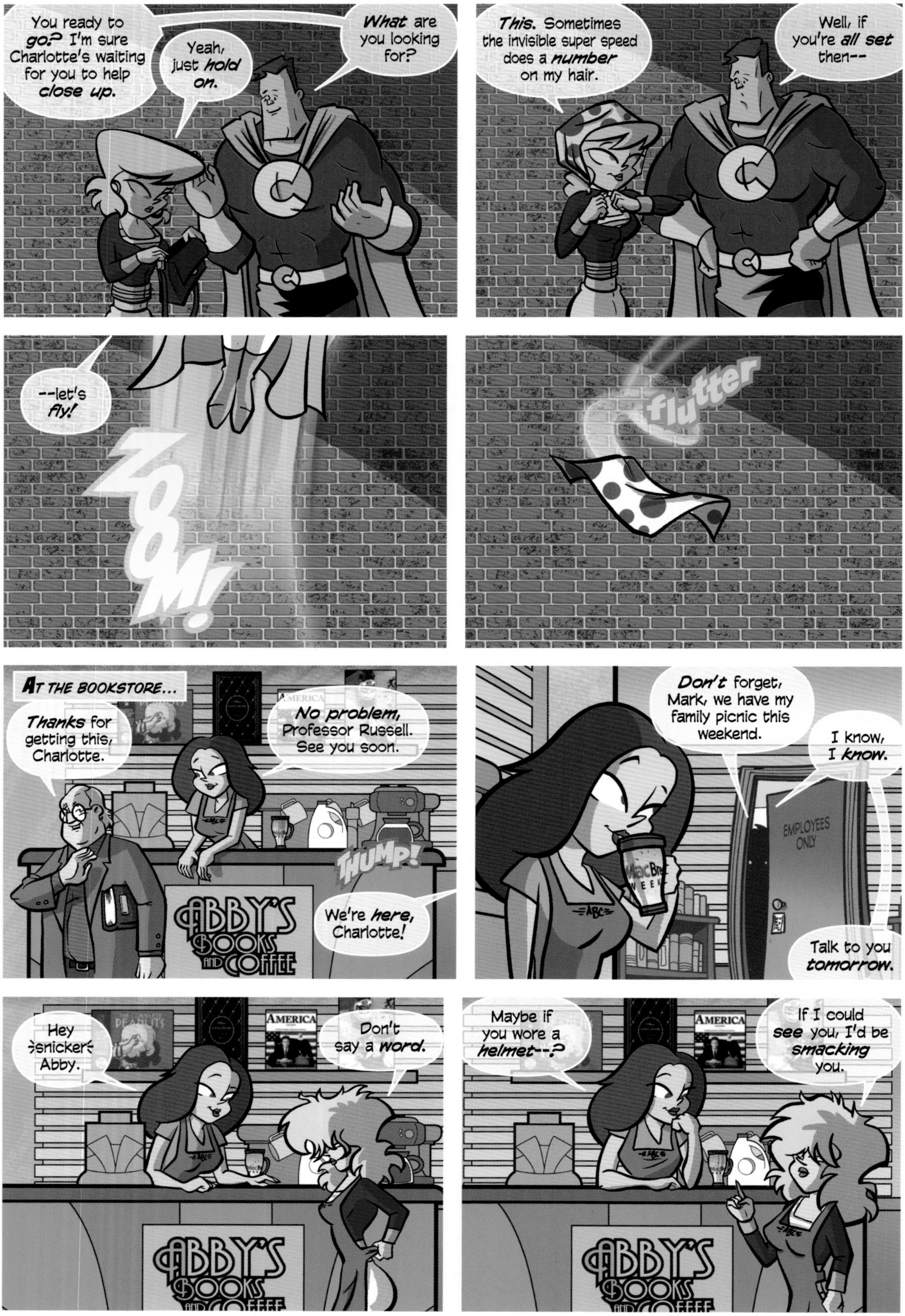
You ready to go? I'm sure Charlotte's waiting for you to help close up.
Yeah, just hold on.
What are you looking for?
This. Sometimes the invisible super speed does a number on my hair.
Well, if you're all set then--
--let's fly!
ZOOM!
flutter
AT THE BOOKSTORE...
Thanks for getting this, Charlotte.
No problem, Professor Russell. See you soon.
THUMP!
We're here, Charlotte!
ABBY'S BOOKS AND COFFEE
Don't forget, Mark, we have my family picnic this weekend.
I know, I know.
EMPLOYEES ONLY
Talk to you tomorrow.
Hey ≯snicker≮ Abby.
Don't say a word.
Maybe if you wore a helmet--?
If I could see you, I'd be smacking you.

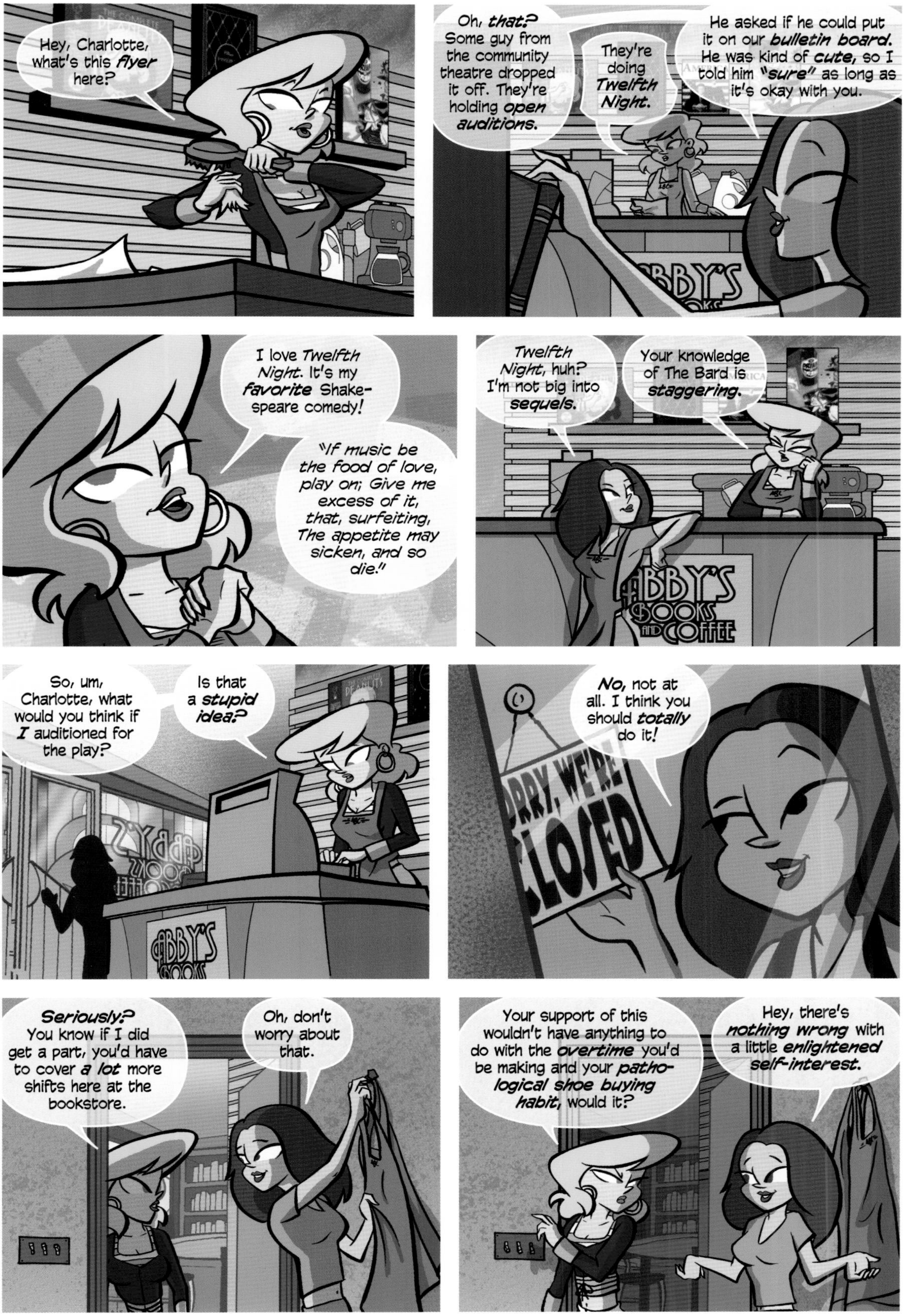

Hey, Charlotte, what's this *flyer* here?
Oh, *that?* Some guy from the community theatre dropped it off. They're holding *open auditions.*
They're doing *Twelfth Night.*
He asked if he could put it on our *bulletin board.* He was kind of *cute,* so I told him *"sure"* as long as it's okay with you.
I love *Twelfth Night*. It's my *favorite* Shake-speare comedy!
"If music be the food of love, play on; Give me excess of it, that, surfeiting, The appetite may sicken, and so die."
Twelfth Night, huh? I'm not big into *sequels.*
Your knowledge of The Bard is *staggering.*
ABBY'S BOOKS AND COFFEE
So, um, Charlotte, what would you think if *I* auditioned for the play?
Is that a *stupid idea?*
No, not at all. I think you should *totally* do it!
Seriously? You know if I did get a part, you'd have to cover *a lot* more shifts here at the bookstore.
Oh, don't worry about that.
Your support of this wouldn't have anything to do with the *overtime* you'd be making and your *patho-logical shoe buying habit,* would it?
Hey, there's *nothing wrong* with a little *enlightened self-interest.*

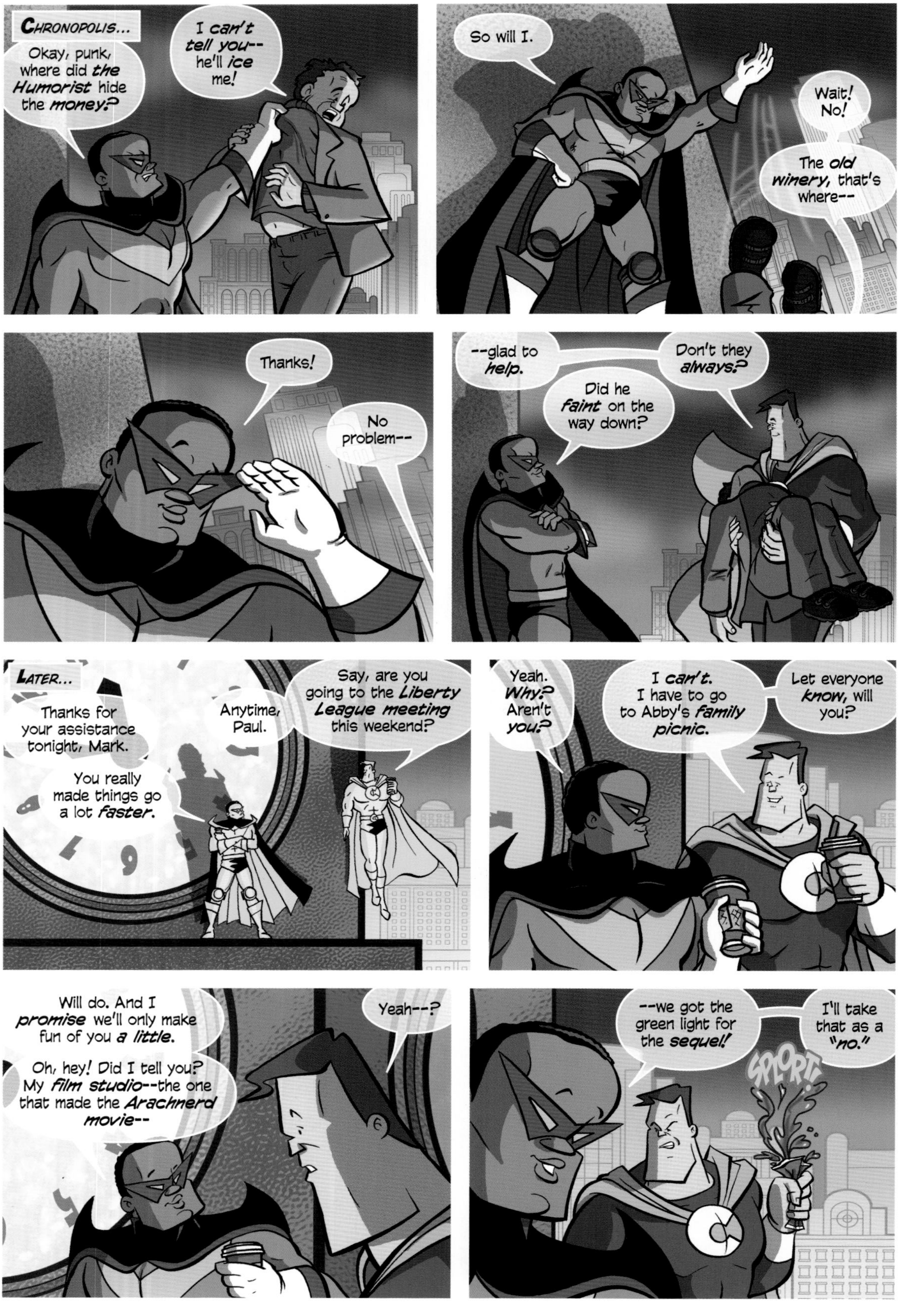
CHRONOPOLIS...
Okay, punk, where did *the Humorist* hide the *money?*
I *can't tell you--* he'll *ice* me!
So will I.
Wait! No!
The *old winery,* that's where--
Thanks!
No problem--
--glad to *help.*
Did he *faint* on the way down?
Don't they *always?*
LATER...
Thanks for your assistance tonight, Mark.
You really made things go a lot *faster.*
Anytime, Paul.
Say, are you going to the *Liberty League meeting* this weekend?
Yeah. *Why?* Aren't *you?*
I *can't.* I have to go to Abby's *family picnic.*
Let everyone *know,* will you?
Will do. And I *promise* we'll only make fun of you *a little.*
Oh, hey! Did I tell you? My *film studio*--the one that made the *Arachnerd movie*--
Yeah--?
--we got the green light for the *sequel!*
I'll take that as a *"no."*
SPLORT!

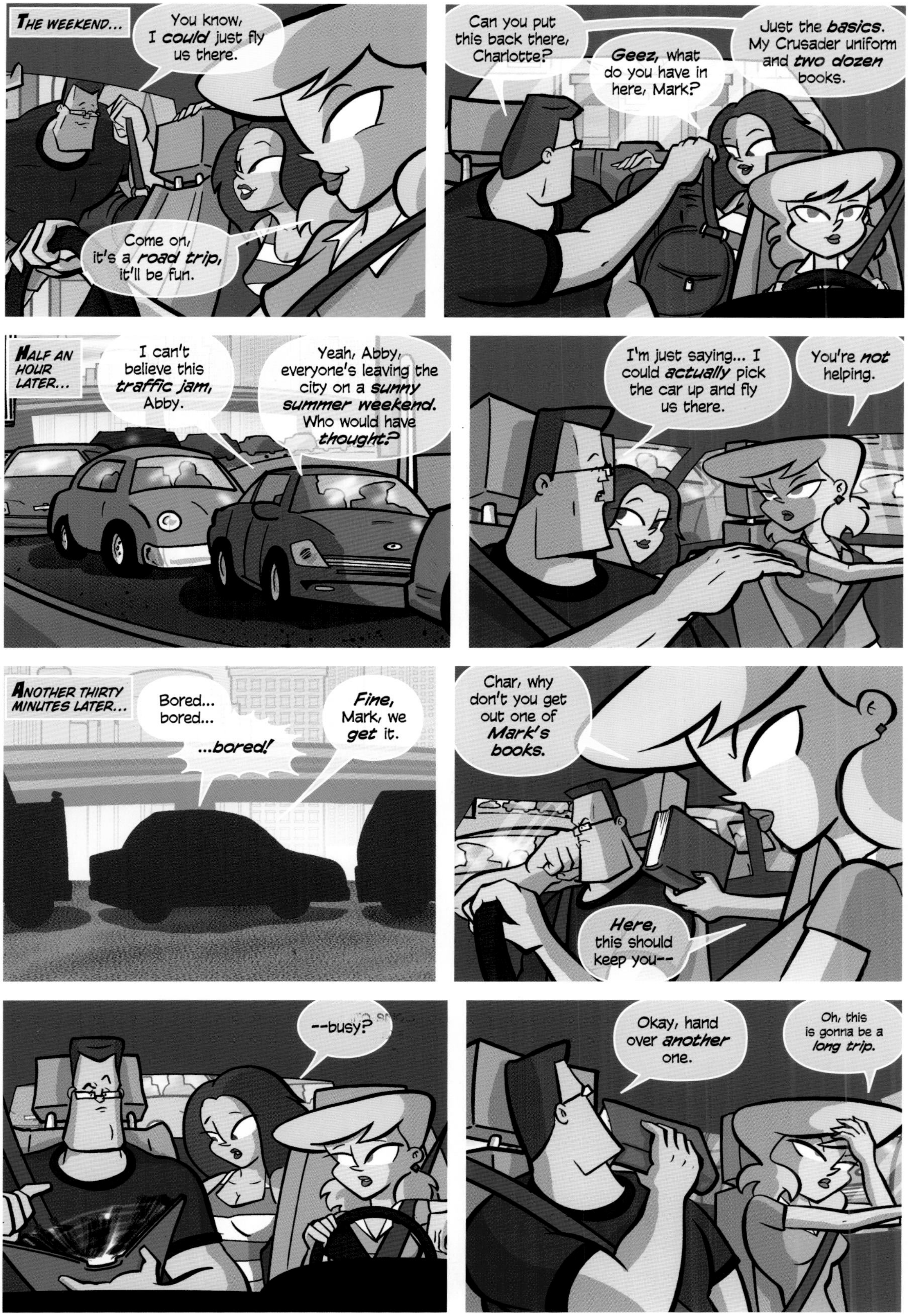
THE WEEKEND...
You know, I *could* just fly us there.
Come on, it's a *road trip*, it'll be fun.
Can you put this back there, Charlotte?
Geez, what do you have in here, Mark?
Just the *basics.* My Crusader uniform and *two dozen* books.
HALF AN HOUR LATER...
I can't believe this *traffic jam,* Abby.
Yeah, Abby, everyone's leaving the city on a *sunny summer weekend.* Who would have *thought?*
I'm just saying... I could *actually* pick the car up and fly us there.
You're *not* helping.
ANOTHER THIRTY MINUTES LATER...
Bored... bored...
...*bored!*
Fine, Mark, we *get* it.
Char, why don't you get out one of *Mark's books.*
Here, this should keep you--
--busy?
Okay, hand over *another* one.
Oh, this is gonna be a *long trip.*

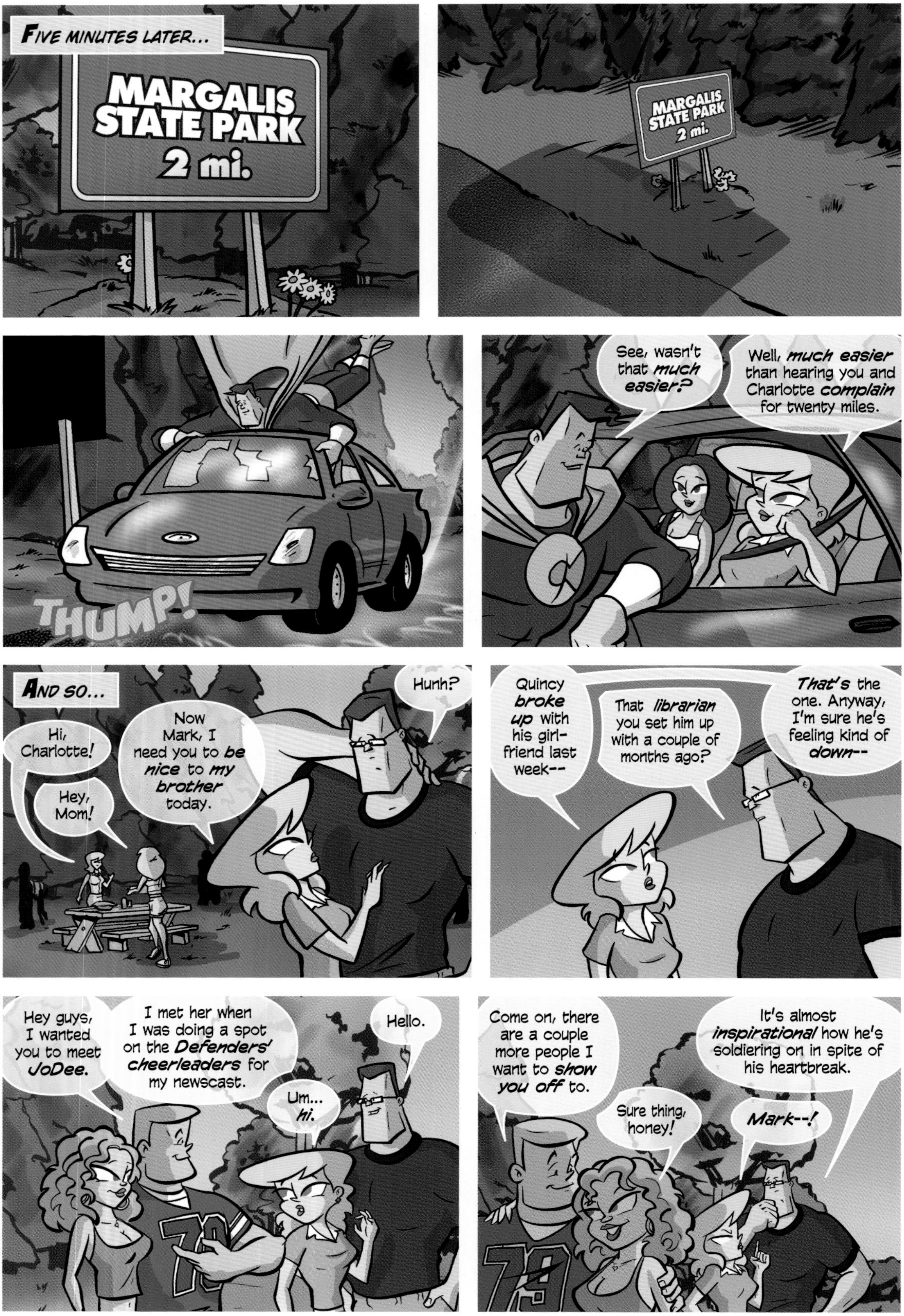

FIVE MINUTES LATER...
MARGALIS STATE PARK 2 mi.
MARGALIS STATE PARK 2 mi.
THUMP!
See, wasn't that *much easier?*
Well, *much easier* than hearing you and Charlotte *complain* for twenty miles.
AND SO...
Hi, Charlotte!
Hey, Mom!
Now Mark, I need you to *be nice* to *my brother* today.
Hunh?
Quincy *broke up* with his girl-friend last week--
That *librarian* you set him up with a couple of months ago?
That's the one. Anyway, I'm sure he's feeling kind of *down*--
Hey guys, I wanted you to meet *JoDee.*
I met her when I was doing a spot on the *Defenders' cheerleaders* for my newscast.
Um... *hi.*
Hello.
Come on, there are a couple more people I want to *show you off* to.
Sure thing, honey!
It's almost *inspirational* how he's soldiering on in spite of his heartbreak.
Mark--!

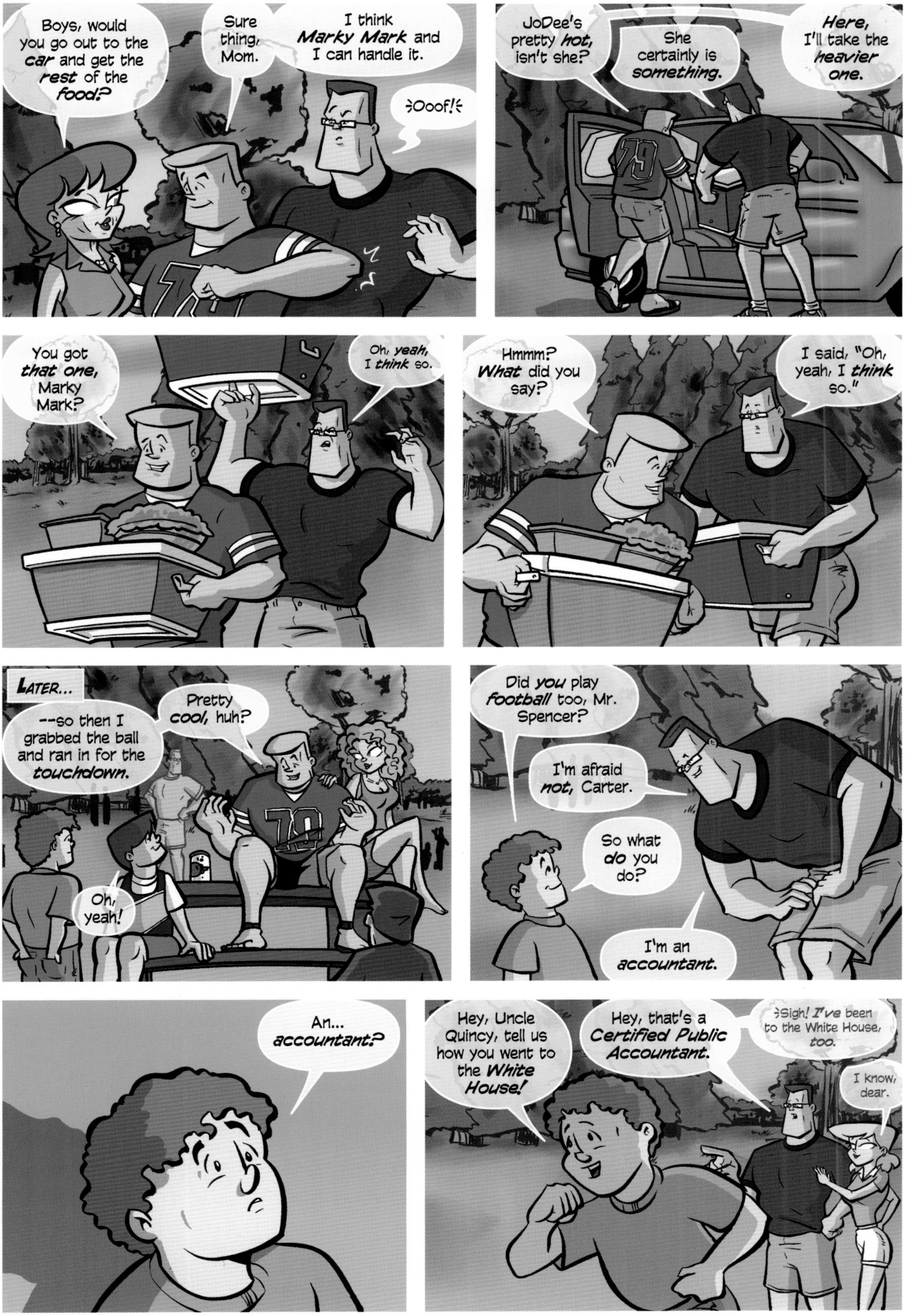
Boys, would you go out to the car and get the rest of the food?
Sure thing, Mom.
I think Marky Mark and I can handle it.
Ooof!
JoDee's pretty hot, isn't she?
She certainly is something.
Here, I'll take the heavier one.
You got that one, Marky Mark?
Oh, yeah, I think so.
Hmmm? What did you say?
I said, "Oh, yeah, I think so."
LATER...
--so then I grabbed the ball and ran in for the touchdown.
Pretty cool, huh?
Oh, yeah!
Did you play football too, Mr. Spencer?
I'm afraid not, Carter.
So what do you do?
I'm an accountant.
An... accountant?
Hey, Uncle Quincy, tell us how you went to the White House!
Hey, that's a Certified Public Accountant.
Sigh! I've been to the White House, too.
I know, dear.

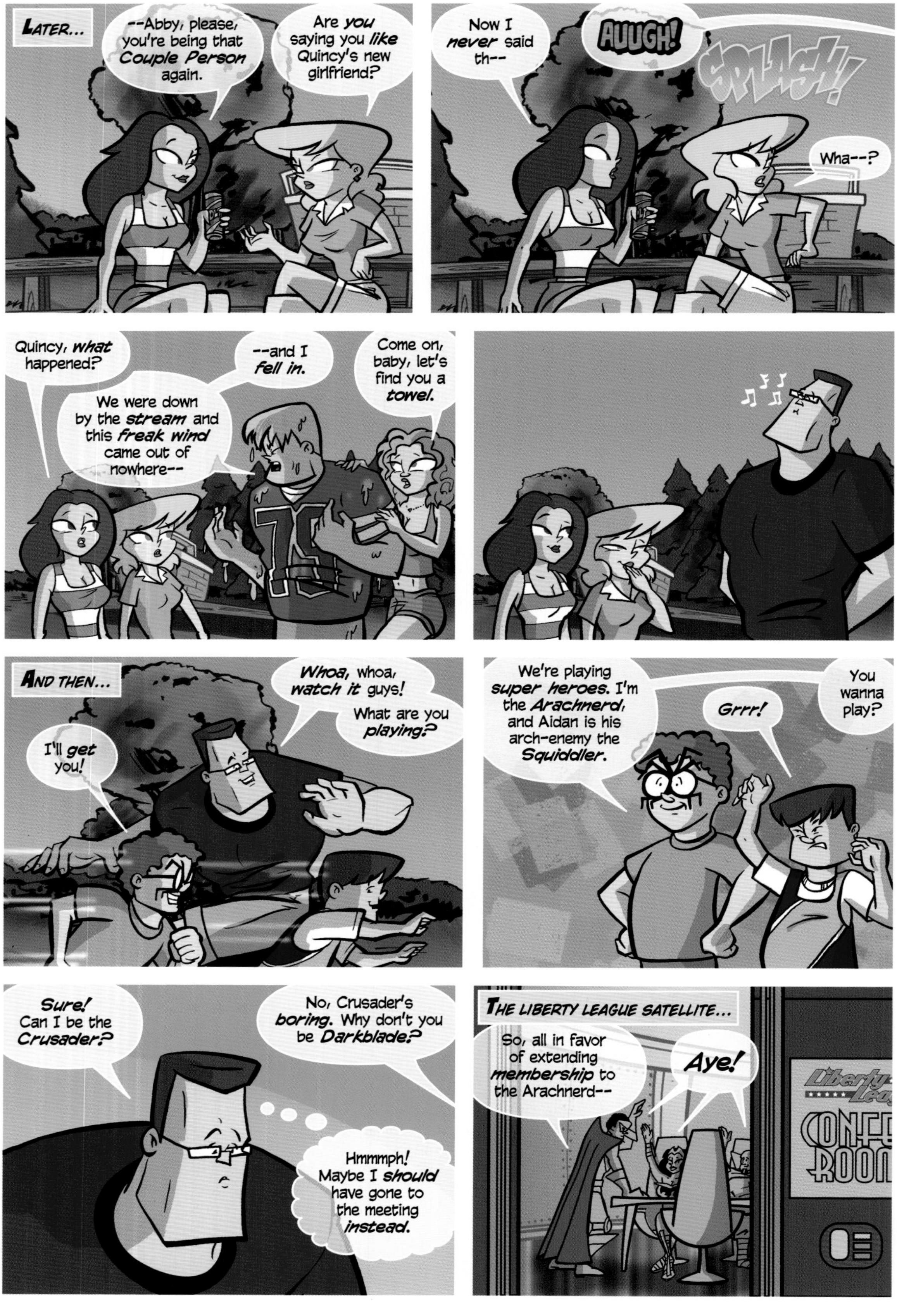
LATER...
--Abby, please, you're being that *Couple Person* again.
Are *you* saying you *like* Quincy's new girlfriend?
Now I *never* said th--
AUUGH!
SPLASH!
Wha--?
Quincy, *what* happened?
We were down by the *stream* and this *freak wind* came out of nowhere--
--and I *fell in.*
Come on, baby, let's find you a *towel.*
AND THEN...
I'll *get* you!
Whoa, whoa, *watch it* guys!
What are you *playing?*
We're playing *super heroes.* I'm the *Arachnerd,* and Aidan is his arch-enemy the *Squiddler.*
Grrr!
You wanna play?
Sure! Can I be the *Crusader?*
No, Crusader's *boring.* Why don't you be *Darkblade?*
Hmmmph! Maybe I *should* have gone to the meeting *instead.*
THE LIBERTY LEAGUE SATELLITE...
So, all in favor of extending *membership* to the Arachnerd--
Aye!

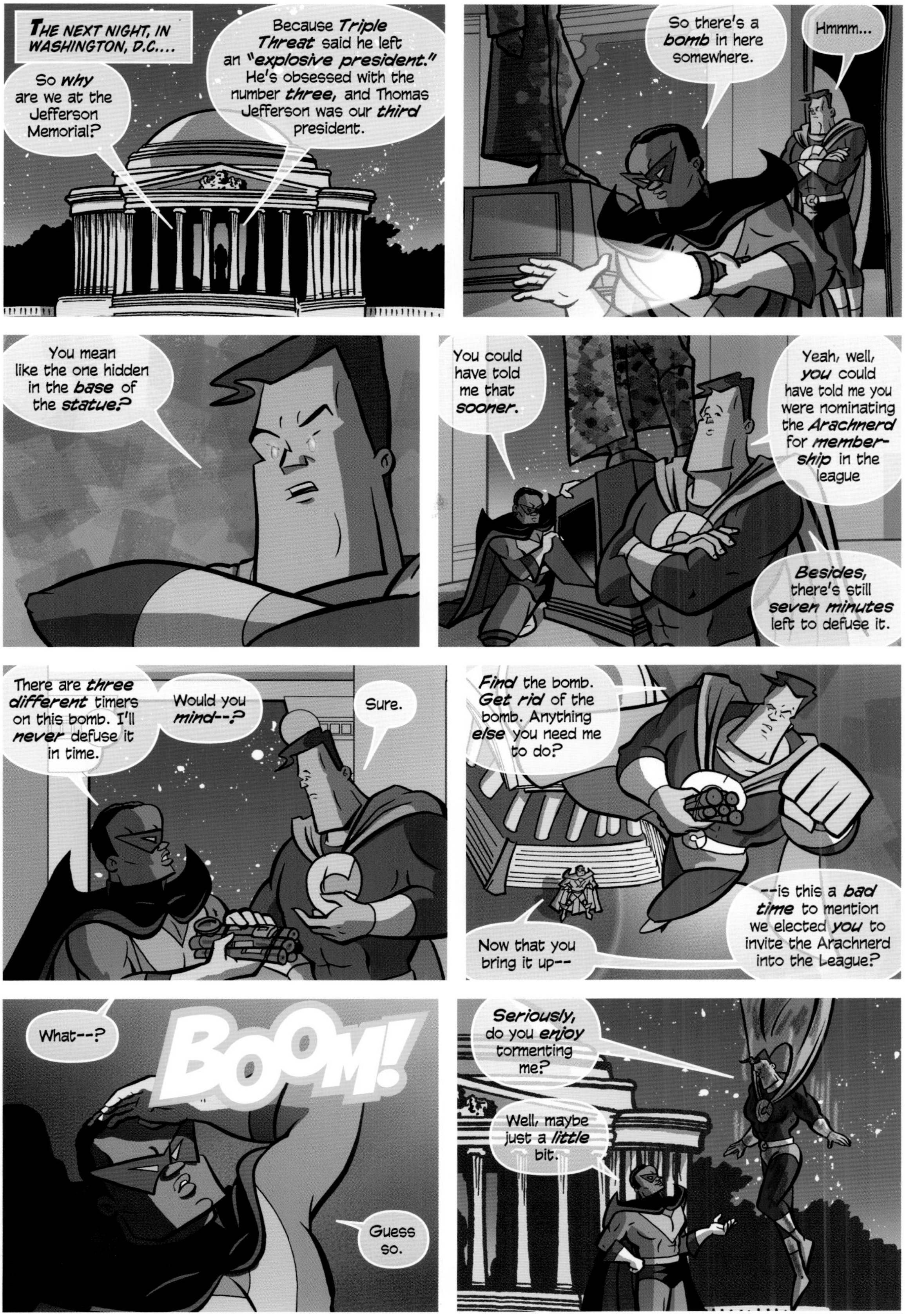
THE NEXT NIGHT, IN WASHINGTON, D.C....
So why are we at the Jefferson Memorial?
Because Triple Threat said he left an "explosive president." He's obsessed with the number three, and Thomas Jefferson was our third president.
So there's a bomb in here somewhere.
Hmmm...
You mean like the one hidden in the base of the statue?
You could have told me that sooner.
Yeah, well, you could have told me you were nominating the Arachnerd for membership in the league
Besides, there's still seven minutes left to defuse it.
There are three different timers on this bomb. I'll never defuse it in time.
Would you mind--?
Sure.
Find the bomb. Get rid of the bomb. Anything else you need me to do?
Now that you bring it up--
--is this a bad time to mention we elected you to invite the Arachnerd into the League?
What--?
BOOM!
Guess so.
Seriously, do you enjoy tormenting me?
Well, maybe just a little bit.

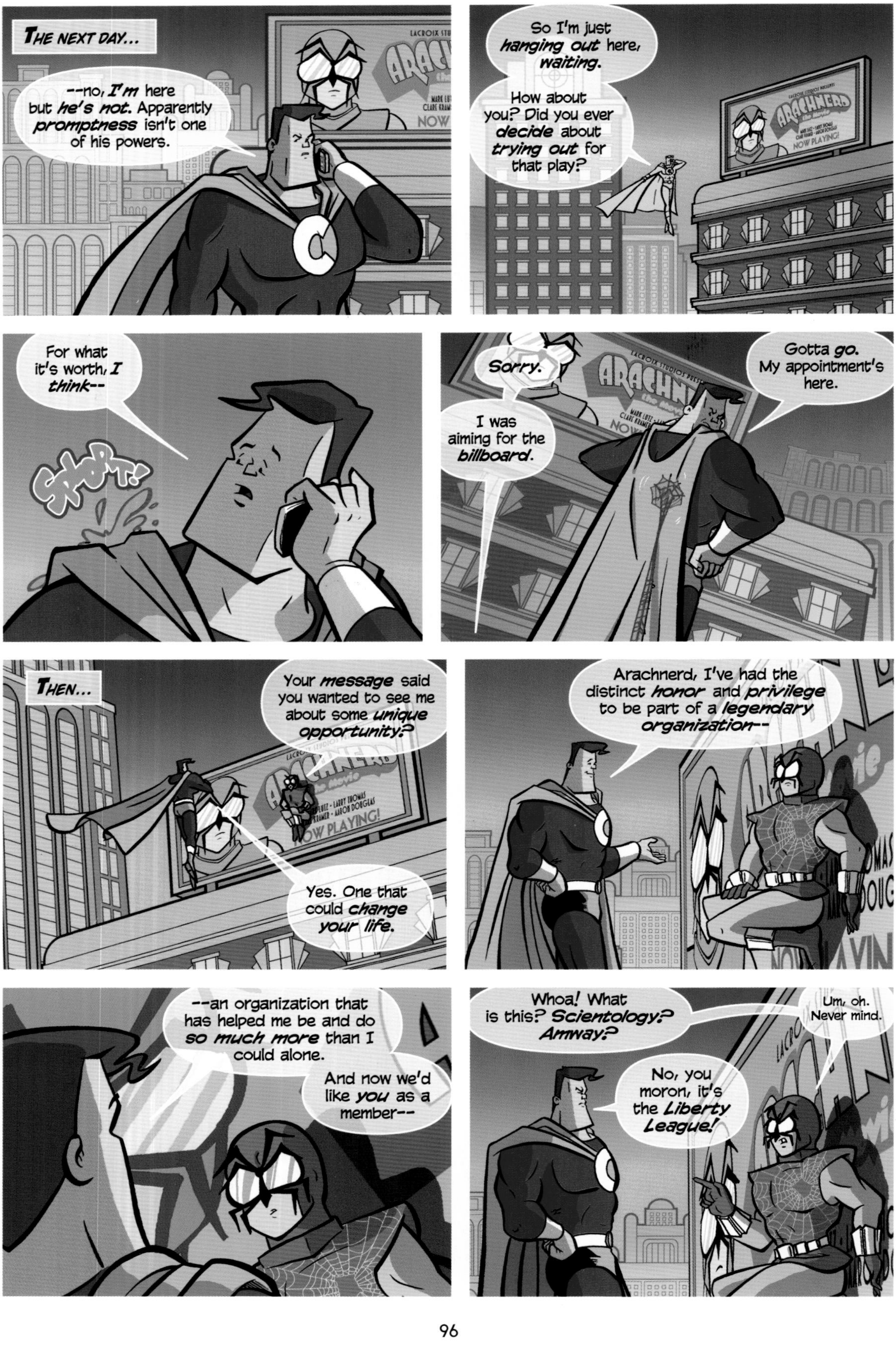
THE NEXT DAY...
--no, I'm here but he's not. Apparently promptness isn't one of his powers.
So I'm just hanging out here, waiting.
How about you? Did you ever decide about trying out for that play?
For what it's worth, I think--
SPLORT!
Sorry.
I was aiming for the billboard.
Gotta go. My appointment's here.
THEN...
Your message said you wanted to see me about some unique opportunity?
Yes. One that could change your life.
Arachnerd, I've had the distinct honor and privilege to be part of a legendary organization--
--an organization that has helped me be and do so much more than I could alone.
And now we'd like you as a member--
Whoa! What is this? Scientology? Amway?
No, you moron, it's the Liberty League!
Um, oh. Never mind.

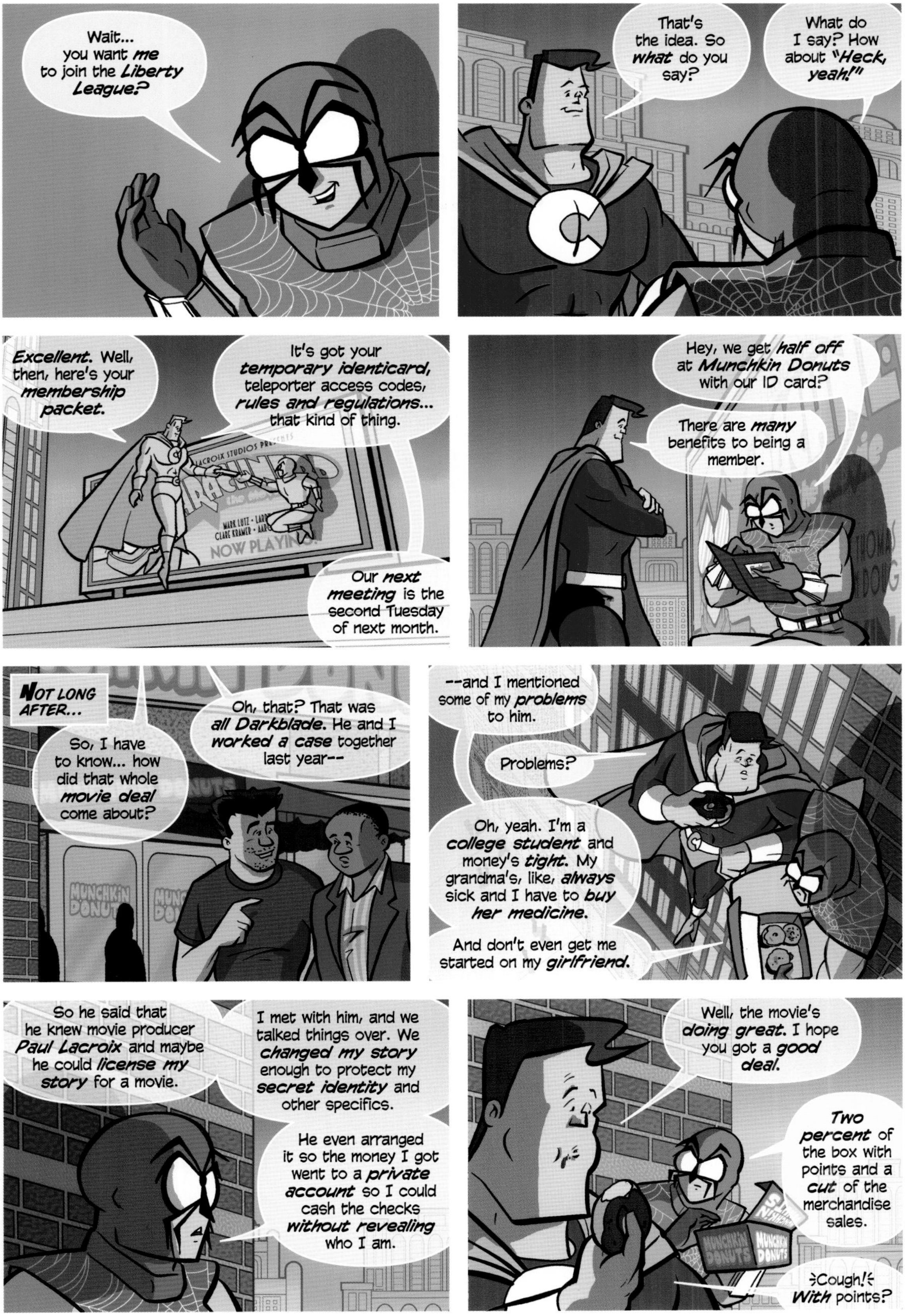
Wait... you want *me* to join the *Liberty League?*
That's the idea. So *what* do you say?
What do I say? How about *"Heck, yeah!"*
Excellent. Well, then, here's your *membership packet.*
It's got your *temporary identicard,* teleporter access codes, *rules and regulations...* that kind of thing.
LACROIX STUDIOS PRESENTS
Our *next meeting* is the second Tuesday of next month.
Hey, we get *half off* at *Munchkin Donuts* with our ID card?
There are *many* benefits to being a member.
NOT LONG AFTER...
So, I have to know... how did that whole *movie deal* come about?
Oh, that? That was *all Darkblade.* He and I *worked a case* together last year--
MUNCHKIN DONUTS
--and I mentioned some of my *problems* to him.
Problems?
Oh, yeah. I'm a *college student* and money's *tight.* My grandma's, like, *always* sick and I have to *buy her medicine.*
And don't even get me started on my *girlfriend.*
So he said that he knew movie producer *Paul Lacroix* and maybe he could *license my story* for a movie.
I met with him, and we talked things over. We *changed my story* enough to protect my *secret identity* and other specifics.
He even arranged it so the money I got went to a *private account* so I could cash the checks *without revealing* who I am.
Well, the movie's *doing great.* I hope you got a *good deal.*
Two percent of the box with points and a *cut* of the merchandise sales.
MUNCHKIN DONUTS
Cough! *With* points?

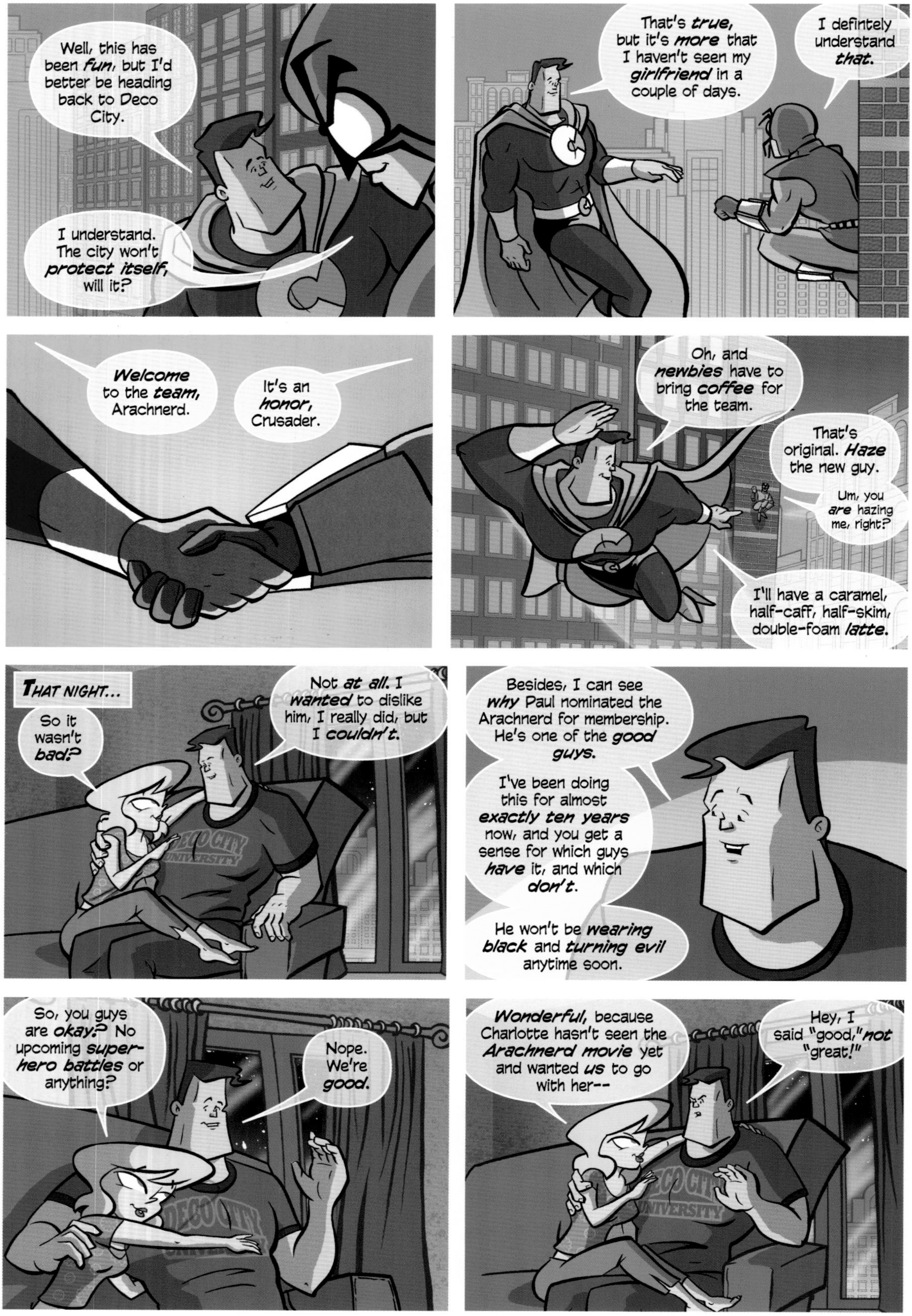

Well, this has been fun, but I'd better be heading back to Deco City.
I understand. The city won't protect itself, will it?
That's true, but it's more that I haven't seen my girlfriend in a couple of days.
I defintely understand that.
Welcome to the team, Arachnerd.
It's an honor, Crusader.
Oh, and newbies have to bring coffee for the team.
That's original. Haze the new guy.
Um, you are hazing me, right?
I'll have a caramel, half-caff, half-skim, double-foam latte.
THAT NIGHT...
So it wasn't bad?
Not at all. I wanted to dislike him, I really did, but I couldn't.
Besides, I can see why Paul nominated the Arachnerd for membership. He's one of the good guys.
I've been doing this for almost exactly ten years now, and you get a sense for which guys have it, and which don't.
He won't be wearing black and turning evil anytime soon.
So, you guys are okay? No upcoming super-hero battles or anything?
Nope. We're good.
Wonderful, because Charlotte hasn't seen the Arachnerd movie yet and wanted us to go with her--
Hey, I said "good," not "great!"

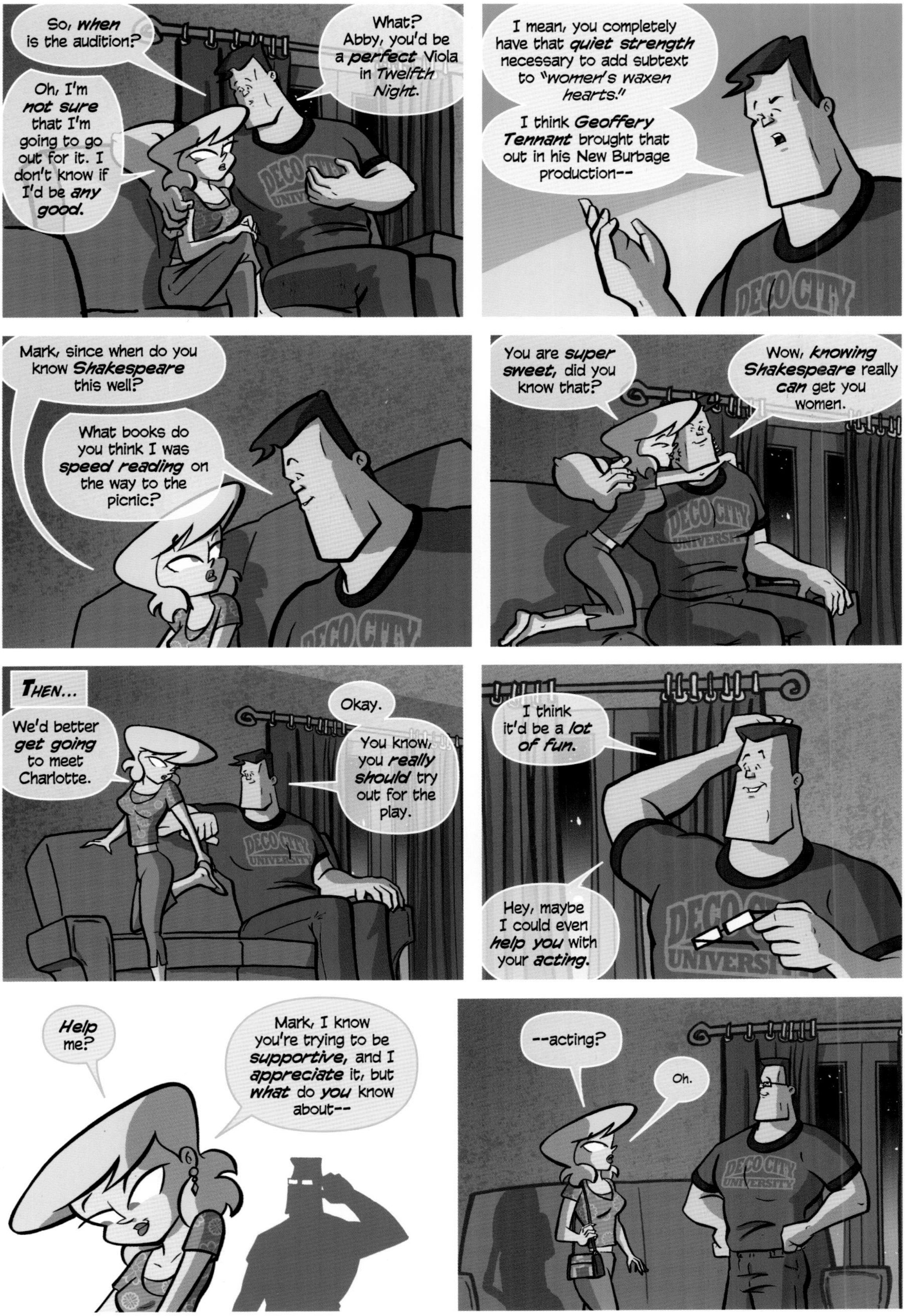
So, when is the audition?
Oh, I'm not sure that I'm going to go out for it. I don't know if I'd be any good.
What? Abby, you'd be a perfect Viola in Twelfth Night.
I mean, you completely have that quiet strength necessary to add subtext to "women's waxen hearts."
I think Geoffery Tennant brought that out in his New Burbage production--
Mark, since when do you know Shakespeare this well?
What books do you think I was speed reading on the way to the picnic?
You are super sweet, did you know that?
Wow, knowing Shakespeare really can get you women.
THEN...
We'd better get going to meet Charlotte.
Okay.
You know, you really should try out for the play.
I think it'd be a lot of fun.
Hey, maybe I could even help you with your acting.
Help me?
Mark, I know you're trying to be supportive, and I appreciate it, but what do you know about--
--acting?
Oh.

THE LIBERTY LEAGUE SATELLITE...

So how is *this* going to help me prepare for the *audition*, Mark?

I figured that some experience in a *theatre environment* would help you get used to being on a *stage*.

Trust me, Abby.

So you've brought me into a satellite in *geosynchronous orbit?* Interesting.

This is our *Battle Room*. It's a *holographic simulator* that helps us train for combat.

Kind of like the *Holodeck* on *Star Trek*, except it *doesn't break down* near as much.

KLIK!

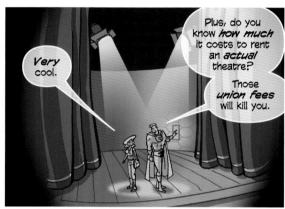

Plus, do you know *how much* it costs to rent an *actual* theatre?

Those *union fees* will kill you.

Very cool.

TWO HOURS LATER...

How easy is it for the proper false In women's waxen hearts to set their forms! Alas, our frailty is the cause, not we, For such as we are made if such we be.

Clap! Clap!

Excellent!

Really? You think so?

Absolutely! You've really found the character and you've got *iambic pentameter* down.

It's pretty impress--

TWHISHH!

What--?

Oh, *sorry*. I didn't know anyone was *using* the Battle Room.

Hi, *Mark...* Abby.

Hey, Zoe.

This is some *holographic simulation* to help me deal with *hecklers*, right?

'Fraid *not*, dear.

SHORTLY...

So, what are you two doing in the *Battle Room?*

I'm preparing to audition for a role in *Twelfth Night.*

I think the *number two holo emitter* is out of alignment. *Excuse me* a minute.

Shakespeare? I've always *loved* his work. *What role* are you hoping for?

Viola. She's--

--she's the character that gets shipwrecked and *pretends to be a man,* right?

That's the one.

Abby, *you're perfect* for that part.

Really? Um...thanks.

Hey, *wait a minute...*

LATER...

So are you *nervous* at all?

A little bit. I've never done *anything* like this before.

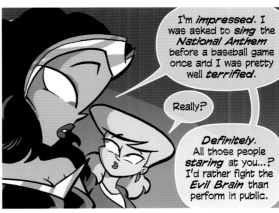

I'm *impressed.* I was asked to *sing* the *National Anthem* before a baseball game once and I was pretty well *terrified.*

Really?

Definitely. All those people *staring* at you...? I'd rather fight the *Evil Brain* than perform in public.

Oh, but I'm sure *you'll* do fine. Good luck, Abby.

Gee, thanks.

Don't worry, you'll be great.

How can you be so *sure?*

Because you were *acting* like you *didn't* want to slug her, and I *totally* bought it.

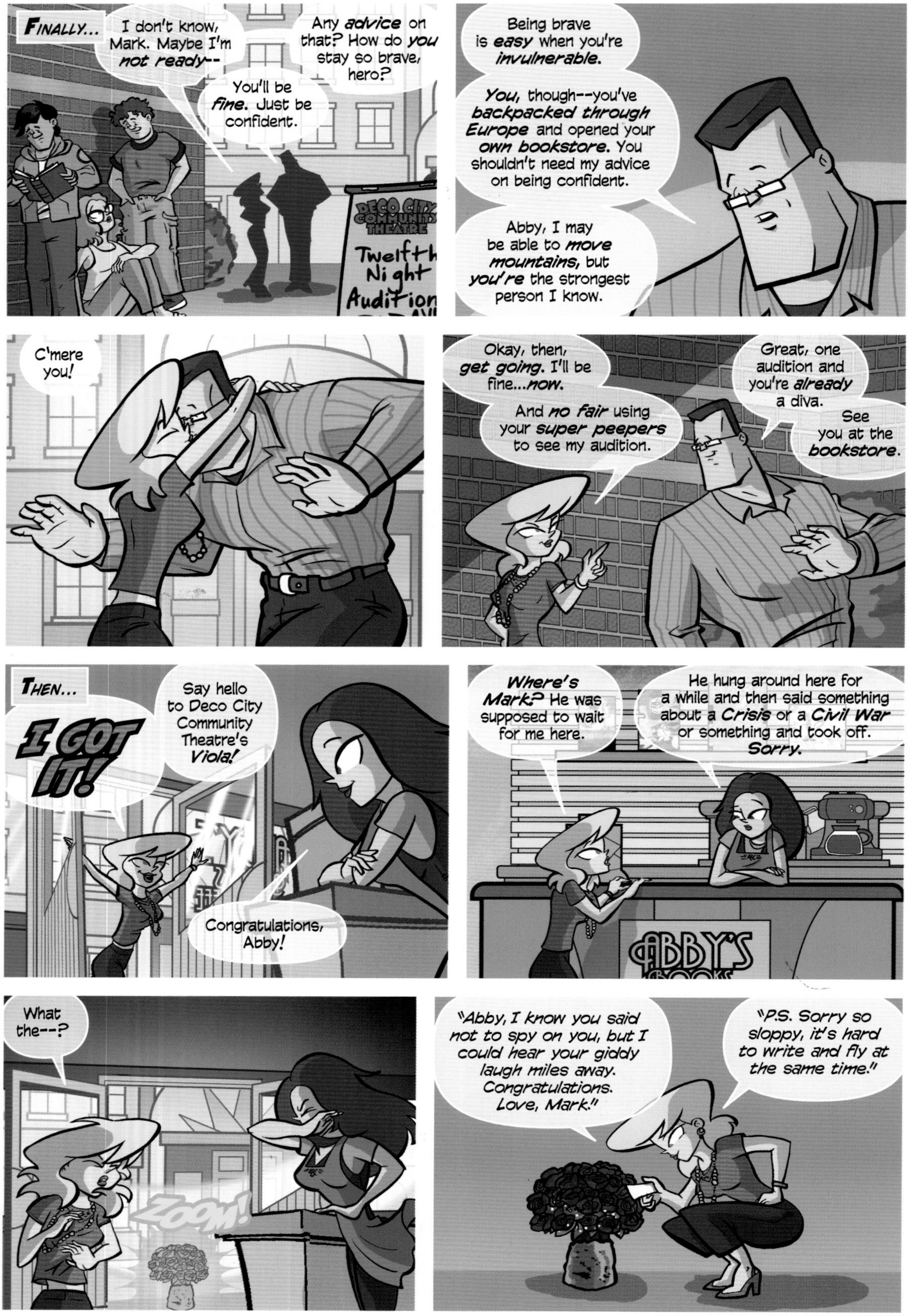
FINALLY...
I don't know, Mark. Maybe I'm *not ready*--
You'll be *fine*. Just be confident.
Any *advice* on that? How do *you* stay so brave, hero?
DECO CITY COMMUNITY THEATRE
Twelfth Night Audition
Being brave is *easy* when you're *invulnerable*.
You, though--you've *backpacked through Europe* and opened your *own bookstore*. You shouldn't need my advice on being confident.
Abby, I may be able to *move mountains*, but *you're* the strongest person I know.
C'mere you!
Okay, then, *get going*. I'll be fine...*now*.
And *no fair* using your *super peepers* to see my audition.
Great, one audition and you're *already* a diva.
See you at the *bookstore*.
THEN...
I GOT IT!
Say hello to Deco City Community Theatre's *Viola!*
Congratulations, Abby!
Where's Mark? He was supposed to wait for me here.
He hung around here for a while and then said something about a *Crisis* or a *Civil War* or something and took off. *Sorry.*
ABBY'S
What the--?
ZOOM!
"Abby, I know you said not to spy on you, but I could hear your giddy laugh miles away. Congratulations. Love, Mark."
"P.S. Sorry so sloppy, it's hard to write and fly at the same time."

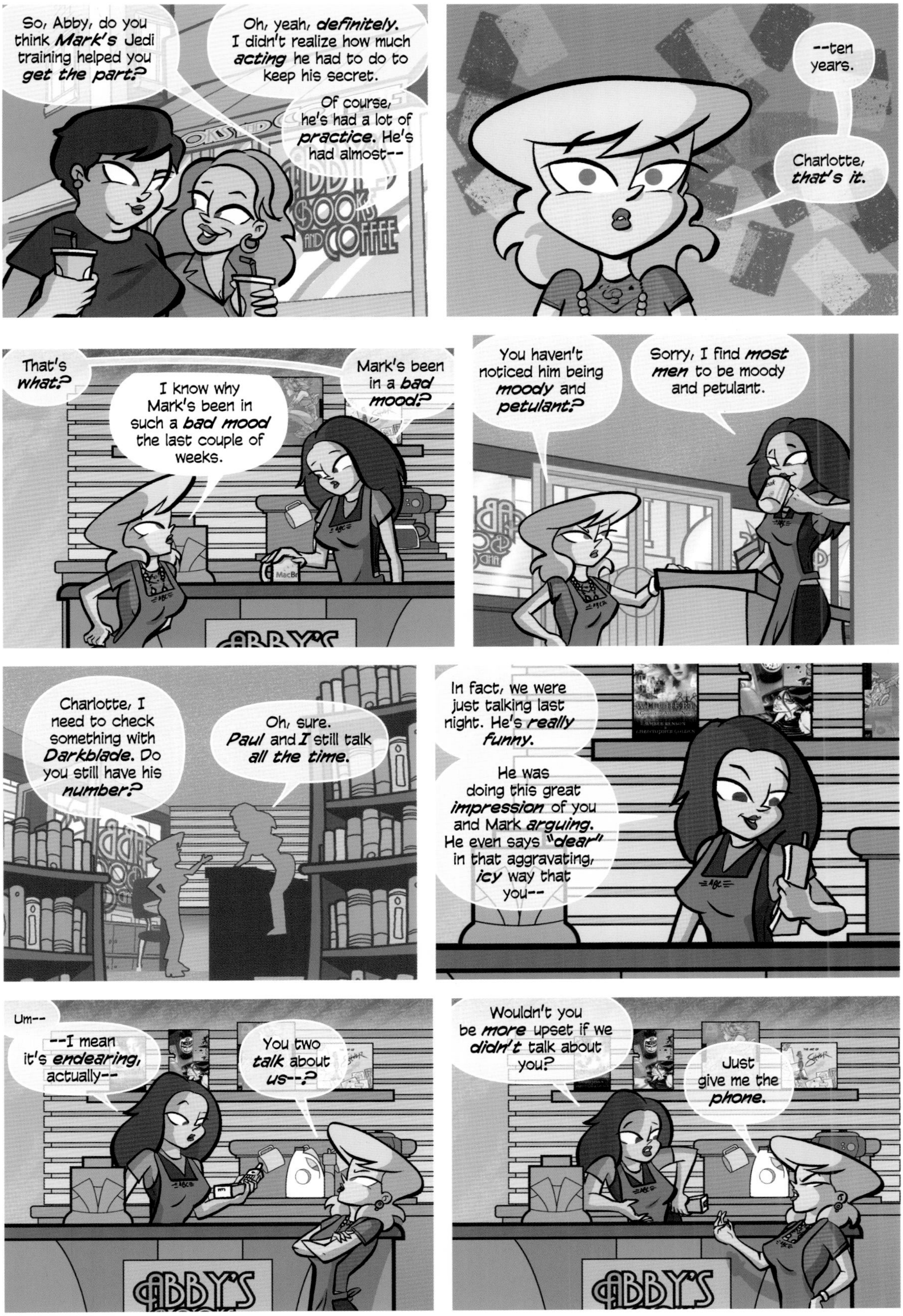
So, Abby, do you think *Mark's* Jedi training helped you *get the part?*
Oh, yeah, *definitely.* I didn't realize how much *acting* he had to do to keep his secret.
Of course, he's had a lot of *practice.* He's had almost--
--ten years.
Charlotte, *that's it.*
That's *what?*
I know why Mark's been in such a *bad mood* the last couple of weeks.
Mark's been in a *bad mood?*
You haven't noticed him being *moody* and *petulant?*
Sorry, I find *most men* to be moody and petulant.
Charlotte, I need to check something with *Darkblade.* Do you still have his *number?*
Oh, sure. *Paul* and *I* still talk *all the time.*
In fact, we were just talking last night. He's *really funny.*
He was doing this great *impression* of you and Mark *arguing.* He even says *"dear"* in that aggravating, *icy* way that you--
Um--
--I mean it's *endearing,* actually--
You two *talk* about *us--?*
Wouldn't you be *more* upset if we *didn't* talk about you?
Just give me the *phone.*

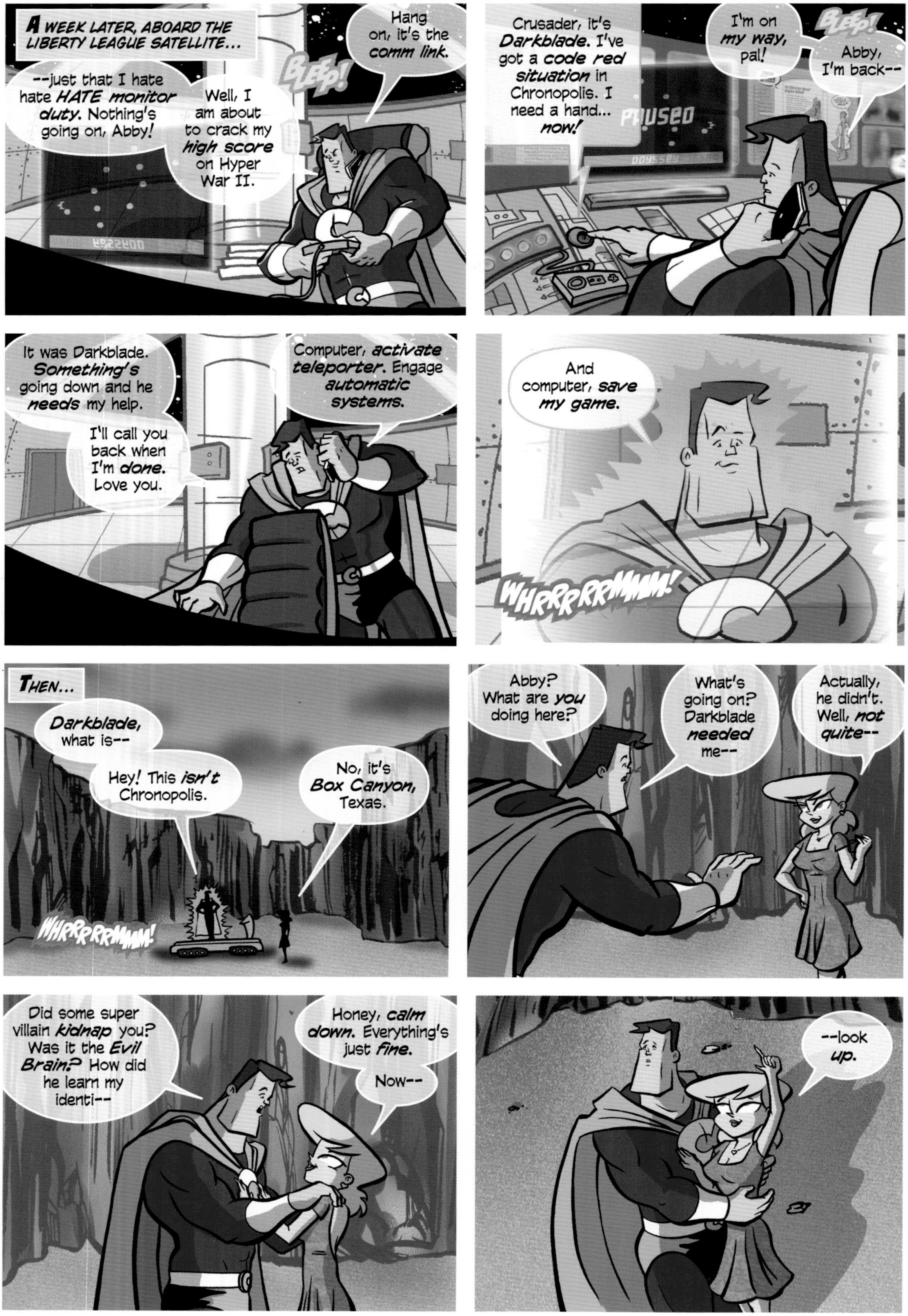

A WEEK LATER, ABOARD THE LIBERTY LEAGUE SATELLITE...
--just that I hate hate *HATE monitor duty.* Nothing's going on, Abby!
Well, I am about to crack my *high score* on Hyper War II.
BLEEP!
Hang on, it's the *comm link.*
Crusader, it's *Darkblade.* I've got a *code red situation* in Chronopolis. I need a hand... *now!*
PAUSED
I'm on *my way,* pal!
BLEEP!
Abby, I'm back--
It was Darkblade. *Something's* going down and he *needs* my help.
I'll call you back when I'm *done.* Love you.
Computer, *activate teleporter.* Engage *automatic systems.*
And computer, *save my game.*
WHRRRRRMMM!
THEN...
Darkblade, what is--
Hey! This *isn't* Chronopolis.
No, it's *Box Canyon,* Texas.
WHRRRRRMMM!
Abby? What are *you* doing here?
What's going on? Darkblade *needed* me--
Actually, he didn't. Well, *not quite--*
Did some super villain *kidnap* you? Was it the *Evil Brain?* How did he learn my identi--
Honey, *calm down.* Everything's just *fine.*
Now--
--look *up.*

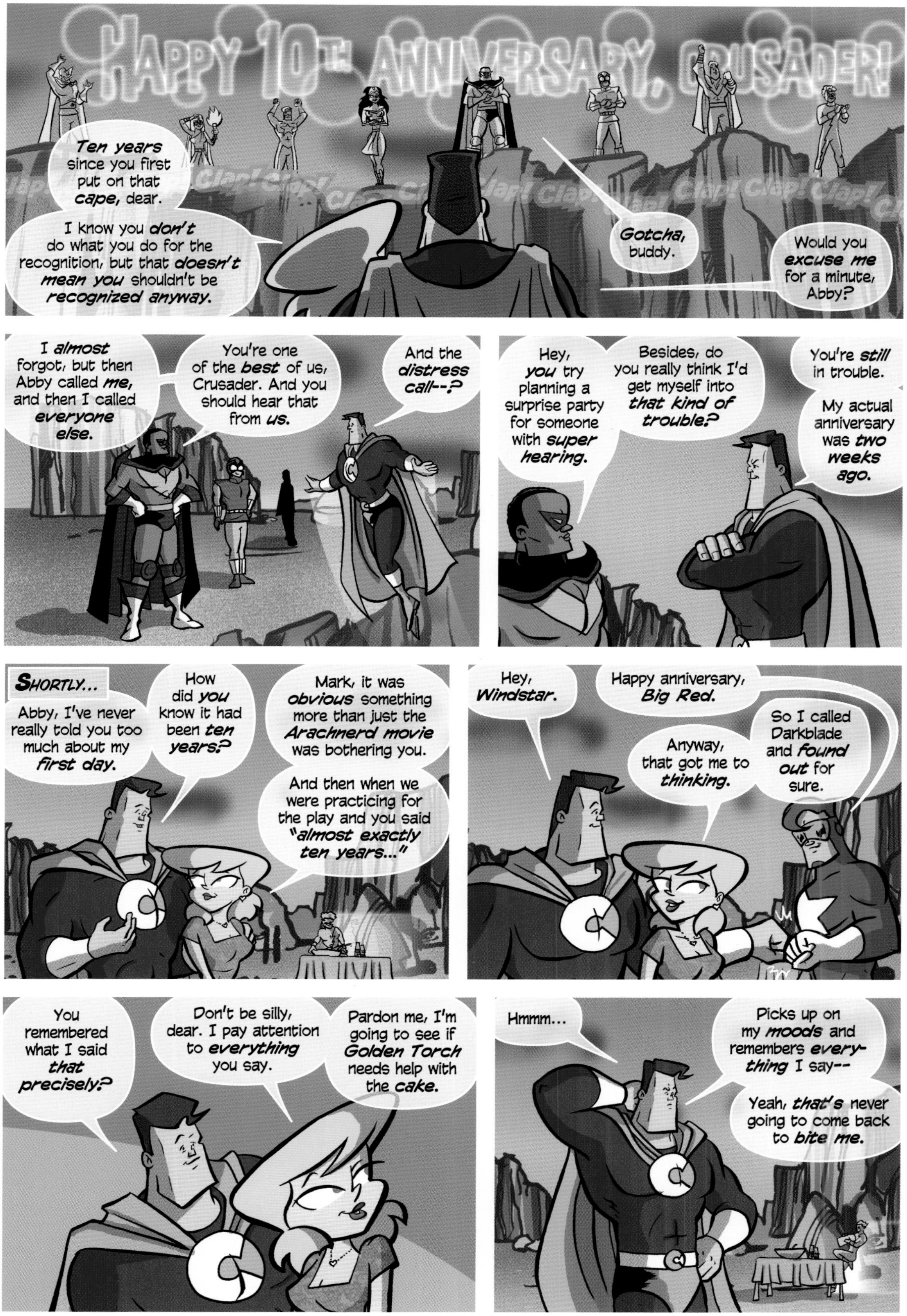
HAPPY 10TH ANNIVERSARY, CRUSADER!
Ten years since you first put on that cape, dear.
I know you don't do what you do for the recognition, but that doesn't mean you shouldn't be recognized anyway.
Clap! Clap! Clap! Clap! Clap! Clap!
Gotcha, buddy.
Would you excuse me for a minute, Abby?
I almost forgot, but then Abby called me, and then I called everyone else.
You're one of the best of us, Crusader. And you should hear that from us.
And the distress call--?
Hey, you try planning a surprise party for someone with super hearing.
Besides, do you really think I'd get myself into that kind of trouble?
You're still in trouble.
My actual anniversary was two weeks ago.
SHORTLY...
Abby, I've never really told you too much about my first day.
How did you know it had been ten years?
Mark, it was obvious something more than just the Arachnerd movie was bothering you.
And then when we were practicing for the play and you said "almost exactly ten years..."
Hey, Windstar.
Happy anniversary, Big Red.
Anyway, that got me to thinking.
So I called Darkblade and found out for sure.
You remembered what I said that precisely?
Don't be silly, dear. I pay attention to everything you say.
Pardon me, I'm going to see if Golden Torch needs help with the cake.
Hmmm...
Picks up on my moods and remembers every-thing I say--
Yeah, that's never going to come back to bite me.

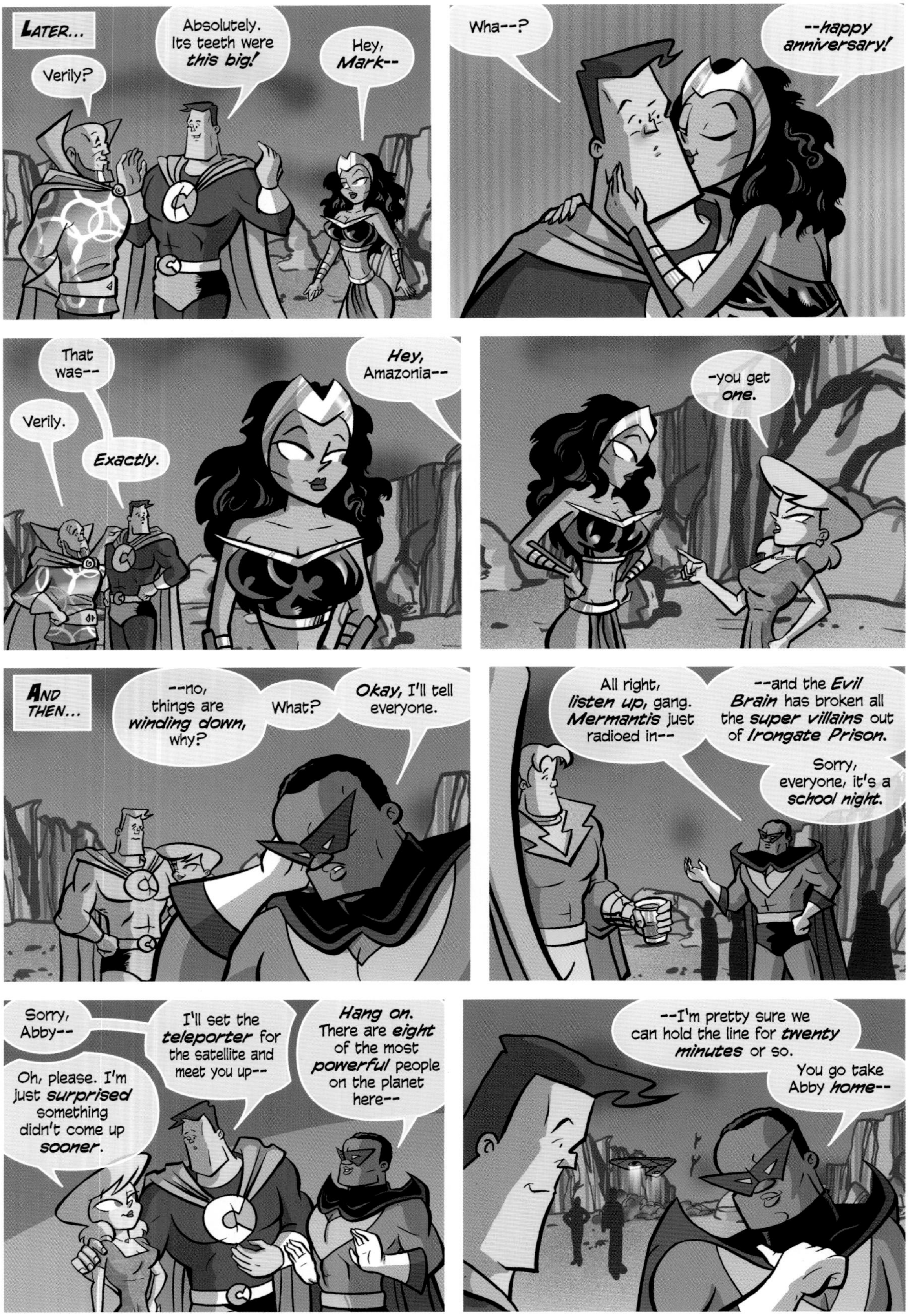
LATER...
Verily?
Absolutely. Its teeth were this big!
Hey, Mark--
Wha--?
--happy anniversary!
That was--
Verily.
Exactly.
Hey, Amazonia--
-you get one.
AND THEN...
--no, things are winding down, why?
What?
Okay, I'll tell everyone.
All right, listen up, gang. Mermantis just radioed in--
--and the Evil Brain has broken all the super villains out of Irongate Prison.
Sorry, everyone, it's a school night.
Sorry, Abby--
Oh, please. I'm just surprised something didn't come up sooner.
I'll set the teleporter for the satellite and meet you up--
Hang on. There are eight of the most powerful people on the planet here--
--I'm pretty sure we can hold the line for twenty minutes or so.
You go take Abby home--

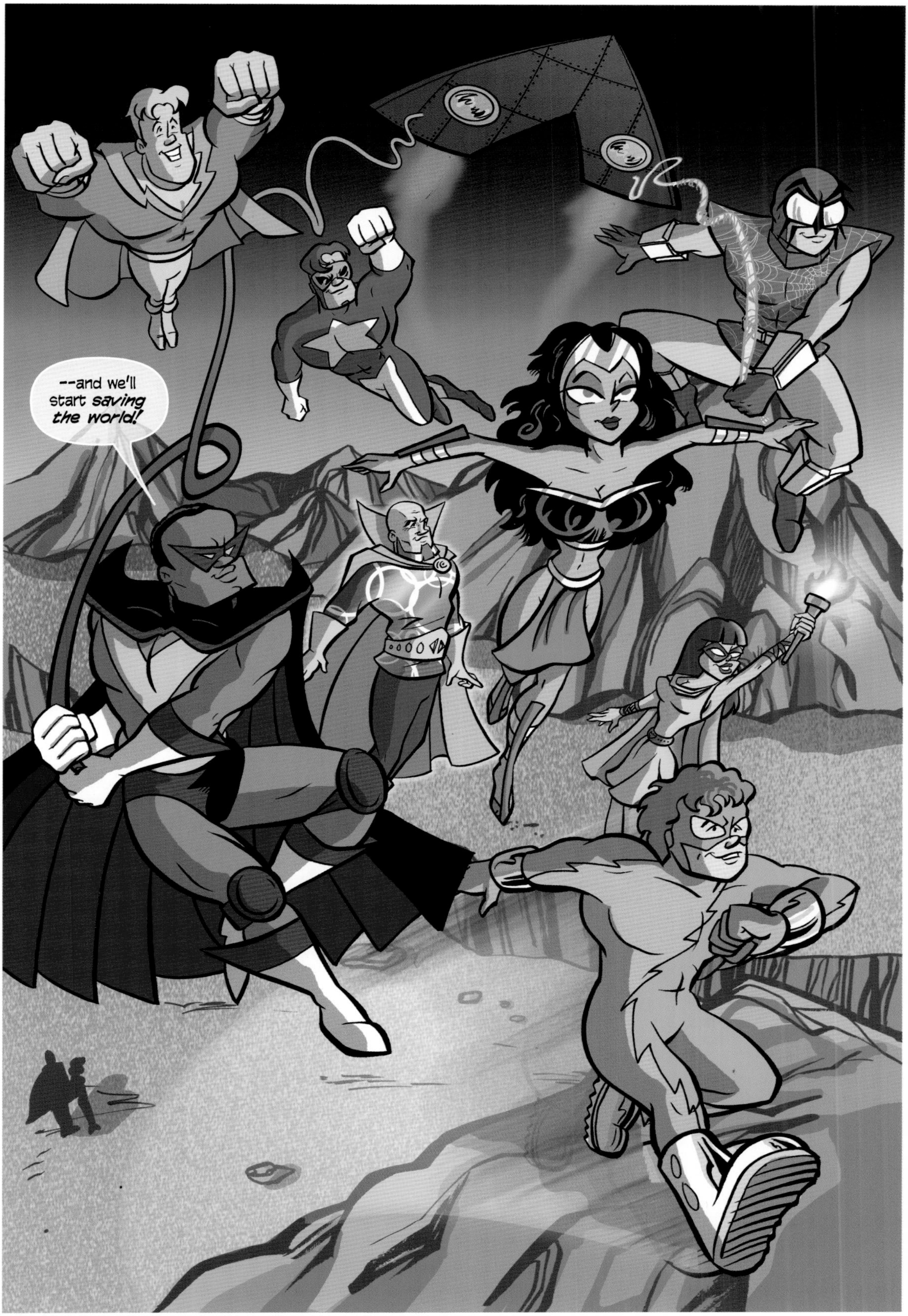
--and we'll start *saving the world!*

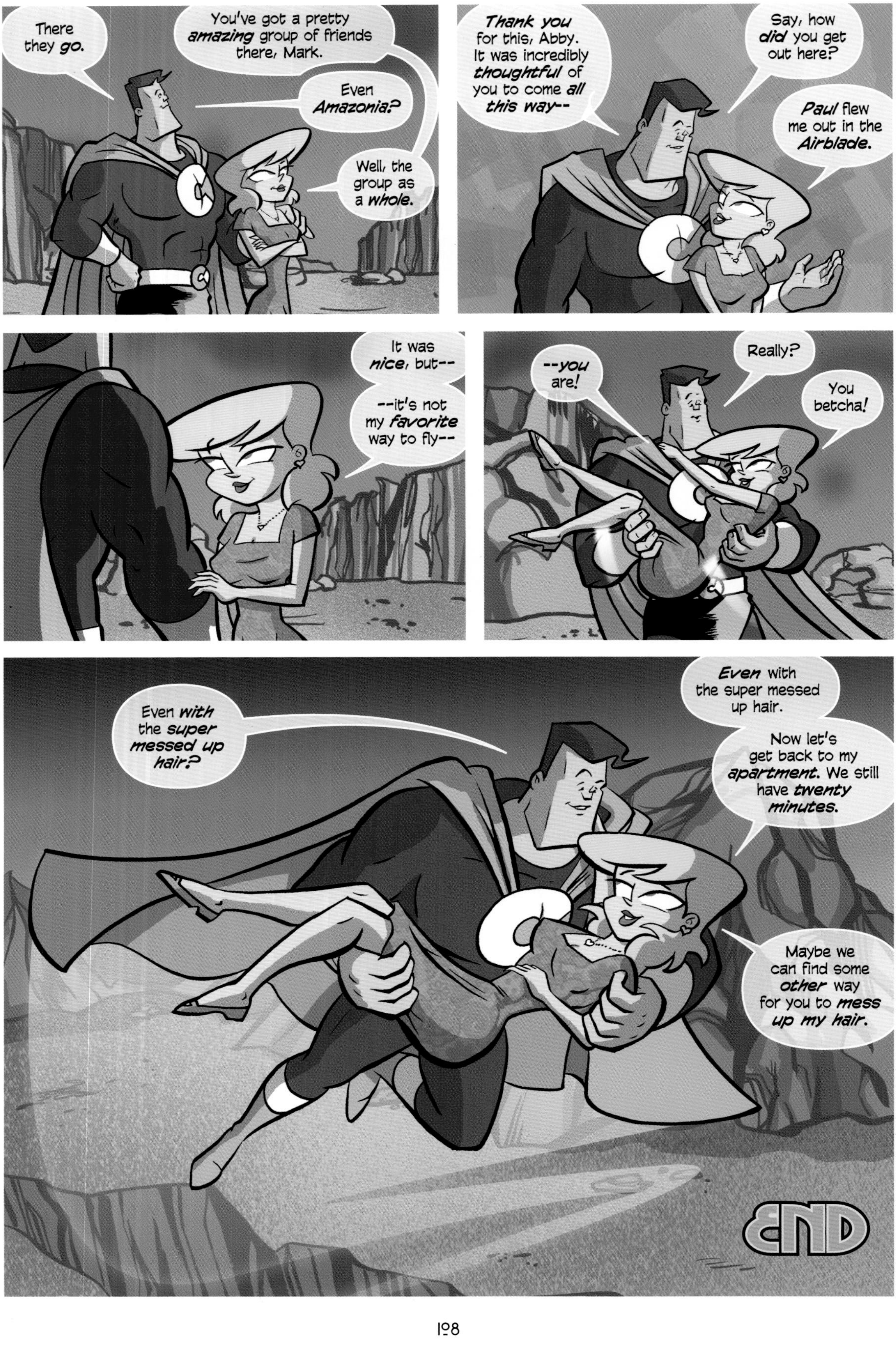
There they *go.*
You've got a pretty *amazing* group of friends there, Mark.
Even *Amazonia?*
Well, the group as a *whole.*
Thank you for this, Abby. It was incredibly *thoughtful* of you to come *all this way--*
Say, how *did* you get out here?
Paul flew me out in the *Airblade.*
It was *nice*, but--
--it's not my *favorite* way to fly--
--you are!
Really?
You betcha!
Even *with* the *super messed up hair?*
Even with the super messed up hair.
Now let's get back to my *apartment.* We still have *twenty minutes.*
Maybe we can find some *other* way for you to *mess up my hair.*
END

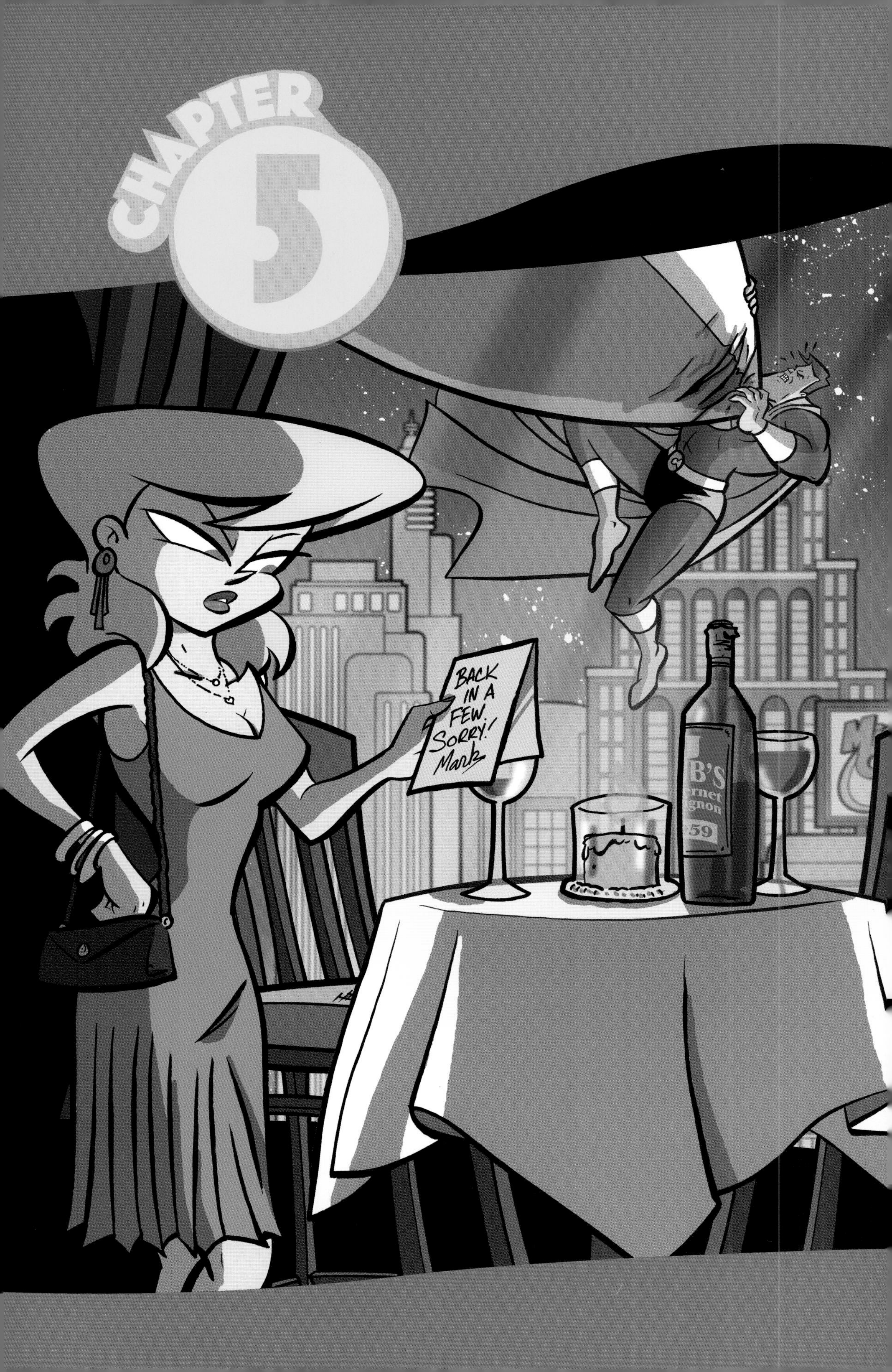
CHAPTER
5
BACK IN A FEW. SORRY!
Mark

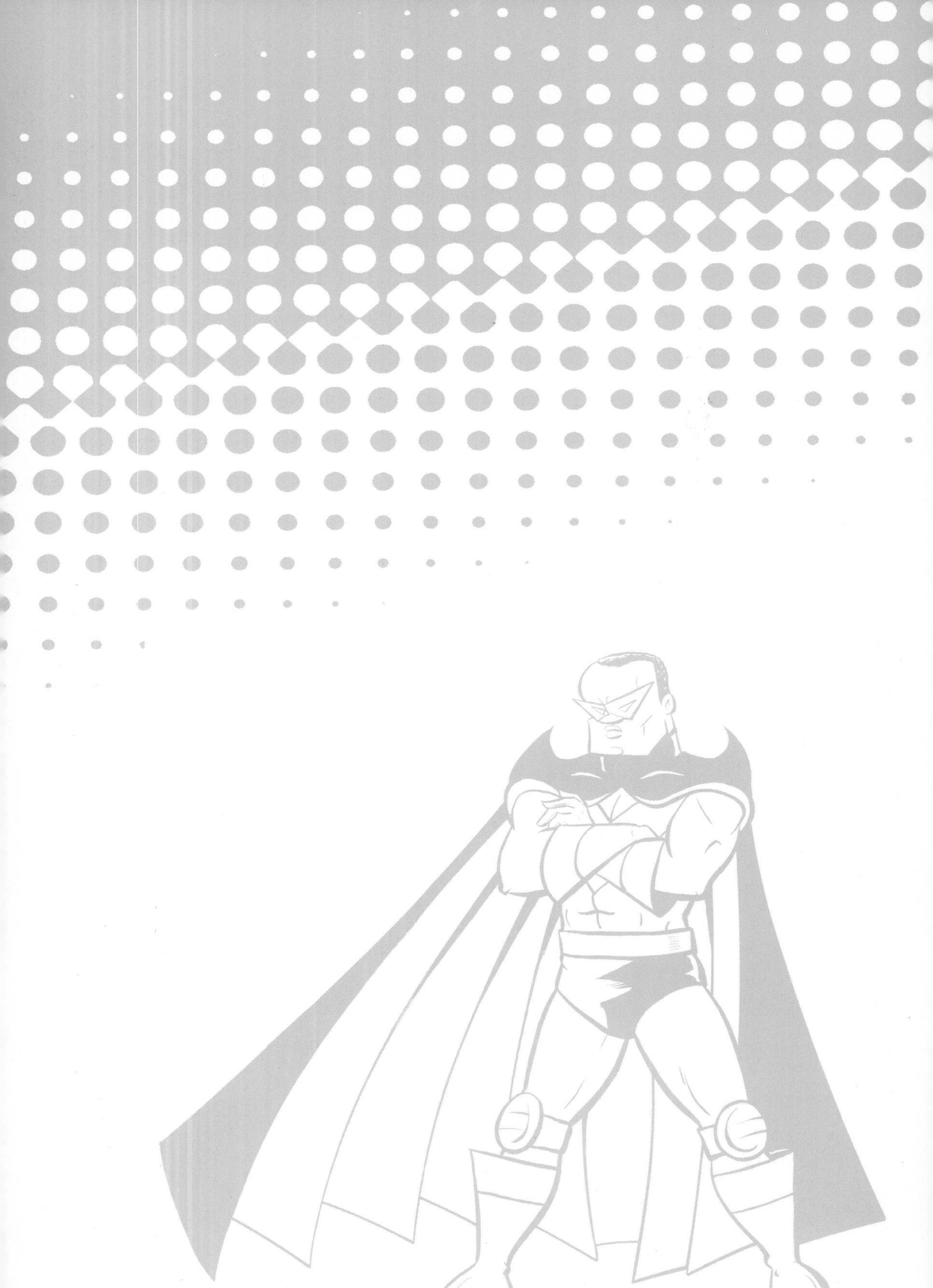

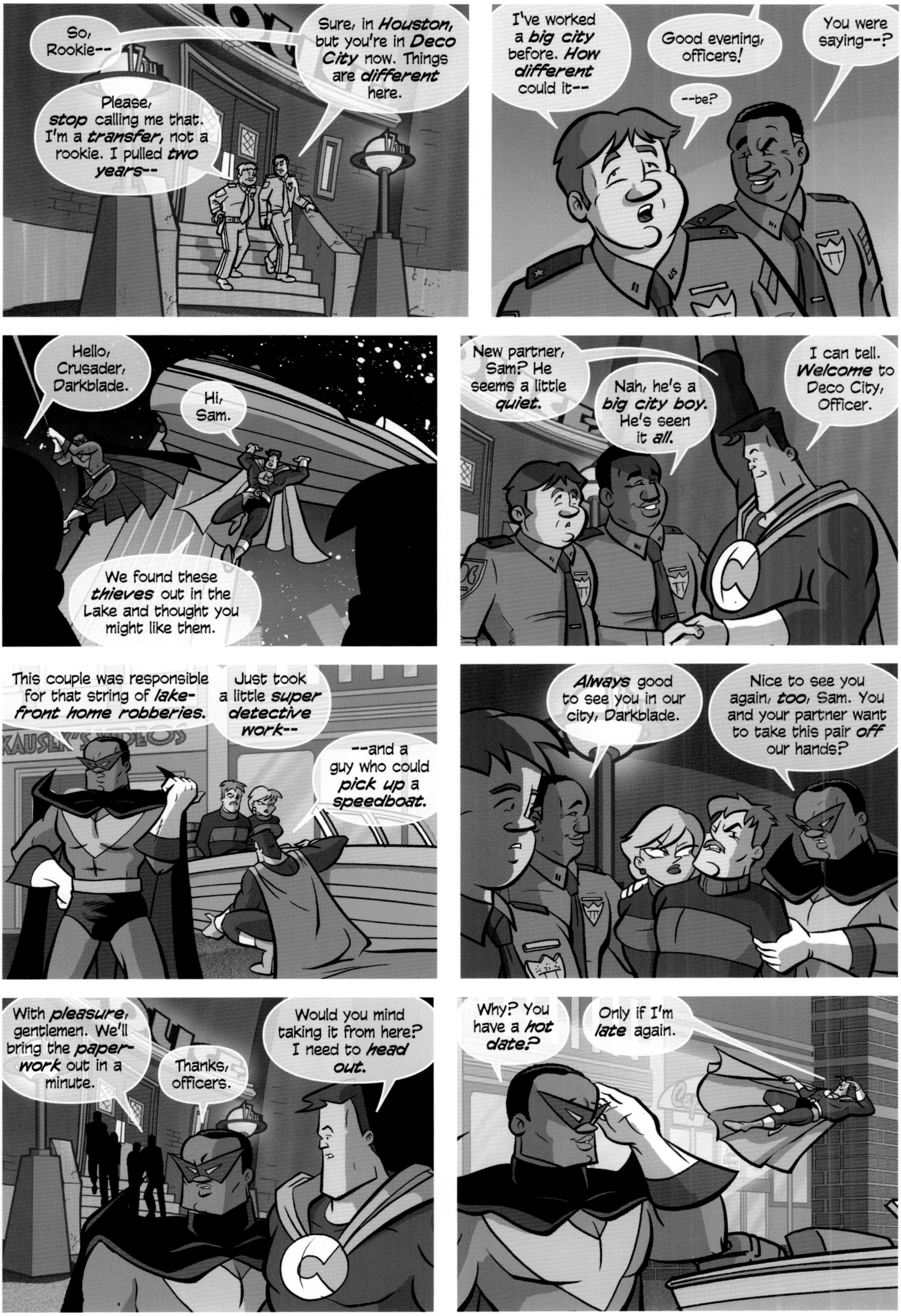

So, Rookie--
Sure, in Houston, but you're in Deco City now. Things are different here.
Please, stop calling me that. I'm a transfer, not a rookie. I pulled two years--
I've worked a big city before. How different could it--
Good evening, officers!
You were saying--?
--be?
Hello, Crusader, Darkblade.
Hi, Sam.
We found these thieves out in the Lake and thought you might like them.
New partner, Sam? He seems a little quiet.
Nah, he's a big city boy. He's seen it all.
I can tell. Welcome to Deco City, Officer.
This couple was responsible for that string of lake-front home robberies.
Just took a little super detective work--
--and a guy who could pick up a speedboat.
Always good to see you in our city, Darkblade.
Nice to see you again, too, Sam. You and your partner want to take this pair off our hands?
With pleasure, gentlemen. We'll bring the paper-work out in a minute.
Thanks, officers.
Would you mind taking it from here? I need to head out.
Why? You have a hot date?
Only if I'm late again.

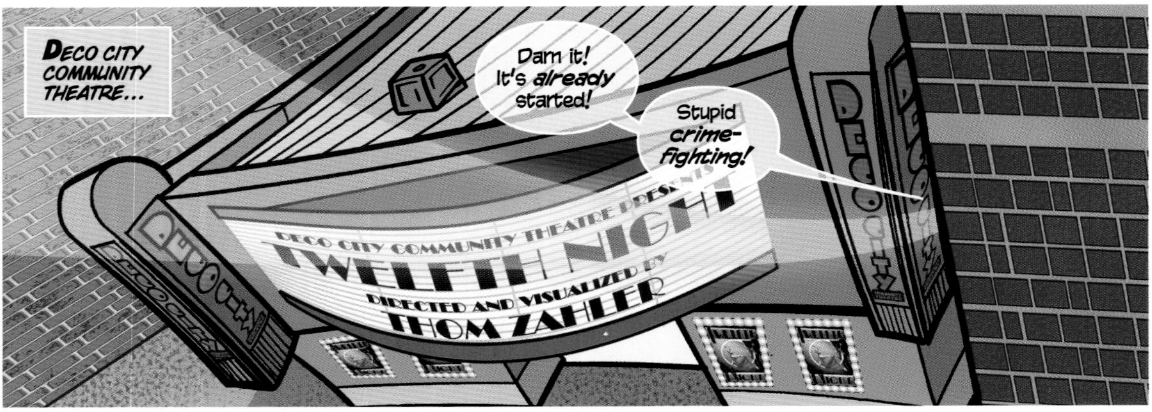
DECO CITY COMMUNITY THEATRE...
Darn it! It's already started!
Stupid crime-fighting!
DECO CITY COMMUNITY THEATRE PRESENTS
TWELFTH NIGHT
DIRECTED AND VISUALIZED BY
THOM ZAHLER

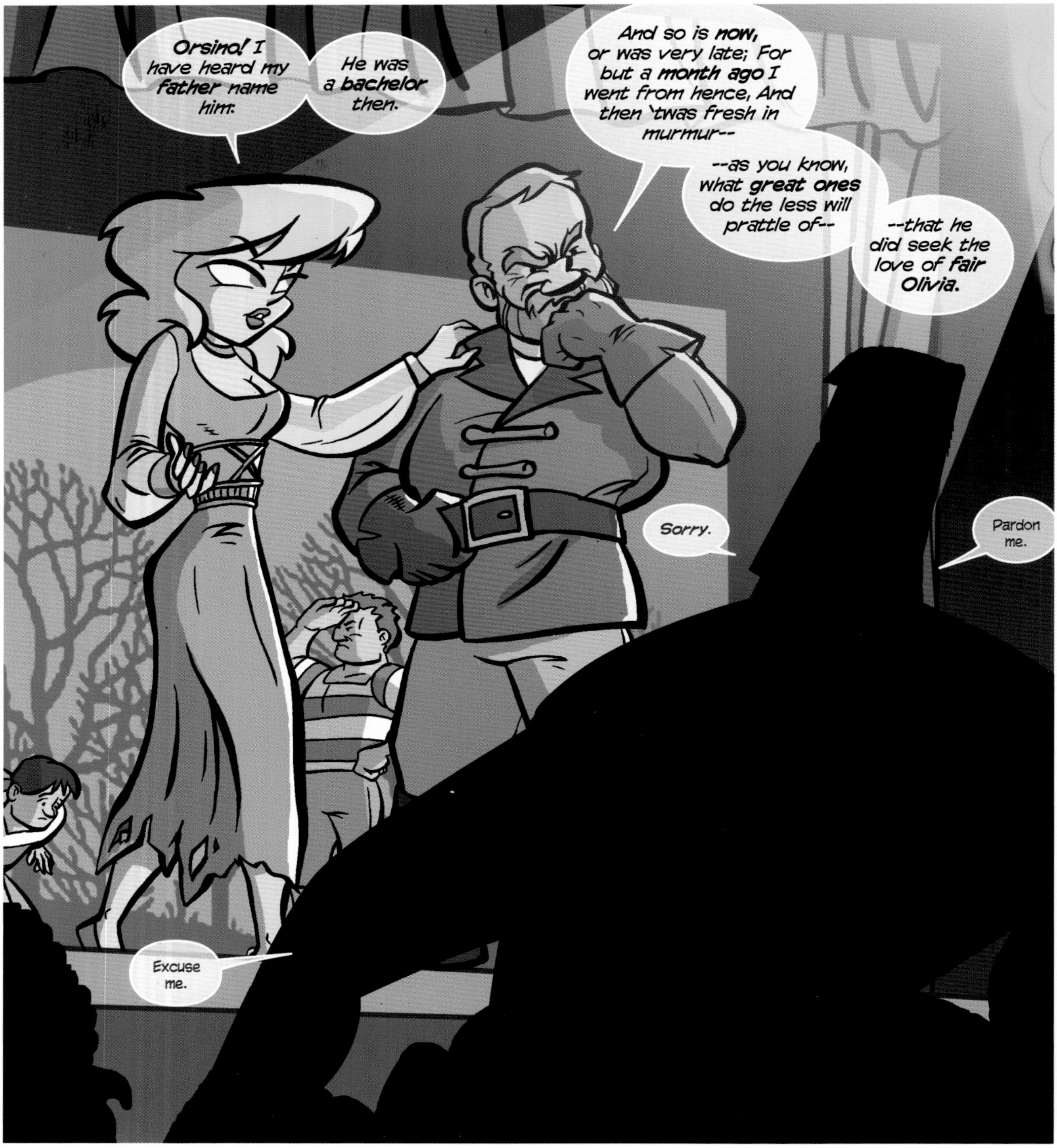
Orsino! I have heard my father name him.
He was a bachelor then.
And so is now, or was very late; For but a month ago I went from hence, And then 'twas fresh in murmur--
--as you know, what great ones do the less will prattle of--
--that he did seek the love of fair Olivia.
Sorry.
Pardon me.
Excuse me.

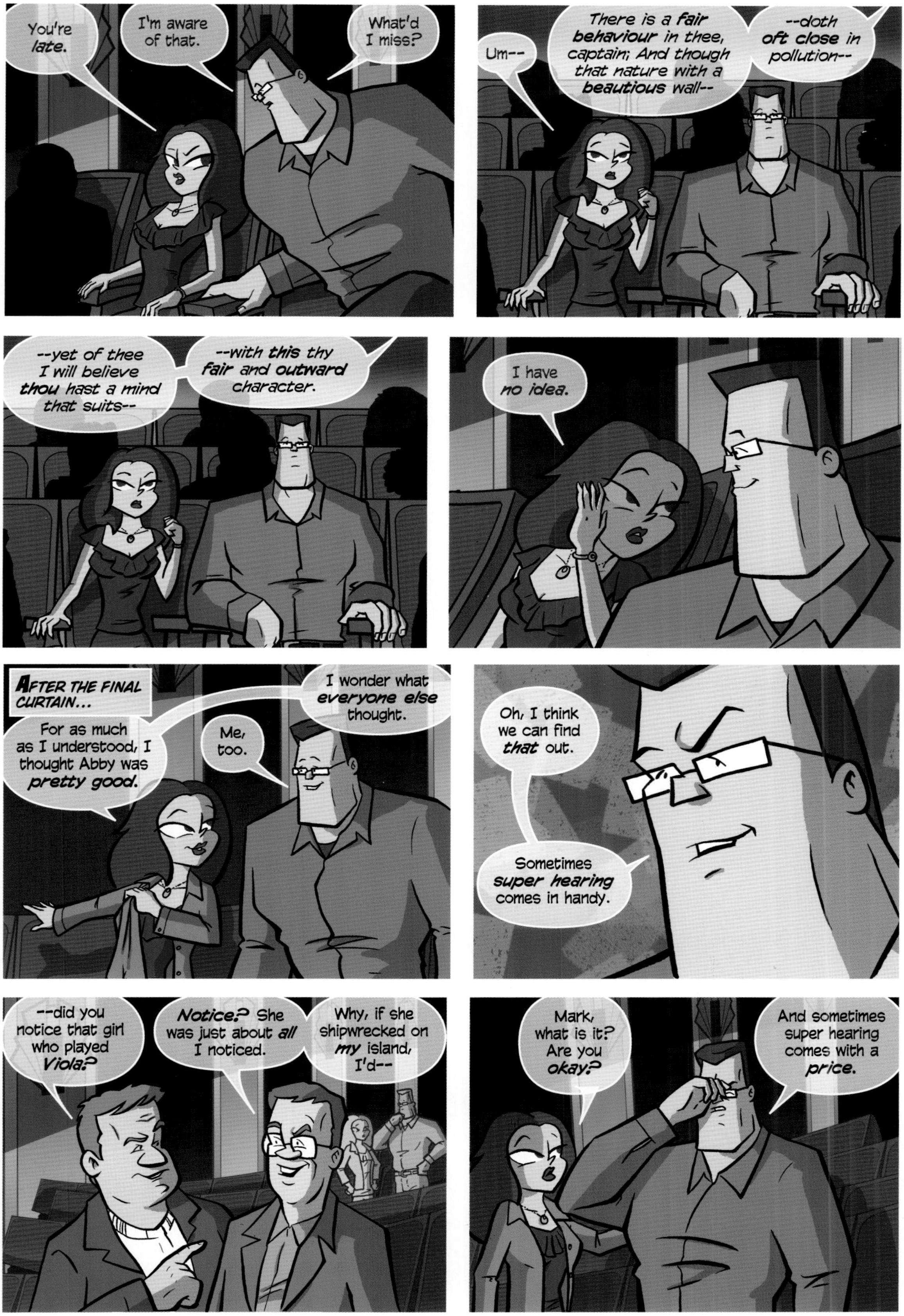
You're late.
I'm aware of that.
What'd I miss?
Um--
There is a fair behaviour in thee, captain; And though that nature with a beautious wall--
--doth oft close in pollution--
--yet of thee I will believe thou hast a mind that suits--
--with this thy fair and outward character.
I have no idea.
AFTER THE FINAL CURTAIN...
For as much as I understood, I thought Abby was pretty good.
Me, too.
I wonder what everyone else thought.
Oh, I think we can find that out.
Sometimes super hearing comes in handy.
--did you notice that girl who played Viola?
Notice? She was just about all I noticed.
Why, if she shipwrecked on my island, I'd--
Mark, what is it? Are you okay?
And sometimes super hearing comes with a price.

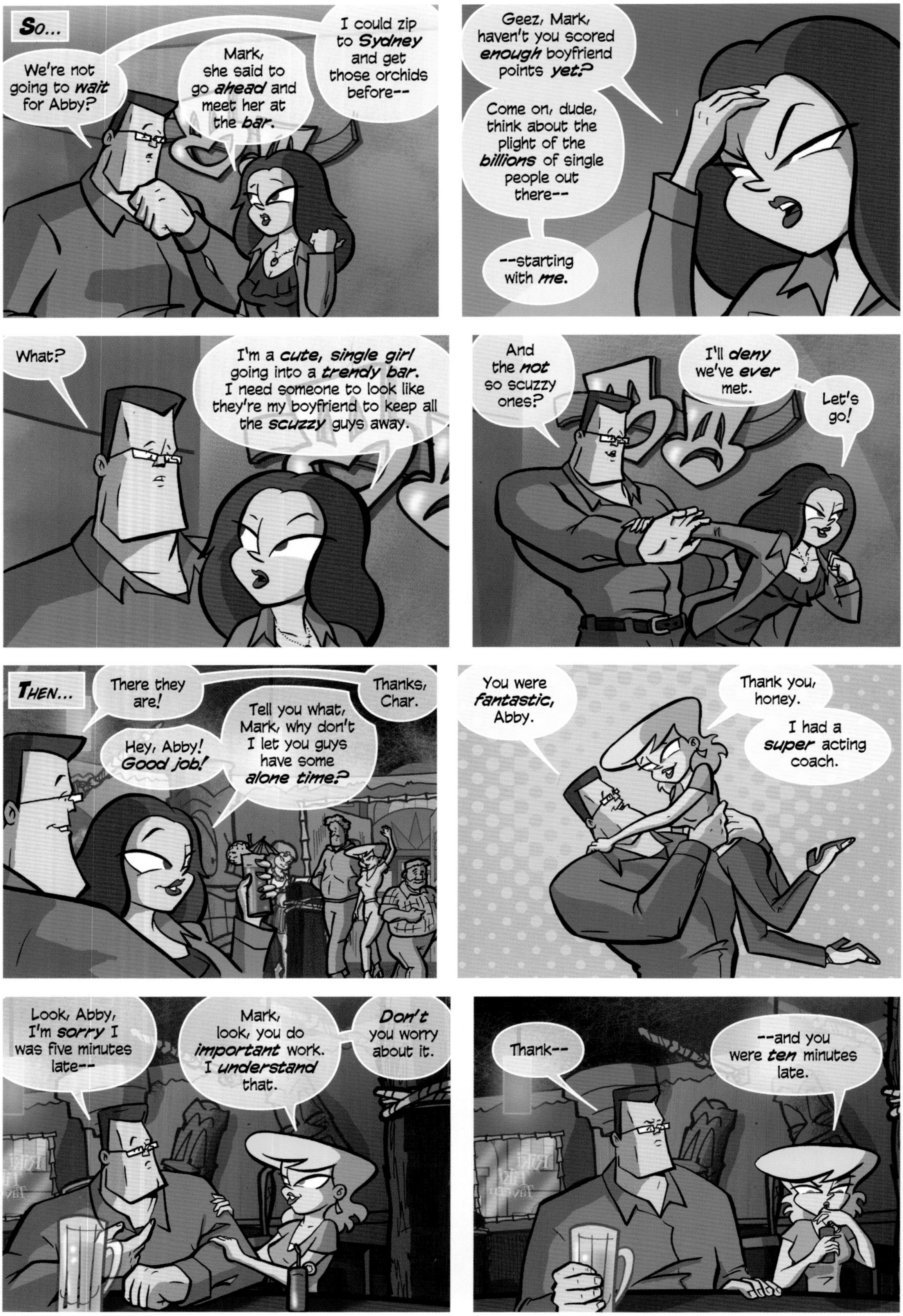
So...
We're not going to *wait* for Abby?
Mark, she said to go *ahead* and meet her at the *bar*.
I could zip to *Sydney* and get those orchids before--
Geez, Mark, haven't you scored *enough* boyfriend points *yet?*
Come on, dude, think about the plight of the *billions* of single people out there--
--starting with *me*.
What?
I'm a *cute, single girl* going into a *trendy bar*. I need someone to look like they're my boyfriend to keep all the *scuzzy* guys away.
And the *not* so scuzzy ones?
I'll *deny* we've *ever* met.
Let's go!
Then...
There they are!
Thanks, Char.
Hey, Abby! *Good job!*
Tell you what, Mark, why don't I let you guys have some *alone time?*
You were *fantastic*, Abby.
Thank you, honey.
I had a *super* acting coach.
Look, Abby, I'm *sorry* I was five minutes late--
Mark, look, you do *important* work. I *understand* that.
Don't you worry about it.
Thank--
--and you were *ten* minutes late.

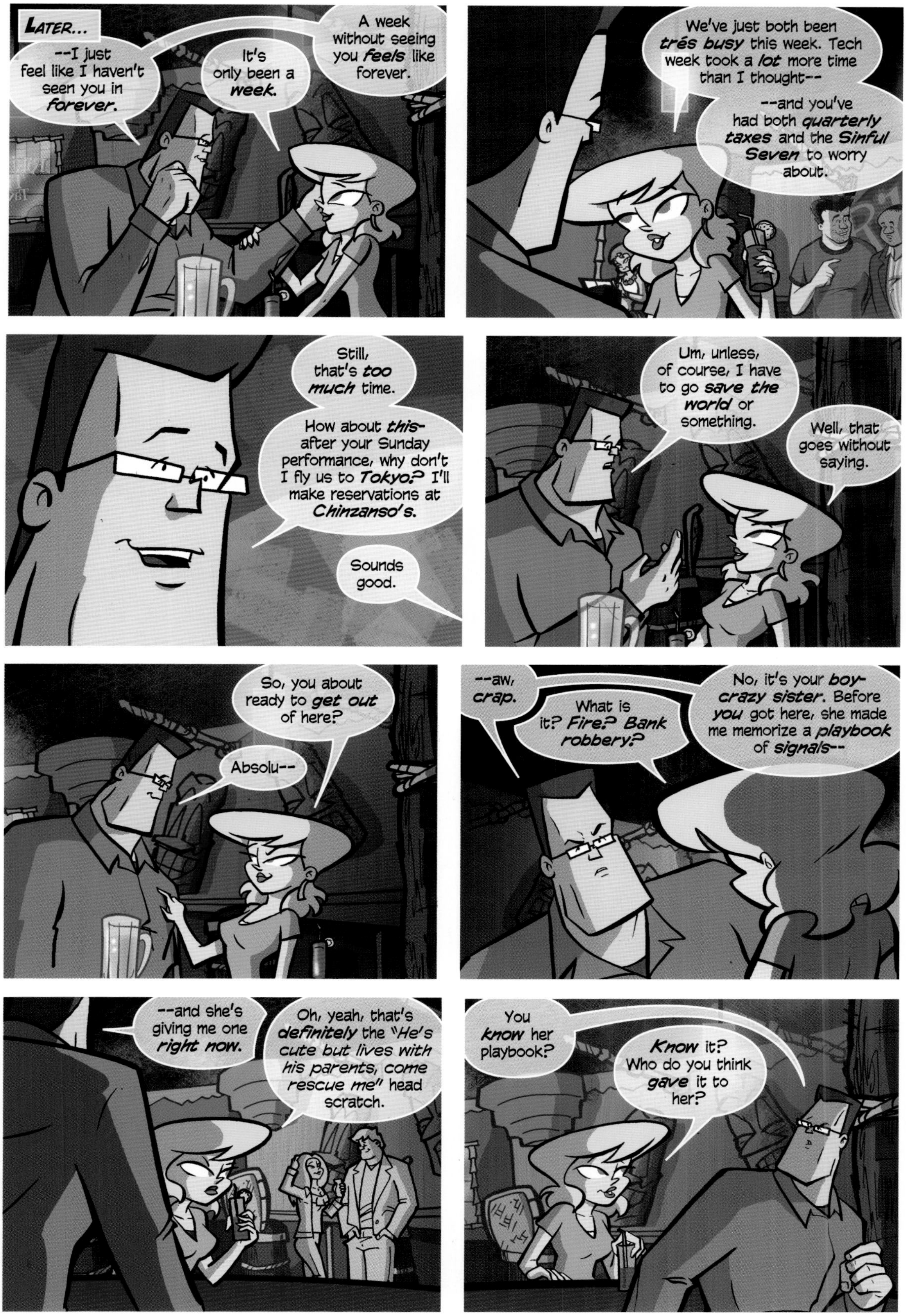
LATER...
--I just feel like I haven't seen you in *forever*.
It's only been a *week*.
A week without seeing you *feels* like forever.
We've just both been *trés busy* this week. Tech week took a *lot* more time than I thought--
--and you've had both *quarterly taxes* and the *Sinful Seven* to worry about.
Still, that's *too much* time.
How about *this*- after your Sunday performance, why don't I fly us to *Tokyo?* I'll make reservations at *Chinzanso's*.
Sounds good.
Um, unless, of course, I have to go *save the world* or something.
Well, that goes without saying.
So, you about ready to *get out* of here?
Absolu--
--aw, *crap.*
What is it? *Fire? Bank robbery?*
No, it's your *boy-crazy sister*. Before *you* got here, she made me memorize a *playbook* of *signals*--
--and she's giving me one *right now*.
Oh, yeah, that's *definitely* the "*He's cute but lives with his parents, come rescue me*" head scratch.
You *know* her playbook?
Know it? Who do you think *gave* it to her?

THE NEXT MORNING...

Finally, I'm not the one who's *late* for once.

What happened?

Hit snooze. A *lot*.

ABBY'S

≷Yawn!≷ It was just *so* *much*, the *play*, the *after-party*...

I don't know *how* I'm going to do it again *tonight*.

When did *you* leave the bar last night?

I dunno. A couple *hours* after you two took off.

And you're *conscious?* What's your secret?

Well, generally we *single people* have far more *stamina* than those of you in relationships--

ABBY'S BOOKS AND COFFEE

--but in *your* case I'm just going to chalk it up to you being much, *much* older than me.

Just *shut up* and pour me some *coffee*, whippersnapper.

ABBY'S

Don't worry, I've got something that will *wake you up.*

Please tell me it's something with *two creams* and *three sugars*.

Here you go.

Thank you. You're now my favorite little sister.

Oh, hey-- *Mark called* just before you got here.

ABBY'S

Come to me, oh sweet, sweet elixir of life that men call "Joe."

What did Mark *say?*

He wanted me to let you know that *his mother* is *coming into town* next week.

ABBY'S

≷Sputter!≷ *What? Mark's MOM?*

See? I *told* you I had *something* to wake you up.

BBY'S

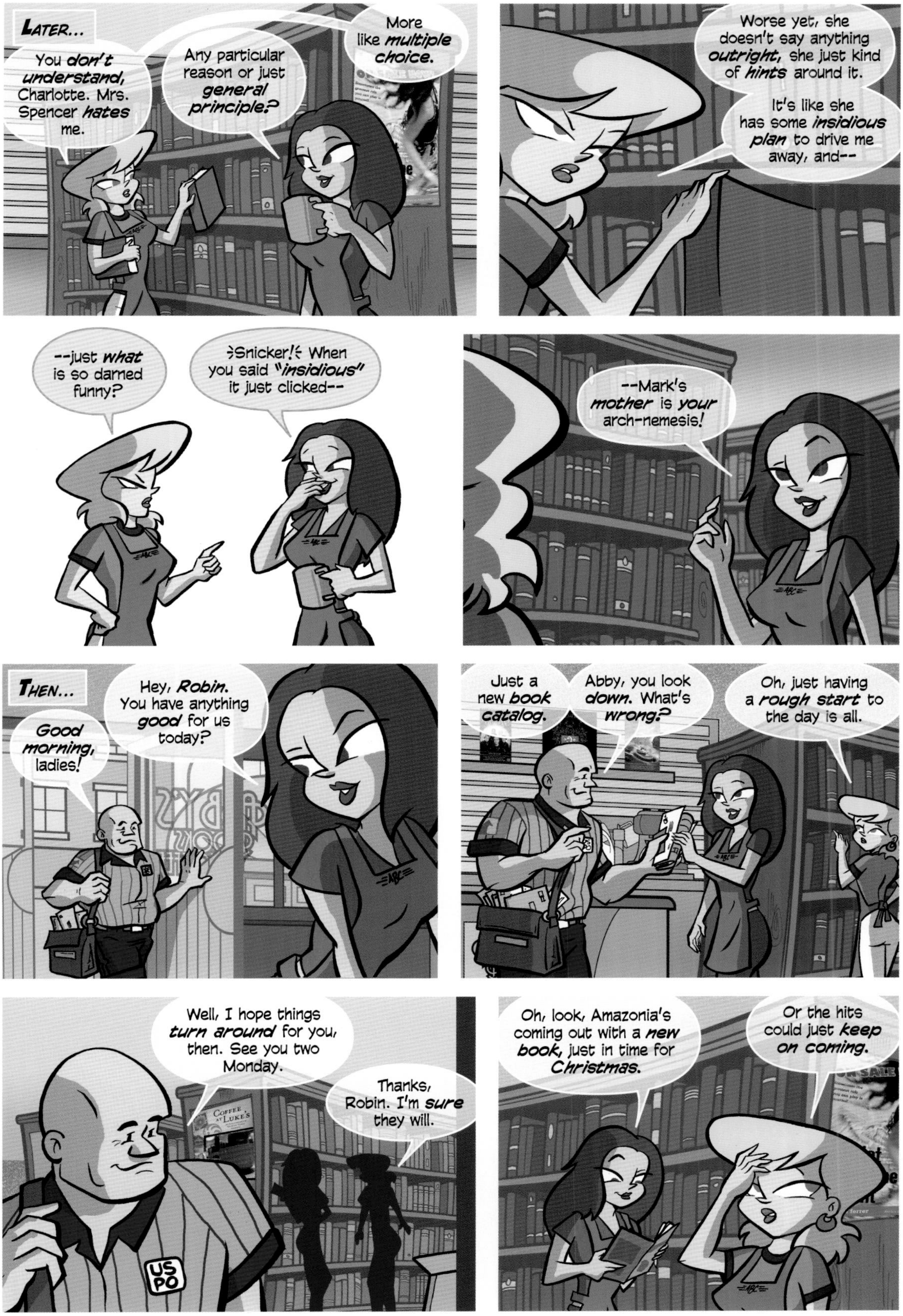
LATER...
You don't understand, Charlotte. Mrs. Spencer hates me.
Any particular reason or just general principle?
More like multiple choice.
Worse yet, she doesn't say anything outright, she just kind of hints around it.
It's like she has some insidious plan to drive me away, and--
--just what is so darned funny?
Snicker! When you said "insidious" it just clicked--
--Mark's mother is your arch-nemesis!
THEN...
Good morning, ladies!
Hey, Robin. You have anything good for us today?
Just a new book catalog.
Abby, you look down. What's wrong?
Oh, just having a rough start to the day is all.
Well, I hope things turn around for you, then. See you two Monday.
Thanks, Robin. I'm sure they will.
COFFEE AT LUKE'S
US PO
Oh, look, Amazonia's coming out with a new book, just in time for Christmas.
Or the hits could just keep on coming.

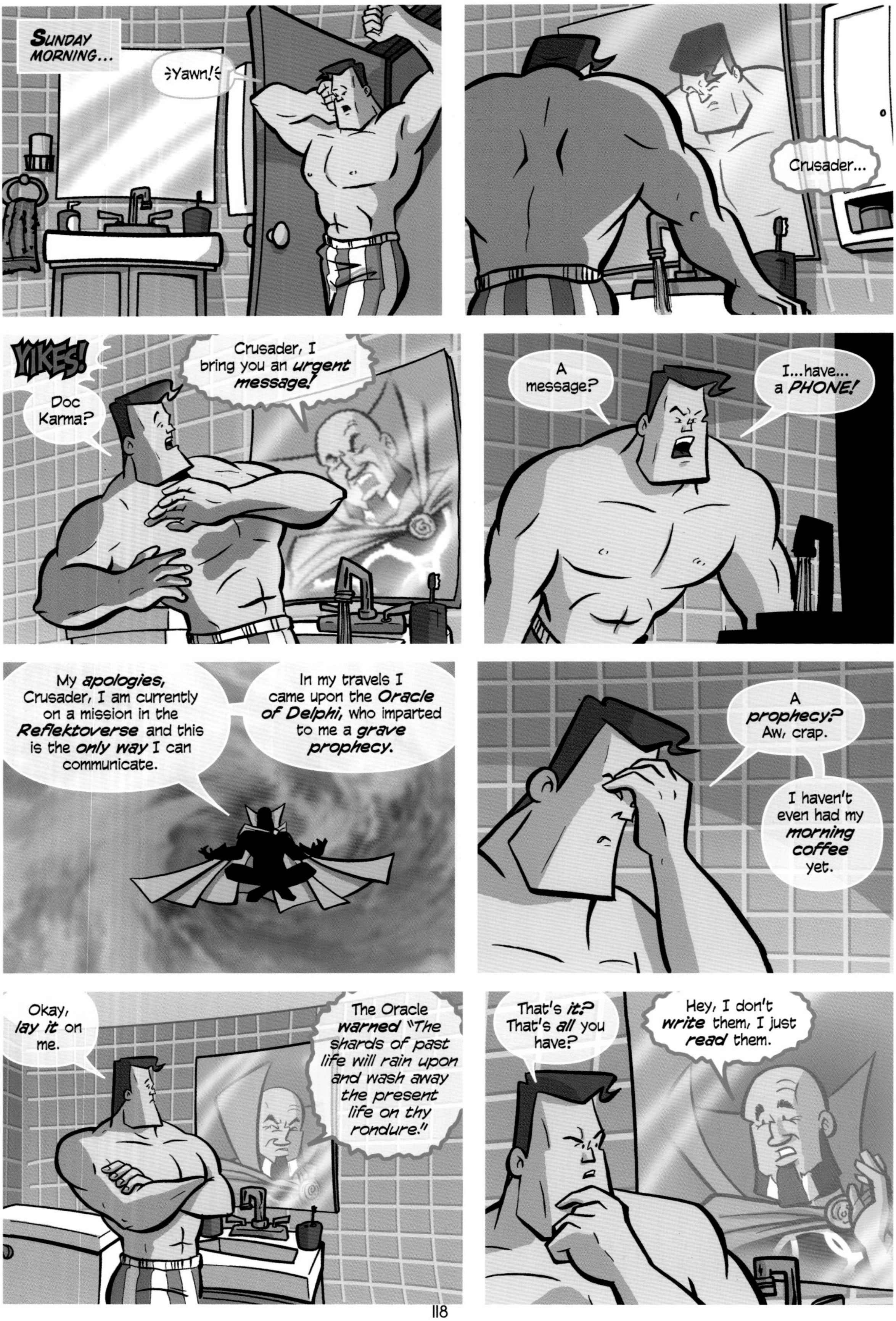

SUNDAY MORNING...
Yawn!
Crusader...
YIKES!
Doc Karma?
Crusader, I bring you an *urgent message!*
A message?
I...have... a *PHONE!*
My *apologies,* Crusader, I am currently on a mission in the *Reflektoverse* and this is the *only way* I can communicate.
In my travels I came upon the *Oracle of Delphi,* who imparted to me a *grave prophecy.*
A *prophecy?* Aw, crap.
I haven't even had my *morning coffee* yet.
Okay, *lay it* on me.
The Oracle *warned "The shards of past life will rain upon and wash away the present life on thy rondure."*
That's *it?* That's *all* you have?
Hey, I don't *write* them, I just *read* them.

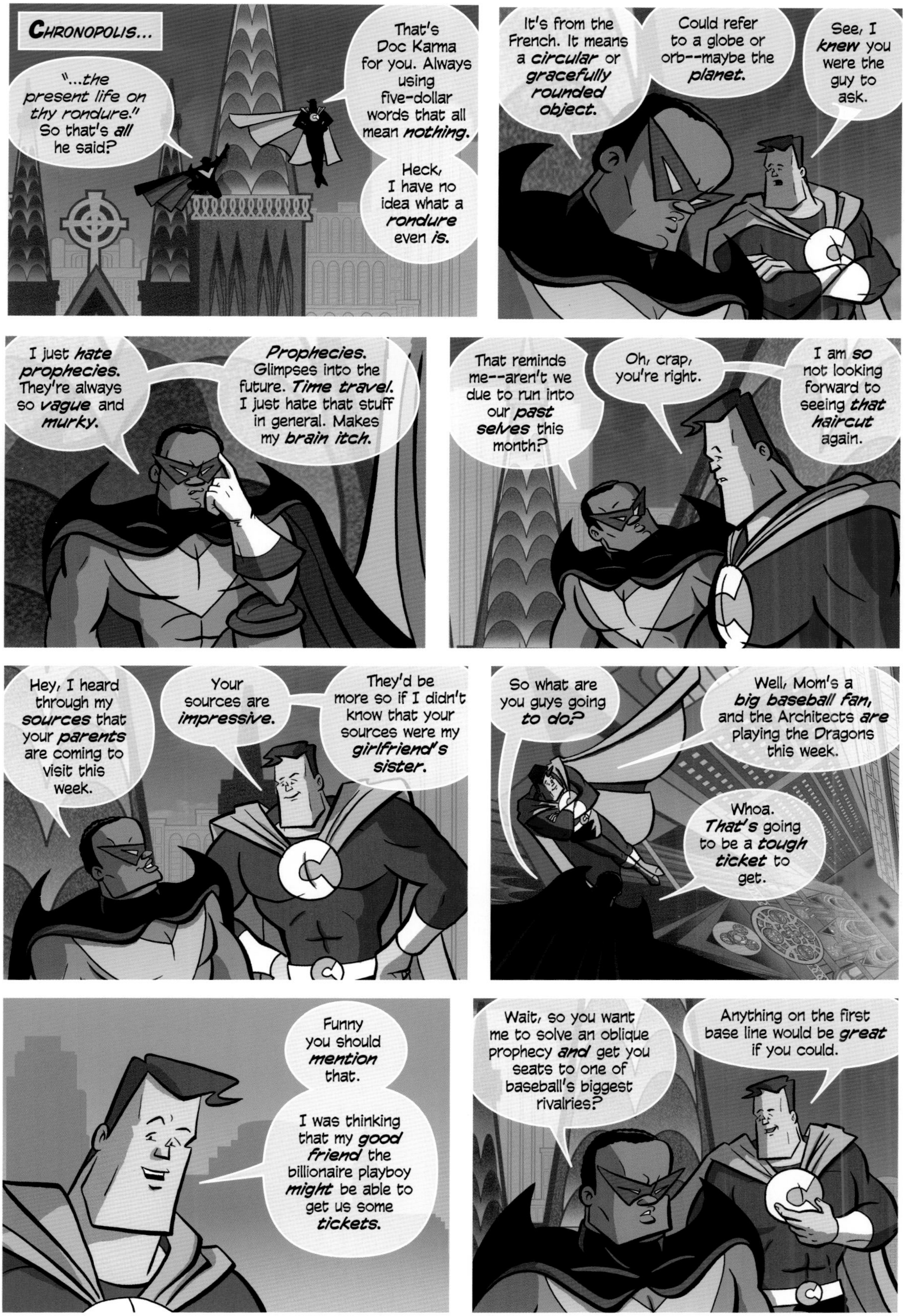

CHRONOPOLIS...
"...the present life on thy rondure." So that's all he said?
That's Doc Karma for you. Always using five-dollar words that all mean nothing.
Heck, I have no idea what a rondure even is.
It's from the French. It means a circular or gracefully rounded object.
Could refer to a globe or orb--maybe the planet.
See, I knew you were the guy to ask.
I just hate prophecies. They're always so vague and murky.
Prophecies. Glimpses into the future. Time travel. I just hate that stuff in general. Makes my brain itch.
That reminds me--aren't we due to run into our past selves this month?
Oh, crap, you're right.
I am so not looking forward to seeing that haircut again.
Hey, I heard through my sources that your parents are coming to visit this week.
Your sources are impressive.
They'd be more so if I didn't know that your sources were my girlfriend's sister.
So what are you guys going to do?
Well, Mom's a big baseball fan, and the Architects are playing the Dragons this week.
Whoa. That's going to be a tough ticket to get.
Funny you should mention that.
I was thinking that my good friend the billionaire playboy might be able to get us some tickets.
Wait, so you want me to solve an oblique prophecy and get you seats to one of baseball's biggest rivalries?
Anything on the first base line would be great if you could.

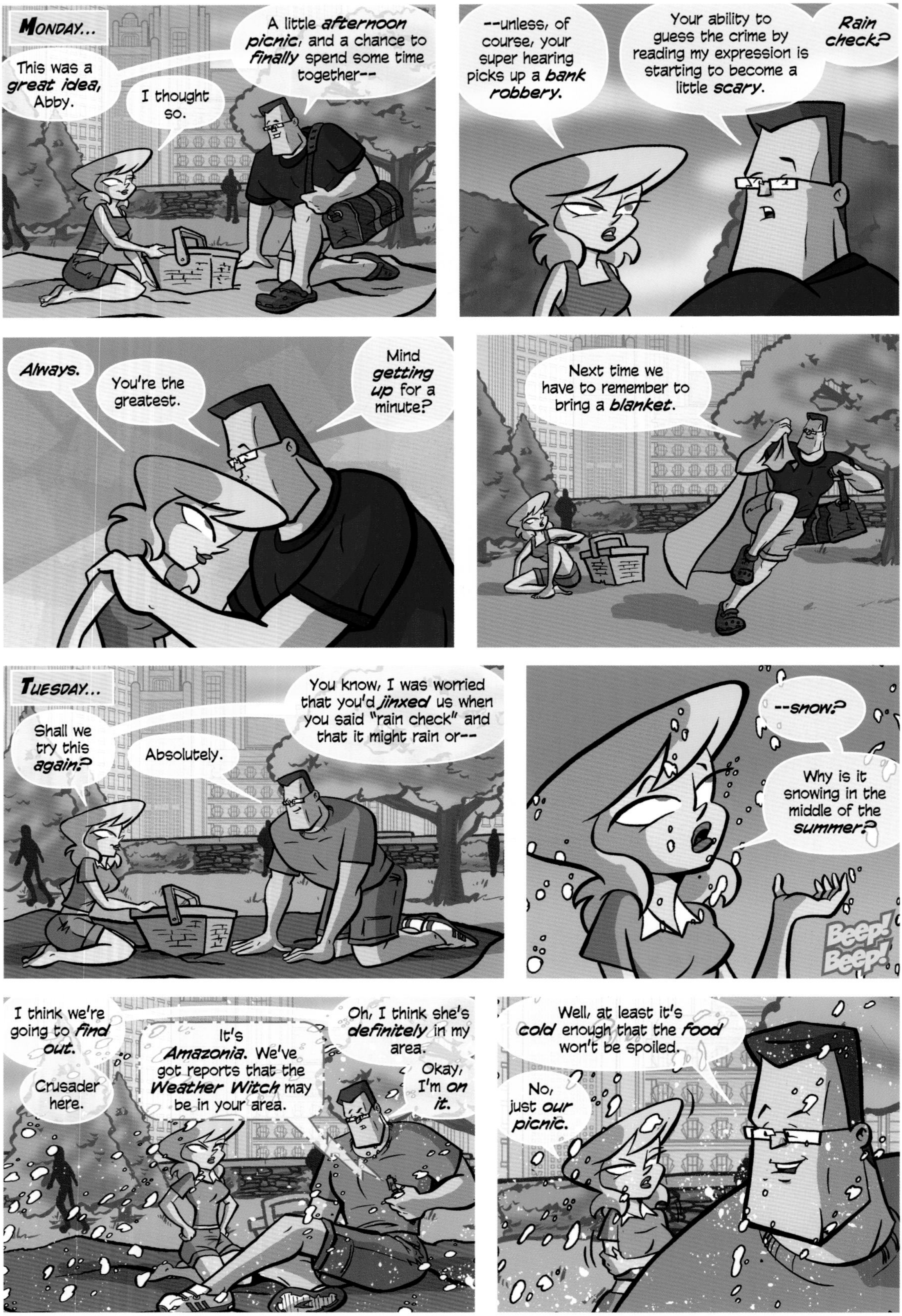
MONDAY...
This was a great idea, Abby.
I thought so.
A little afternoon picnic, and a chance to finally spend some time together--
--unless, of course, your super hearing picks up a bank robbery.
Your ability to guess the crime by reading my expression is starting to become a little scary.
Rain check?
Always.
You're the greatest.
Mind getting up for a minute?
Next time we have to remember to bring a blanket.
TUESDAY...
Shall we try this again?
Absolutely.
You know, I was worried that you'd jinxed us when you said "rain check" and that it might rain or--
--snow?
Why is it snowing in the middle of the summer?
Beep! Beep!
I think we're going to find out.
Crusader here.
It's Amazonia. We've got reports that the Weather Witch may be in your area.
Oh, I think she's definitely in my area.
Okay, I'm on it.
Well, at least it's cold enough that the food won't be spoiled.
No, just our picnic.

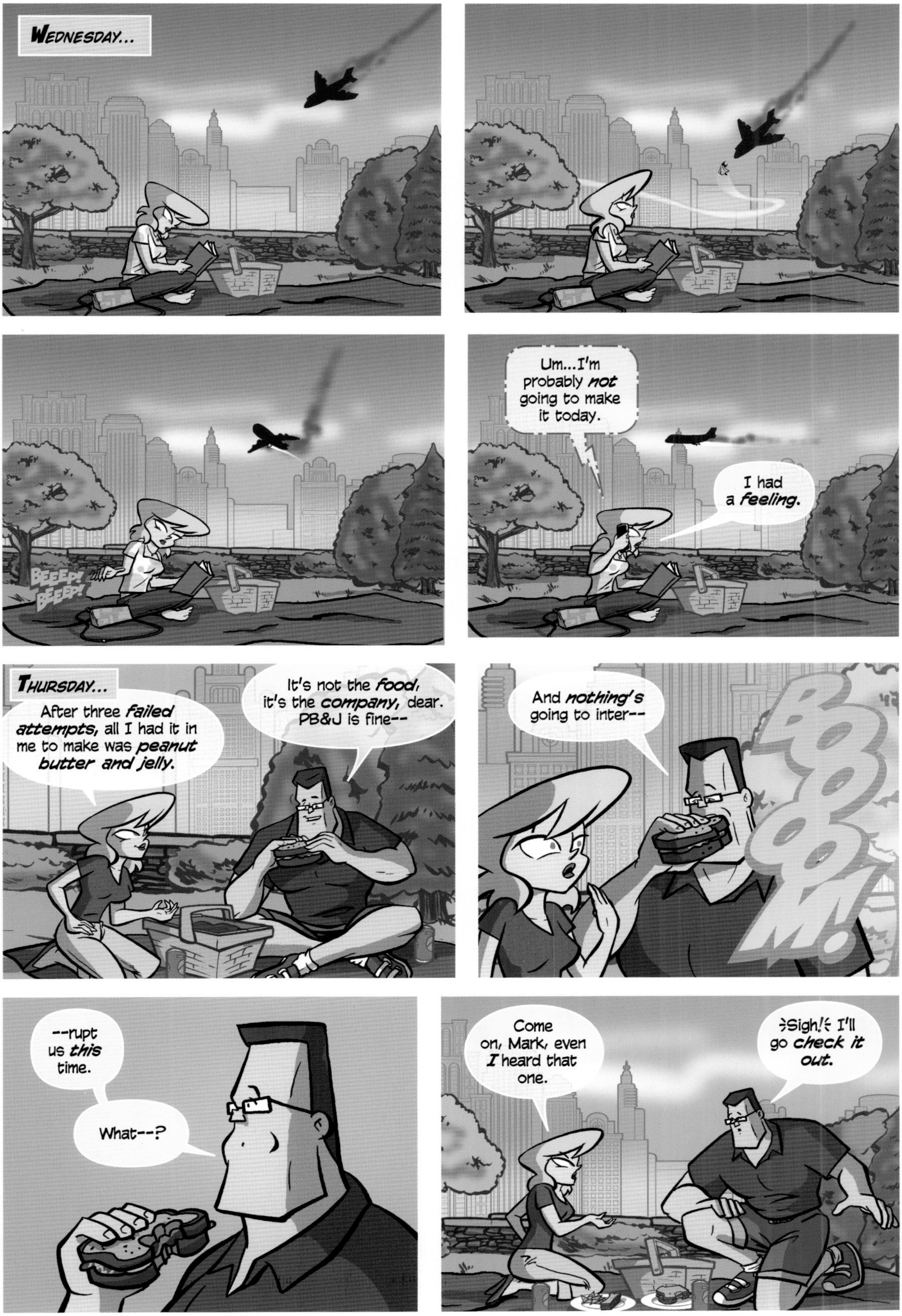
WEDNESDAY...
BEEEP! BEEEP!
Um...I'm probably *not* going to make it today.
I had a *feeling*.
THURSDAY...
After three *failed attempts*, all I had it in me to make was *peanut butter and jelly*.
It's not the *food*, it's the *company*, dear. PB&J is fine--
And *nothing's* going to inter--
BOOOM!
--rupt us *this* time.
What--?
Come on, Mark, even *I* heard that one.
Sigh! I'll go *check it out*.

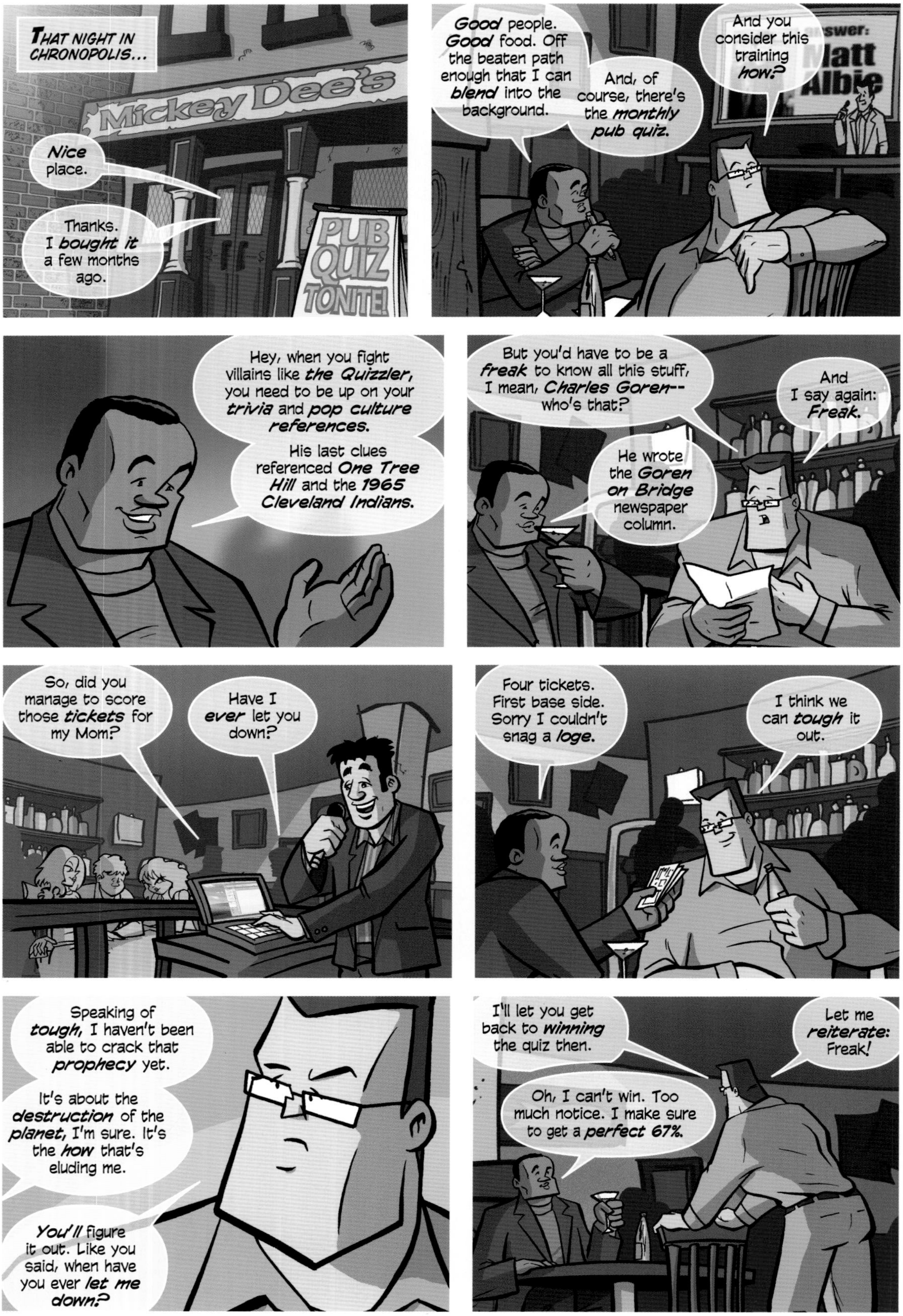
THAT NIGHT IN CHRONOPOLIS...
Mickey Dee's
Nice place.
Thanks. I bought it a few months ago.
PUB QUIZ TONITE!
Good people. Good food. Off the beaten path enough that I can blend into the background.
And, of course, there's the monthly pub quiz.
And you consider this training how?
Hey, when you fight villains like the Quizzler, you need to be up on your trivia and pop culture references.
His last clues referenced One Tree Hill and the 1965 Cleveland Indians.
But you'd have to be a freak to know all this stuff, I mean, Charles Goren-- who's that?
He wrote the Goren on Bridge newspaper column.
And I say again: Freak.
So, did you manage to score those tickets for my Mom?
Have I ever let you down?
Four tickets. First base side. Sorry I couldn't snag a loge.
I think we can tough it out.
Speaking of tough, I haven't been able to crack that prophecy yet.
It's about the destruction of the planet, I'm sure. It's the how that's eluding me.
You'll figure it out. Like you said, when have you ever let me down?
I'll let you get back to winning the quiz then.
Let me reiterate: Freak!
Oh, I can't win. Too much notice. I make sure to get a perfect 67%.

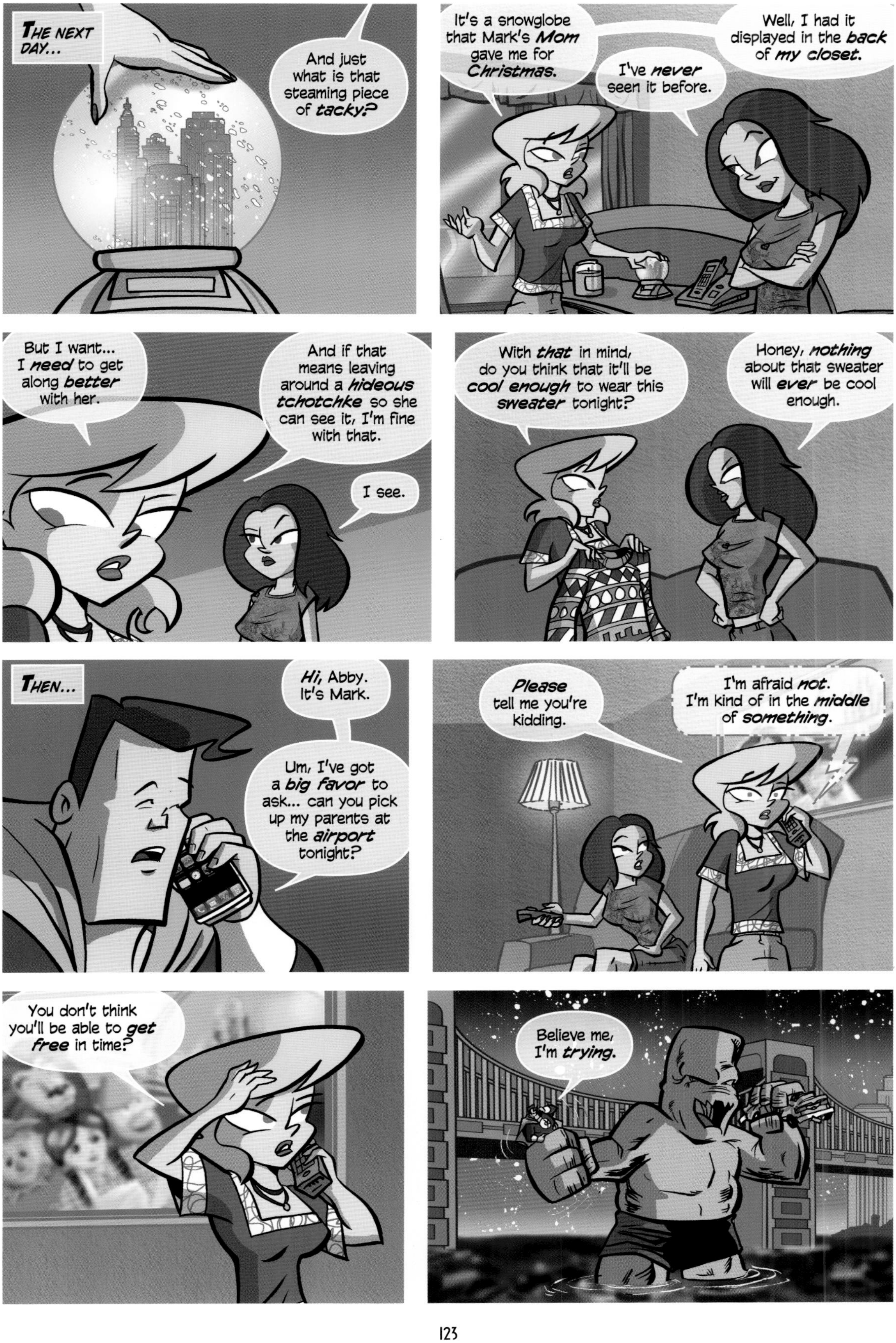
THE NEXT DAY...
And just what is that steaming piece of tacky?
It's a snowglobe that Mark's Mom gave me for Christmas.
I've never seen it before.
Well, I had it displayed in the back of my closet.
But I want... I need to get along better with her.
And if that means leaving around a hideous tchotchke so she can see it, I'm fine with that.
I see.
With that in mind, do you think that it'll be cool enough to wear this sweater tonight?
Honey, nothing about that sweater will ever be cool enough.
THEN...
Hi, Abby. It's Mark.
Um, I've got a big favor to ask... can you pick up my parents at the airport tonight?
Please tell me you're kidding.
I'm afraid not. I'm kind of in the middle of something.
You don't think you'll be able to get free in time?
Believe me, I'm trying.

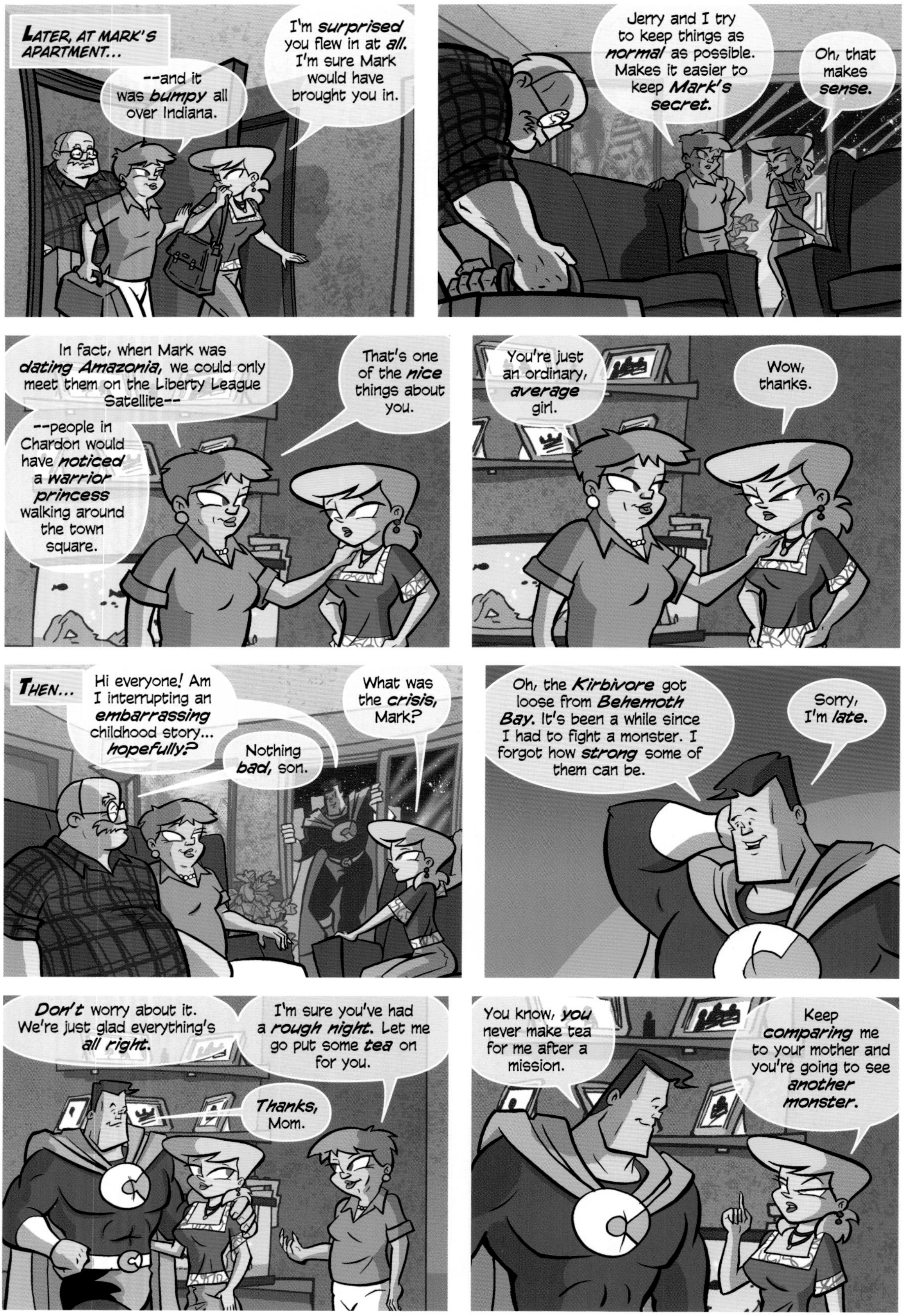
LATER, AT MARK'S APARTMENT...
--and it was bumpy all over Indiana.
I'm surprised you flew in at all. I'm sure Mark would have brought you in.
Jerry and I try to keep things as normal as possible. Makes it easier to keep Mark's secret.
Oh, that makes sense.
In fact, when Mark was dating Amazonia, we could only meet them on the Liberty League Satellite--
--people in Chardon would have noticed a warrior princess walking around the town square.
That's one of the nice things about you.
You're just an ordinary, average girl.
Wow, thanks.
THEN...
Hi everyone! Am I interrupting an embarrassing childhood story... hopefully?
Nothing bad, son.
What was the crisis, Mark?
Oh, the Kirbivore got loose from Behemoth Bay. It's been a while since I had to fight a monster. I forgot how strong some of them can be.
Sorry, I'm late.
Don't worry about it. We're just glad everything's all right.
I'm sure you've had a rough night. Let me go put some tea on for you.
Thanks, Mom.
You know, you never make tea for me after a mission.
Keep comparing me to your mother and you're going to see another monster.

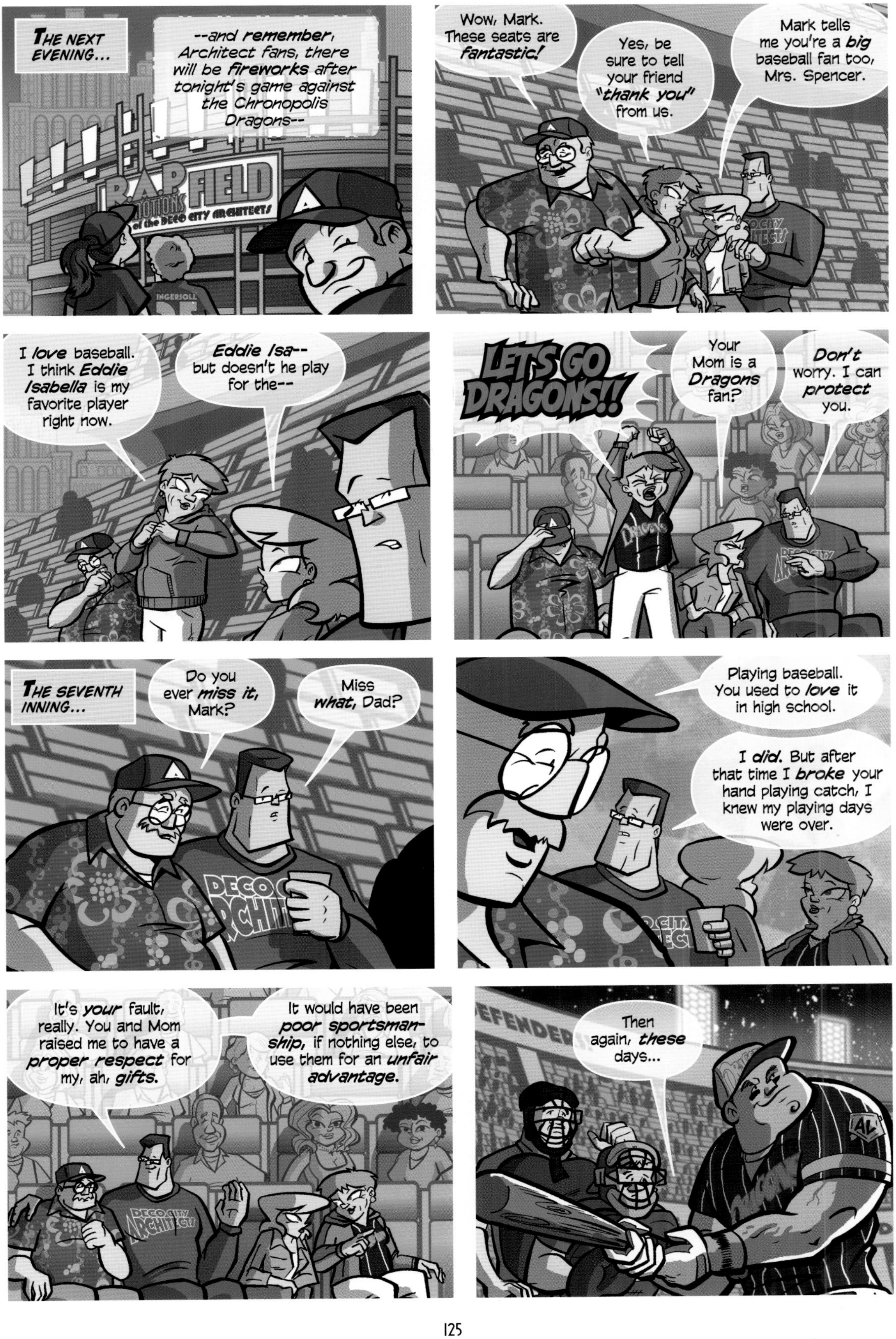
THE NEXT EVENING...
--and *remember*, Architect fans, there will be *fireworks* after tonight's game against the Chronopolis Dragons--
R.A.P. FIELD
Wow, Mark. These seats are *fantastic!*
Yes, be sure to tell your friend *"thank you"* from us.
Mark tells me you're a *big* baseball fan too, Mrs. Spencer.
I *love* baseball. I think *Eddie Isabella* is my favorite player right now.
Eddie Isa-- but doesn't he play for the--
LET'S GO DRAGONS!!
Your Mom is a *Dragons* fan?
Don't worry. I can *protect* you.
THE SEVENTH INNING...
Do you ever *miss it*, Mark?
Miss *what*, Dad?
Playing baseball. You used to *love* it in high school.
I *did*. But after that time I *broke* your hand playing catch, I knew my playing days were over.
It's *your* fault, really. You and Mom raised me to have a *proper respect* for my, ah, *gifts*.
It would have been *poor sportsmanship*, if nothing else, to use them for an *unfair advantage*.
Then again, *these* days...

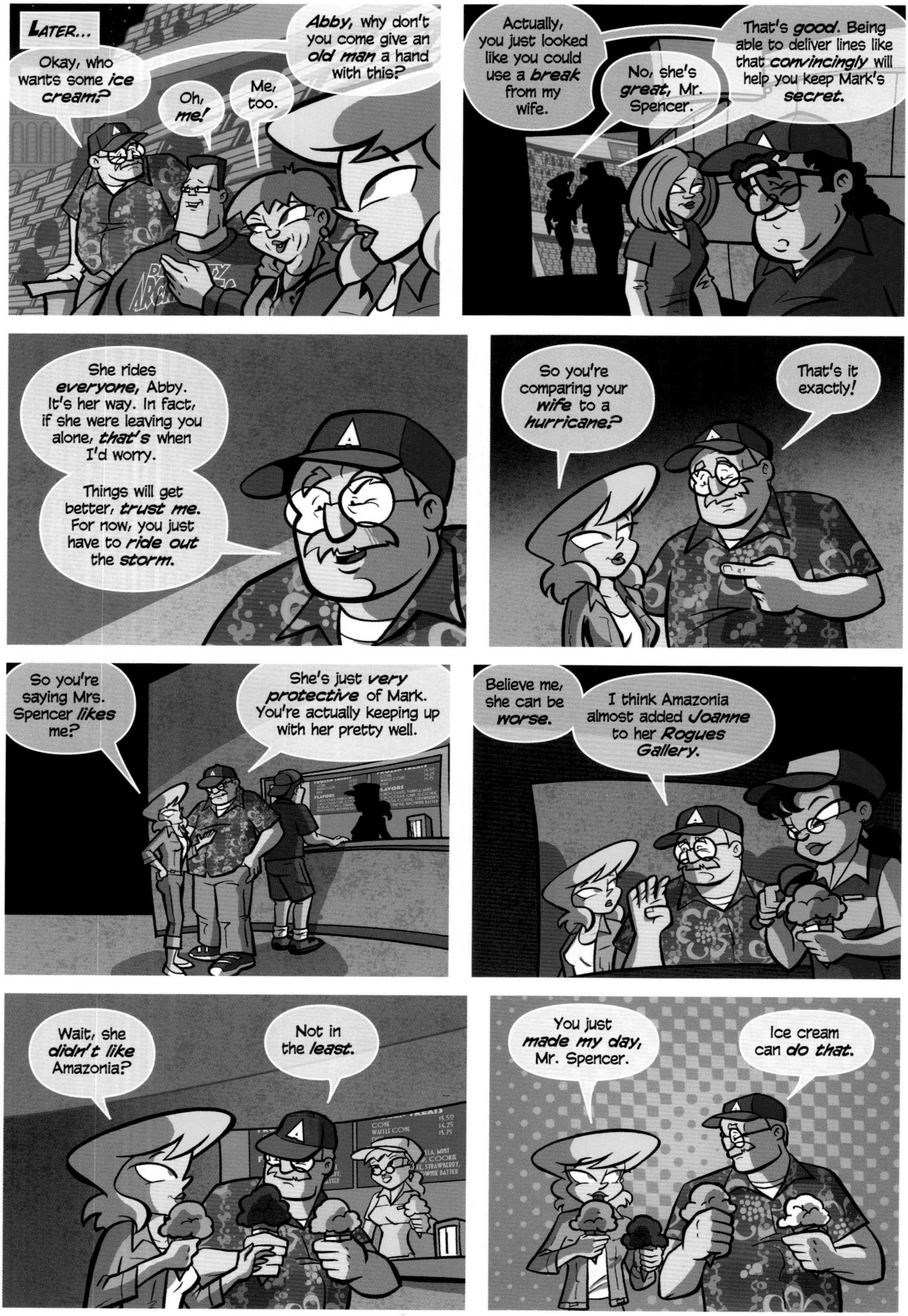
LATER...
Okay, who wants some *ice cream?*
Oh, *me!*
Me, too.
Abby, why don't you come give an *old man* a hand with this?
Actually, you just looked like you could use a *break* from my wife.
No, she's *great,* Mr. Spencer.
That's *good.* Being able to deliver lines like that *convincingly* will help you keep Mark's *secret.*
She rides *everyone,* Abby. It's her way. In fact, if she were leaving you alone, *that's* when I'd worry.
Things will get better, *trust me.* For now, you just have to *ride out* the *storm.*
So you're comparing your *wife* to a *hurricane?*
That's it exactly!
So you're saying Mrs. Spencer *likes* me?
She's just *very protective* of Mark. You're actually keeping up with her pretty well.
Believe me, she can be *worse.*
I think Amazonia almost added *Joanne* to her *Rogues Gallery.*
Wait, she *didn't like* Amazonia?
Not in the *least.*
You just *made my day,* Mr. Spencer.
Ice cream can *do that.*

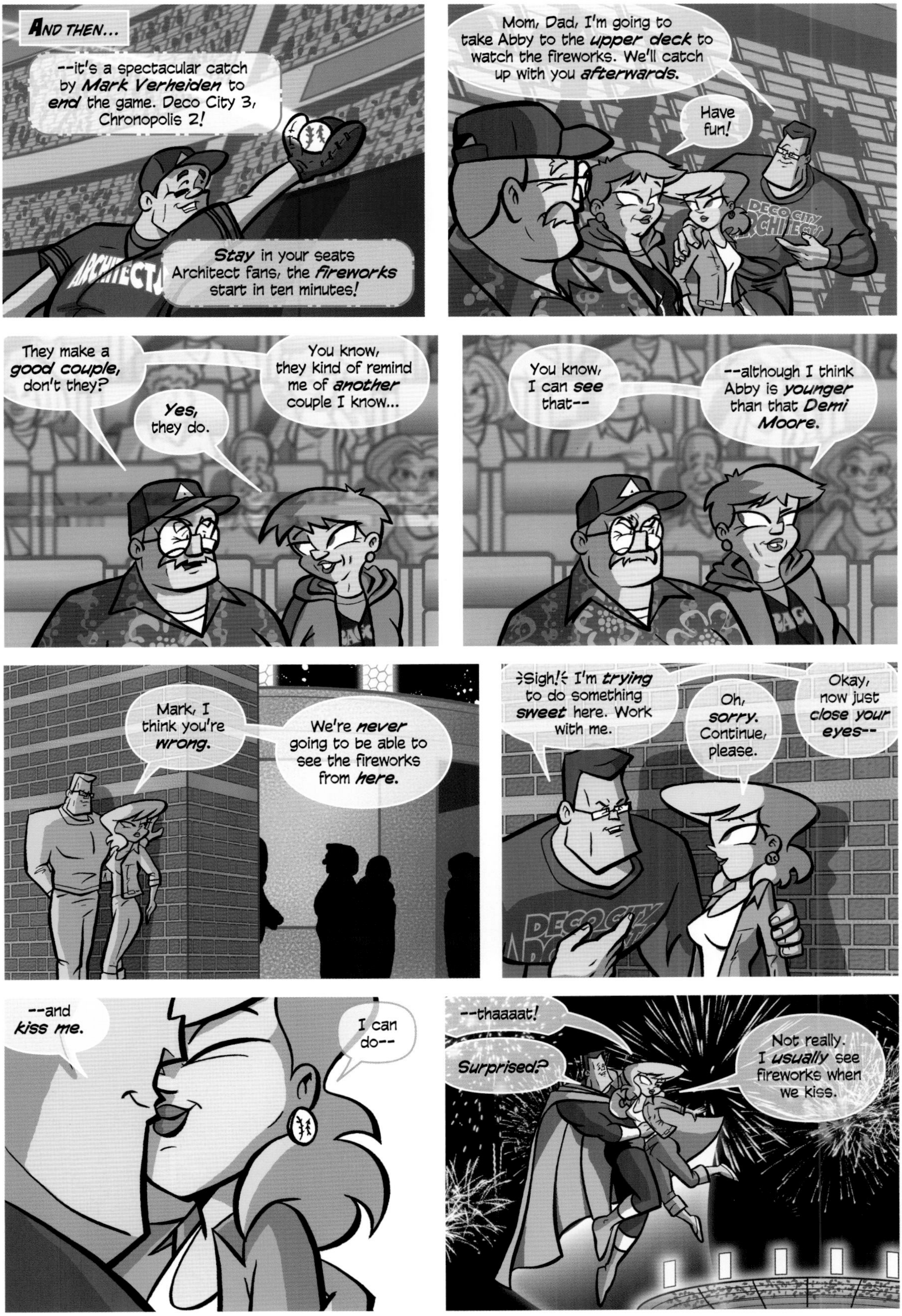
AND THEN...
--it's a spectacular catch by Mark Verheiden to end the game. Deco City 3, Chronopolis 2!
Stay in your seats Architect fans, the fireworks start in ten minutes!
Mom, Dad, I'm going to take Abby to the upper deck to watch the fireworks. We'll catch up with you afterwards.
Have fun!
They make a good couple, don't they?
Yes, they do.
You know, they kind of remind me of another couple I know...
You know, I can see that--
--although I think Abby is younger than that Demi Moore.
Mark, I think you're wrong.
We're never going to be able to see the fireworks from here.
Sigh! I'm trying to do something sweet here. Work with me.
Oh, sorry. Continue, please.
Okay, now just close your eyes--
--and kiss me.
I can do--
--thaaaat!
Surprised?
Not really. I usually see fireworks when we kiss.

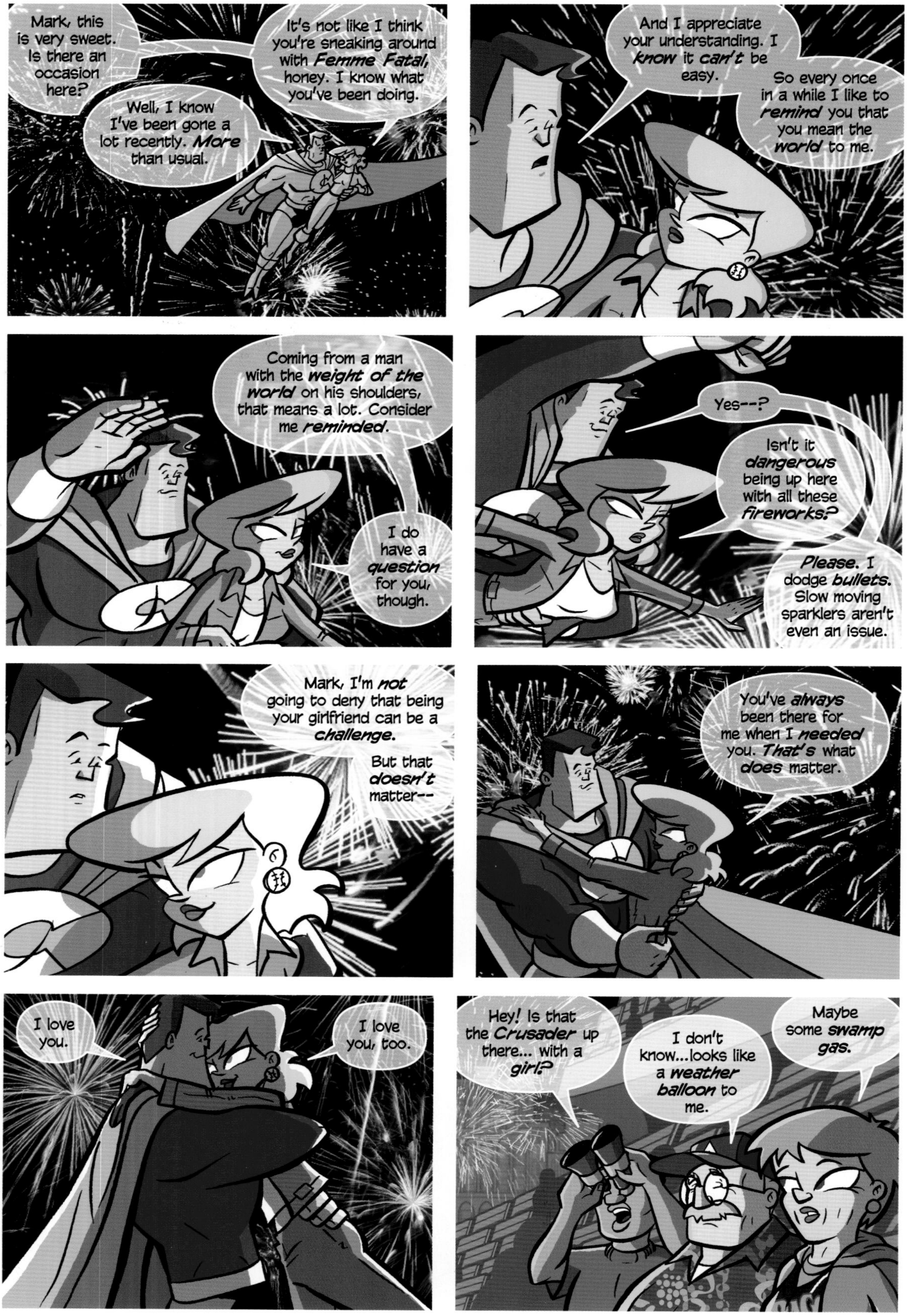

Mark, this is very sweet. Is there an occasion here?
It's not like I think you're sneaking around with *Femme Fatal,* honey. I know what you've been doing.
Well, I know I've been gone a lot recently. *More* than usual.
And I appreciate your understanding. I *know* it *can't* be easy.
So every once in a while I like to *remind* you that you mean the *world* to me.
Coming from a man with the *weight of the world* on his shoulders, that means a lot. Consider me *reminded*.
I do have a *question* for you, though.
Yes--?
Isn't it *dangerous* being up here with all these *fireworks?*
Please. I dodge *bullets*. Slow moving sparklers aren't even an issue.
Mark, I'm *not* going to deny that being your girlfriend can be a *challenge*.
But that *doesn't* matter--
You've *always* been there for me when I *needed* you. *That's* what *does* matter.
I love you.
I love you, too.
Hey! Is that the *Crusader* up there... with a *girl?*
I don't know...looks like a *weather balloon* to me.
Maybe some *swamp gas*.

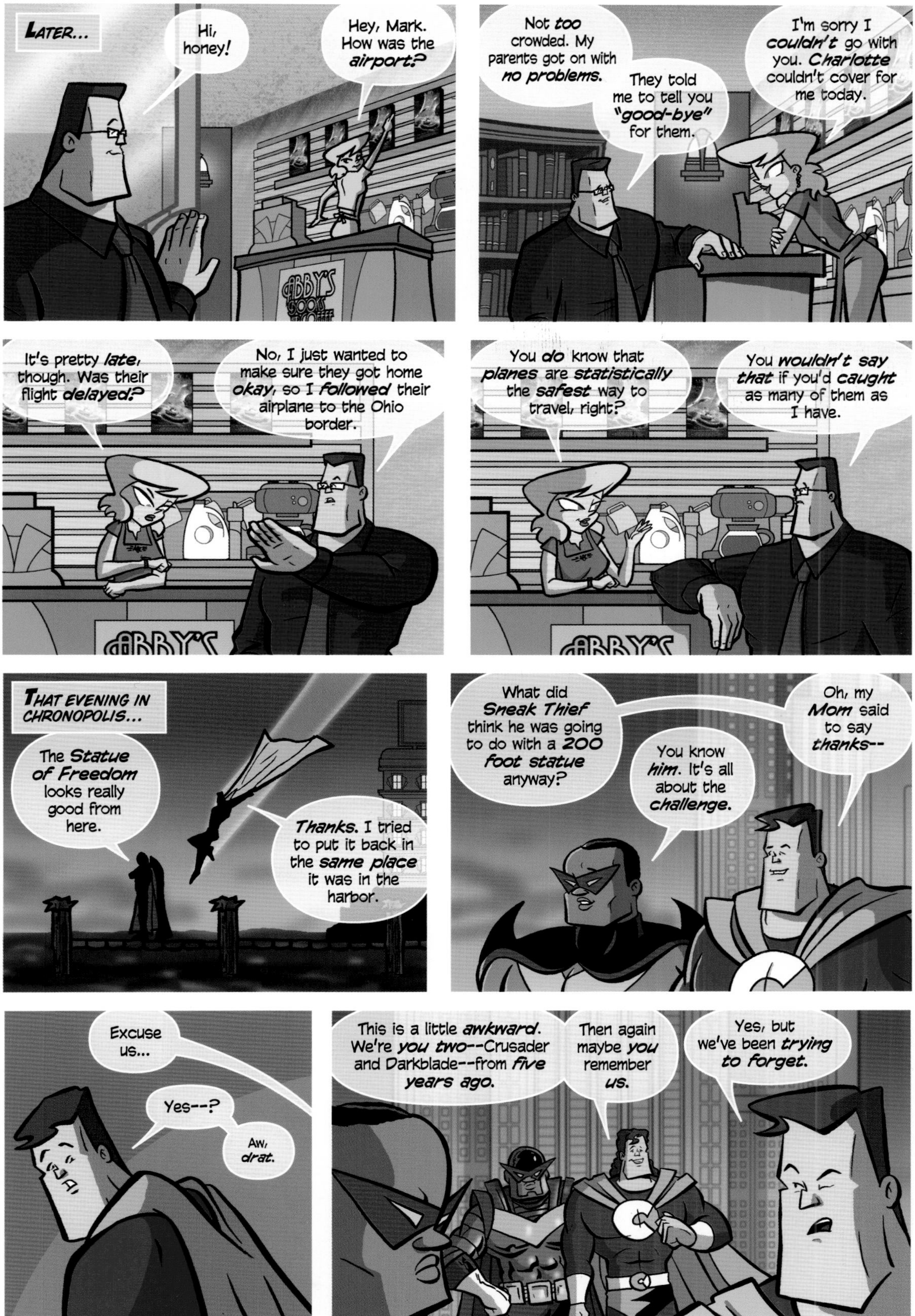
LATER...
Hi, honey!
Hey, Mark. How was the airport?
Not too crowded. My parents got on with no problems.
They told me to tell you "good-bye" for them.
I'm sorry I couldn't go with you. Charlotte couldn't cover for me today.
It's pretty late, though. Was their flight delayed?
No, I just wanted to make sure they got home okay, so I followed their airplane to the Ohio border.
You do know that planes are statistically the safest way to travel, right?
You wouldn't say that if you'd caught as many of them as I have.
THAT EVENING IN CHRONOPOLIS...
The Statue of Freedom looks really good from here.
Thanks. I tried to put it back in the same place it was in the harbor.
What did Sneak Thief think he was going to do with a 200 foot statue anyway?
You know him. It's all about the challenge.
Oh, my Mom said to say thanks--
Excuse us...
Yes--?
Aw, drat.
This is a little awkward. We're you two--Crusader and Darkblade--from five years ago.
Then again maybe you remember us.
Yes, but we've been trying to forget.

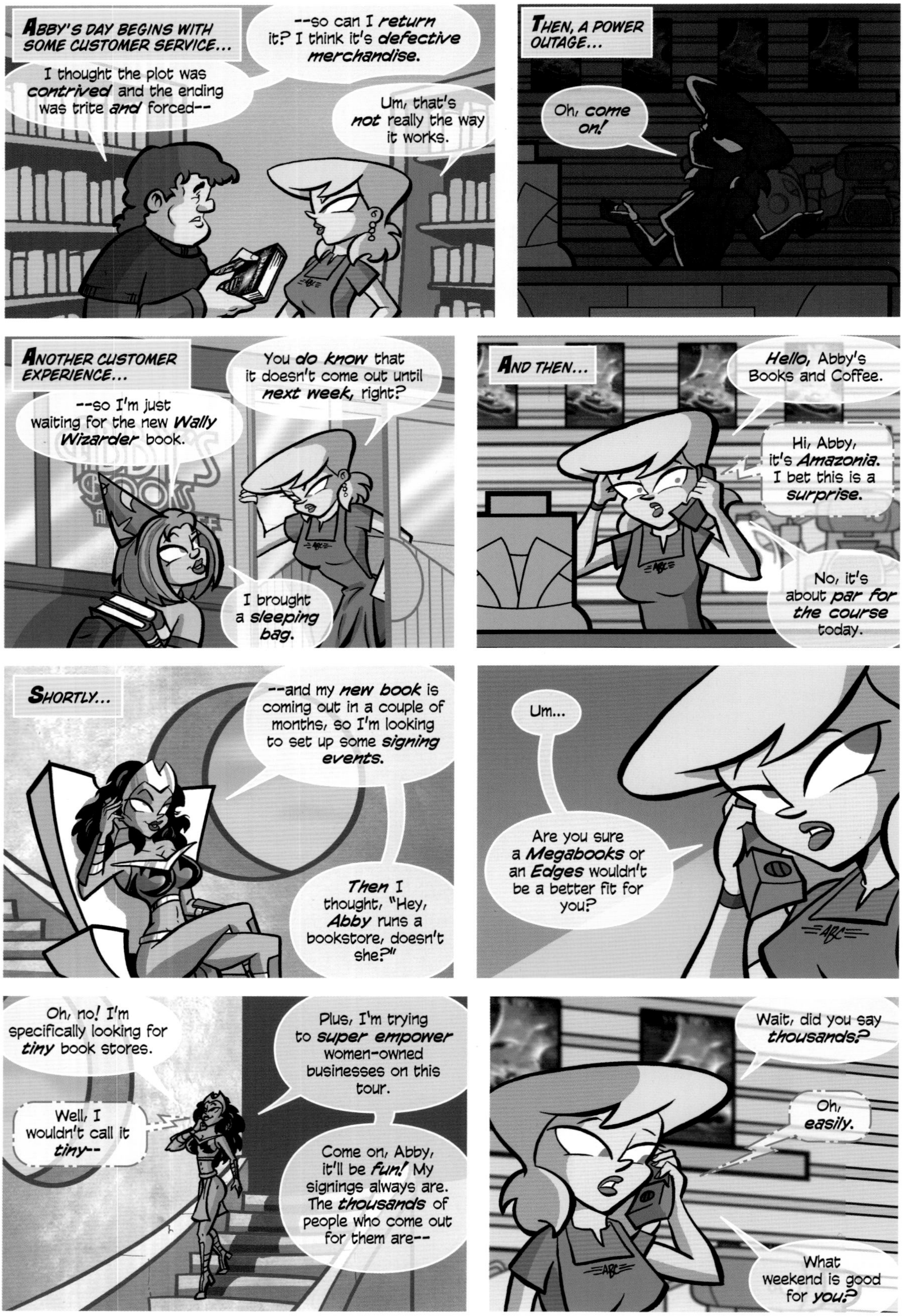
ABBY'S DAY BEGINS WITH SOME CUSTOMER SERVICE...
I thought the plot was contrived and the ending was trite and forced--
--so can I return it? I think it's defective merchandise.
Um, that's not really the way it works.
THEN, A POWER OUTAGE...
Oh, come on!
ANOTHER CUSTOMER EXPERIENCE...
--so I'm just waiting for the new Wally Wizarder book.
You do know that it doesn't come out until next week, right?
I brought a sleeping bag.
AND THEN...
Hello, Abby's Books and Coffee.
Hi, Abby, it's Amazonia. I bet this is a surprise.
No, it's about par for the course today.
SHORTLY...
--and my new book is coming out in a couple of months, so I'm looking to set up some signing events.
Then I thought, "Hey, Abby runs a bookstore, doesn't she?"
Um...
Are you sure a Megabooks or an Edges wouldn't be a better fit for you?
Oh, no! I'm specifically looking for tiny book stores.
Well, I wouldn't call it tiny--
Plus, I'm trying to super empower women-owned businesses on this tour.
Come on, Abby, it'll be fun! My signings always are. The thousands of people who come out for them are--
Wait, did you say thousands?
Oh, easily.
What weekend is good for you?

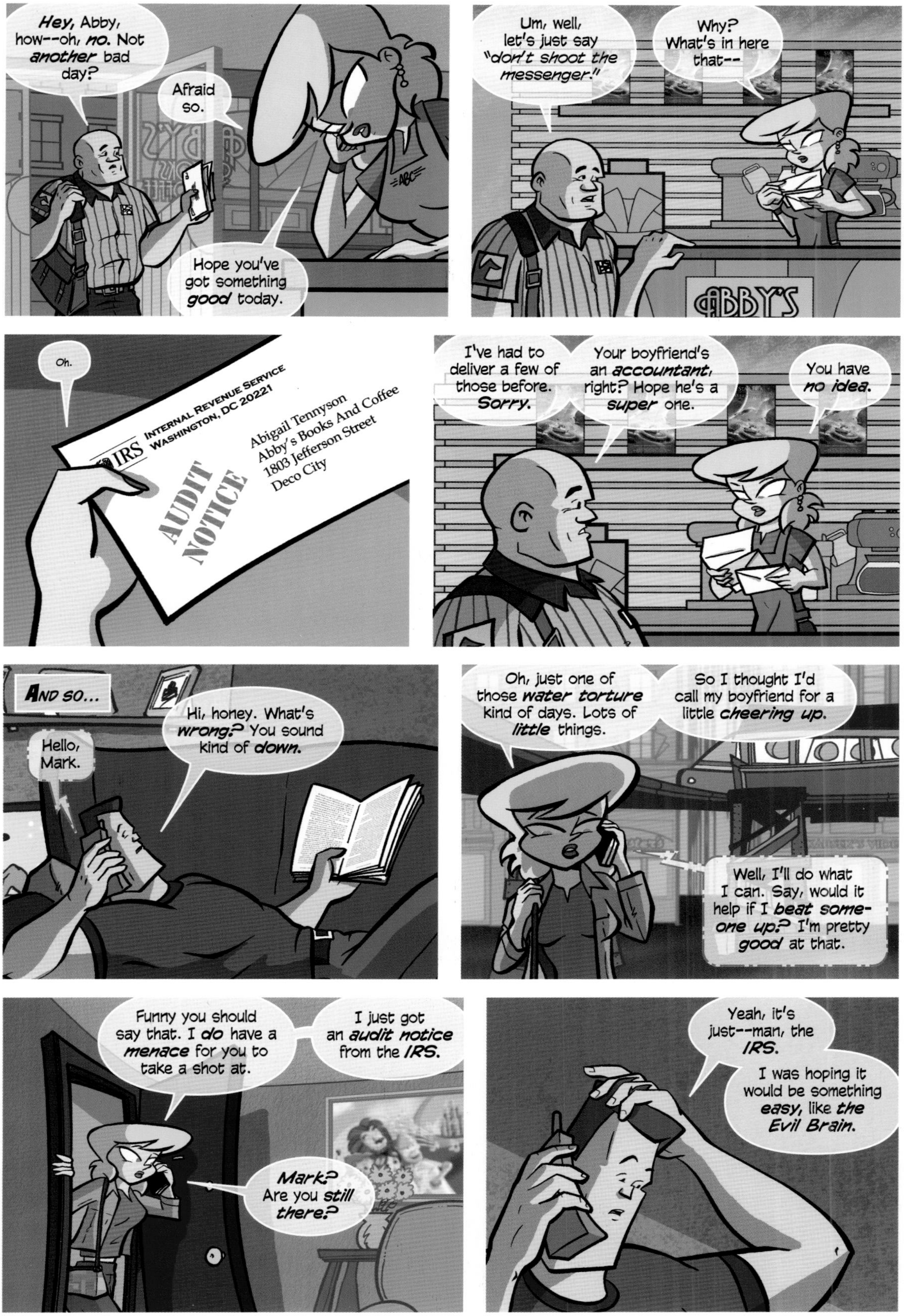
Hey, Abby, how--oh, no. Not another bad day?
Afraid so.
Hope you've got something good today.
Um, well, let's just say "don't shoot the messenger."
Why? What's in here that--
Oh.
INTERNAL REVENUE SERVICE
WASHINGTON, DC 20221
IRS
Abigail Tennyson
Abby's Books And Coffee
1803 Jefferson Street
Deco City
AUDIT NOTICE
I've had to deliver a few of those before. Sorry.
Your boyfriend's an accountant, right? Hope he's a super one.
You have no idea.
AND SO...
Hello, Mark.
Hi, honey. What's wrong? You sound kind of down.
Oh, just one of those water torture kind of days. Lots of little things.
So I thought I'd call my boyfriend for a little cheering up.
Well, I'll do what I can. Say, would it help if I beat someone up? I'm pretty good at that.
Funny you should say that. I do have a menace for you to take a shot at.
I just got an audit notice from the IRS.
Mark? Are you still there?
Yeah, it's just--man, the IRS.
I was hoping it would be something easy, like the Evil Brain.

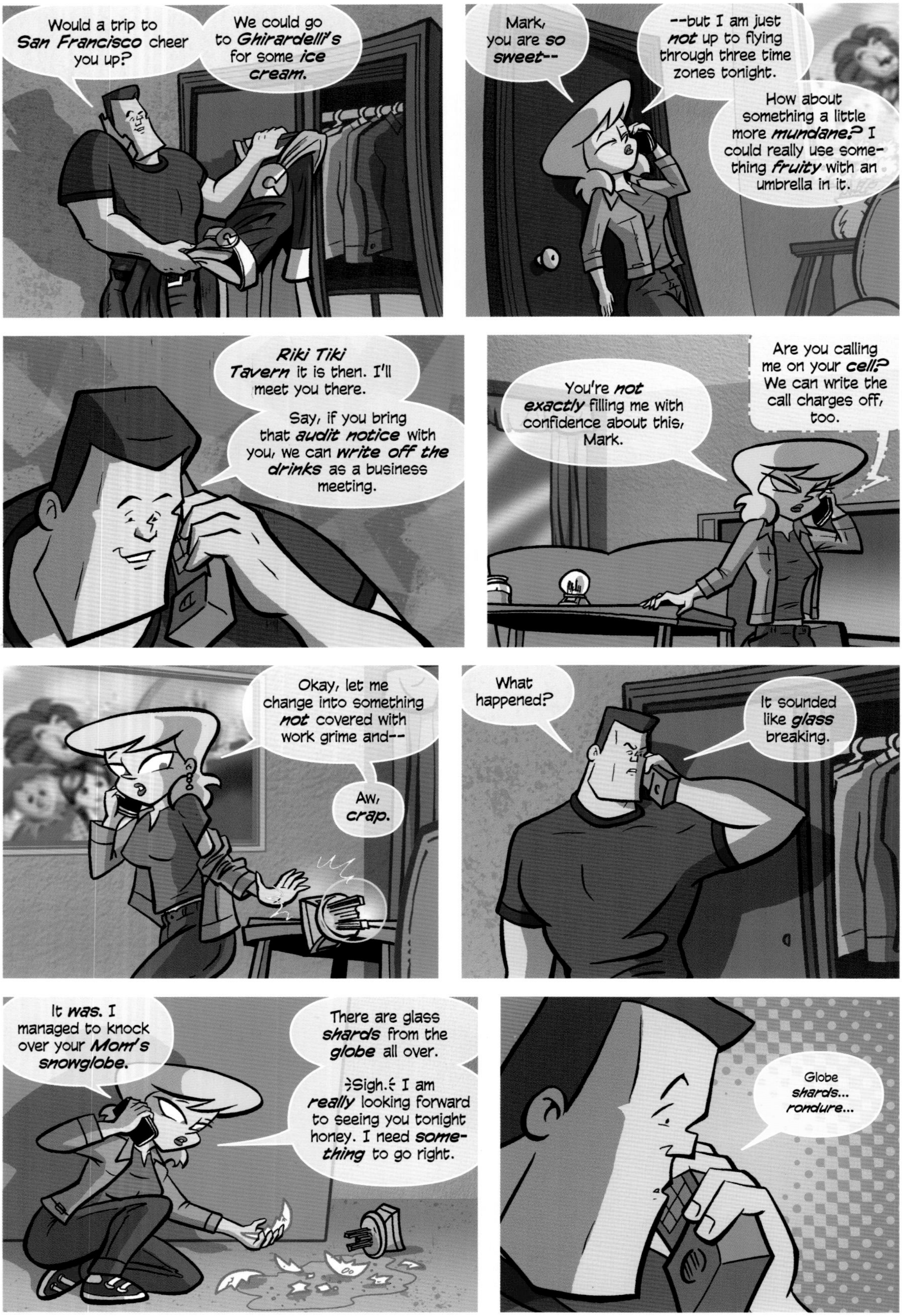

Would a trip to San Francisco cheer you up?
We could go to Ghirardelli's for some ice cream.
Mark, you are so sweet--
--but I am just not up to flying through three time zones tonight.
How about something a little more mundane? I could really use something fruity with an umbrella in it.
Riki Tiki Tavern it is then. I'll meet you there.
Say, if you bring that audit notice with you, we can write off the drinks as a business meeting.
You're not exactly filling me with confidence about this, Mark.
Are you calling me on your cell? We can write the call charges off, too.
Okay, let me change into something not covered with work grime and--
Aw, crap.
What happened?
It sounded like glass breaking.
It was. I managed to knock over your Mom's snowglobe.
There are glass shards from the globe all over.
⊰Sigh.⊱ I am really looking forward to seeing you tonight honey. I need something to go right.
Globe shards... rondure...

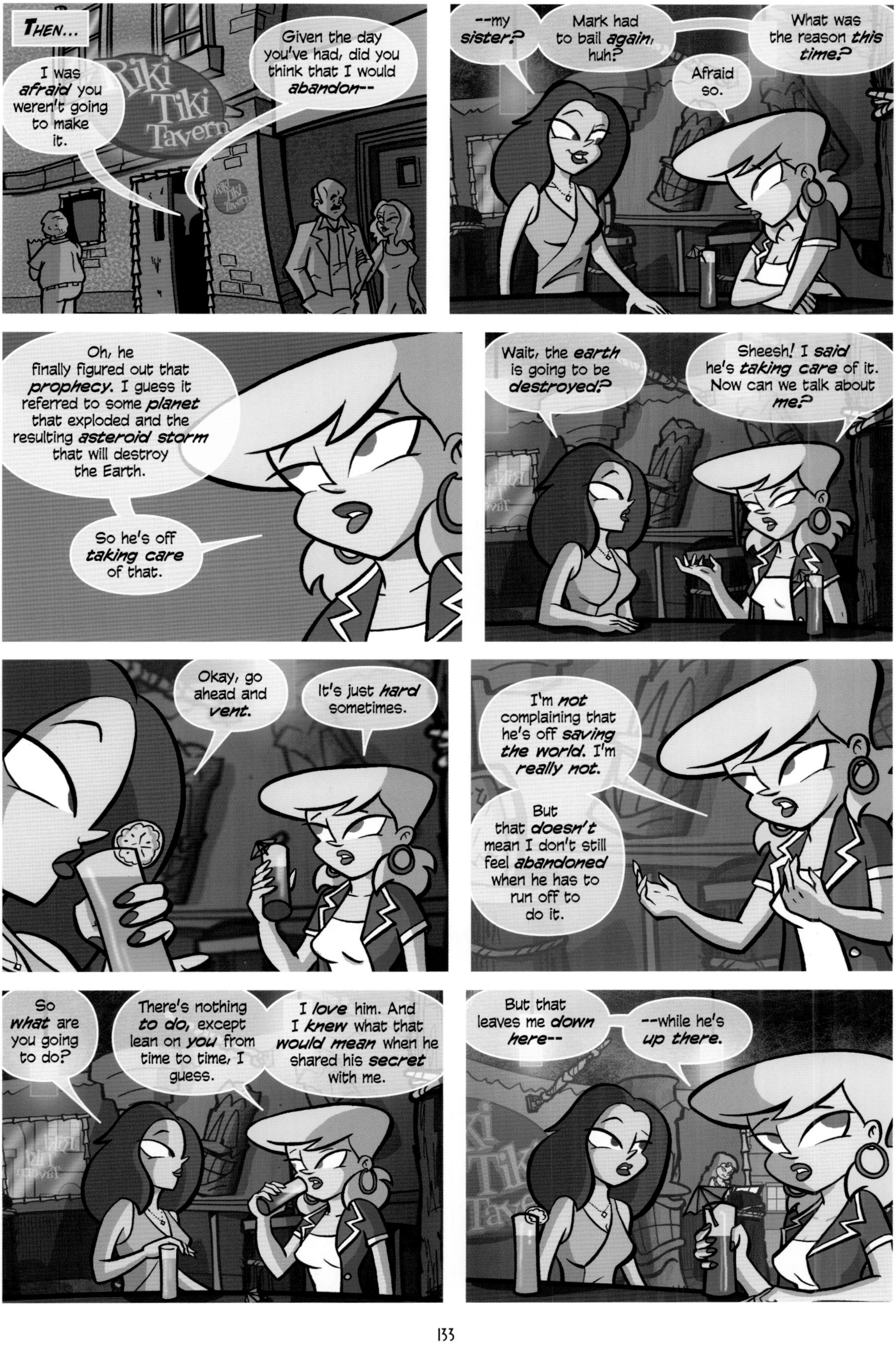
THEN...
I was *afraid* you weren't going to make it.
Riki Tiki Tavern
Given the day you've had, did you think that I would *abandon--*
--my *sister?*
Mark had to bail *again*, huh?
Afraid so.
What was the reason *this time?*
Oh, he finally figured out that *prophecy*. I guess it referred to some *planet* that exploded and the resulting *asteroid storm* that will destroy the Earth.
So he's off *taking care* of that.
Wait, the *earth* is going to be *destroyed?*
Sheesh! I *said* he's *taking care* of it. Now can we talk about *me?*
Okay, go ahead and *vent*.
It's just *hard* sometimes.
I'm *not* complaining that he's off *saving the world*. I'm *really not*.
But that *doesn't* mean I don't still feel *abandoned* when he has to run off to do it.
So *what* are you going to do?
There's nothing *to do*, except lean on *you* from time to time, I guess.
I *love* him. And I *knew* what that *would mean* when he shared his *secret* with me.
But that leaves me *down here--*
--while he's *up there*.

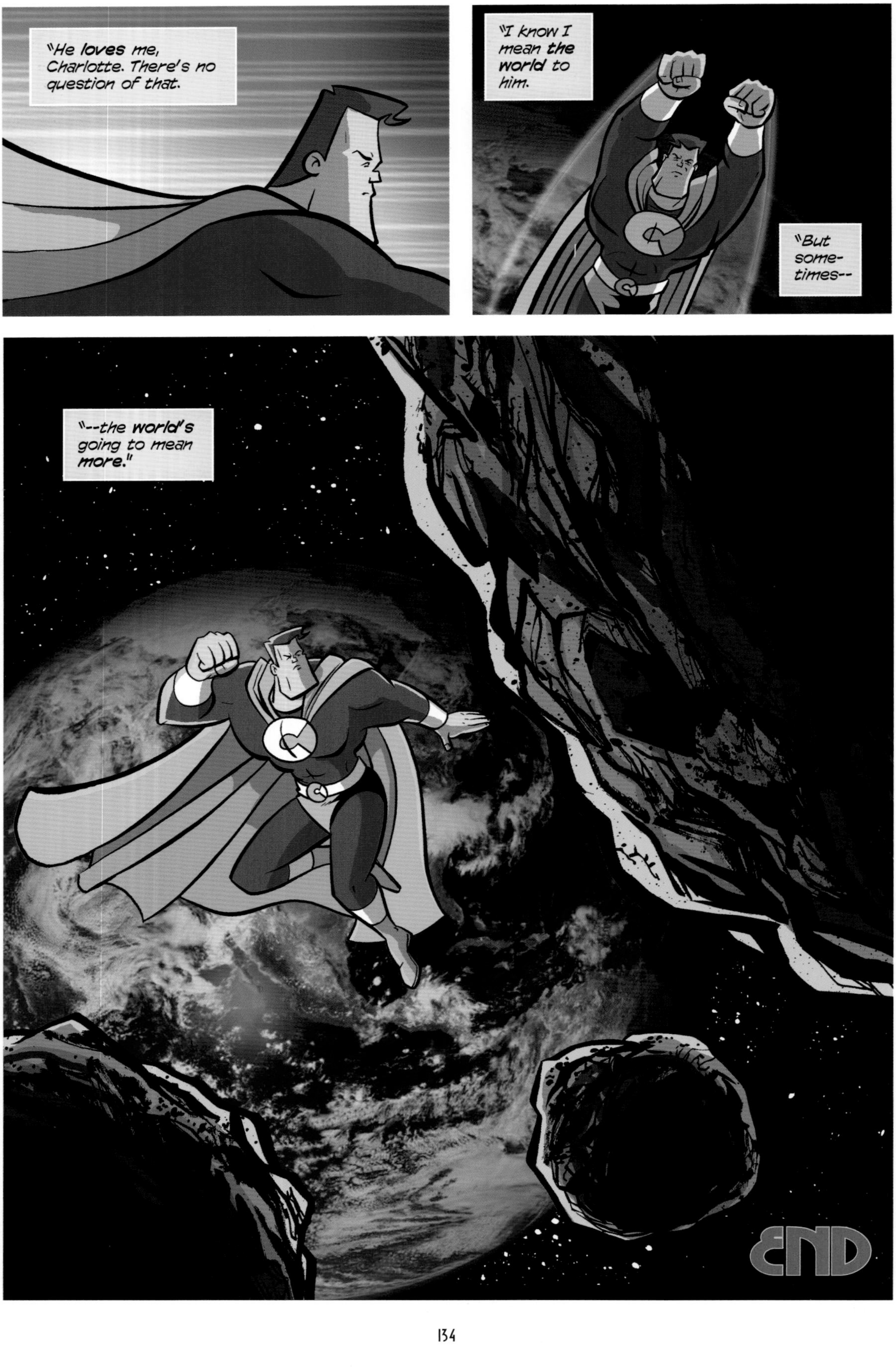
"He loves me, Charlotte. There's no question of that.
"I know I mean the world to him.
"But some-times--
"--the world's going to mean more."
END

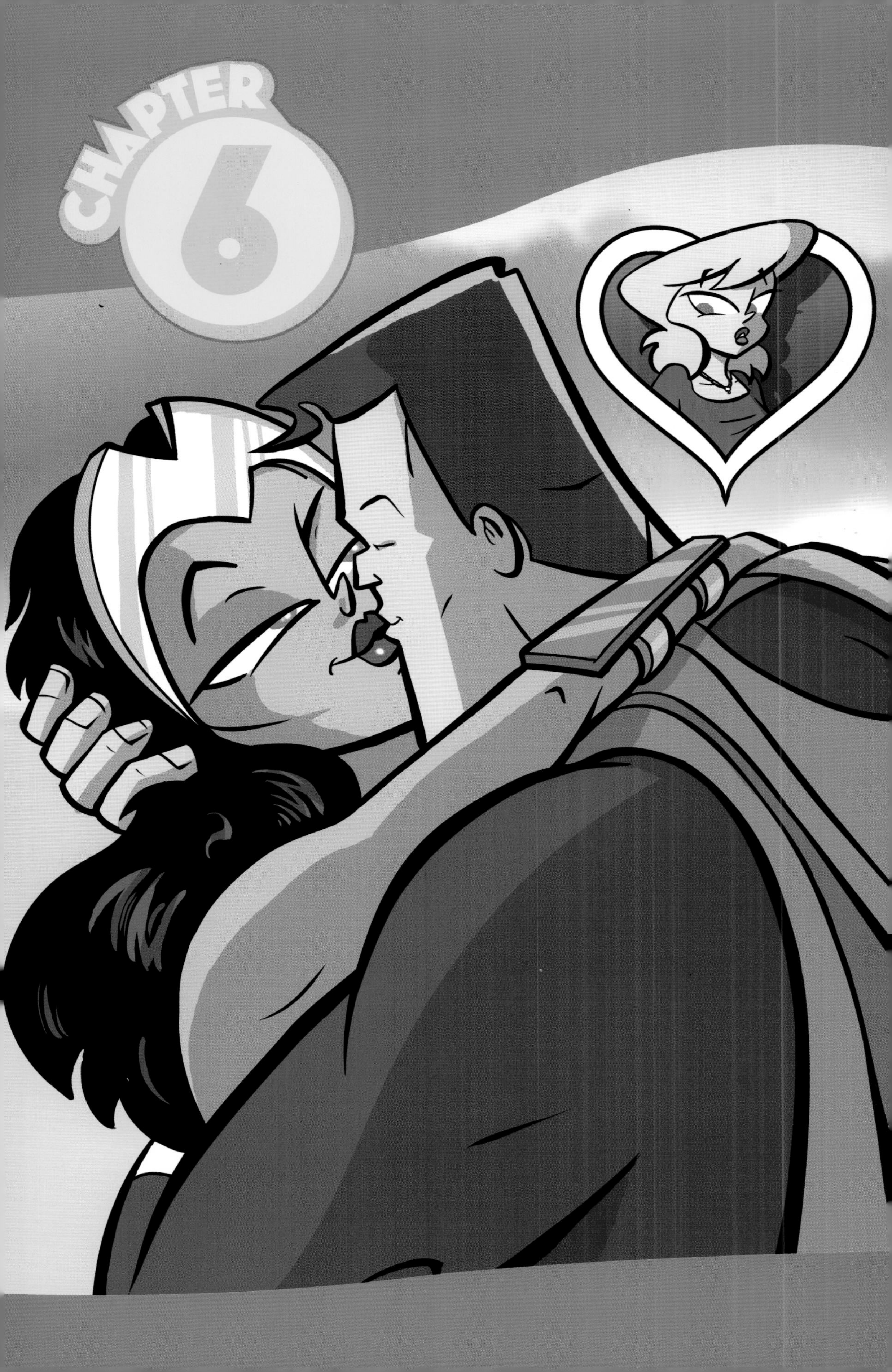
CHAPTER 6

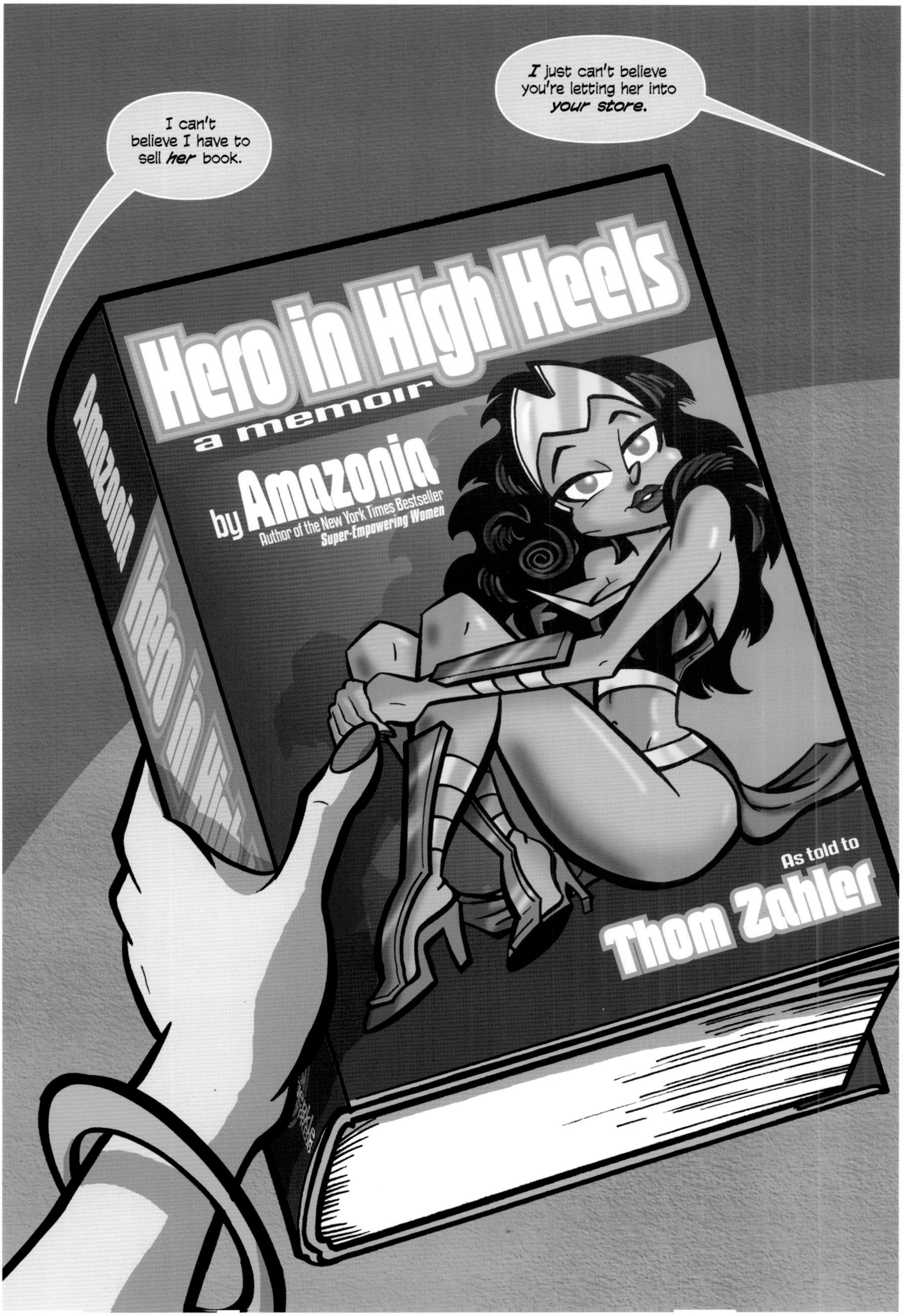
I can't believe I have to sell *her* book.
I just can't believe you're letting her into *your store.*
Hero in High Heels
a memoir
by Amazonia
Author of the New York Times Bestseller Super-Empowering Women
As told to
Thom Zahler
Amazonia
Hero in High Heels

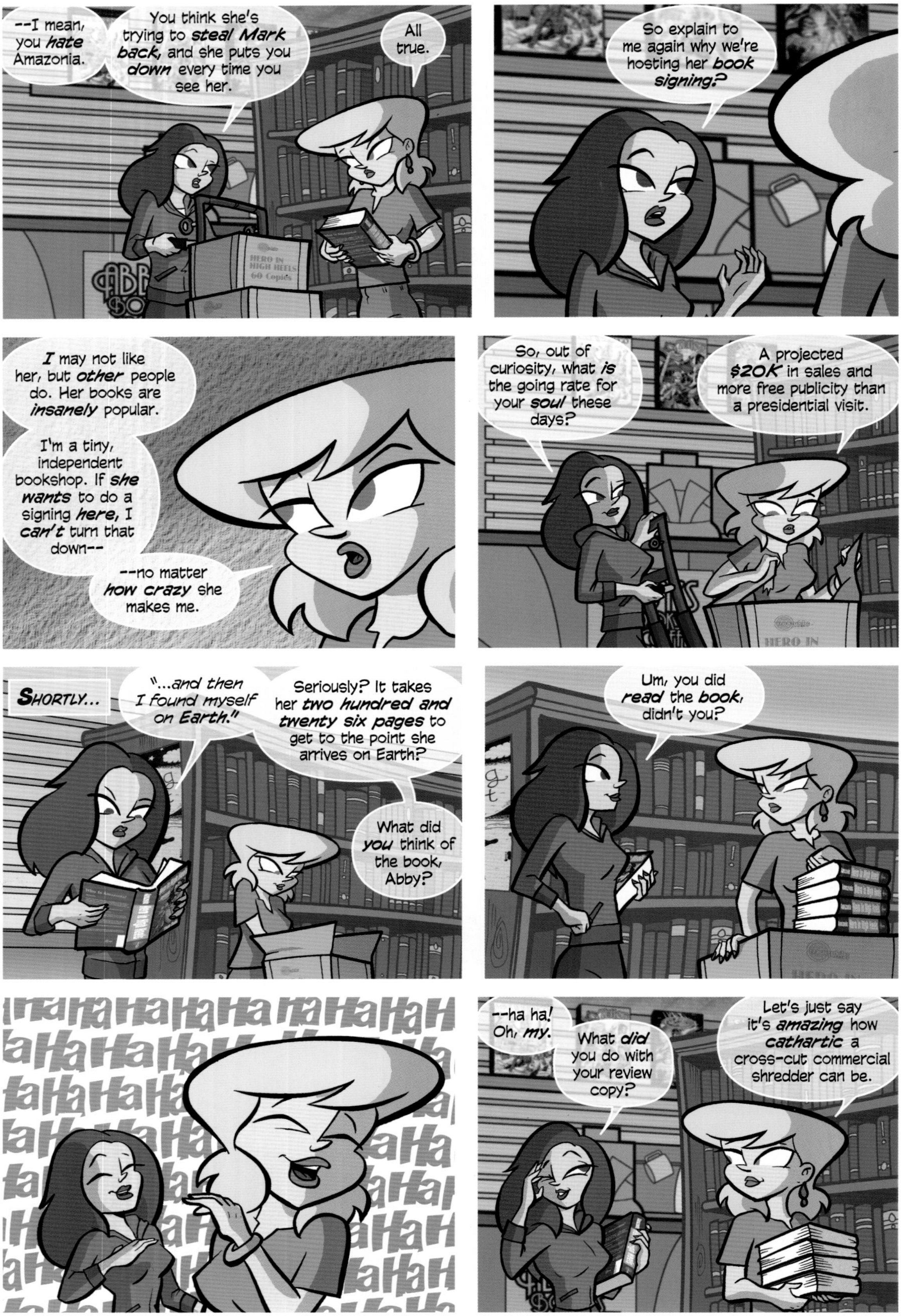
--I mean, you *hate* Amazonia.
You think she's trying to ***steal Mark back,*** and she puts you ***down*** every time you see her.
All true.
So explain to me again why we're hosting her ***book signing?***
I may not like her, but ***other*** people do. Her books are ***insanely*** popular.
I'm a tiny, independent bookshop. If ***she wants*** to do a signing ***here,*** I ***can't*** turn that down--
--no matter ***how crazy*** she makes me.
So, out of curiosity, what ***is*** the going rate for your ***soul*** these days?
A projected ***$20K*** in sales and more free publicity than a presidential visit.
SHORTLY...
"...*and then I found myself on Earth."*
Seriously? It takes her ***two hundred and twenty six pages*** to get to the point she arrives on Earth?
What did ***you*** think of the book, Abby?
Um, you did ***read*** the ***book,*** didn't you?
HaHaHaHaHaHaHaHaHaHaHaHa
--ha ha! Oh, ***my.***
What ***did*** you do with your review copy?
Let's just say it's ***amazing*** how ***cathartic*** a cross-cut commercial shredder can be.

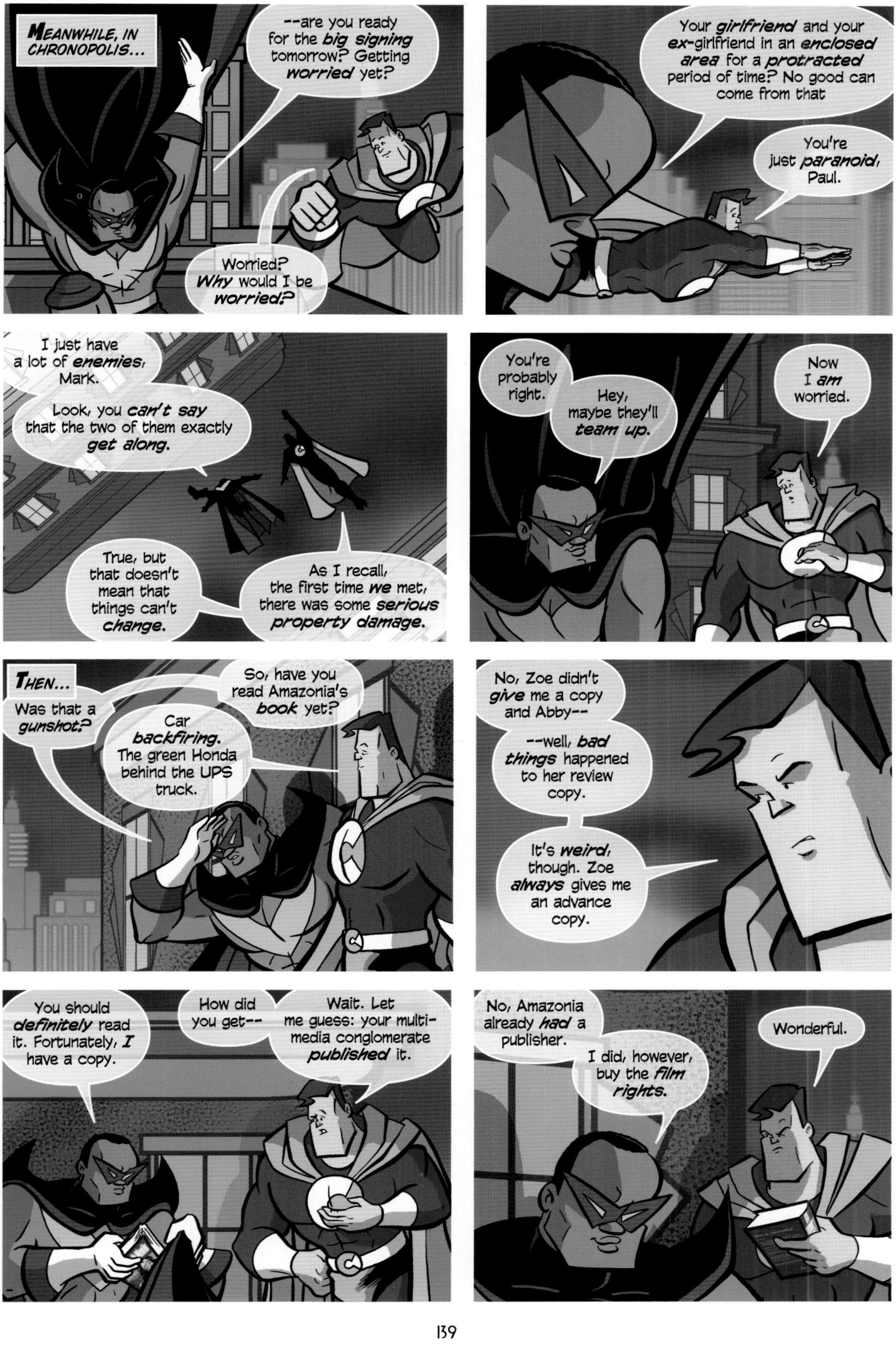
MEANWHILE, IN CHRONOPOLIS...
--are you ready for the big signing tomorrow? Getting worried yet?
Worried? Why would I be worried?
Your girlfriend and your ex-girlfriend in an enclosed area for a protracted period of time? No good can come from that
You're just paranoid, Paul.
I just have a lot of enemies, Mark.
Look, you can't say that the two of them exactly get along.
True, but that doesn't mean that things can't change.
As I recall, the first time we met, there was some serious property damage.
You're probably right.
Hey, maybe they'll team up.
Now I am worried.
THEN...
Was that a gunshot?
So, have you read Amazonia's book yet?
Car backfiring. The green Honda behind the UPS truck.
No, Zoe didn't give me a copy and Abby--
--well, bad things happened to her review copy.
It's weird, though. Zoe always gives me an advance copy.
You should definitely read it. Fortunately, I have a copy.
How did you get--
Wait. Let me guess: your multi-media conglomerate published it.
No, Amazonia already had a publisher.
I did, however, buy the film rights.
Wonderful.

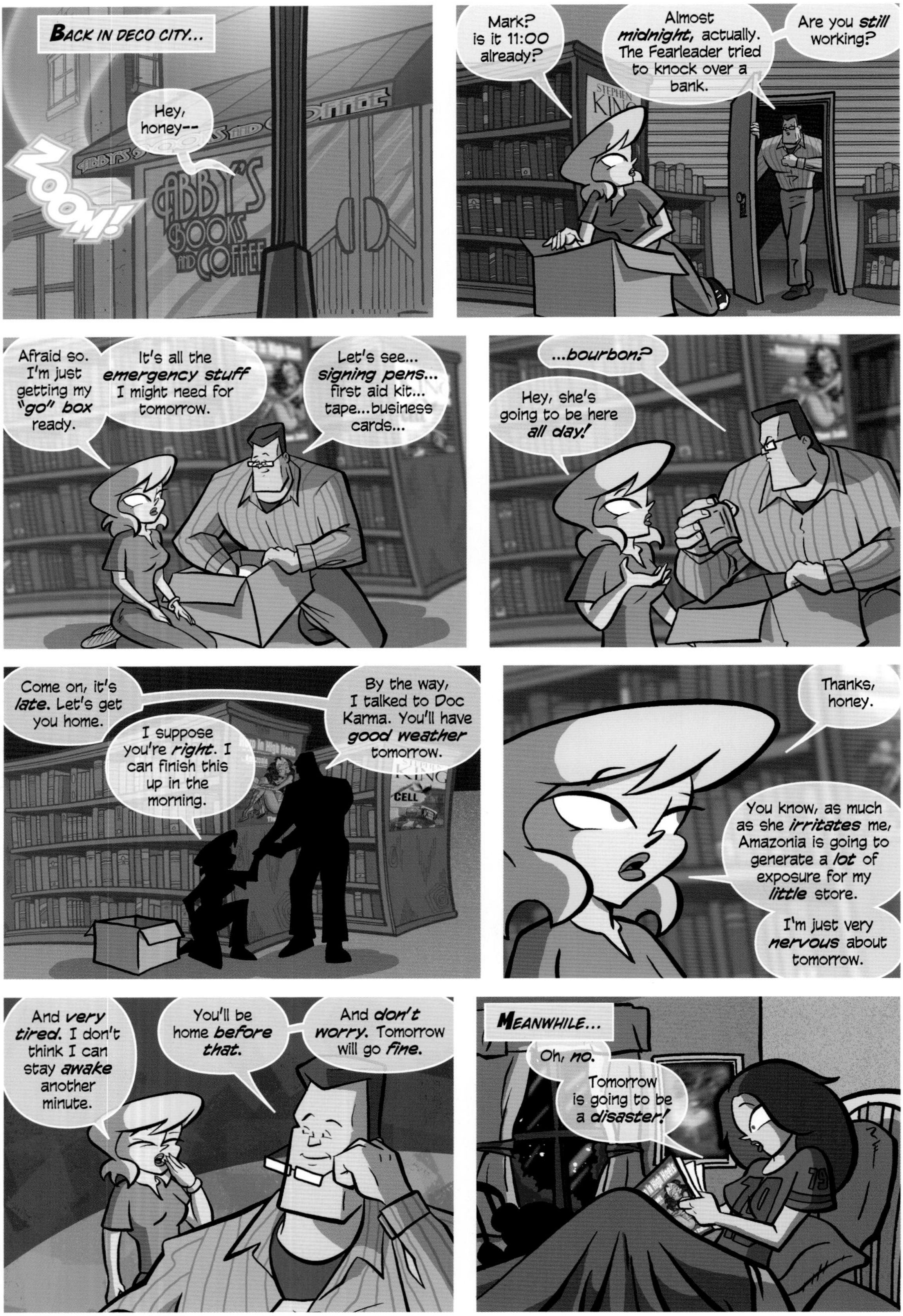

BACK IN DECO CITY...
Hey, honey--
ZOOM!
ABBY'S BOOKS AND COFFEE
Mark? is it 11:00 already?
Almost *midnight*, actually. The Fearleader tried to knock over a bank.
Are you *still* working?
Afraid so. I'm just getting my *"go" box* ready.
It's all the *emergency stuff* I might need for tomorrow.
Let's see... *signing pens*... first aid kit... tape...business cards...
...*bourbon?*
Hey, she's going to be here *all day!*
Come on, it's *late*. Let's get you home.
I suppose you're *right*. I can finish this up in the morning.
By the way, I talked to Doc Karma. You'll have *good weather* tomorrow.
Thanks, honey.
You know, as much as she *irritates* me, Amazonia is going to generate a *lot* of exposure for my *little* store.
I'm just very *nervous* about tomorrow.
And *very tired*. I don't think I can stay *awake* another minute.
You'll be home *before that*.
And *don't worry*. Tomorrow will go *fine*.
MEANWHILE...
Oh, *no*.
Tomorrow is going to be a *disaster!*

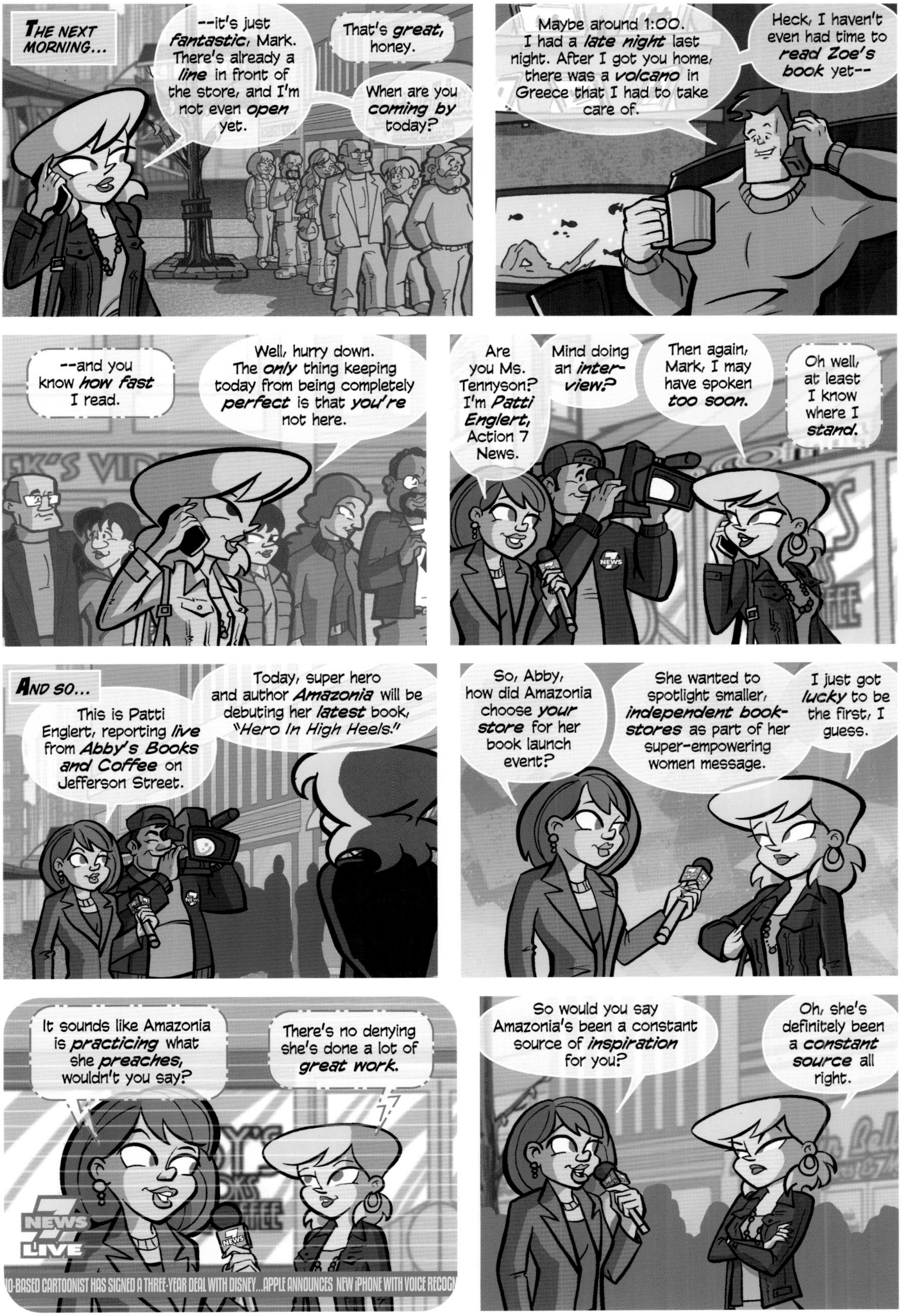
THE NEXT MORNING...
--it's just fantastic, Mark. There's already a line in front of the store, and I'm not even open yet.
That's great, honey.
When are you coming by today?
Maybe around 1:00. I had a late night last night. After I got you home, there was a volcano in Greece that I had to take care of.
Heck, I haven't even had time to read Zoe's book yet--
--and you know how fast I read.
Well, hurry down. The only thing keeping today from being completely perfect is that you're not here.
Are you Ms. Tennyson? I'm Patti Englert, Action 7 News.
Mind doing an inter-view?
Then again, Mark, I may have spoken too soon.
Oh well, at least I know where I stand.
AND SO...
This is Patti Englert, reporting live from Abby's Books and Coffee on Jefferson Street.
Today, super hero and author Amazonia will be debuting her latest book, "Hero In High Heels."
So, Abby, how did Amazonia choose your store for her book launch event?
She wanted to spotlight smaller, independent book-stores as part of her super-empowering women message.
I just got lucky to be the first, I guess.
It sounds like Amazonia is practicing what she preaches, wouldn't you say?
There's no denying she's done a lot of great work.
CARTOONIST HAS SIGNED A THREE-YEAR DEAL WITH DISNEY...APPLE ANNOUNCES NEW iPHONE WITH VOICE
So would you say Amazonia's been a constant source of inspiration for you?
Oh, she's definitely been a constant source all right.

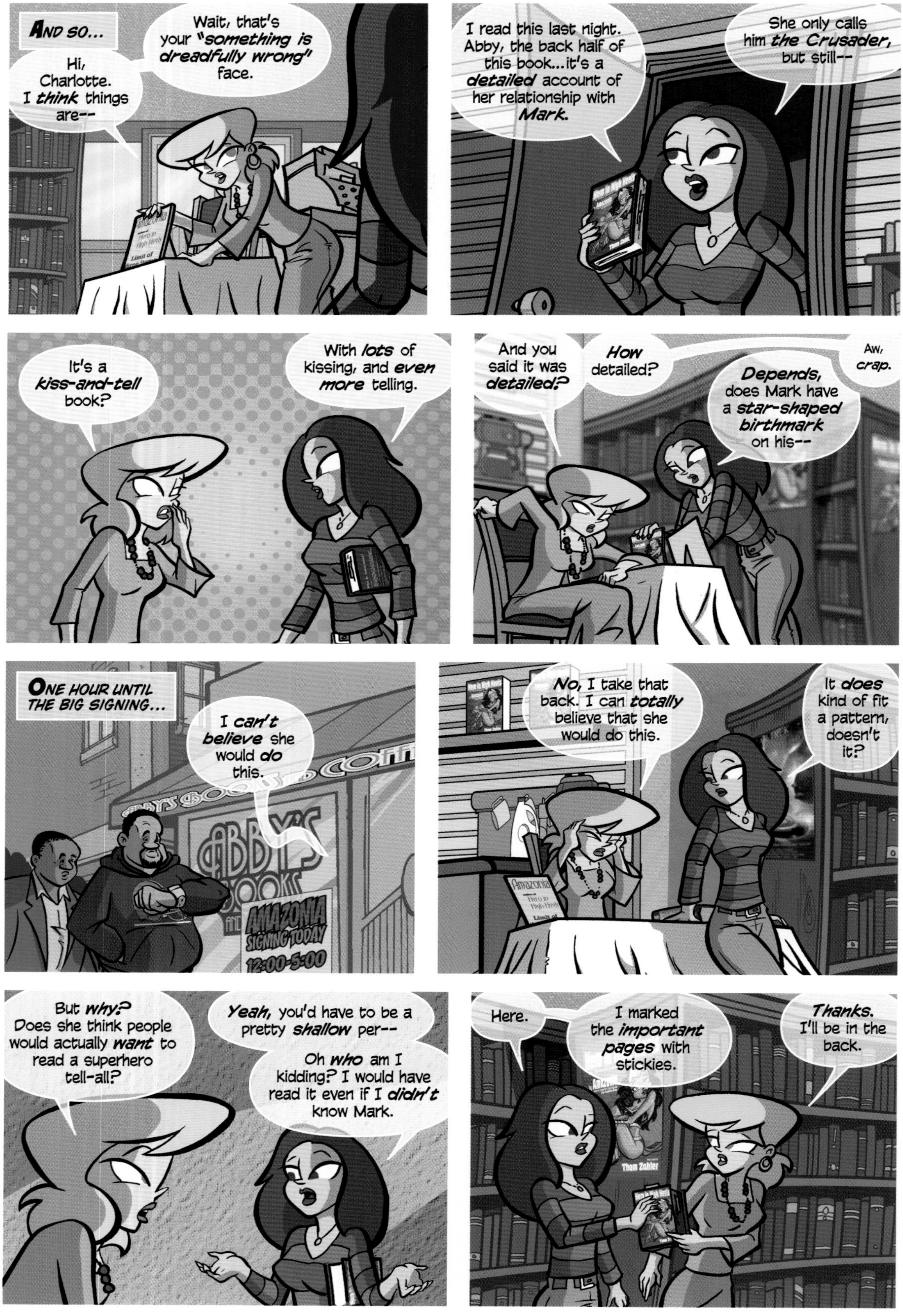
AND SO...
Hi, Charlotte. I *think* things are--
Wait, that's your *"something is dreadfully wrong"* face.
I read this last night. Abby, the back half of this book...it's a *detailed* account of her relationship with *Mark.*
She only calls him *the Crusader,* but still--
It's a *kiss-and-tell* book?
With *lots* of kissing, and *even more* telling.
And you said it was *detailed?*
How detailed?
Depends, does Mark have a *star-shaped birthmark* on his--
Aw, *crap.*
ONE HOUR UNTIL THE BIG SIGNING...
I *can't believe* she would *do* this.
ABBY'S BOOKS
AMAZONIA SIGNING TODAY 12:00-5:00
No, I take that back. I can *totally* believe that she would do this.
It *does* kind of fit a pattern, doesn't it?
Amazonia
Hero to High Heels
But *why?* Does she think people would actually *want* to read a superhero tell-all?
Yeah, you'd have to be a pretty *shallow* per--
Oh *who* am I kidding? I would have read it even if I *didn't* know Mark.
Here.
I marked the *important pages* with stickies.
Thanks. I'll be in the back.

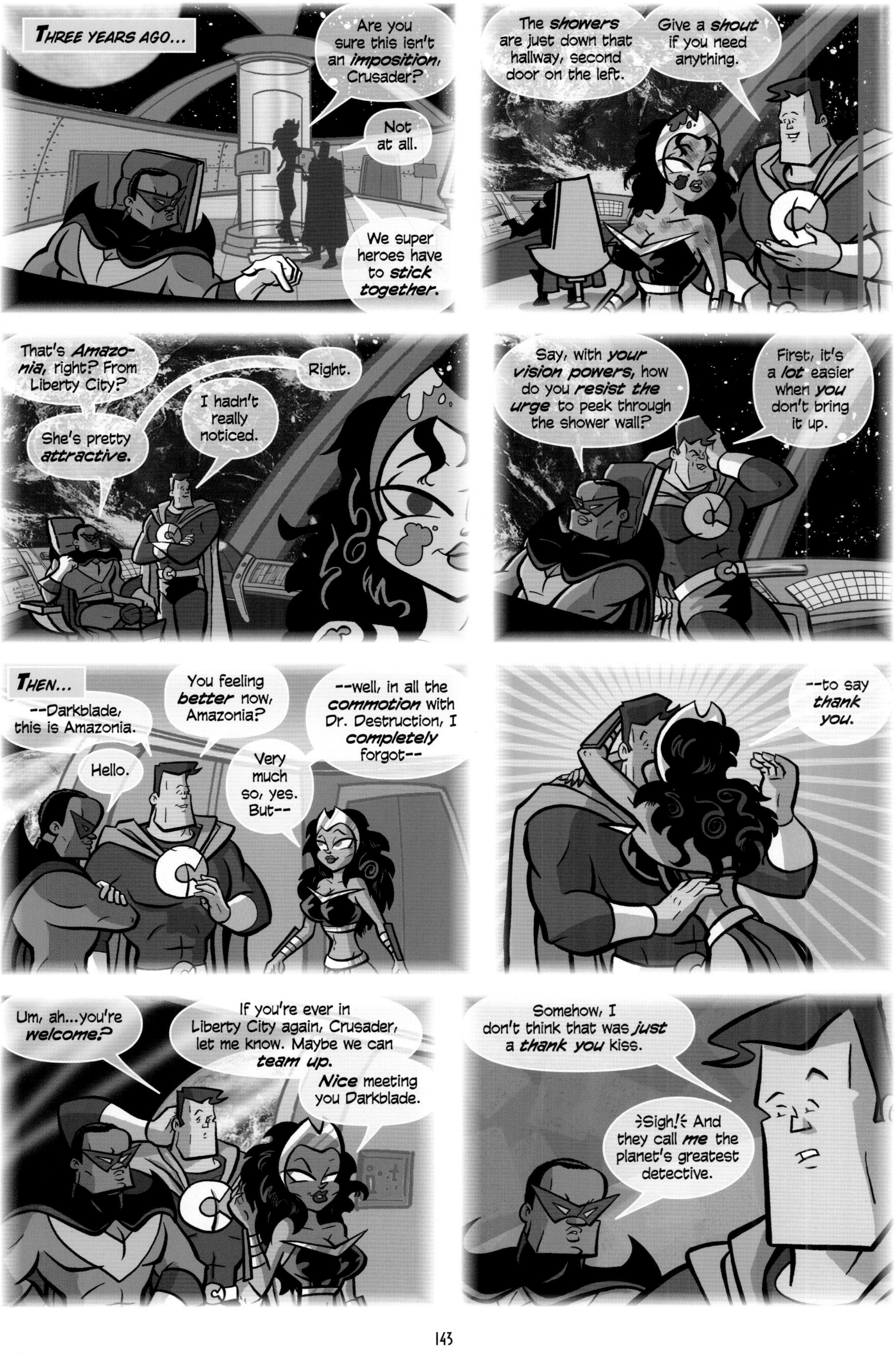
THREE YEARS AGO...
Are you sure this isn't an imposition, Crusader?
Not at all.
We super heroes have to stick together.
The showers are just down that hallway, second door on the left.
Give a shout if you need anything.
That's Amazonia, right? From Liberty City?
Right.
She's pretty attractive.
I hadn't really noticed.
Say, with your vision powers, how do you resist the urge to peek through the shower wall?
First, it's a lot easier when you don't bring it up.
THEN...
--Darkblade, this is Amazonia.
Hello.
You feeling better now, Amazonia?
Very much so, yes. But--
--well, in all the commotion with Dr. Destruction, I completely forgot--
--to say thank you.
Um, ah...you're welcome?
If you're ever in Liberty City again, Crusader, let me know. Maybe we can team up.
Nice meeting you Darkblade.
Somehow, I don't think that was just a thank you kiss.
Sigh! And they call me the planet's greatest detective.

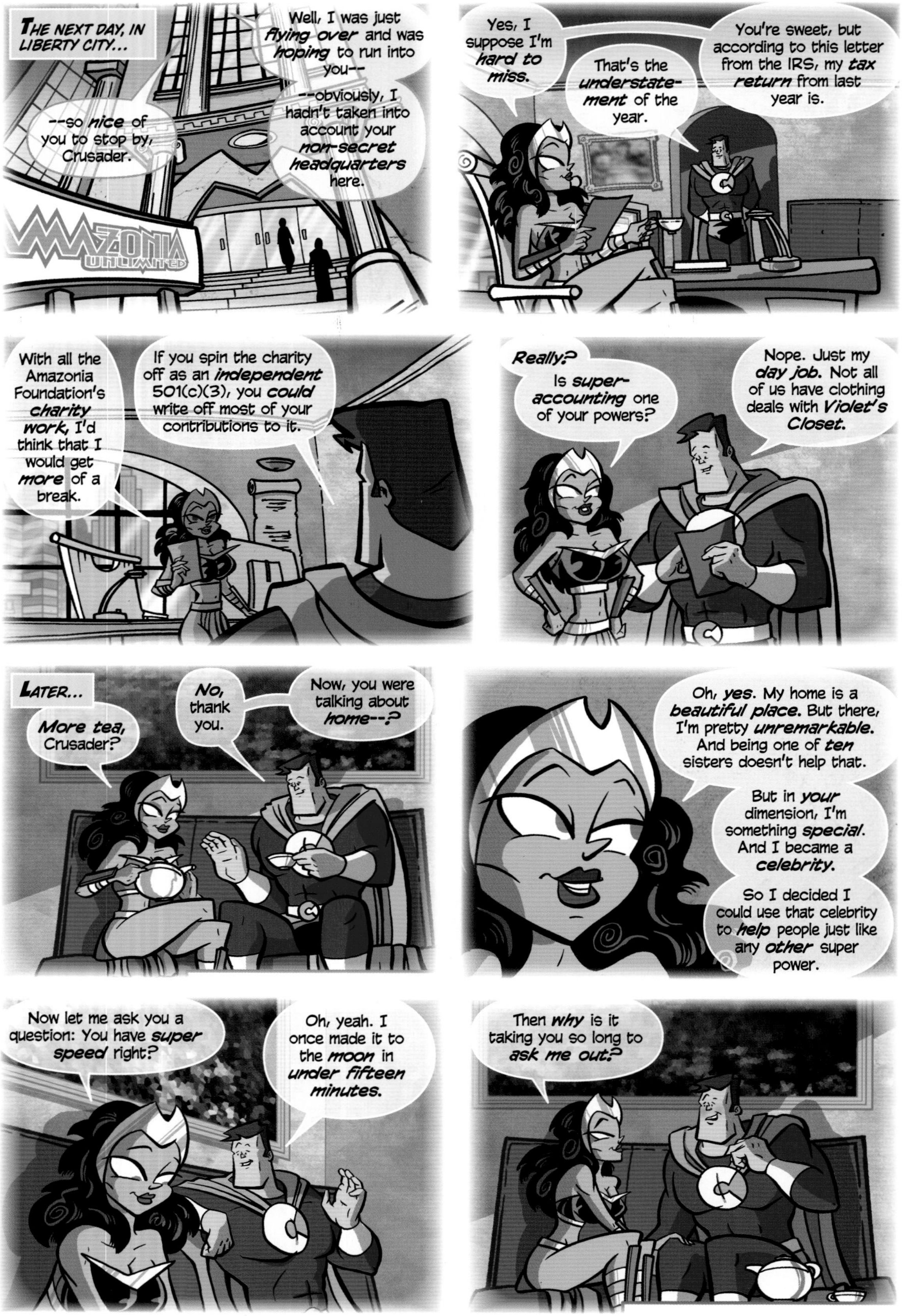
THE NEXT DAY, IN LIBERTY CITY...
--so nice of you to stop by, Crusader.
Well, I was just flying over and was hoping to run into you--
--obviously, I hadn't taken into account your non-secret headquarters here.
AMAZONIA UNLIMITED
Yes, I suppose I'm hard to miss.
That's the understatement of the year.
You're sweet, but according to this letter from the IRS, my tax return from last year is.
With all the Amazonia Foundation's charity work, I'd think that I would get more of a break.
If you spin the charity off as an independent 501(c)(3), you could write off most of your contributions to it.
Really? Is super-accounting one of your powers?
Nope. Just my day job. Not all of us have clothing deals with Violet's Closet.
LATER...
More tea, Crusader?
No, thank you.
Now, you were talking about home--?
Oh, yes. My home is a beautiful place. But there, I'm pretty unremarkable. And being one of ten sisters doesn't help that.
But in your dimension, I'm something special. And I became a celebrity.
So I decided I could use that celebrity to help people just like any other super power.
Now let me ask you a question: You have super speed right?
Oh, yeah. I once made it to the moon in under fifteen minutes.
Then why is it taking you so long to ask me out?

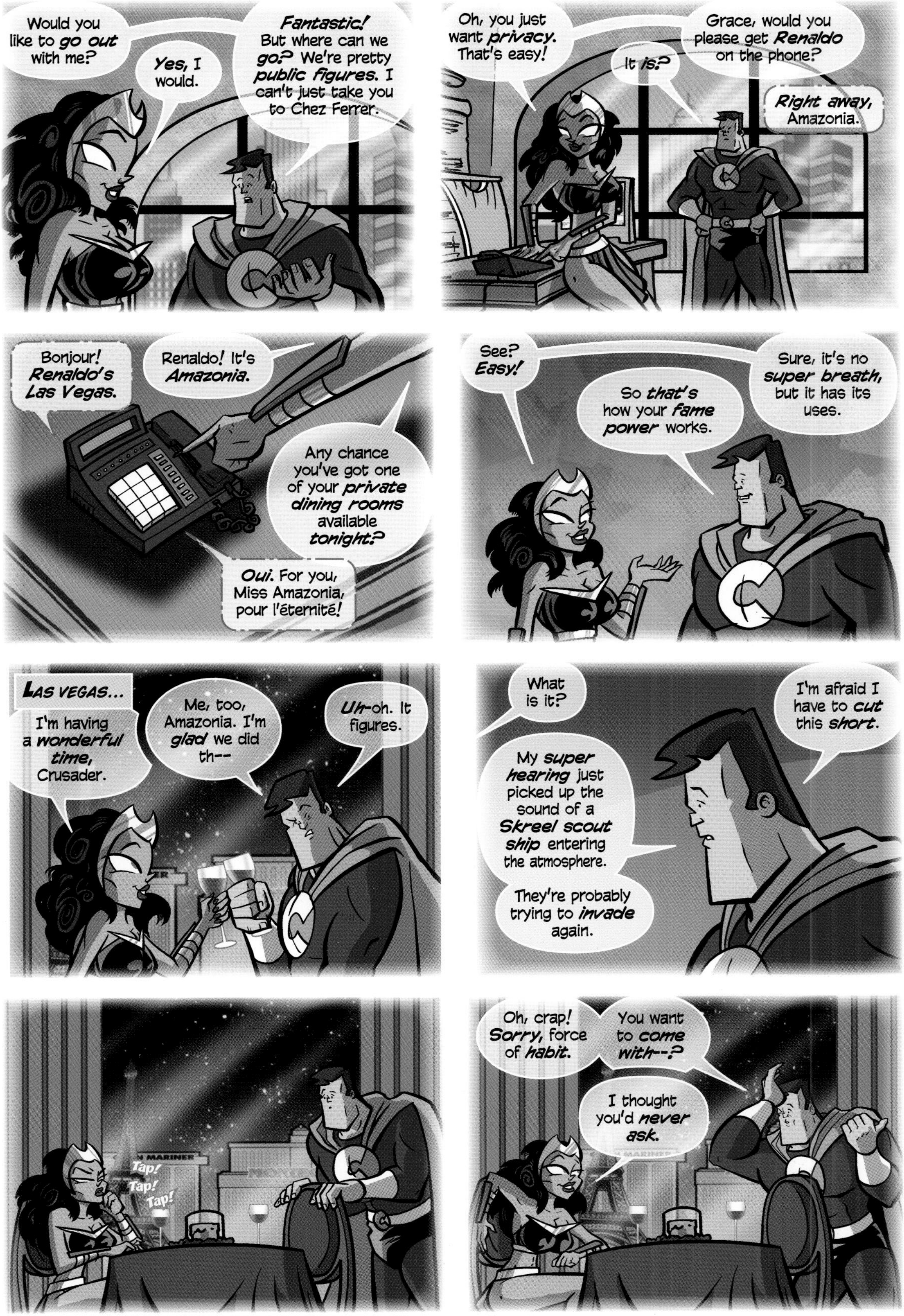
Would you like to go out with me?
Yes, I would.
Fantastic! But where can we go? We're pretty public figures. I can't just take you to Chez Ferrer.
Oh, you just want privacy. That's easy!
It is?
Grace, would you please get Renaldo on the phone?
Right away, Amazonia.
Bonjour! Renaldo's Las Vegas.
Renaldo! It's Amazonia.
Any chance you've got one of your private dining rooms available tonight?
Oui. For you, Miss Amazonia, pour l'éternité!
See? Easy!
So that's how your fame power works.
Sure, it's no super breath, but it has its uses.
LAS VEGAS...
I'm having a wonderful time, Crusader.
Me, too, Amazonia. I'm glad we did th--
Uh-oh. It figures.
What is it?
I'm afraid I have to cut this short.
My super hearing just picked up the sound of a Skreel scout ship entering the atmosphere.
They're probably trying to invade again.
Tap!
Tap!
Tap!
Oh, crap! Sorry, force of habit.
You want to come with--?
I thought you'd never ask.

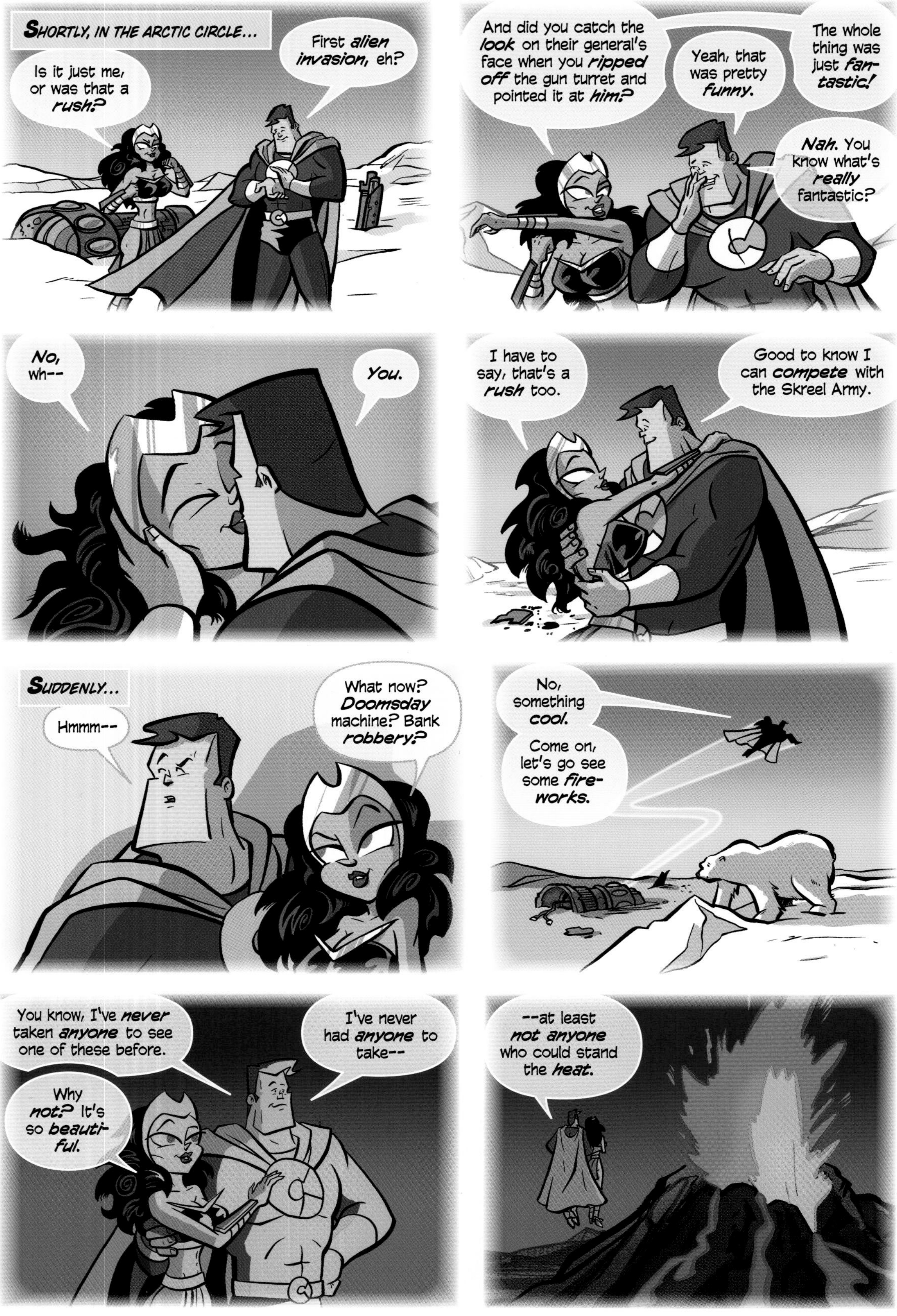

SHORTLY, IN THE ARCTIC CIRCLE...
Is it just me, or was that a rush?
First alien invasion, eh?
And did you catch the look on their general's face when you ripped off the gun turret and pointed it at him?
Yeah, that was pretty funny.
The whole thing was just fantastic!
Nah. You know what's really fantastic?
No, wh--
You.
I have to say, that's a rush too.
Good to know I can compete with the Skreel Army.
SUDDENLY...
Hmmm--
What now? Doomsday machine? Bank robbery?
No, something cool.
Come on, let's go see some fireworks.
You know, I've never taken anyone to see one of these before.
Why not? It's so beautiful.
I've never had anyone to take--
--at least not anyone who could stand the heat.

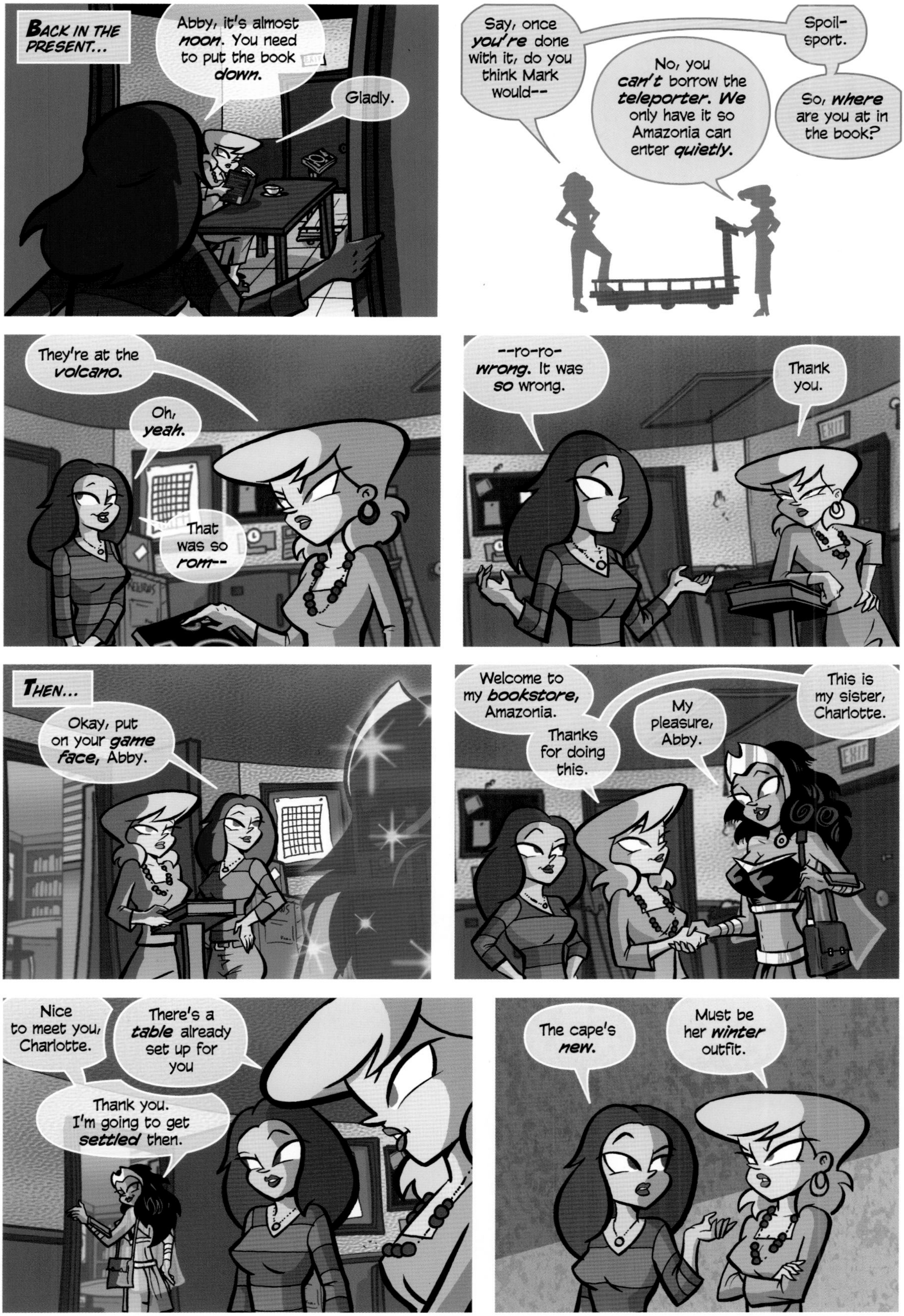
BACK IN THE PRESENT...
Abby, it's almost **noon**. You need to put the book **down**.
EXIT
Gladly.
Say, once **you're** done with it, do you think Mark would--
No, you **can't** borrow the **teleporter**. **We** only have it so Amazonia can enter **quietly**.
Spoil-sport.
So, **where** are you at in the book?
They're at the **volcano**.
Oh, **yeah**.
That was so **rom**--
--ro-ro- **wrong**. It was **so** wrong.
Thank you.
EXIT
THEN...
Okay, put on your **game face**, Abby.
Welcome to my **bookstore**, Amazonia.
Thanks for doing this.
My pleasure, Abby.
This is my sister, Charlotte.
EXIT
Nice to meet you, Charlotte.
There's a **table** already set up for you
Thank you. I'm going to get **settled** then.
The cape's **new**.
Must be her **winter** outfit.

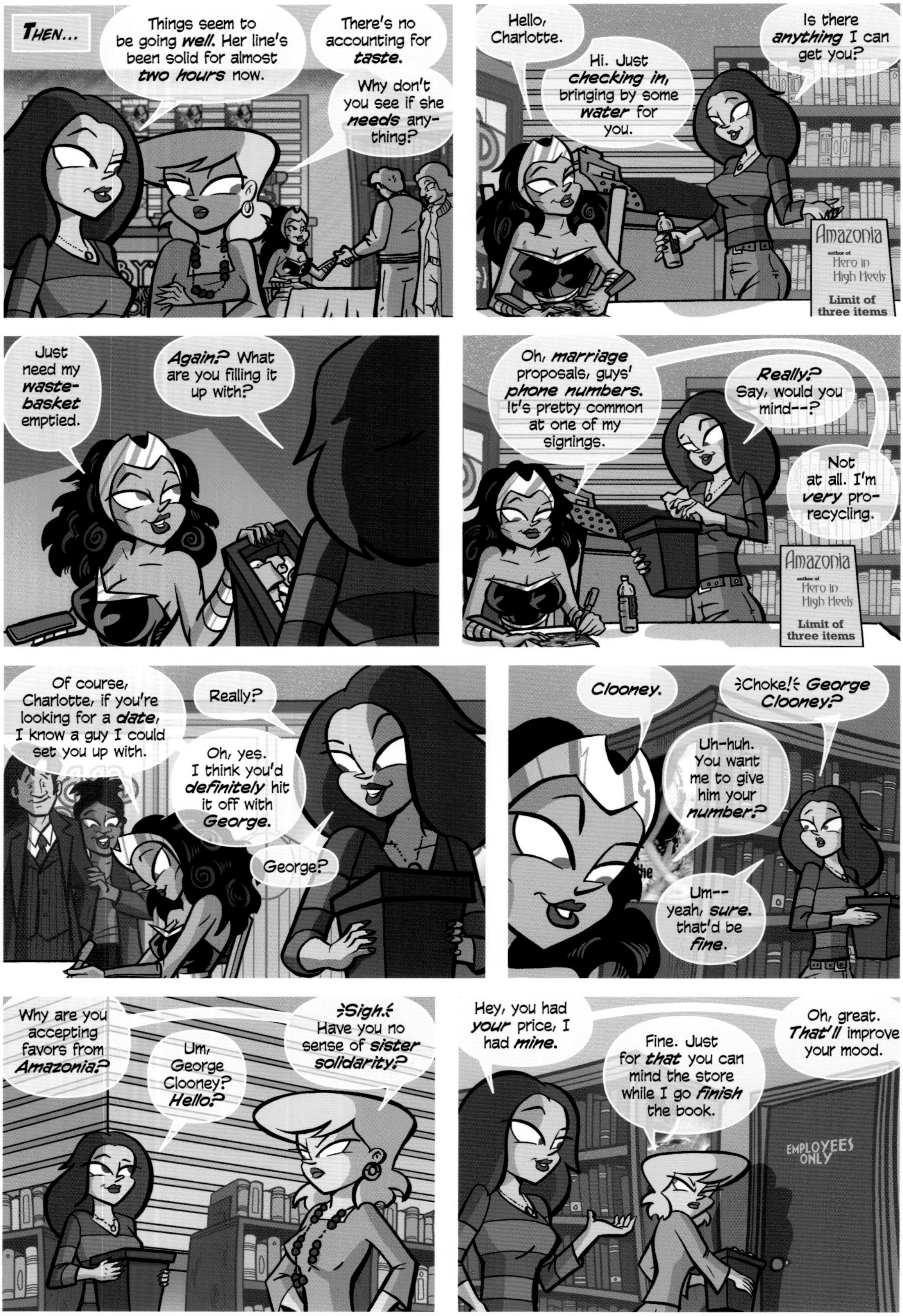
THEN...
Things seem to be going *well.* Her line's been solid for almost *two hours* now.
There's no accounting for *taste.*
Why don't you see if she *needs* anything?
Hello, Charlotte.
Hi. Just *checking in,* bringing by some *water* for you.
Is there *anything* I can get you?
Amazonia author of Hero in High Heels
Limit of three items
Just need my *wastebasket* emptied.
Again? What are you filling it up with?
Oh, *marriage* proposals, guys' *phone numbers.* It's pretty common at one of my signings.
Really? Say, would you mind--?
Not at all. I'm *very* pro-recycling.
Amazonia author of Hero in High Heels
Limit of three items
Of course, Charlotte, if you're looking for a *date,* I know a guy I could set you up with.
Really?
Oh, yes. I think you'd *definitely* hit it off with *George.*
George?
Clooney.
⁝Choke!⁝ *George Clooney?*
Uh-huh. You want me to give him your *number?*
Um-- yeah, *sure.* that'd be *fine.*
Why are you accepting favors from *Amazonia?*
Um, George Clooney? *Hello?*
⁝Sigh.⁝ Have you no sense of *sister solidarity?*
Hey, you had *your* price, I had *mine.*
Fine. Just for *that* you can mind the store while I go *finish* the book.
Oh, great. *That'll* improve your mood.
EMPLOYEES ONLY

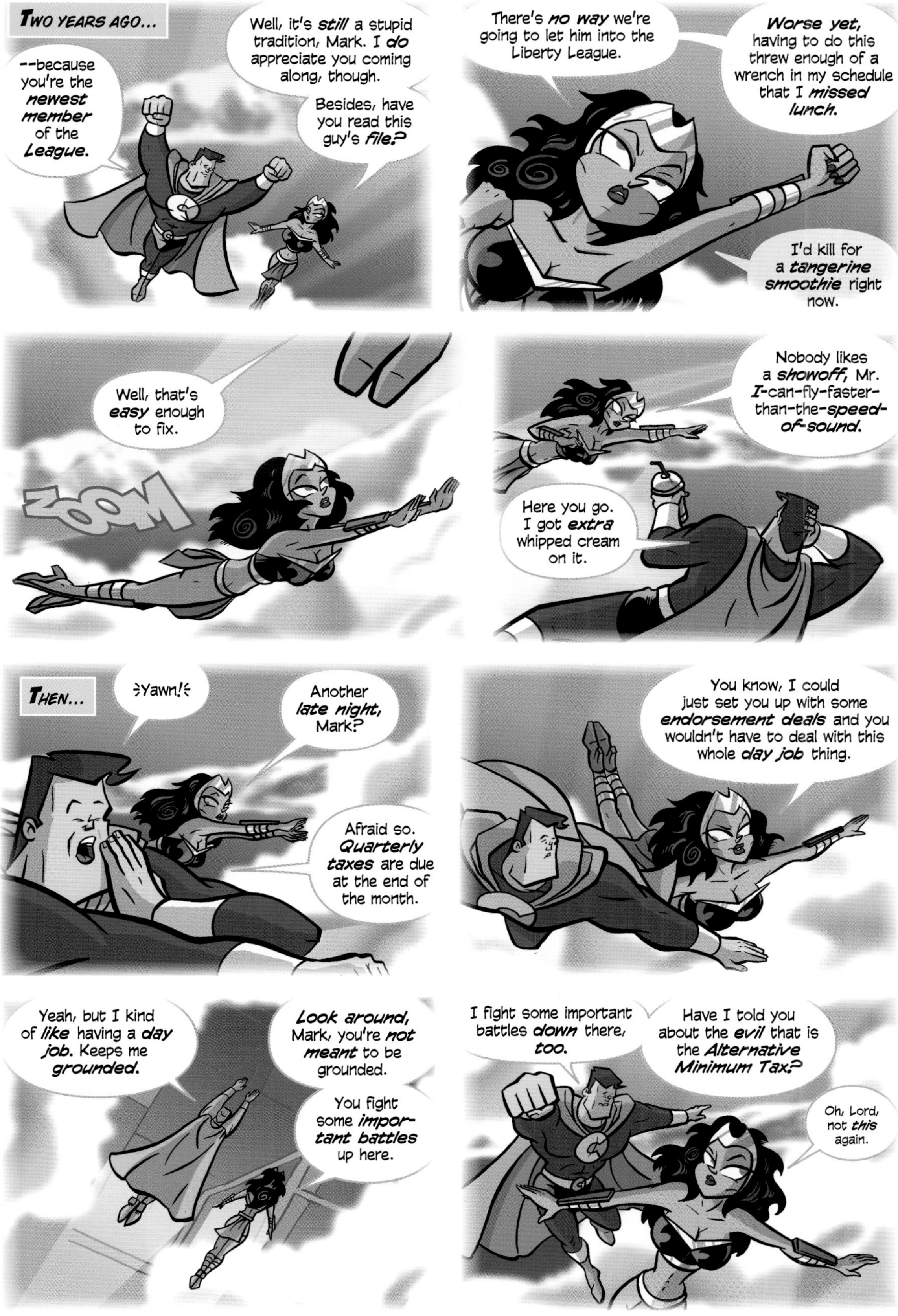

Two years ago...
--because you're the newest member of the League.
Well, it's still a stupid tradition, Mark. I do appreciate you coming along, though.
Besides, have you read this guy's file?
There's no way we're going to let him into the Liberty League.
Worse yet, having to do this threw enough of a wrench in my schedule that I missed lunch.
I'd kill for a tangerine smoothie right now.
Well, that's easy enough to fix.
ZOOM
Nobody likes a showoff, Mr. I-can-fly-faster-than-the-speed-of-sound.
Here you go. I got extra whipped cream on it.
Then...
Yawn!
Another late night, Mark?
Afraid so. Quarterly taxes are due at the end of the month.
You know, I could just set you up with some endorsement deals and you wouldn't have to deal with this whole day job thing.
Yeah, but I kind of like having a day job. Keeps me grounded.
Look around, Mark, you're not meant to be grounded.
You fight some important battles up here.
I fight some important battles down there, too.
Have I told you about the evil that is the Alternative Minimum Tax?
Oh, Lord, not this again.

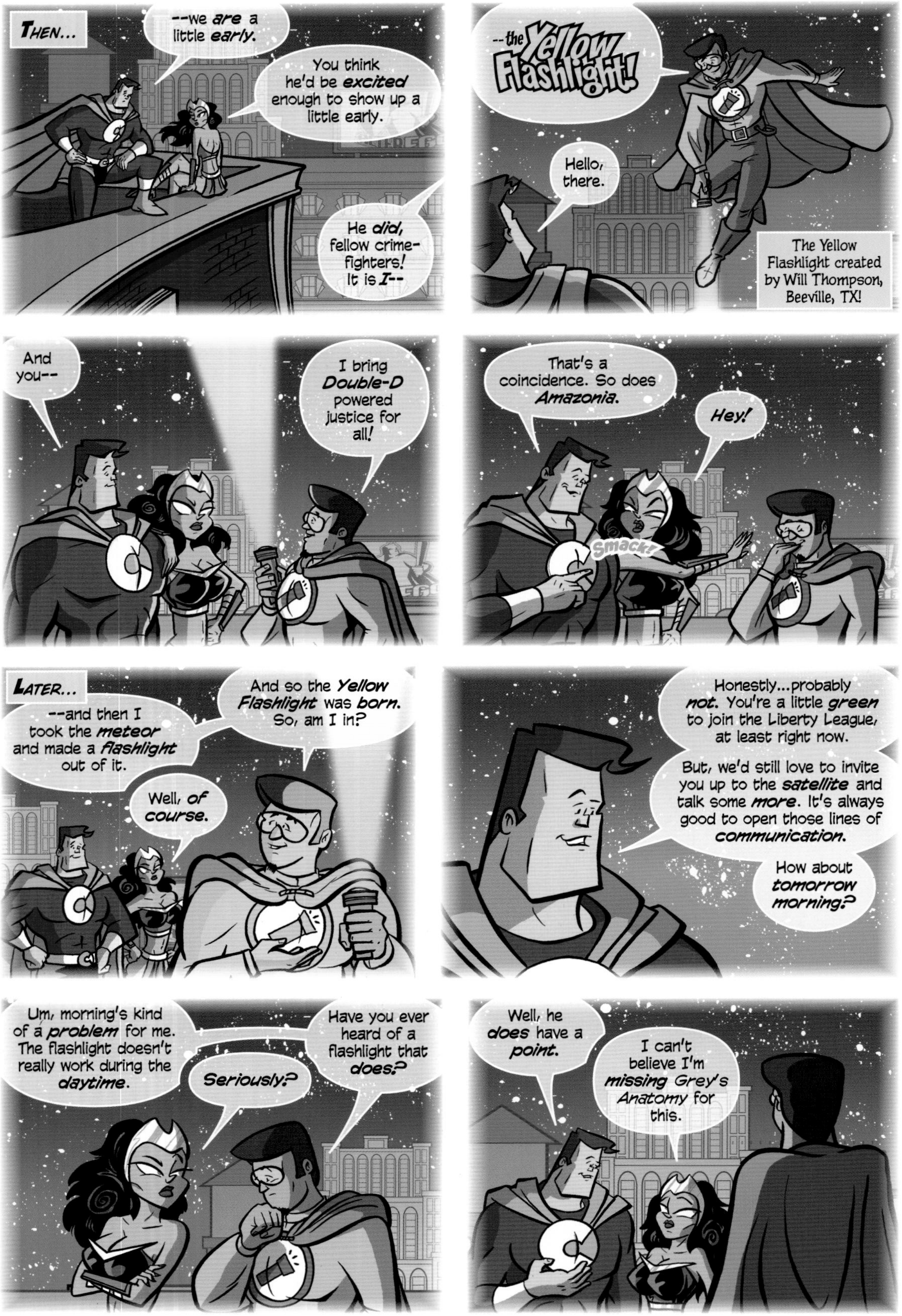
THEN...
--we are a little early.
You think he'd be excited enough to show up a little early.
He did, fellow crime-fighters! It is I--
--the Yellow Flashlight!
Hello, there.
The Yellow Flashlight created by Will Thompson, Beeville, TX!
And you--
I bring Double-D powered justice for all!
That's a coincidence. So does Amazonia.
Hey!
Smack!
LATER...
--and then I took the meteor and made a flashlight out of it.
And so the Yellow Flashlight was born. So, am I in?
Well, of course.
Honestly...probably not. You're a little green to join the Liberty League, at least right now.
But, we'd still love to invite you up to the satellite and talk some more. It's always good to open those lines of communication.
How about tomorrow morning?
Um, morning's kind of a problem for me. The flashlight doesn't really work during the daytime.
Seriously?
Have you ever heard of a flashlight that does?
Well, he does have a point.
I can't believe I'm missing Grey's Anatomy for this.

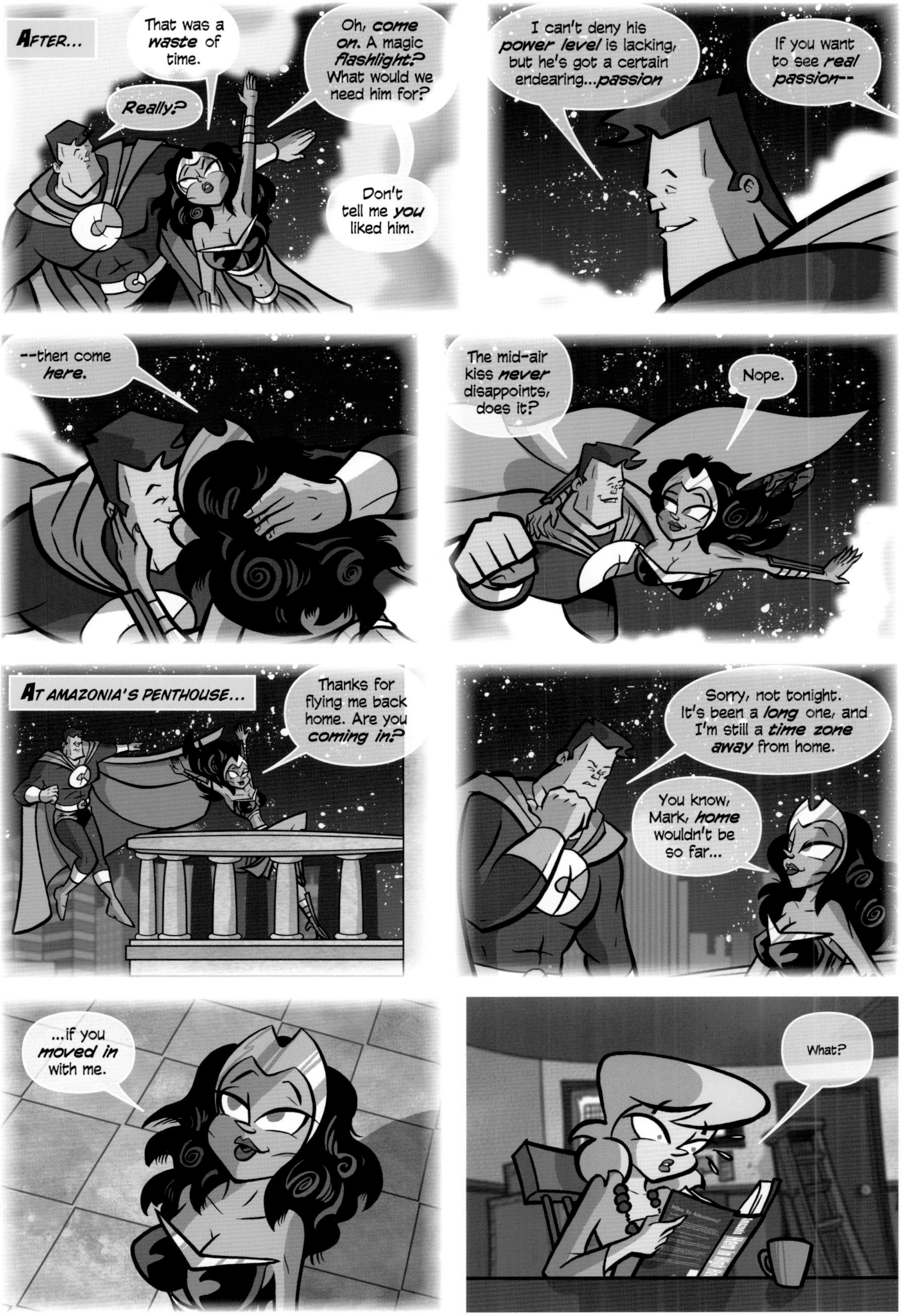

AFTER...
That was a waste of time.
Really?
Oh, come on. A magic flashlight? What would we need him for?
Don't tell me you liked him.
I can't deny his power level is lacking, but he's got a certain endearing...passion
If you want to see real passion--
--then come here.
The mid-air kiss never disappoints, does it?
Nope.
AT AMAZONIA'S PENTHOUSE...
Thanks for flying me back home. Are you coming in?
Sorry, not tonight. It's been a long one, and I'm still a time zone away from home.
You know, Mark, home wouldn't be so far...
...if you moved in with me.
What?

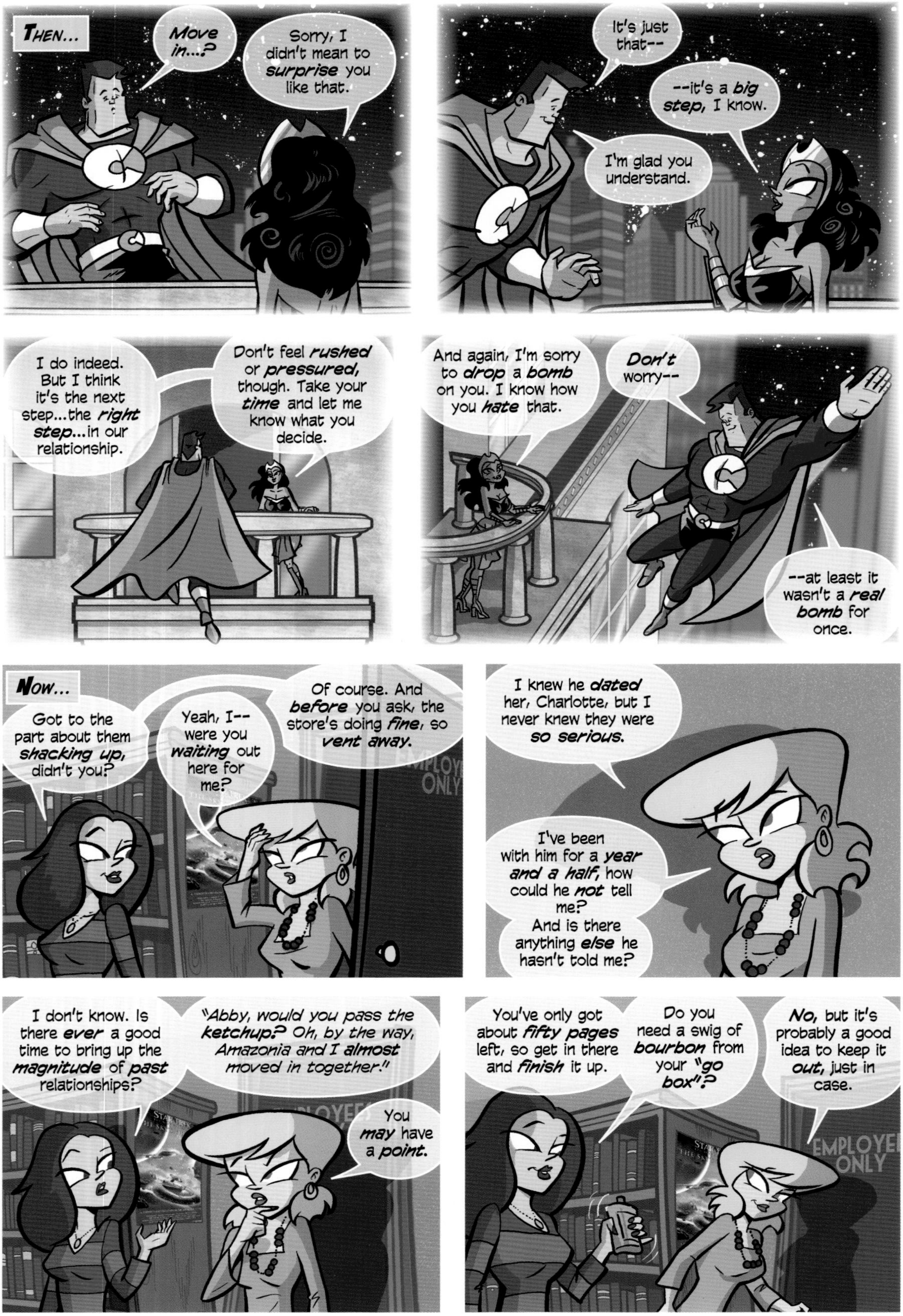
THEN...
Move in...?
Sorry, I didn't mean to surprise you like that.
It's just that--
--it's a big step, I know.
I'm glad you understand.
I do indeed. But I think it's the next step...the right step...in our relationship.
Don't feel rushed or pressured, though. Take your time and let me know what you decide.
And again, I'm sorry to drop a bomb on you. I know how you hate that.
Don't worry--
--at least it wasn't a real bomb for once.
NOW...
Got to the part about them shacking up, didn't you?
Yeah, I-- were you waiting out here for me?
Of course. And before you ask, the store's doing fine, so vent away.
I knew he dated her, Charlotte, but I never knew they were so serious.
I've been with him for a year and a half, how could he not tell me?
And is there anything else he hasn't told me?
I don't know. Is there ever a good time to bring up the magnitude of past relationships?
"Abby, would you pass the ketchup? Oh, by the way, Amazonia and I almost moved in together."
You may have a point.
You've only got about fifty pages left, so get in there and finish it up.
Do you need a swig of bourbon from your "go box"?
No, but it's probably a good idea to keep it out, just in case.

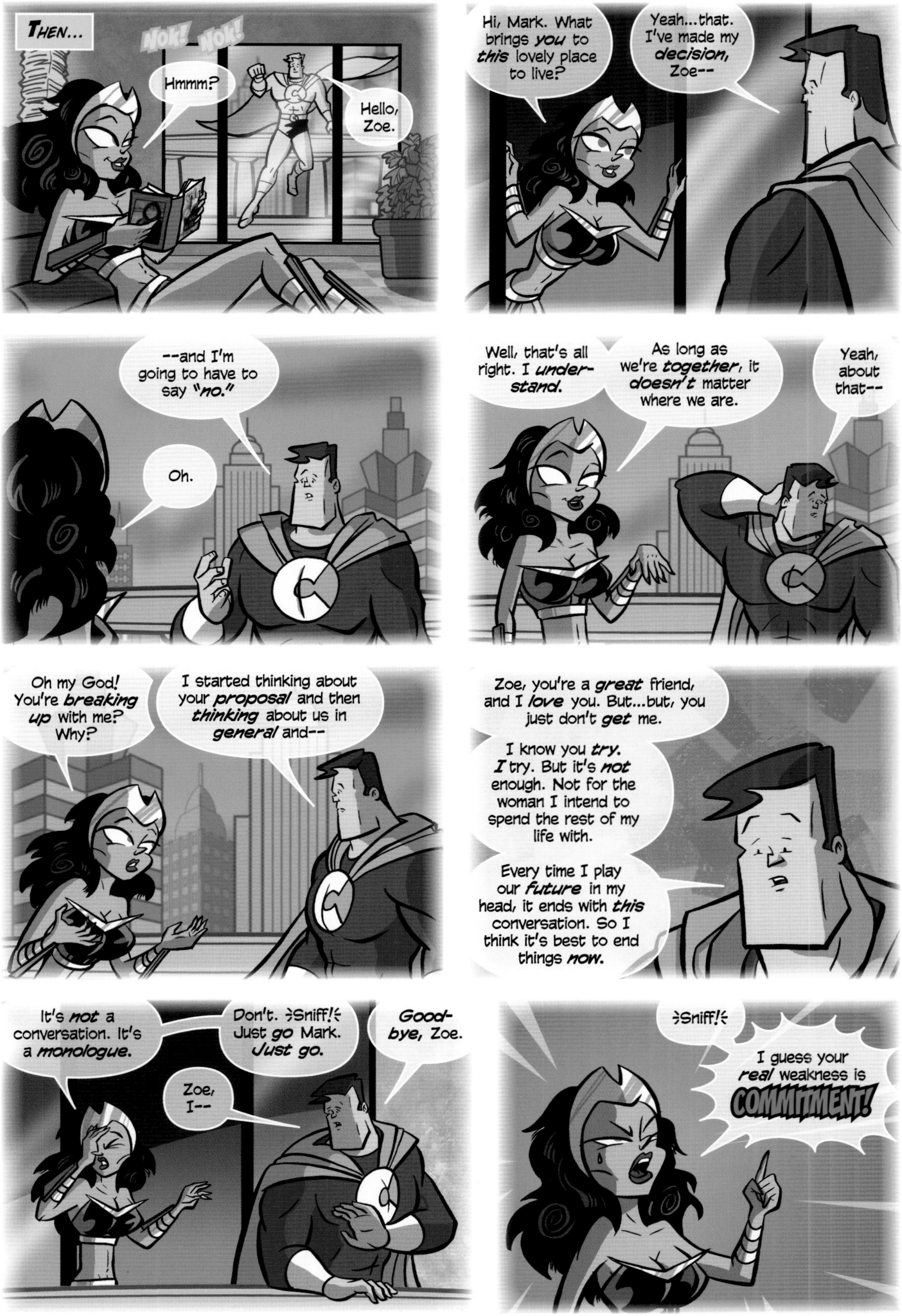

THEN...
NOK! NOK!
Hmmm?
Hello, Zoe.
Hi, Mark. What brings *you* to *this* lovely place to live?
Yeah...that. I've made my *decision*, Zoe--
--and I'm going to have to say "*no*."
Oh.
Well, that's all right. I *under-stand*.
As long as we're *together*, it *doesn't* matter where we are.
Yeah, about that--
Oh my God! You're *breaking up* with me? Why?
I started thinking about your *proposal* and then *thinking* about us in *general* and--
Zoe, you're a *great* friend, and I *love* you. But...but, you just don't *get* me.
I know you *try*. *I* try. But it's *not* enough. Not for the woman I intend to spend the rest of my life with.
Every time I play our *future* in my head, it ends with *this* conversation. So I think it's best to end things *now*.
It's *not* a conversation. It's a *monologue*.
Zoe, I--
Don't. *Sniff!* Just *go* Mark. *Just go*.
Good-bye, Zoe.
Sniff!
I guess your *real* weakness is COMMITMENT!

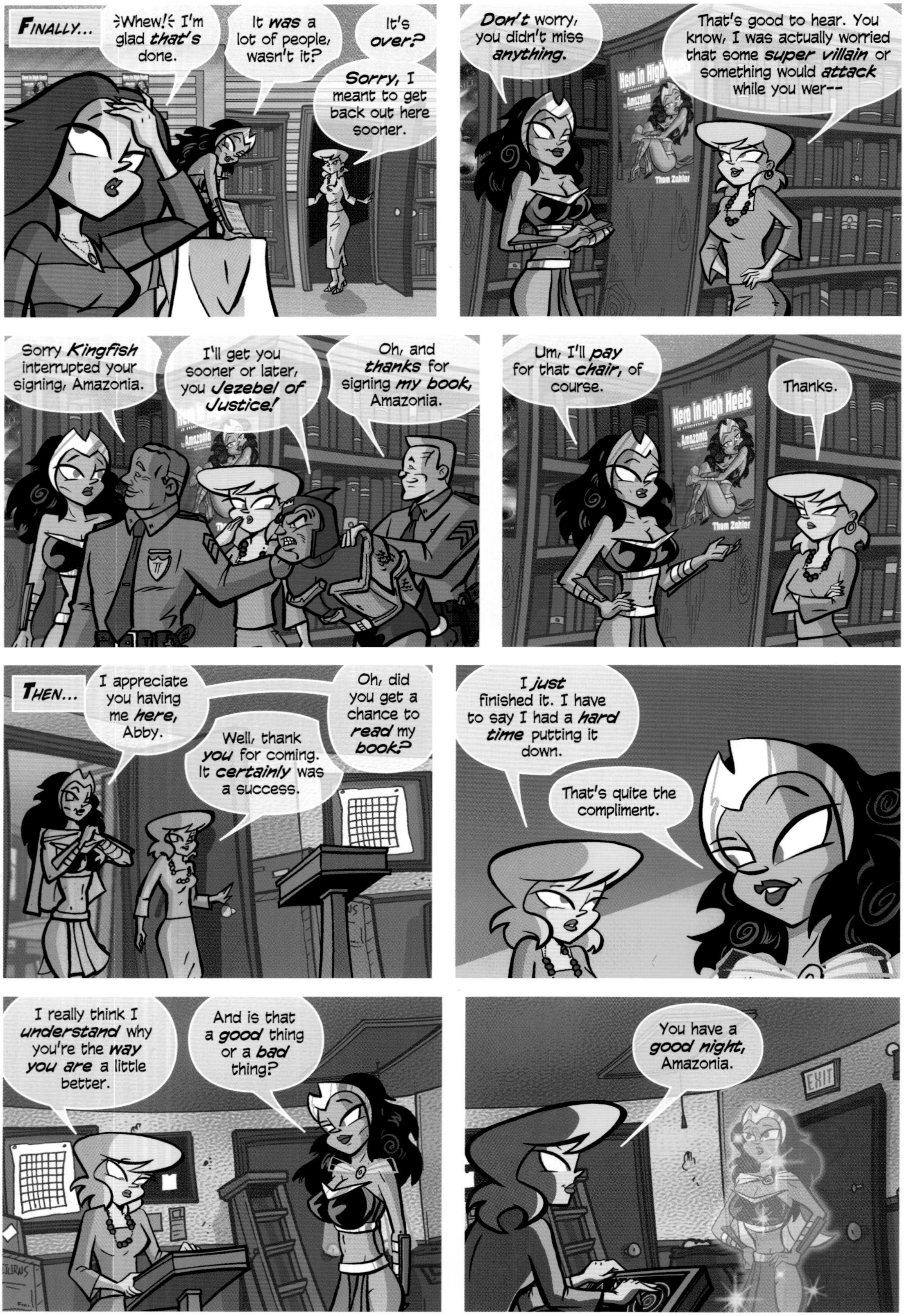
FINALLY...
Whew! I'm glad that's done.
It was a lot of people, wasn't it?
It's over?
Sorry, I meant to get back out here sooner.
Don't worry, you didn't miss anything.
That's good to hear. You know, I was actually worried that some super villain or something would attack while you wer--
Hero in High Heels
Amazonia
Thom Zahler
Sorry Kingfish interrupted your signing, Amazonia.
I'll get you sooner or later, you Jezebel of Justice!
Oh, and thanks for signing my book, Amazonia.
Um, I'll pay for that chair, of course.
Thanks.
Hero in High Heels
a memoir
Amazonia
Thom Zahler
THEN...
I appreciate you having me here, Abby.
Well, thank you for coming. It certainly was a success.
Oh, did you get a chance to read my book?
I just finished it. I have to say I had a hard time putting it down.
That's quite the compliment.
I really think I understand why you're the way you are a little better.
And is that a good thing or a bad thing?
You have a good night, Amazonia.
EXIT

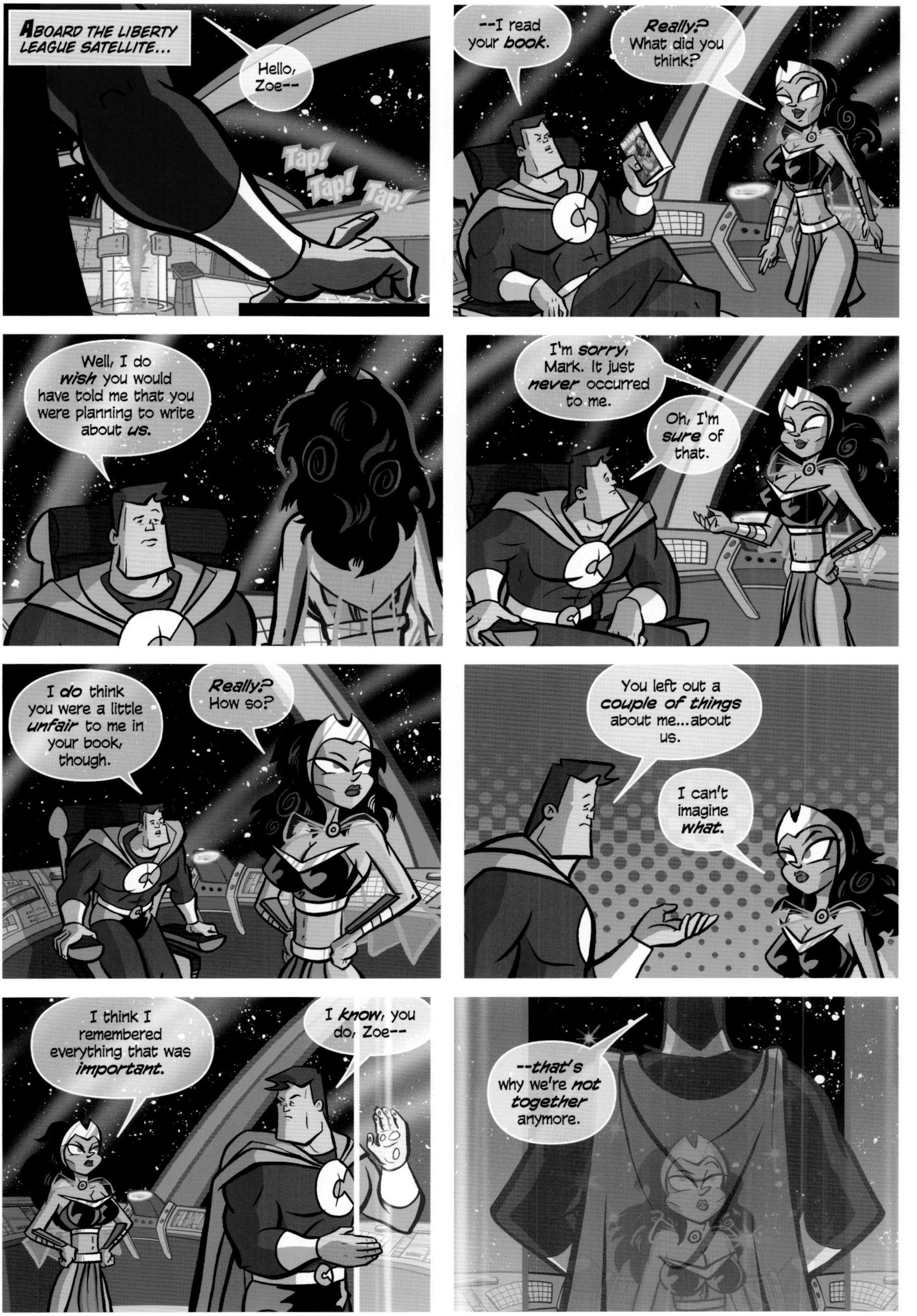
ABOARD THE LIBERTY LEAGUE SATELLITE...
Hello, Zoe--
Tap! Tap! Tap!
--I read your book.
Really? What did you think?
Well, I do wish you would have told me that you were planning to write about us.
I'm sorry, Mark. It just never occurred to me.
Oh, I'm sure of that.
I do think you were a little unfair to me in your book, though.
Really? How so?
You left out a couple of things about me...about us.
I can't imagine what.
I think I remembered everything that was important.
I know, you do, Zoe--
--that's why we're not together anymore.

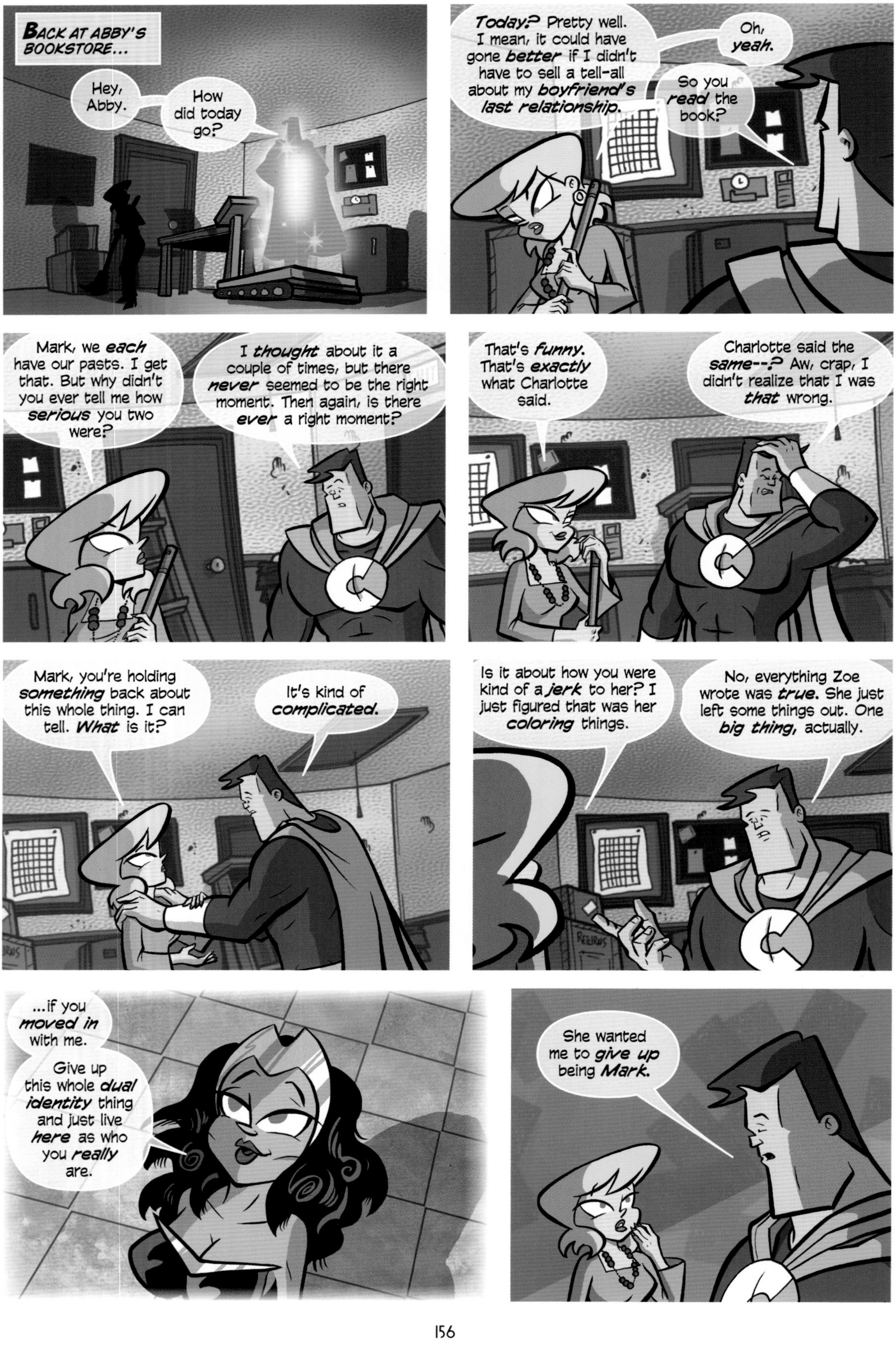
BACK AT ABBY'S BOOKSTORE...
Hey, Abby.
How did today go?
Today? Pretty well. I mean, it could have gone better if I didn't have to sell a tell-all about my boyfriend's last relationship.
Oh, yeah.
So you read the book?
Mark, we each have our pasts. I get that. But why didn't you ever tell me how serious you two were?
I thought about it a couple of times, but there never seemed to be the right moment. Then again, is there ever a right moment?
That's funny. That's exactly what Charlotte said.
Charlotte said the same--? Aw, crap, I didn't realize that I was that wrong.
Mark, you're holding something back about this whole thing. I can tell. What is it?
It's kind of complicated.
Is it about how you were kind of a jerk to her? I just figured that was her coloring things.
No, everything Zoe wrote was true. She just left some things out. One big thing, actually.
...if you moved in with me.
Give up this whole dual identity thing and just live here as who you really are.
She wanted me to give up being Mark.

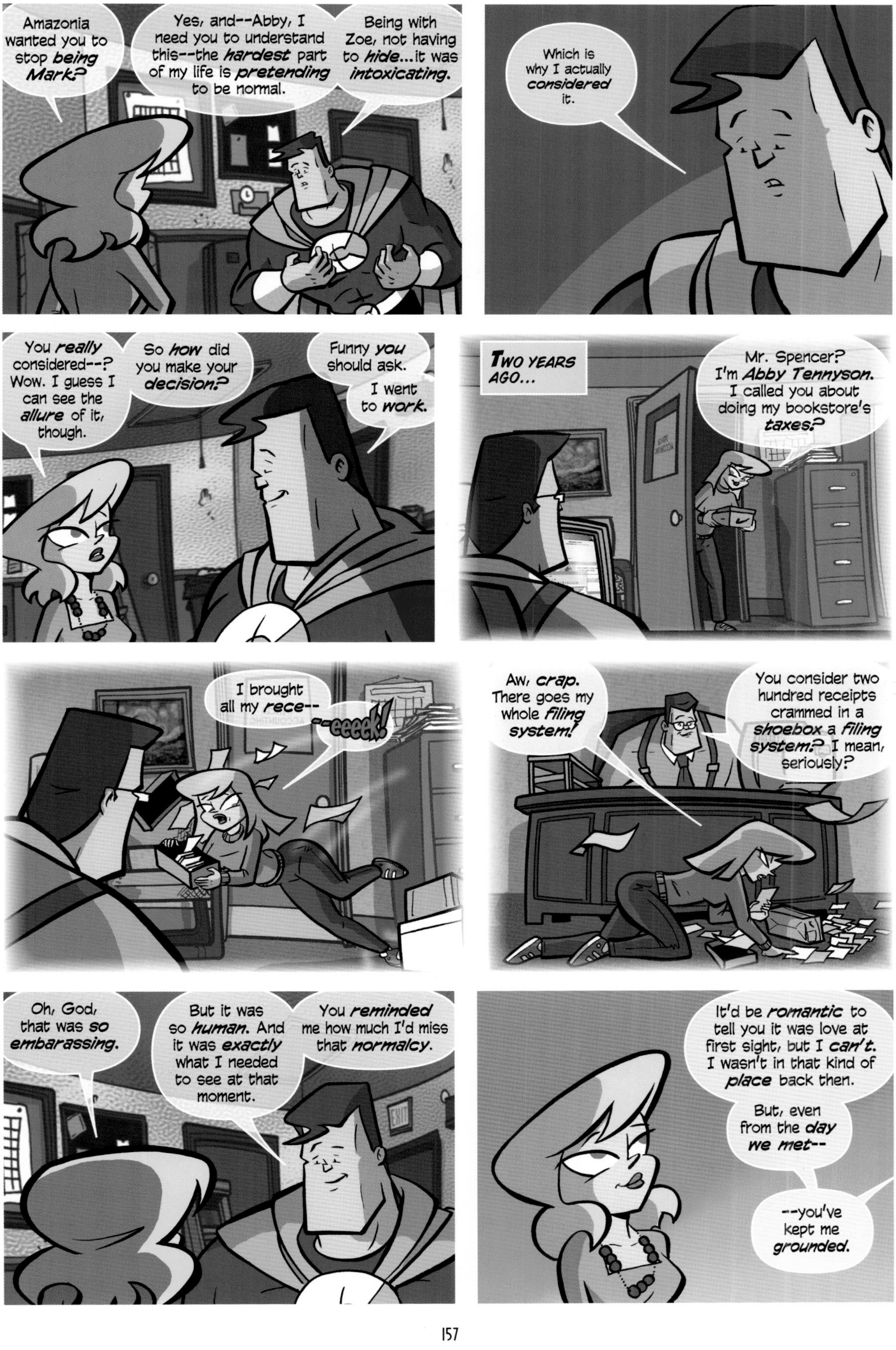
Amazonia wanted you to stop being Mark?
Yes, and--Abby, I need you to understand this--the hardest part of my life is pretending to be normal.
Being with Zoe, not having to hide...it was intoxicating.
Which is why I actually considered it.
You really considered--? Wow. I guess I can see the allure of it, though.
So how did you make your decision?
Funny you should ask.
I went to work.
TWO YEARS AGO...
Mr. Spencer? I'm Abby Tennyson. I called you about doing my bookstore's taxes?
I brought all my rece--
--eeeek!
Aw, crap. There goes my whole filing system!
You consider two hundred receipts crammed in a shoebox a filing system? I mean, seriously?
Oh, God, that was so embarassing.
But it was so human. And it was exactly what I needed to see at that moment.
You reminded me how much I'd miss that normalcy.
It'd be romantic to tell you it was love at first sight, but I can't. I wasn't in that kind of place back then.
But, even from the day we met--
--you've kept me grounded.

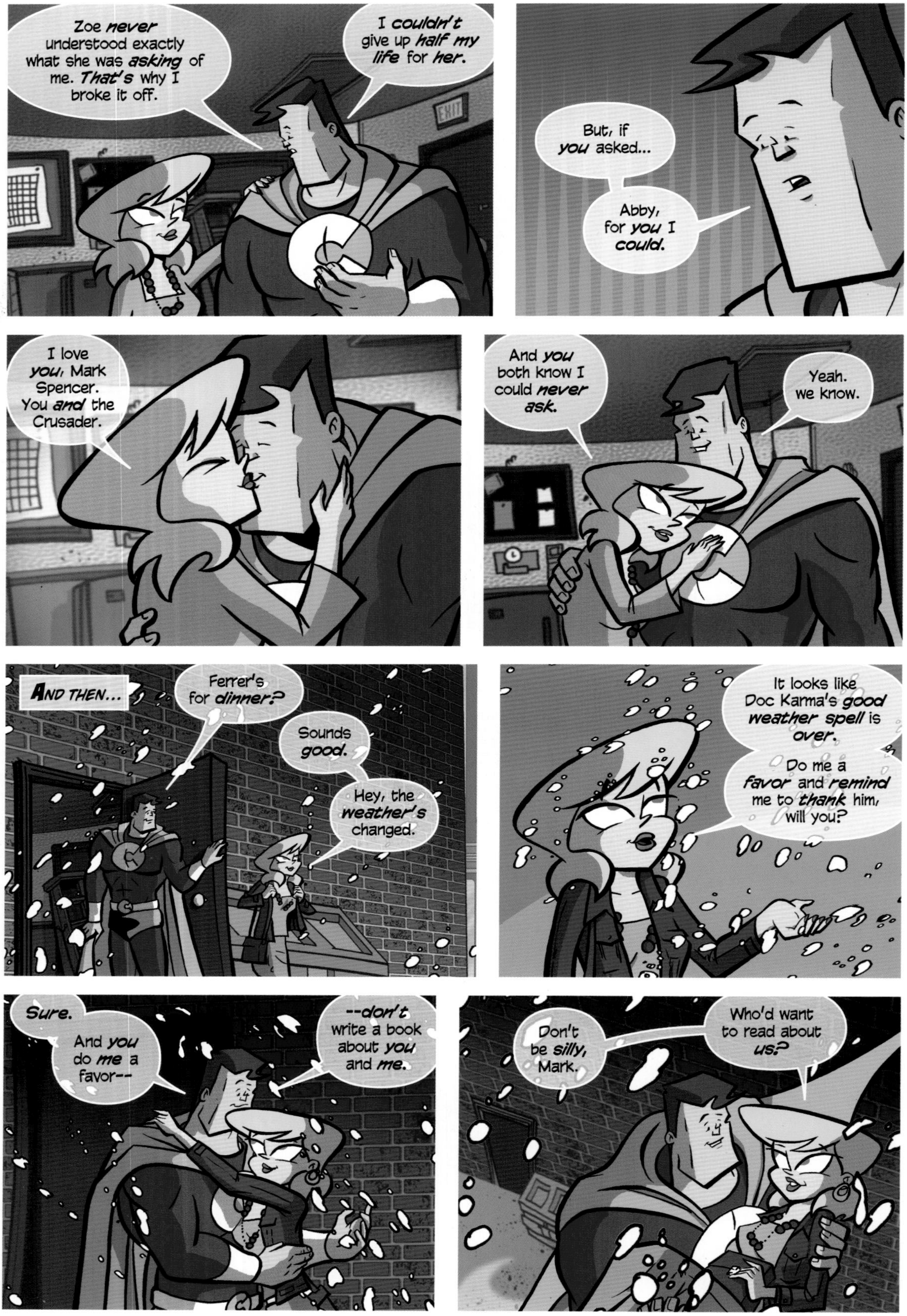
Zoe never understood exactly what she was asking of me. That's why I broke it off.
I couldn't give up half my life for her.
EXIT
But, if you asked...
Abby, for you I could.
I love you, Mark Spencer. You and the Crusader.
And you both know I could never ask.
Yeah. we know.
AND THEN...
Ferrer's for dinner?
Sounds good.
Hey, the weather's changed.
It looks like Doc Karma's good weather spell is over.
Do me a favor and remind me to thank him, will you?
Sure.
And you do me a favor--
--don't write a book about you and me.
Don't be silly, Mark.
Who'd want to read about us?

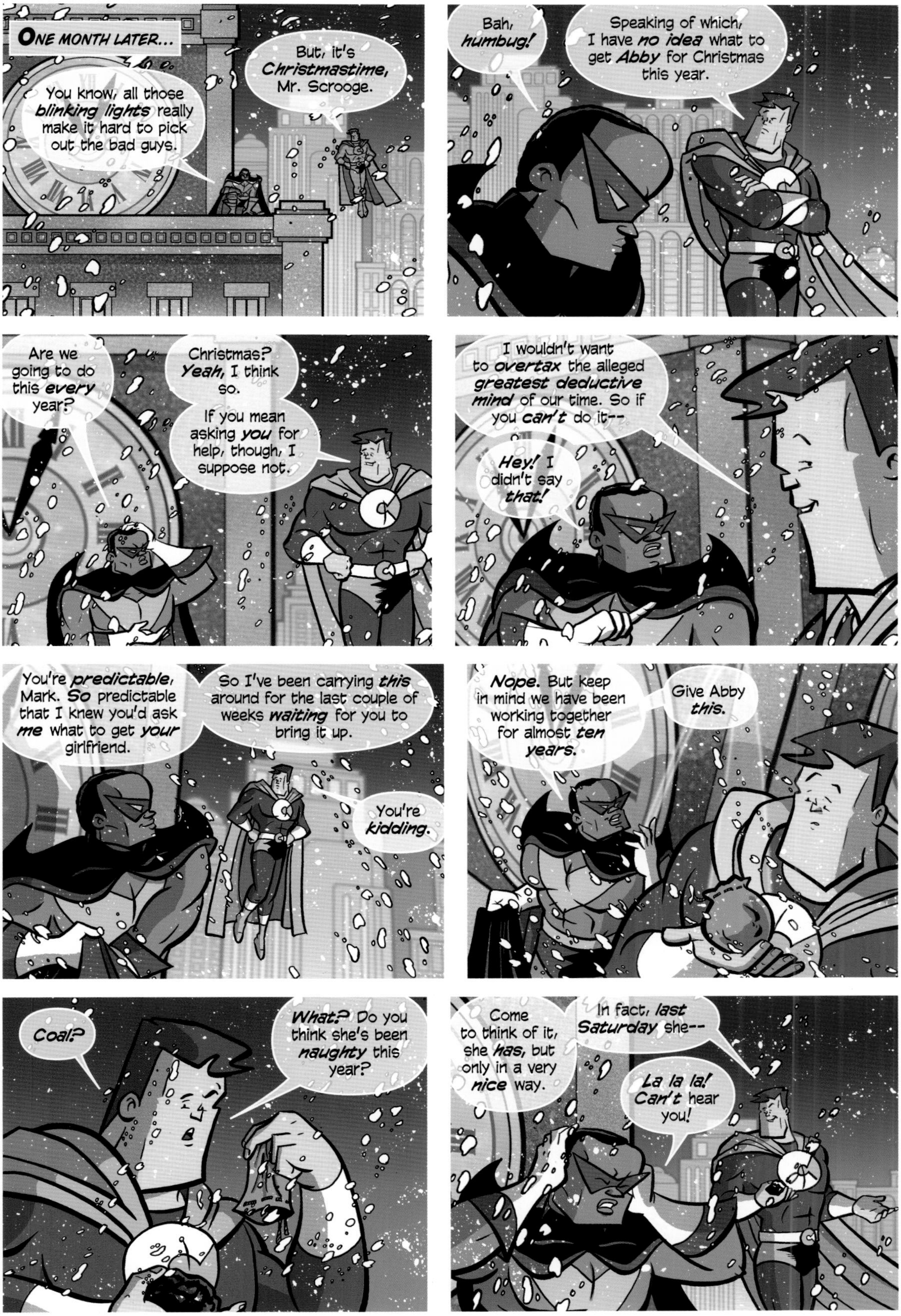

One month later...
You know, all those blinking lights really make it hard to pick out the bad guys.
But, it's Christmastime, Mr. Scrooge.
Bah, humbug!
Speaking of which, I have no idea what to get Abby for Christmas this year.
Are we going to do this every year?
Christmas? Yeah, I think so.
If you mean asking you for help, though, I suppose not.
I wouldn't want to overtax the alleged greatest deductive mind of our time. So if you can't do it--
Hey! I didn't say that!
You're predictable, Mark. So predictable that I knew you'd ask me what to get your girlfriend.
So I've been carrying this around for the last couple of weeks waiting for you to bring it up.
You're kidding.
Nope. But keep in mind we have been working together for almost ten years.
Give Abby this.
Coal?
What? Do you think she's been naughty this year?
Come to think of it, she has, but only in a very nice way.
In fact, last Saturday she--
La la la! Can't hear you!

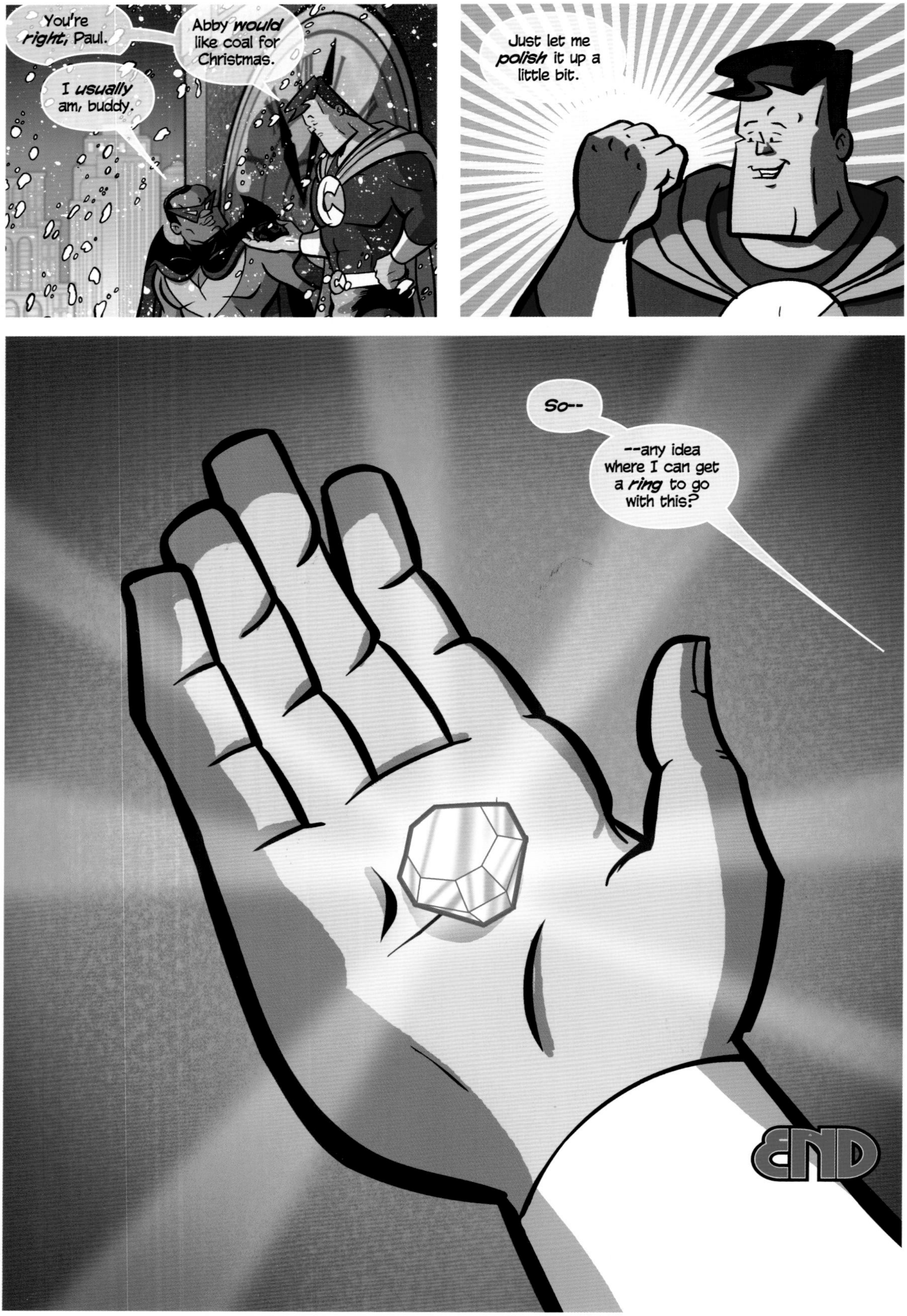
You're *right,* Paul.
Abby *would* like coal for Christmas.
I *usually* am, buddy.
Just let me *polish* it up a little bit.
So--
--any idea where I can get a *ring* to go with this?
END

IN THE BEGINNING...

A few years ago, I entered one of those reality show contests for something called *Situation: Comedy.* You had to write a spec sitcom pilot, and the turn-around time was insanely short. I wrote a romantic comedy script called *Long Distance* (the scriptbook of that is available at Amazon.com, just sayin').

I meant it as a one-off project, but I found I really liked it. I'm a big sitcom fan, especially of Aaron Sorkin's *SportsNight,* and writing a dialogue-based comedy really struck a chord with me. About that time, I was looking for a new comic project. I also wanted something that wasn't the huge 100-plus page committment that my previous *Raider* graphic novels were.

Then I had that chocolate-and-peanut butter moment: I liked sitcoms, and I liked superheroes. And I had just written that romantic comedy and... hey, what if I did all three?

I knew I wanted to do something more cartoony than my previous work. I experimented with a bunch of styles and designs before coming up with a look for the Crusader.

I had a few requirements: he had to have a chest emblem, a neckline that would allow his uniform to show underneath a button down shirt, and cape. Despite *The Incredibles* bagging on superheroes wearing capes, there **had** to be a cape.

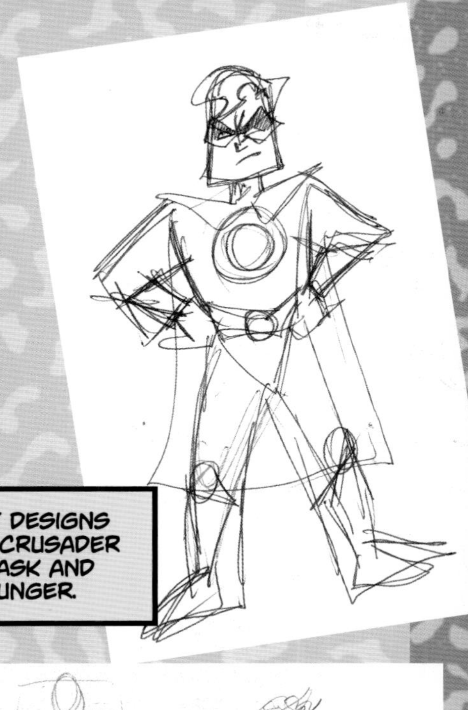

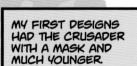

MY FIRST DESIGNS HAD THE CRUSADER WITH A MASK AND MUCH YOUNGER.

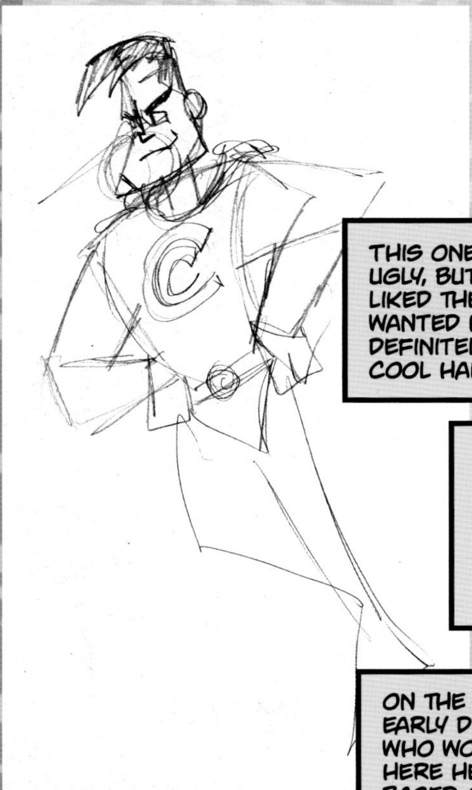

THIS ONE'S PRETTY UGLY, BUT I KIND OF LIKED THE HAIR. I WANTED HIM TO DEFINITELY HAVE COOL HAIR.

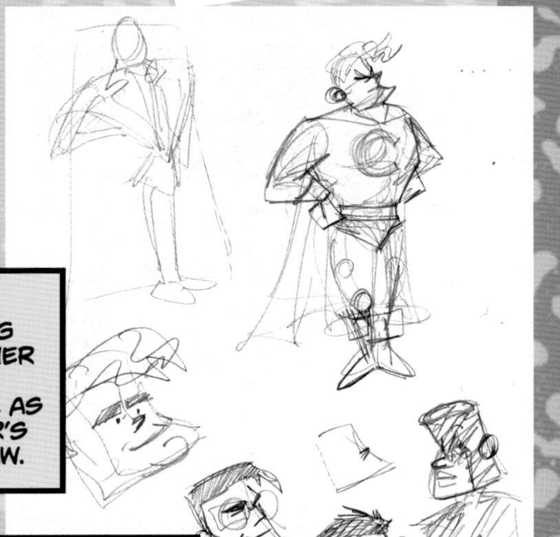

I STARTED EXPERIMENTING WITH CARTOONIER PROPORTIONS HERE, AS WELL AS THE CRUSADER'S PROMINENT JAW.

ON THE FAR RIGHT, YOU CAN SEE AN EARLY DESIGN FOR THE CHARACTER WHO WOULD BECOME DARKBLADE. HERE HE WAS MORE AN ELECTRIC-BASED CHARACTER.

I LOVE IT WHEN A PLAN COMES TOGETHER...

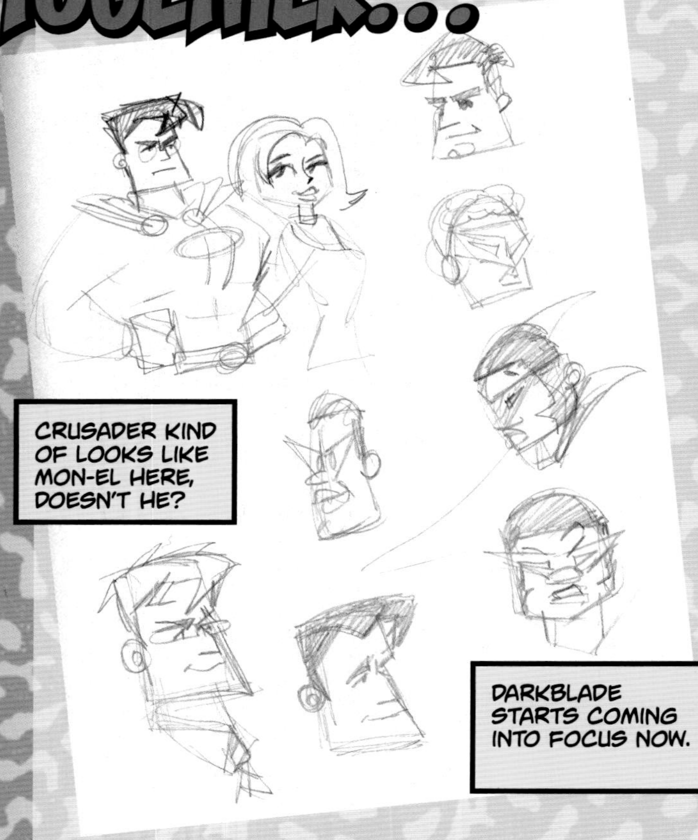

CRUSADER KIND OF LOOKS LIKE MON-EL HERE, DOESN'T HE?
DARKBLADE STARTS COMING INTO FOCUS NOW.

With the superhero sitcom idea firmly in place, I needed to give him a supporting cast.

Abby was the most important, obviously. But I didn't want her to be just "the girlfriend." She needed to be interesting by herself. I thought of making her a lawyer, so that she'd interact with Mark as the Crusader more, but that seemed to be a constant conflict of interest.

My second idea was to have her work at an advertising agency. I'd done that myself, so I knew there was funny to be had there. Then I decided that the ad business might be funny enough to do as a separate (and, as yet, unstarted) project.

Something about Sela Ward's character in *Once and Again,* and the way the bookstore worked in the series gave me the inspiration to make her own a small book shop.

In going through my sketchbooks, I don't seem to have any roughs of Charlotte, and very few of Abby. I was probably worried most about the superhero uniforms, knowing that I'd be stuck with those designs over the run of the series.

I also think that, somehow, Charlotte appeared in my head fully formed. She may be my favorite character in the series.

As far as names, Mark gets his from my friend Mark Lutz. Abby was named after Abigail Adams, as I was on a *1776* jag at the time, and loved her character. Paul's named after my friend and writer Paul D. Storrie, and Charlotte after another friend and writer, Charlotte Fullerton.

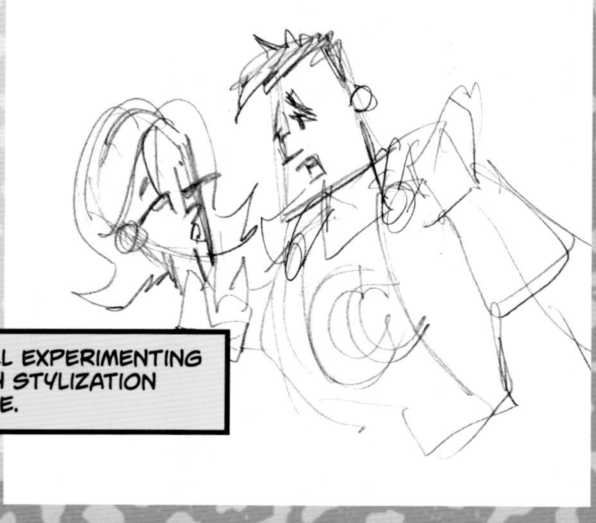

STILL EXPERIMENTING WITH STYLIZATION HERE.

TIME FOR FRIENDS....

I always liked the Seventies version of Superman and Batman where they were best friends, and applied that to *Love and Capes*. I think the idea of Crusader and Darkblade confiding in each other as they protect their respective cities is an important tent pole of the book.

The great thing about playing with archetypes is that you don't have to spend a lot of time on the set-up, and then you can play against it. So, Darkblade is the gruff dark avenger, but he's also capable of giving Mark relationship advice.

AND THE RUNNING "DRINKING COFFEE" GAG BEGINS...

I don't know why, but I didn't want the two of them to operate in the same city, and with the Crusader's speed, distance wasn't a problem.

Deco City is based on Chicago. I love the way that city looks, and before starting LNC, I had designed an art deco themed website for a writer friend of mine. The art deco style was just too much fun to play with.

There are references to Deco City being in the central time zone, and it has an elevated train, like the Windy City.

Chronopolis is based on New York, and it was there that I figured the hook for that city. I was seeing *Wicked* with my brother, and the set has a wonderful gear-and-clocktower motif. Setting the pair in front of a clocktower made the scenes pop visually.

So I decided that Chronopolis was the clocktower capital of the world, hence the name, and the many large timepieces behind them.

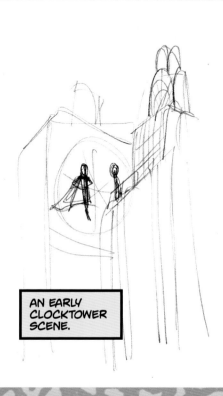

AN EARLY CLOCKTOWER SCENE.

PUTTING IT TOGETHER...

How was I supposed to know?
When the Lord of Atlantis asks "Do you like lobsters" you're not supposed to say "Yes, with butter!"
But I--
Did you see any seafood there? Sheesh. He talks to those things. It'd be like him asking to grow on your cat!

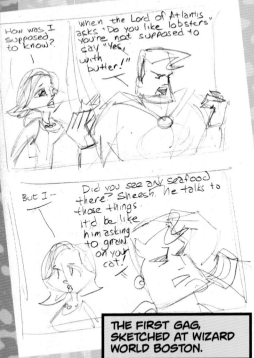

THE FIRST GAG, SKETCHED AT WIZARD WORLD BOSTON.

I started to really like the series, and was trying to figure out the pace. I came up with the idea of the four-panel comic strip grid for a couple of reasons.

The first is that it set a cadence. There'd be a joke (or a beat) every four panels, making sure that I didn't skimp on the funny. And the comic book caption boxes made scene transitions easy.

The second is that I wasn't sure the book would succeed, so I wanted to have the ability to repurpose it as a web strip. That half-page format works much better on monitors than trying to fit a full comic book page.

Oddly, putting the book online in that way helped it succeed as a comic book. It helped promote it.

I also started setting rules for the book. All superheroics would take place off camera. This kept the focus on the relationship, and, should the series ever become an actual sitcom, it makes it cheaper to film.

Second, while the book is a comedy, the superhero stuff is serious. I describe it as having the tone of the George Reeves *Adventures of Superman*. The crimes and plots are real, but the Crusader is never really worried.

Love and Capes has been described as a superhero parody, but it's not, really. The heroics are straight. Most of the villains are "serious." It's just that everything else is funny. Like *Scrubs* is funny, but it doesn't mean the doctor stuff is played for laughs.

SO, DO YOU HAVE A WEAKNESS?
WHAT KIND OF QUESTION IS THAT?
YOU KNOW, A WEAKNESS, KRYPTONITE, YELLOW FIRE?
I KNOW WHAT A WEAKNESS IS. HOW CAN YOU ASK THAT?
I JUST WANT TO GET TO KNOW YOU. BESIDES, SHOULDN'T I KNOW SO I DON'T ACCIDENTALLY COOK YOU SOMETHING THAT YOU CAN'T HAVE.
IT'S A WEAKNESS, NOT AN ALLERGY!
DON'T YOU TRUST ME? YOU SAID YOU LOVE ME. BUT YOU DON'T TRUST ME?
LAST GUY I KNOW WHO TOLD HIS GIRLFRIEND HIS WEAKNESS WOUND UP ON THE FRONT PAGE OF THE PAPER
I WOULDN'T DO THAT.
RIGHT. LIKE YOU DIDN'T TELL YOUR SISTER I WAS CAPT. CRUSADER
ONE LITTLE MISTAKE.
YOU WANT TO KNOW MY WEAKNESS?
YEAH
FINE
IT'S YOU. MY WEAKNESS IS YOU. I'VE STOOD IN THE HEART OF THE SUN, BUT I MELT WHEN YOU SMILE
IT'S YOU
I LOVE YOU
SMEK
SPENT MY WHOLE LIFE FIGHTING CRIME, THINK I DON'T KNOW HOW TO DODGE A FEW BULLETS?

THE PAGE TO THE RIGHT, I THINK, IS THE HEART OF THE BOOK, AND MOST REPRESENTATIVE OF THE STORIES TO COME.

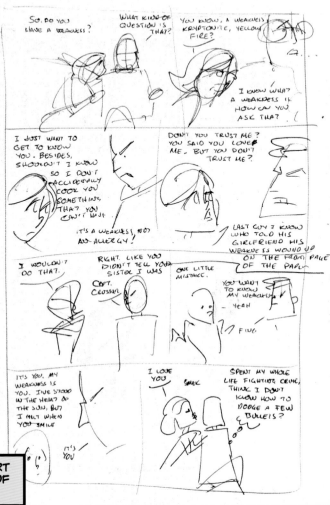

THE WORLD MUST BE PEOPLED...

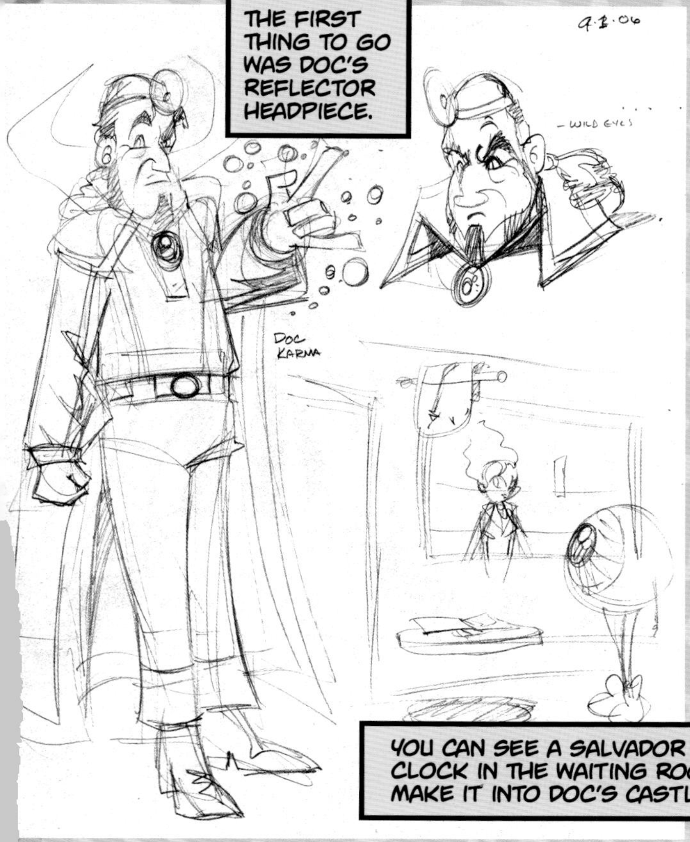
9.1.06
DOC KARMA

THE FIRST THING TO GO WAS DOC'S REFLECTOR HEADPIECE.

YOU CAN SEE A SALVADOR DALI-ESQUE MELTED CLOCK IN THE WAITING ROOM HERE, WHICH DID MAKE IT INTO DOC'S CASTLE.

And here's where things almost went off the rails.

One of the other rules I came up with for the book was that I would introduce one new superhero per issue (a rule which I promptly broke to make #4 pay off the way it did).

So I decided to introduce the doctor of my superhero universe. But my first attempt at Doc Karma went too broad. I had ideas of a bizarre waiting room, a telepathic, flame-haired receptionist, walking eyeballs, and floating furniture.

Fortunately, I pulled things back and made the comedy much more understated, and for the best.

It should come as no surprise that I'm a big Superman fan. And I think the Man of Steel doesn't get his props when compared to the more popular Batman and Spider-Man. That jealousy became Mark's jealousy towards many of the other superhero characters.

It gives Mark a nice flaw to exploit for some funny scenes, and probably how the most powerful superhero on the planet would react to not getting a movie made about him.

Knowing that #4 would come out at Free Comic Book Day 2007, which was also tied into the third *Spider-Man* movie, I decided to create The Arachnerd.

He's clearly inspired by Spider-Man, but he borrows his color scheme from another spider character: DC's Tarantula.

I'm particularly proud of the wacky spider mask he wears.

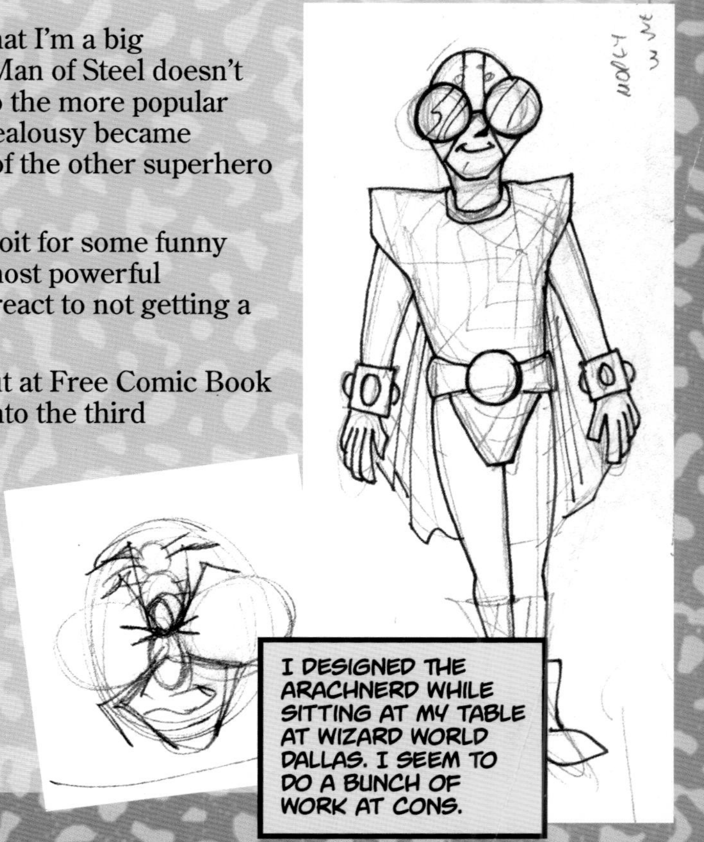

I DESIGNED THE ARACHNERD WHILE SITTING AT MY TABLE AT WIZARD WORLD DALLAS. I SEEM TO DO A BUNCH OF WORK AT CONS.

FRIENDS LIKE THESE...

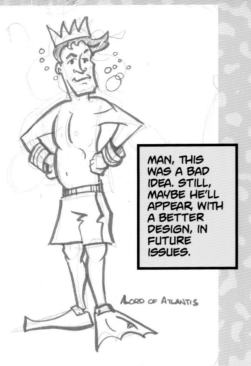

MAN, THIS WAS A BAD IDEA. STILL, MAYBE HE'LL APPEAR, WITH A BETTER DESIGN, IN FUTURE ISSUES.
LORD OF ATLANTIS

In issue three, I decided to take Mark and Abby to Atlantis, finally doing the first joke I'd ever written for the series.

But, if you notice, we never meet Mermantis, Lord of Atlantis. Why? Because I could never come up with a cool enough design for him. The design to the left came about during the "too wacky" phase that I was in. Man, that could have been a train wreck.

And then Major Might replaced Mermantis as the focus of the Atlantis story. I don't think the story suffers for his absence, either.

It's also why Mermantis is left on the satellite in #4, while the rest of the Liberty League make an appearance.

Amazonia, much like her character, just showed up and took over. I didn't expect her to be as popular as she was, and actually reworked issue #2 to make sure she had an appearance, however brief.

In thinking of a bit for her in issue #4, I came up with the "she writes a book" idea that became the focus of issue #6. I'd always known the scene that would end that issue, but I didn't have anything else planned out. And then I realized I could use the book as the reason to flashback to Zoe and Mark's previous relationship.

I mentioned before that I love Aaron Sorkin, and #6 owes a lot to the last few episodes of *Studio 60 on the Sunset Strip,* where they kept cutting between the past and present to further the story.

As far as Zoe, well, I guess sometimes a good idea comes around and you just run with it.

PART OF AMAZONIA'S LOOK AND ATTITUDE IS BASED ON ANGELINA JOLIE.

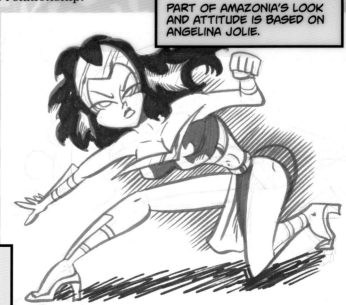

THERE'S A LOT MORE BEHIND THE SCENES TRIVIA AT THE LOVE AND CAPES WEBSITE: ***WWW.LOVEANDCAPES.COM***

Putting It Together
How a Page is Created from Start to Finish!

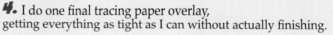

1. Most pages start in the shower. Seriously. I've found that I get most of my best ideas in the shower, so I've started keeping those shower crayons nearby. My roughs at this point are near illegible, but they make sense to me.

2. I have a piece of illustration board with the 8-panel grid ruled on it. I throw a sheet of tracing paper over it and start blocking out the page. You'll notice all the panels don't line up. Everything's still pretty rough here.

3. I lay another sheet of tracing paper on top of the first and start tightening things up, working out the structure of figures and backgrounds. Hands that I've roughed out as mittens need to get fingers. Here's where perspective gets worked out. This page took only one try. I've had pages that took as many as five at this stage, just to get things right.

4. I do one final tracing paper overlay, getting everything as tight as I can without actually finishing.

5. Now it's time to ink. I throw a sheet of marker paper over the final pencils, and put that on a lightbox so I can see through it. I use a brush (Windsor Newton Series 7 #2) for most of the figures, and tech pens and Micron markers for more mechanical things. You'll notice that I draw repeated backgrounds (like the couch) only once. They'll be repeated and duplicated in the next steps. Also, large black areas are left open, as I'll fill in the blacks once I scan them in.

6. I scan everything into Adobe Photoshop, and fill in the black areas there. Using a Wacom Graphics Tablet, I start coloring each panel individually. The panels always have extra area around the edges, so that I have room to play once I start putting the whole page together. Also, I have some stored backgrounds (like the city buildings in the first four panels) that I can place in Photoshop. Some things still get cut or changed: notice the lamp I drew never appears in the final. Coloring's a huge process… maybe I'll do a feature just on that sometime.

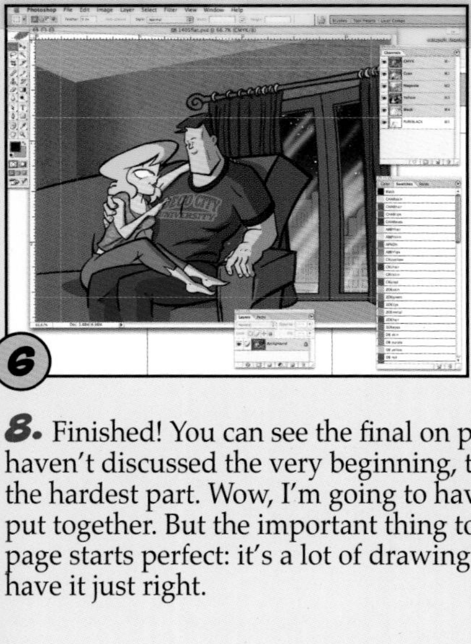

7. With each panel finished, I go into Adobe Illustrator and bring in each panel, fitting it into the 8-panel grid. This is where I do the lettering, too. Again, it's a huge and techie process, and one that deserves its own section someday.

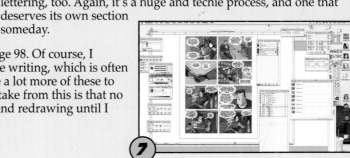

8. Finished! You can see the final on page 98. Of course, I haven't discussed the very beginning, the writing, which is often the hardest part. Wow, I'm going to have a lot more of these to put together. But the important thing to take from this is that no page starts perfect: it's a lot of drawing and redrawing until I have it just right.

ABOUT THE CREATOR

WRITTEN AND DRAWN BY THOMAS F. ZAHLER

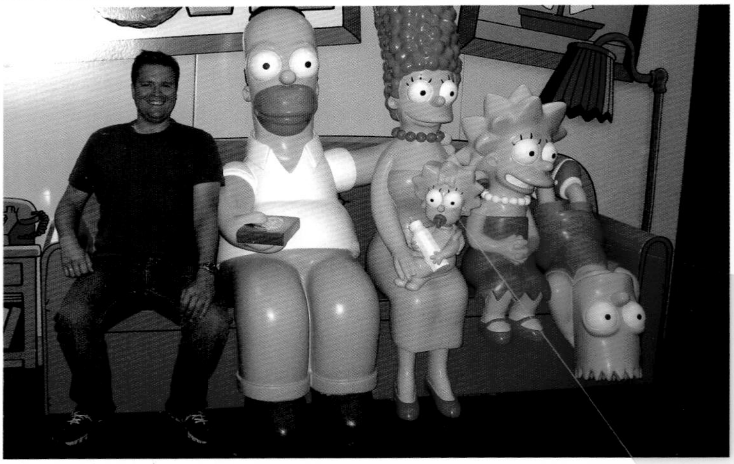

Kidnapped as a child by the legendary Pirates of the Dover Coast, young Thom Zahler was taught to sail the Seven Seas and to draw funny pictures. At least one of those skills would serve him well later in life.

He escaped his servitude in an unparalleled adventure of action, danger, excitement, and romance that doesn't bear going into right now, and returned to his native village of Timberlake to begin his life anew as a cartoonist.

Since then, he has drawn for fun and profit… mostly profit. His work has been seen in national advertising campaigns, in newspapers and magazines, and of course, in comic books.

By making the Faustian bargain of trading sleep for coffee, Zahler has managed to also become the president of the Timberlake governing council, a game show contestant, the co-author of "'Til Death", a *Star Trek: The Next Generation* short story published in the *Sky's the Limit* anthology, and a frequent guest on Cleveland television and radio.

Thom Zahler will return in *Thom Zahler vs. The League of Monsters.*

SPECIAL THANKS TO:
DEITRI VILLARREAL, PAUL D. STORRIE,
SANDI SCHEIDERER, JILL A. SMITH,
ROGER PRICE, PAUL MEROLLE,
CHRISTINE MARGALIS,
JESSE JACKSON,
MIKE HORKAN, MATT HALEY,
CHARLOTTE FULLERTON,
CARIDAD FERRER,
HARLAN & SUSAN ELLISON
AND MIKE BOKAUSEK

VISIT THOM ZAHLER'S BLOG AT WWW.THOMZ.COM/WORDPRESS